Joshua

J. Gordon McConville &
Stephen N. Williams

WILLIAM B. EERDMANS PUBLISHING COMPANY
GRAND RAPIDS, MICHIGAN / CAMBRIDGE, U.K.

© 2010 J. Gordon McConville and Stephen N. Williams
All rights reserved

Published 2010 by
Wm. B. Eerdmans Publishing Co.
2140 Oak Industrial Drive N.E., Grand Rapids, Michigan 49505 /
P.O. Box 163, Cambridge CB3 9PU U.K.
www.eerdmans.com

Library of Congress Cataloging-in-Publication Data

McConville, J. G. (J. Gordon)
    Joshua / J. Gordon McConville & Stephen N. Williams.
       p.   cm.   — (The Two horizons Old Testament commentary)
    Includes bibliographical references (p.   ).
    ISBN 978-0-8028-2702-9 (pbk.: alk. paper)
    1. Bible. O.T. Joshua — Commentaries.   2. Bible. O.T. Joshua — Theology.
    I. Williams, Stephen N. (Stephen Nantlais)   II. Title.

BS1295.53.M43   2010
222′.206 — dc22

                                                                                            2009045880

Unless otherwise noted, the Scripture quotations in this publication are from the HOLY BIBLE: NEW INTERNATIONAL VERSION. Copyright © 1973, 1978, 1984 by the International Bible Society. Used by permission of Zondervan Bible Publishers.

This book is fondly dedicated to

> *Betty McConville*
> *and*
> *Megan Williams*

who taught their sons where to look for a light on their path and a lamp for their feet.

Contents

Preface	x
Abbreviations	xi
Introduction to Joshua (Gordon McConville)	1
The Book	1
The Audience of Joshua	2
Dating and Historicity	3
Reading Joshua as Scripture	8
Joshua and Theology	10
Commentary on Joshua (Gordon McConville)	13
Theological Horizons of Joshua (Stephen Williams)	93
Theology in the Book of Joshua	95
The Question of the Land	95
Possession and Loss	95
The New Testament and the Land	99
Back to the Land?	103
The Question of Genocide	108
The Grim Tale	108
What and Why?	113
Did God Really Say . . . ?	116
Radical Accommodation	120

Conclusion	123
Idolatry	125
At Stake	125
Practices of the Nations	127
The Practice of Israel	131
A Matter of Life and Death	133
Touching on Beauty	137
Covenant	140
Behind the Covenant	142
Covenant and Privilege	145
Covenant and Law	148
Conclusion	153
God of Miracle and Mystery	154
Something Rich and Strange	154
Approaching the Miraculous	156
What Exactly Are We Told?	158
The Scientific Question	161
The Half-Seen World	165
Joshua and Biblical Theology (Gordon McConville)	171
Introduction	171
Key Themes of the Book of Joshua	172
Joshua and Genesis	172
Joshua and Exodus	174
Joshua and Leviticus	175
Joshua and Numbers	177
Joshua and Deuteronomy	179
Joshua and Judges–Kings	183
Conclusion	186
Joshua in Biblical Theology	187
The Problem of Evil and Violence	188
Joshua–Kings: Chaos, History, and Violence	190
Joshua, Chaos, and History in the Rest of the Old Testament	193

Conclusion	196
A Response to Gordon McConville (Stephen Williams)	200
Reading Joshua Today (Stephen Williams)	206
The Question of History	207
The God of Joshua	214
God as Personal	217
God of Power	220
The Character of God	223
Divine Lordship	228
A Response to Stephen Williams (Gordon McConville)	230
Bibliography	236
Author Index	246
Scripture Index	249

Preface

The Two Horizons Old Testament series has afforded a welcome opportunity for the two authors to work together on this volume on Joshua. Gordon McConville and Stephen Williams share Celtic and Presbyterian origins and a long friendship. We are delighted to have been able to collaborate, as specialists in the Old Testament and Systematic Theology respectively, in a project whose aim is to bring together biblical exegesis and Christian theology. While such collaboration is not prescriptive for the series, it seems to us to be an ideal occasion for it. The resulting volume is one that neither author could have written alone and has dimensions that we could not fully anticipate at the outset.

Each read and commented on all the work of the other as it progressed, and our separate contributions have been affected by this process in ways that can hardly be accounted for. While each section of the volume can be attributed to one hand or the other, there is an important sense in which it comes entirely from both together. Any decent collaboration will have differences of perspective, and we have acknowledged these in responses to each other's contribution in the final part of the volume. They are differences born of unity and owing something perhaps to the distinctive disciplinary constraints of Biblical Studies and Systematic Theology. But this is the very dialogue that we believe has made the project worth the effort. Personal opinions are not held here as absolute and immovable. Rather, collaborative interpretation is part and parcel of the story of the theological reception of Scripture down the centuries. Notwithstanding all the above, Stephen Williams would also like to thank Desmond Alexander for helpful discussions of relevant topics; as he works in a different institution from Gordon McConville, separated by a stretch of water, it was valuable to have the input of one of the OT scholars on-site.

GORDON MCCONVILLE and STEPHEN WILLIAMS   October 2008

Abbreviations

AB	Anchor Bible
ABD	*Anchor Bible Dictionary,* ed. David Noel Freedman. 6 vols. (New York: Doubleday, 1992)
ANET	*Ancient Near Eastern Texts Relating to the Old Testament,* ed. James B. Pritchard (Princeton: Princeton University Press, 1954)
ANF	Ante-Nicene Fathers
AOTC	Apollos Old Testament Commentary
BASOR	*Bulletin of the American Schools of Oriental Research*
BBC	Blackwell Biblical Commentaries
BETL	Bibliotheca ephemeridum theologicarum lovaniensium
BibJS	Biblical and Judaic Studies
BWANT	Beiträge zur Wissenschaft vom Alten und Neuen Testament
BZAW	Beihefte zur *Zeitschrift für die alttestamentliche Wissenschaft*
CBQ	*Catholic Biblical Quarterly*
CSCD	Cambridge Studies in Christian Doctrine
CTJ	*Calvin Theological Journal*
ESV	English Standard Version
FAT	Forschungen zum Alten Testament
HTKAT	Herders theologischer Kommentar zum Alten Testament
IB	*Interpreter's Bible,* ed. George Arthur Buttrick. 12 vols. (Nashville: Abingdon, 1951-57)
IBS	Irish Biblical Studies
ICC	International Critical Commentary
IDBSup	*Interpreter's Dictionary of the Bible: Supplementary Volume,* ed. Keith Crim. (Nashville: Abingdon, 1976)
ITQ	*Irish Theological Quarterly*
JBL	*Journal of Biblical Literature*

Abbreviations

JPSV	Jewish Publication Society Version
JSOT	*Journal for the Study of the Old Testament*
JSOTSup	*Journal for the Study of the Old Testament,* Supplement Series
LB	Late Bronze
LHB/OTS	Library of Hebrew Bible/Old Testament Studies
LXX	Septuagint
MT	Masoretic Text
NAB	New American Bible
NAC	New American Commentary
NIB	*The New Interpreter's Bible,* ed. Leander Keck et al. 12 vols. (Nashville: Abingdon, 1994-2004)
NIBC	New International Biblical Commentary
NICOT	New International Commentary on the Old Testament
NIV	New International Version
NJB	New Jerusalem Bible
NPNF[1]	Nicene and Post-Nicene Fathers, series 1
NRSV	New Revised Standard Version
ÖBS	Österreichische biblische Studien
OBT	Overtures to Biblical Theology
OTL	Old Testament Library
OTS	Old Testament Studies
REB	Revised English Bible
RSV	Revised Standard Version
SBT	Studies in Biblical Theology
SBTS	Sources for Biblical and Theological Study
SHANE	Studies in the History of the Ancient Near East
SHS	Scripture and Hermeneutics Series
SJT	*Scottish Journal of Theology*
Them	*Themelios*
ThTo	*Theology Today*
TOTC	Tyndale Old Testament Commentaries
TynBul	*Tyndale Bulletin*
VT	*Vetus Testamentum*
VTSup	Vetus Testamentum Supplements
WBC	Word Biblical Commentary
WMANT	Wissenschaftliche Monographien zum Alten und Neuen Testament
WTJ	*Westminster Theological Journal*

Introduction

The Book

The book of Joshua occupies a pivotal place in the Old Testament's opening narrative. It tells of the fulfilment of the promise of land for Israel, made to Abraham in Genesis (Gen 12:1-3). Thus it stands at the end of the Pentateuch (Genesis-Deuteronomy), which takes the reader from the creation of the world, through the election of Israel, its foundation as the covenant people of God, a vision for its social and religious life through law, and the death of Moses, to the point at which the people is equipped and ready to enter the land. Deuteronomy must be followed by something like Joshua if the history of Israel with God is to continue.

Joshua is therefore not just a fulfilment, but also the presupposition of the account of the life of Israel that follows. If Israel had not entered the land, the famous stories of Gideon and Samson, of Saul, David and Solomon, of the prophets and kings of Israel and Judah could never have been told. As Israel under Joshua crosses the great divide of the River Jordan, so the book itself is a threshold, marking the passage from a people without land to a people with land. The building blocks are henceforth in place, and the stage set for the great drama that will show how Israel will fare as God's covenant people, and ultimately as his "light to the nations."

Joshua is no mere division marker, however. It resumes the action narrative that has been in pause since the end of the book of Numbers. The curtain goes up on the great cultural conflict with Canaan, foreshadowed in the earlier narrative and articulated in Deuteronomy. Roughly the first half of the book (Joshua 1–12) is devoted to the possession of the land and confronts the reader with the reality of it, in piece-by-piece expansion into its length and breadth and by means of war. The narrative shows how the covenant antici-

1

pated on the plains of Moab is enacted, with an important echo in Josh 8:30-35 of the ceremony commanded in Deuteronomy 27.

Roughly the second half of the book (chs. 13–24) relates the distribution of the land to the tribes. Once again the theoretical is given substance. Tribal Israel will not only have to hold this land against enemies, it will have to demarcate territory between its parts, and this means the rigorous, painstaking delineation of boundaries. It also means making practical provision for the landless Levites (ch. 21) and for the special problem of the one accused of murder, who flees from his own jurisdiction (ch. 20). This section, and the whole book, culminates with a further great covenantal ceremony at Shechem (ch. 24).

The Audience of Joshua

The audience of Joshua may be considered in connection with the book's place in the large block of Genesis-Kings.[1] When these books are read as a connected whole, their first audience has to be sought at the end point of the whole block, namely in 2 Kings 25, which tells of the destruction of the Jerusalem temple, the exile of the people of Judah to Babylon, and the release of King Jehoiachin from prison (2 Kgs 25:27-30). It is clear from the book of Joshua itself that the reader's perspective is assumed to be some time after the events related, as evident in the expression "to this day" (e.g., Josh 8:28-29; 9:27; 10:27). This feature indicates that the events are told, in some sense, to account for situations that exist later and that are already familiar to readers.

The account of the Gibeonites (Joshua 9), for example, explains why a non-Israelite population exists in the heart of Israel and is engaged in supporting its worship. It is difficult to place this story at any particular time in Judah's history. The phrase "house of my God" (9:23) could refer to the Jerusalem temple, which is frequently called the "house" of the Lord in the Old Testament (as in 2 Sam 7:13), but it need not do so, as is clear from 1 Sam 1:24, where the pre-Davidic sanctuary at Shiloh is described as "the house of the Lord." The Gibeonites were apparently persecuted by Saul, as indicated by their expulsion from their city Beeroth (2 Sam 4:2-3; cf. Josh 9:17), and they subsequently obtained permission from David to take revenge (2 Sam 21:1-6).

---

1. Genesis-Kings is a continuous narrative, though no doubt composed from many sources. In modern scholarship it is now sometimes known as the "primary history;" see Freedman, "The Law and the Prophets," 250-65; and also his "Canon of the OT," 130-36. The history as told in Chronicles, Ezra, and Nehemiah is a separate literary block, completed at a later time than Genesis-Kings. The two blocks complement each other in a number of ways, but Joshua belongs properly to the first.

Later, Solomon's establishment of a forced levy of foreign groups will have affected them, since the Gibeonites were "Hivites" (1 Kgs 9:20-21; cf. Josh 9:7). It is possible to read the Gibeonite story as a portrayal of their decline from a protected status, as under David, to one of slavery and so to uncover successive stages of its composition.[2] While such a reconstruction is uncertain, it is important to realize that a narrative like this one will have had the capacity for differences in meaning at different stages of Israel's history.

It follows that the notion of an audience of the narrative need not refer to the first hearers only. The identity of these first hearers would in any case be hypothetical and could not determine the interpretation. The reader should reckon rather with a succession of audiences, none of them capable of being identified with certainty. Even the exilic audience indicated by the end-point of Genesis-Kings is hypothetical, since little can be known of the specific situation of such an audience, not even whether it was Palestinian or Babylonian. Nor should that audience become determinative for interpreting the book.

However, the setting of Joshua in Genesis-Kings is an unavoidable factor in its interpretation, because it involves, not only the development of the story beyond the confines of the book of Joshua, but also echoes and analogies between the books. One echo is that between Joshua and King Josiah, both of whom put the law of Moses rigorously into effect (Josh 1:8; 24:26; 2 Kgs 23:1-3). Another exists in the concept of the possession of land, since the narrative of occupation under Joshua finds its opposite in that of its loss in Kings. Since Joshua is offered to us in the setting of Genesis-Kings, its message has to be understood in that context too. That is, the possession of land must be considered in the context of its later loss; the existence of Israel as a nation is not presented as a permanent fact, but as something that could unravel, as history demonstrates (see also the final comment on 4:20-24). The Israel that became a nation in its own land could return to being a subject people in a land dominated by a foreign empire, and so have to find a new way of being God's people. With Jewish people henceforth scattered permanently throughout the lands of Babylon and beyond, there would be no return to the situation portrayed in Joshua.

Dating and Historicity

The question of the date of the book has been broached above in connection with the audience. While the book is set in a block that is at least exilic, this

---

2. Nelson offers an interpretation of this sort; *Joshua*, 123-29.

does not remove the question of its origin. How does the account of conquest and settlement relate to the actual origins of Israel in the land that came to bear its name?

The events narrated in Joshua are placed between the Mosaic era, that is, the period of Israelite captivity in Egypt together with its sequel in exodus and wilderness wanderings, and the time of the "judges," namely the period before the rise of the monarchy, when Israel was tribal in form. Since the beginning of King David's reign is usually put at 1010 B.C., Joshua and the judges (the subject of the book of Judges) must be placed in the late second millennium. Precise dating of Joshua, however, is hardly possible. The Old Testament provides chronological data which, at face value, put Moses and Joshua as early as the fifteenth century.[3] Yet among scholars who accept the historicity of exodus and land-occupation in some form, most have opted instead for a date in the thirteenth century and supposed that the text in Kings is based on figures that are intended to refer broadly to generations, or phases in history, rather than to exact spans of time.[4] A further reference point is the Egyptian victory memorial known as the Merneptah Stela (ca. 1230), which refers to "Israel" among the inhabitants and city-states of Palestine. This places an entity known as Israel in Palestine by that date.

The prevailing scholarly view, however, is that Joshua is not a factual account of historical events. The Merneptah Stela notwithstanding, it is not possible to confirm from sources outside the Bible either that Israel existed as a unified people at that time or that it occupied the land by conquest. It is notoriously difficult to match the archaeological evidence concerning the major cities in the narrative to the premise of a conquest in the thirteenth century, although there have been serious attempts to do so.[5] The archaeology, rather, is thought to suggest that Israel was part of the indigenous population, and emerged into a distinct group out of a specific social and cultural context.[6] Its religion likewise only gradually became distinct from the ambient Canaanite

---

3. An important text is 1 Kgs 6:1, which puts the exodus 480 years before Solomon began to build the temple in ca. 960 B.C., which gives a date of about 1440.

4. Typical is Bright, *A History of Israel*, 121-22, who dated the Israelites' labor on the cities of Pithom and Raamses to the reigns of Sethos I (1305-1290) and Ramesses II (1290-1224). This is echoed by Albertz, *A History of Israelite Religion in the Old Testament Period*, 1:45, who found the origins of Yahweh religion in a group of foreign conscripts put to forced labor by the Ramessides.

5. Albright, "Archaeology and the Date of the Hebrew Conquest of Palestine"; Kitchen, *Ancient Orient and Old Testament*, 57-75; Miller, "The Israelite Occupation of Canaan." See also the review and critique of theories of Israel's settlement in the land and an argument for the arrival of Israel in the fifteenth century B.C. by Bimson, "The Origins of Israel in Canaan."

6. See e.g., Finkelstein and Silberman, *The Bible Unearthed*.

religion, so that on one account aniconic mono-Yahwism is a late entrant in Israel, displacing and airbrushing earlier Israelite religion.[7]

Other factors involved in making a decision about history include the nature of the writing. Joshua is undoubtedly theological in character, since it aims, like much of the Old Testament, to persuade its audience to remain faithful to Yahweh, God of Israel. Theology and history, of course, are not necessarily at odds with each other. On the contrary, Christian theology has at its heart claims about events that happened in history. Even so, there is no formula for determining in advance the way in which theology and history relate to each other in any given text. The theological character of Joshua comes across strongly in certain narratives, not least chs. 3–6, which narrate the crossing of the Jordan and the siege and sacking of Jericho. In the commentary that follows, it is suggested that this is not a straightforward factual account of the battle for a city, rather a demonstration that the people of Yahweh could not be resisted. A resistance by the people of Jericho is mentioned in 24:11, but there is nothing of this in ch. 6, suggesting that ch. 6 is stylized, composed for a very specific purpose (see comment there). If this is so, the question naturally arises for the modern reader why the ancient writer would write in such a way. A general answer lies in the obvious point that people in different times and places simply have different understandings of what is involved in telling history. More specifically, the book of Joshua can be assigned to a genre of writing widely exemplified in the ancient Near East, namely the "conquest account," whose purpose was to demonstrate that conquests were successfully undertaken at the behest of the particular nation's god. Joshua then becomes Yahweh's and Israel's version of a kind of literature well known to people at the time.[8] Such accounts were naturally shaped to the purpose of demonstrating the god's supreme power over events.

None of this means that an Israelite conquest of Canaan did not happen. However, as we have observed, at the least the author of Joshua does not intend to furnish a realistic description of the taking of Jericho (though the same cannot be said about the account at Ai in ch. 8). The issue for theological interpretation therefore is: in what sense does the book of Joshua have to be "historical" in order to be valid theologically? The question is engaged more fully later in the volume (in Stephen Williams's section, "Reading Joshua Today"). But we make some preliminary observations at this point.

To address the question of historicity in Joshua is to enter another kind

---

7. This view is articulated by Smith, *The Origins of Biblical Monotheism*.
8. The "conquest account" is well described and documented by Younger, *Ancient Conquest Accounts*.

of discourse from the narrative. In archaeological investigations, it is a question of levels of occupation and destruction, distinguishing types of pottery and dwellings, imagining the original disposition of piles of rubble as walls, reckoning with the effects of erosion. All these factors play a large part in the discussion of Jericho in particular, which is still widely held not to have been occupied as a walled city at the likeliest time of Joshua's conquest (the late thirteenth century). The archaeological record at Jericho is difficult to read, however, and the relation between it and the Joshua narrative continues to be debated. Indeed, every site named in the book raises its own special questions, so that a full account of the relation between the history and the literature would be a vast undertaking, of a sort that the Two Horizons Commentary cannot accommodate. Readers are referred to more technical volumes for such inquiries.[9]

For our present purposes it is appropriate to ask about the nature of the relationship between historical inquiry and the narrative of Joshua. As a question in theological interpretation it goes back well over a century and includes the contribution of Rudolf Bultmann to the debate about the Jesus of history and the Christ of faith. After Bultmann, many interpreters have resisted his strong distinction between faith and history, fact and interpretation.[10] The proclamation of the resurrection of Jesus has no meaning apart from his actual resurrection, and this was apparently the understanding of the New Testament writers (as Paul in 1 Cor 15:13-14). In principle, the same holds true for the study of the history of Israel. Iain Provan and others have argued for the inseparability of history, interpretation, and faith for Old Testament theology and the proper place of philosophy and tradition in historiography, in answer to an influential "minimalist" school of thought that finds that the Old Testament story lacks a basis in historical fact.[11] A Christian reading of Joshua inhabits the Jewish-Christian tradition, in which God's ancient gift of land to Israel plays a part. This by no means preempts historical inquiry as such; it only puts a question against a specific form of it, commonly styled as scientific. On the contrary, the concept of a people chosen by

---

9. For an account of the archaeology of Jericho, see Bienkowski, *Jericho in the Late Bronze Age*. For a more general account of Iron Age archaeology, see Mazar, "The Iron Age I." For a reading of Joshua that discusses historical issues in support of the Joshua narrative, see Hess, *Joshua*.

10. See e.g., Thiselton, *The Two Horizons*, e.g., 213-23, 246-51.

11. Provan, "Ideologies, Literary and Critical: Reflections on Recent Writing on the History of Israel," *JBL* 114 (1995) 585-606. In the same volume of *JBL* was a response by Thompson, "A Neo-Albrightian School in History and Biblical Scholarship?" Provan responded in turn with "In the Stable with the Dwarves"; note esp. 243-51.

God to be the bearer of his salvation to the world requires a correlate in historical actuality.

To describe or articulate the nature of this correlation is more difficult, however, for there is not in the Old Testament a clear and irreducible analogy to the central biblical fact of the resurrection. Even when it is agreed that the Old Testament proclamation requires an actual historical Israel, there remains a work of exegesis and interpretation to judge what kind of historical claim is being made by a particular narrative. The well-known differences between the accounts of Samuel-Kings and Chronicles, for example, raise precisely this question. They compel the reader either to try to harmonize, an approach perhaps invited by the LXX title of Chronicles (*ta paraleipomena*, "things omitted"), but which can lead to unnatural readings, or to suppose that the writers of the texts had different criteria regarding the rendering and interpretation of events than most modern readers. The degree of conformity to a modern perception no doubt varies between Old Testament texts, so that one might judge (as scholarship predominantly has done) that Kings is broadly more "historical" than Chronicles. The same may also be true within books. As we have suggested, the stylized account of the fall of Jericho seems less realistic than the account of the capture of Ai (though this point is made without prejudice to an investigation of the texts with this question in mind). In the commentary section of the present volume, the question of historicity is not primarily in view. This is because we think that the work of interpretation does not need to specify the limits of the historical "core." Indeed, the force of the message in the book cannot depend on a demonstration of this, for none can ever be made, and the reader who required it would be in an impossible position. Indeed one would have to say that the Old Testament writers generally have not felt constrained to give such readers what they seek.

None of this is said in order to qualify the position taken above, that the proclamation of the Old Testament's message depends on a close relationship between fact and interpretation, history and tradition. It is merely to enter the caveat that all texts are subject to the judgments of their readers concerning their nature and purpose, and this includes judgments about the ways in which they speak about history. The differences among scholars on the historical issues in Joshua are unavoidably a factor in the interpretation of the book, and one that is likely to continue. For this reason, the commentary that follows tends to leave certain specifically historical questions open. This is because the relationship between proclamation and "what actually happened" cannot be precisely articulated, and the validity of the narrative as an expression of the meaning of Israel's history is received within theological tradition as a matter of faith. This is not, however, to pitch faith against reason; belief in

Introduction

what cannot be demonstrated "scientifically" is not always irrational. Rather, it is to say that faith need not depend upon a fully worked out historical hypothesis, nor await the kind of demonstration that ordinary historical methods might one day supply.

Reading Joshua as Scripture

The Two Horizons Commentary series is committed to reading the books of the Bible as Christian Scripture. There is nothing formulaic about this, and no attempt to do it is final. The enterprise is as old as the Christian church and is its ongoing task in every generation, because the interpretation of Scripture is a function of the living church in its engagement with an ever-changing world. This point is borne out by the fact that the church's style of reading of the Bible has varied enormously from age to age; indeed it quite regularly varies at any given time across denominations, spiritualities, and cultures. Such variety is not some regrettable thing that ought to be countered by "correct" readings supplied by an all-knowing modern (Western) generation. On the contrary, modern interpretation increasingly recognizes the importance of hearing the symphony of voices that contribute to the obedient hearing of Scripture.[12] This is not to say that interpretation may not be rigorous or contested. On the contrary, much influential interpretation has been born out of controversy. Even so, what is new and controversial is often at the same time a recovery of lost emphases and insights. And nothing that is new and vital now is above correction itself at some future time.

Granted that the subject of biblical interpretation has a vast literature of its own, what can be said briefly about the elements of it? The most significant corollary of the preceding paragraph is that no single method of interpretation can claim hegemony. This in turn raises the question how Christian interpretation is to regard the enormous work of modern scholarship on the Bible. It is an acute question, because some kinds of critical scholarship have been perceived by some Christian readers as posing a threat to the belief that the voice of God is heard through the Bible. Yet it is impossible to ignore any aspect of research on the biblical text. This is not just because, like Everest, it is there, but because it is in the nature of the texts to invite all kinds of ques-

---

12. The Blackwell Bible Commentaries (ed. John Sawyer, Christopher Rowland, Judith Kovacs) are an example of this contemporary trend, with their special attention to readings, and indeed artistic representations, of biblical books and their characters and themes down the centuries; e.g., Gunn, *Judges*.

tions. Here is a narrative of occurrences involving historical peoples and places, and therefore all kinds of historical, geographical, social, anthropological, and religious questions arise. The pursuit of such questions will be contested, of course, as in any academic discipline. But most readers draw on these kinds of inquiries in one way or another, and we cannot help being informed by them.

However, historical methods cannot hold the field alone. As David Ford has written of hermeneutics generally:

> It refuses to be limited to what the text might have meant to its author or first readers and sees it as having an abundance of potential meaning way beyond those.[13]

The search for the author's intention plays a natural part in the reading of a text, because it belongs to the reader's responsibility to take the text seriously as an act of communication. However, it is common today to recognize that the reading of texts varies with the reader, his or her preunderstanding, position in life, interests, and the questions they are asking. One of the aspects of reading Joshua arises from its character as narrative, and it is in respect of its character as narrative that the reader is often invited to make judgments. Narrative techniques enter into the way in which meaning is conveyed. For example, in Josh 6:1-7 the verb עבר/'ābar, "go over," is repeated several times, in order to chime with the theme of land-possession, recall the crossing of the Reed Sea in Exodus 14–15, and stress the certainty of the conquest. The extraordinary muteness of Jericho adds to the effect. There is an artfulness here that is part of the message. Moreover, narratives do not come with univocal meanings, but invite the reader to participate in interpretation. Recent commentary on Joshua, alive to the possibilities of meaning in narrative, assumes that the meaning may not always, or entirely, lie on the surface.[14] The present commentary therefore considers such questions as whether Joshua and Israel always makes the right choices: did they get it right in the matter of Rahab, or the Gibeonites? Interpreters of narrative sometimes speak of "gaps" in a text, that is, spaces which the reader is invited to fill, and Joshua is a candidate, in common arguably with all Old Testament narrative, to be regarded as a "gapped text."[15] Readers of the present commentary will make their own

---

13. Ford, *Christian Wisdom*, 69.

14. An important example is Hawk, *Joshua*. A precedent had been set by Polzin, *Moses and the Deuteronomist*.

15. On the phenomenon of "gapping" in biblical narrative see Sternberg, *The Poetics of Biblical Narrative*, 230-63.

Introduction

judgments too, and our suggestions of meaning are offered in full acknowledgement of that.

But for Christian reading the most important issue is how, above and beyond an "original" meaning, texts bear witness to Jesus Christ. This is particularly sharp in the case of Old Testament texts, because they bore meanings for their first hearers, and subsequent Jewish communities, before Christ, and thus before they bore Christian meanings. The book of Joshua was important to Jewish readers who needed to know that they had legitimate claims to a territory and that tribes had claims to specific lands within it. How then does this book bear witness to Jesus Christ, who came for the sake of all humanity, and how does it speak to his worldwide church? In Christian interpretation there is, by definition, meaning beyond meaning. One way of expressing this is by the concept of *sensus plenior* (fuller sense). Methods such as allegory and typology have been employed in order to enable Christian readers to hear parts of Scripture such as Joshua. The River Jordan has achieved celebrity well beyond its status as a minor river in Palestine (snubbed by the Syrian Naaman, 2 Kgs 5:10-12), as a figure for death, while the promised land of Canaan stands for the life beyond.[16] It is the task of Christian theology to go on thinking about how each part of Scripture bears witness to God's work in the world, a work that encompasses the history of the people Israel and the life, death, and resurrection of Jesus Christ.[17] In the section "Joshua and Biblical Theology" we address aspects of Christian theology that arise from a reading of Joshua.

Joshua and Theology

The central aim of the present volume is to interpret the book of Joshua in relation to Christian theology. After an exegesis of the text (by Gordon

---

16. An example is the great hymn of William Williams, "Guide Me, O Thou Great Jehovah."
17. The century past has seen hugely significant contributions to this task, in the work of, e.g., von Rad, *Old Testament Theology*; Eichrodt, *Theology of the Old Testament*; and the extensive writings of Childs, including *Biblical Theology of the Old and New Testaments*. Childs's contribution remains contemporary, and has influenced other important scholars such as Seitz, in, e.g., *Word Without End*, and Moberly, *The Bible, Theology, and Faith*. Fundamental to all these, especially Childs and his successors, is the belief in a two-testament witness to Jesus Christ, in which each testament retains its own character. The Old is not nullified by the New, but each goes on illuminating the other. A distinctive reflection on the relation between historical exegesis and biblical and theological interpretation, with worked examples, is offered by Lacocque and Ricoeur, *Thinking Biblically*. See also Goldingay, "Old Testament Theology and the Canon," and the response of Seitz, "Canon, Narrative, and the Old Testament's Literal Sense."

Introduction

McConville), a second section (by Stephen Williams) will further address issues of interpretation such as those raised above, and also consider a number of theological topics, namely, land, covenant, law, miracle, judgment (with the problem of genocide), idolatry. The premise of this part of the book (as of the whole) is that the theological topics engaged in Joshua are not limited to the horizons of the author and first readers of the book, but that the book is part of a much larger testimony concerning them. For example, covenant as a concept embraces the widely varying covenantal events associated with Noah, Abraham, Moses, David, prophetic preaching ("New Covenant"), and finally the covenant sealed by Jesus himself in his atoning death. The theological treatment of covenant involves asking what it is about God and the world that can be expressed in various ways through this idea. So it is with all theological topics. The theological interpretation continues into a third section, in which both authors of the volume offer a reflection on reading Joshua as part of Christian Scripture and then make a short response to each other. As we have noted in the Preface, each author has commented in detail on the other's drafts of the material in all three parts. Inevitably, we differ on some points, but our thinking is close enough for us to be happy with the product as a venture in joint authorship.

Undergirding the whole inquiry is the premise that God has acted in the world from the creation, through his life with historic Israel (Immanuel, "God with us"), his missional command to that people, and ultimately in Jesus Christ, himself representative of both Israel and humanity. Christian interpretation begins with the premise that God is self-consistent and that Scripture testifies to his purposeful action and revelation. This is the hermeneutical ground for reading Joshua as Christian Scripture.

The contemporary theological relevance of Joshua is unmistakable. Its central topic of land resonates not only with the modern contention over the territory of Israel-Palestine, but with the perennial relationship between human beings and land, not only as essential to life and sustenance, but also as identity and "place." Many current world conflicts could be linked to these powerful factors. With the question of the right to possess land comes also that of the nature of God and so of society. In its conflict between Israel and Canaan, the book of Joshua portrays a conflict between cultures, a way of life in obedience to Yahweh God of Israel and regulated by his Torah and another way that is characterized as idolatrous. This is the issue that is really at stake in the midst of the violence of the events narrated.

In their contemporary relevance these are highly controversial, and even dangerous, themes. We are familiar today with conflicts conducted in the name of God and attended by violence, including "ethnic cleansing."

Introduction

Does not Joshua lend credibility to triumphalist nationalisms, in which all ordinary human considerations are subordinated to the drive for the victory of the "chosen"? The book is admittedly dangerous in this way. Yet this makes it all the more urgent to reckon seriously with it in the context of Christian Scripture and theology. Much of what is commanded and done in Joshua cannot be taken as command to any modern people. In what ways, therefore, may we learn from it? Such questions are the stuff of Christian biblical and theological interpretation and action.

Commentary

Joshua 1

1:1-5 The new stage in the story of Israel opens by recalling the death of Moses. (The book of Judges begins in a similar way.) Joshua is already known to readers of the Pentateuch as Moses' "servant" (מְשָׁרֵת/*mĕšārēt*; Exod 24:13; 33:11; Num 11:28), a term which points to a religious role (esp. Exod 33:11). Joshua had accompanied Moses when he went up Mount Sinai to receive the commandments from God (Exod 24:13), on that occasion apparently going further than Nadab, Abihu, and the seventy elders who also set out with Moses (Exod 24:9). This marks him out as preeminent among those who would survive Moses.

From the first verse, God now addresses Joshua directly. The crossing of the Jordan which he is to lead (v. 2) will be symptomatic of the possession of the land, a full circle from the exodus from Egypt, which had also involved a crossing (of the Reed Sea; Exodus 14–15). His special assignment is to lead the people of Israel into the land that God had promised to give them, as far back in the story as Abraham (Gen 12:7). For a moment, God's address shifts to the people as a whole (vv. 3-4), when he expands on the promise of land, in terms close to those of Genesis and Deuteronomy (e.g., Gen 15:18-21; Deut 1:6-8; 11:24; 17:14; 34:1-4). Joshua's role was always to have a military aspect (Num 13:16; 14:6, 30; Deut 31:3, 7-8, 23). It is in this connection that God promises to be with Joshua (v. 5), a promise that has been made to him once already (Deut 31:23c), and which reminds us of God's assurance to Moses himself (Exod 3:12). The continuation, "I will never leave you or forsake you," was first spoken to Israel (Deut 4:31; 31:6), but now to Joshua (as later recalled in Heb 13:5).

1:6-9 The next short paragraph records Joshua's commissioning for the task. It is not a first charge to Joshua, but a reaffirmation, for God had already commissioned him while Moses was still alive (Deut 31:7, 14-15, 23). Indeed, v. 6 virtually repeats Deut 31:7. The charge to "be strong and courageous" is suitable for the military task ahead. But the word used, "cause to inherit" (ESV; cf. "put in possession," NRSV), speaks of more than victory, rather of legitimate occupation. The idea of "inheritance" is a way of expressing Israel's God-given right to the land, frequent in Deuteronomy (Deut 4:21). The story of Joshua will tell first of the victory (chs. 2–12), then of the "causing to inherit," as the tribes in turn receive their portions of the territory (chs. 13–22).

The possession of the land will be in fulfilment of God's promise to their "fathers" (v. 6). In itself, "fathers" might refer to the preceding generation. However, in the context it should be taken to mean Abraham and the generations after him, to whom the promise of the land first came (Gen 12:1-3; 28:13-15), and this is the basis of NRSV's "ancestors." That is, God swore to the patriarchs (Abraham, Isaac, and Jacob) that he would give the land to their descendants. This is the generation that will now benefit from that promise.

The exhortation to be strong and courageous is now repeated (v. 7), and with a new end in view. The repetition is surprising at first glance, for now Joshua's courage is directed towards keeping the law of Moses. This is primarily the laws and commands as given by Moses in Deuteronomy, for it is there that such laws are commanded to be written in the "Book of the Law" (Deut 28:58, 61; 31:9, 24-26). Moreover, any future king of Israel was especially required to keep his own copy of this book and obey the laws in it (Deut 17:18-20). The command to Joshua here is very like that given to the king in that place, so that many have thought that Joshua is a royal figure in all but name.[1] It is not necessary to go so far, however. Rather, the standard for all leaders of Israel is set by these terms.

The focus remains on law-keeping in vv. 7-8, before returning to the military context in v. 9. The turn to law-keeping is sometimes regarded as intrusive at this point and indicative of the special interest of a "nomistic" editor (one with a strong interest in law).[2] However, vv. 6-8 make a point that is fundamental to Joshua, namely that possession of the land, though legitimated first of all by God's gift, can continue to be legitimate only when it is held according to God's law. God's writ will run in the land that he gives to his people.

The narrative's horizon returns to the taking of the land (v. 9). The command to be strong and courageous is given again in this context. This is

---

1. E.g., Nelson, *Joshua*, 119.
2. The classic expression of this point of view was that of Smend, "The Law and the Nations."

clear first from its accompaniment, that Joshua should not fear or be dismayed, which is like what was said to Israel through Moses in Deut 1:21. In that place we saw that this "not fearing" was the test of faith on which the taking of the land would depend, a test which Israel first failed (Deut 1:26-33). The test of faith now comes to Joshua himself. But God reassures him in words which he had already heard from Moses (Deut 31:7). The promise that God would be with him also recalls God's words to Moses himself at the beginning of that leader's own great test of faith (Exod 3:12). There are prophetic overtones here as well (Jer 1:17-19).

1:10-11 Joshua's command here testifies to an organization of the people for war already in place. The "officers" are administrative figures. In Deut 1:15 they are among officials appointed by Moses to ease his burden of leadership, and in Deut 16:18 they are to be appointed alongside judges, in that case to assist in judicial administration. It may be supposed that the officials are here appointed according to tribe, as in those cases. Here (as in Deut 1:15) they are part of a military chain of command. The command itself shows a mix of prudence and faith: they will be prepared for the march, but also go in faith that the struggle is in principle won, because God gives them the land to possess.

Israel is about to "cross" the Jordan, "to take possession of the land the Lord your God is giving you for your own." The phrasing is typical in Deuteronomy (e.g., 9:1; 11:31). The time long heralded has come. Yahweh not only "gives" the land for Israel to "inherit" it, but they will then "possess" it, a term used now for the first time in Joshua, and immediately repeated. These different terms have their own significance. By Yahweh's gift Israel will be the legitimate holders of this land.

1:12-18 The narrative now remembers that part of the land has already been given and possessed, that is, the Transjordanian part (to the east of the River Jordan). This was territory already acquired under Moses by victories over the Amorite kings Sihon and Og and given to the tribes of Reuben, Gad, and half-Manasseh. The story is told in Numbers 32 and Deut 2:26–3:22. This part of the land did not easily fit into the typology of "crossing over" to possess, since Israel did not have to cross over to take it. Its importance, however, is clear from the number of times the narrative returns to it in Numbers-Joshua (see also Num 21:31-35; Josh 12:1-6; 13:8-33).

The description of the Transjordanian settlement is quite in line with the promise of land. The territory is a place where Yahweh is "giving rest" to these tribes, the term used for settling down in peace in the land he is giving (cf. Deut 12:9-10; Josh 11:23; 21:44). The unity of the Transjordanian tribes with the rest of Israel is carefully maintained in the duty laid on them to assist their fellow Israelites in taking the land beyond the Jordan. Yet it looks as if two "lands" are in view here, one on each side of the Jordan (vv. 13, 15), each "possessed" by the different parts of Israel. Whether, therefore, the Transjordanian area is part of the promised land in the strict sense is always somewhat in doubt. Perhaps for this reason Moses could lead in this part of the conquest, though he had been forbidden by God from crossing the Jordan and leading the conquest proper (Deut 1:37-38; 3:23-29).

Even so, the Transjordanians declare their loyalty to Joshua and his right to the obedience Moses had once enjoyed (vv. 16-18). Thus, before the narrative of conquest proper in Joshua, the issue of the unity of Israel is recalled, though not yet finally settled (see ch. 22). The taking of the land beyond the Jordan is part of a project already begun by Moses.

Joshua 2

2:1-7 The narrative of the conquest is prefaced by the story of how a Canaanite prostitute assists the Israelites in their preparation to advance across the Jordan. This is a perhaps unexpected change of mood from ch. 1, which may have raised anticipation of a confident march forward. Instead, Israelites find themselves in collaboration with a Canaanite. Joshua's sending of spies from Shittim (in Moab, Num 33:48-49) is itself unexpected (2:1), since the previous spy mission had ended in failure because the people refused to believe a favorable report (Numbers 13–14; also Deut 1:22-33). In this case, however, based on Rahab's evidence (2:9-11) the spies are able to report that the population of "the land" (vv. 9, 24) is terrified of Israel's approach. This is a reversal of the Israelites' fear on the first occasion, and so it enables the story to carry forward the main line of the narrative of the conquest on an upbeat note. The immediate goal of taking Jericho symptomizes the objective of taking the whole land, as we see from the way in which the mission is expressed in 2:1.

The spies lodge in Rahab's house, perhaps thinking that such a house might offer hope of concealment and also because they might pick up information there. It is a risky strategy, yet spying is bound to be a risky business, and the spies may have decided on boldness for the sake of quick gains. The prostitute's house proves to be the last place in which strangers in town might hope to go unnoticed. Straight-away news reaches the "king of Jericho" that they are there (v. 2), and we realize that the strategy has put them entirely in the hands of others whose own interests must be unpredictable. Rahab, however, seems not to have been implicated in the leakage of their presence, and in the frantic search she sides with the spies, hiding them and throwing the king's guard off the scent. Her role as a prostitute affords an explanation of why these strangers might be in her house (the exchange in vv. 3-4, "came to you/me," can be understood sexually), and this is why she can get away with pretending to know nothing about them.

Her first act, therefore, shows that she is willing to frustrate the interests of Jericho, seen in terms of its own power structures. Why does she do this, considering the risks of being discovered as a traitor? Perhaps she was disaffected. A prostitute and her family, no doubt placed in their lowly social position due to poverty and debt, line up against the "king." In this way the social fissures within Canaanite society are exposed in the prelude to Israel's approach. It is against "kings" that Joshua's Israel is coming (see 12:1 and the list in 12:9-24, headed by the king of Jericho). That is, they were coming against a form of city-state kingship in which all wealth and power were ultimately in the royal domain. In such a society some could become poor and have little hope of remedying their poverty. This may be the background to Rahab's decision to put herself on the wrong side of her own authorities.

2:8-14 Whatever her politics, Rahab turns to theology to explain herself to the spies. She expresses the terror before the advance of Israel that is part of the story of God's promise that it would overcome the peoples of the promised land (vv. 9-11; cf. Exod 15:15-16; Num 22:3). Her words are close to Israel's own records of God's faithfulness, when she recalls the exodus from Egypt, the crossing of the Reed Sea, and the defeat of Sihon and Og, the two Transjordanian kings (v. 10; cf. Deut 11:2-4; Ps 135:8-12). She also uses the name Yahweh in her speech. Her words are often held to express the deuteronomic view of the author of Joshua.[3] However, Rahab's actions make most sense if she does actually think she will come out on the winning side. Her understanding that God has indeed given the land of Canaan to Israel serves to underline that the promised victory is certain.

As the price of protecting the spies she asks them for an agreement, in the form of a solemn oath, not to harm her or her family. As she has "dealt kindly" with them (v. 12 NRSV), so they should do to her. The expression she uses is חסד/*ḥesed*, "faithful" or "steadfast love," the specific quality of covenantal relationship (cf. 1 Sam 20:8). Rahab thus binds the spies to their agreement in the most powerful way she knows. And in accepting her terms with an oath on their own lives, they promise not only *ḥesed*, but for good measure add "truth." The spies thus emphatically commit Israel in advance to this act of mercy, which Joshua will in due course honor, and which will result in at least some Canaanites continuing to live alongside them in the land (Josh 6:22-25).

---

3. See Nelson, *Joshua*, 46.

2:15-21 Rahab, always in control, sends the men off to the hill country. Their spying mission is thus abruptly at an end, accomplished to the extent of what they have learned from Rahab. As they go, they qualify their agreement. To save herself, Rahab must display a "scarlet cord" at her window (possibly a piece of clothing which might be used as a sign of her trade). And she is warned to keep her family in the confines of her house. Only on these conditions will the oath hold.

2:22-24 The spies report everything to Joshua, holding nothing back of their oath to Rahab (as is clear from 6:22-25). Joshua is interested only in what Rahab herself had given away: that the population was terrified of Israel. It is time for the enemy to fear; Israel can put aside its own fear (contrast Deut 1:28-29).

It is nevertheless a disconcerting opening to the story of conquest. The spies, who should have kept their presence secret, fall straight away into the power of Canaanites. They seem unable to report anything of strategic value, beyond the confirmation that the Canaanites are afraid. And they have committed themselves to a party within Jericho, with an oath that runs counter to the command to put the whole city under the ban of destruction. After the confident beginning, the account has now raised the question whether Israel's occupation of Canaan will run as smoothly as hoped.

Rahab herself is the most intriguing character in the story. She is a liminal figure in her own city, a prostitute living in the very wall that will shortly collapse in the Israelite siege (6:20). Paradoxically, this very liminality may be that which alerts her first to a threat from outside, and by the same token an opportunity for salvation. Should she be read as a clever opportunist, who does what is necessary to save herself and her family in the societal meltdown that she foresees? Or should we take her confession of faith in Yahweh at its face value? The narrative itself does not compel a decision on this, any more than it is generally possible to read the intentions of people encountered in life. Her inclusion in the paean to the faithful in Hebrews 11 (v. 31), while it does not in itself resolve the narrative ambiguities of Joshua 2, shows that Rahab can be read sympathetically.

Joshua 3

Following the spies' adventures in Jericho, the scene returns to Shittim (3:1; cf. 2:1) where Joshua and Israel prepare to cross the River Jordan. This is the most important single event in the book, and its telling occupies the next two chapters. The Jordan is the first and most important boundary of the land Israel is about to occupy, and its crossing carries all the symbolic weight of the passage from no-land to land, from not possessing to possessing. The miraculous stopping of the flow of water is like the miracle at the Reed Sea (Exodus 14–15), as the present narrative points out (4:23). As such, it is clearly presented as forming part of the same continuing action of God, in which he does "amazing things" (3:5; cf. Deut 4:34) in order to bring his people from slavery into freedom in a land he would give them.

The event is memorialized in Israel's literature. The prophet Micah recalls "what happened from Shittim to Gilgal" in a series of Yahweh's saving acts of Israel (Mic 6:5-6 NRSV, reflecting on Numbers 22–25). In Ps 66:6 the crossings of Reed Sea and Jordan are echoed together in the parallelism of "sea" (ים/*yām*) and "river" (נהר/*nāhār*) (see also Ps 74:13-15). And Elijah and Elisha replicate Israel's crossing (2 Kgs 2:7-8) at the moment when the older man is about to die and pass his prophetic role to the younger, in another symbolic new beginning.

Lying behind the event is a further memory, the creation myth that appears in different forms in both Babylon and Canaan. In Canaan, Baal slays Yam, the god "Sea," who is also at times called Nahar, "River." Like the Babylonian Tiamat, slain by Marduk, he represents the potential for the created order to succumb to chaos. The memory of this myth explains the poetic celebration of Yahweh's creative power in Ps 74:12-17. And the stories of Reed Sea and Jordan echo it in their own way, demonstrating that Yahweh (and not another god) has the power to call all creation to heel, and at the same time that the elements of creation have no animate power of their own (unlike the myths). Sea and river are merely sea and river, not gods.

The story essentially tells how the people, following the ark of the covenant borne by the priests, cross the Jordan, helped by the miraculous act by which the river is stopped in its normal flow. In the course of this action they also set up memorial stones in the river (4:9) and in Gilgal (4:8, 20). The story is often found to be inconsistent in its details (e.g., because the command in 3:12 is not acted on till 4:2; and because some elements occur twice, such as the taking up of the stones from the river; 4:8-9, 20), and this is attributed to a complex textual prehistory.[4] Most of the perceived discrepancies, however, are intelligible within the progress of the narrative.

3:1-6 "Joshua rose early" is a typical expression in the book indicating haste and readiness to proceed (also 6:15; 7:16; 8:10; cf. 8:14). The departure

---

4. Some see in addition a discrepancy between the priests standing at the edge of the Jordan (3:8, 13, 15) and in the middle (3:17); an inconsistency is found between the time scale in vv. 1, 5 (overnight) and vv. 2-4 (three days). For these and others, see Nelson, *Joshua*, 55.

from Shittim shows that this new resolve is the sequel of the spies' episode. The unity of Joshua and Israel is signalled by the fact that plural verbs immediately follow on the first singular ("they set out . . . came . . . lodged"), confirmed in "he and all the people of Israel." The three-day wait before crossing (v. 2) harks back to 1:11 and may also correspond to the time of the spies' mission (2:22). But now the sense of purpose grows with the busy work of the "officers." This group appears elsewhere in Joshua in conjunction with other bearers of authority in Israel (8:33; 23:2; 24:1); here they have an intermediate role between Joshua and the rank and file (see also Deut 16:18, where their role seems to be connected with that of the "judges").

The ark of the covenant has both military and religious significance. Its role in Israel's wars may be seen when Israel moves as a military unit through the wilderness towards the land (Num 3:5-10; 4; Deut 31:9, 25) and also in the encounters with the Philistines (1 Samuel 4–6). On these occasions the duty of its care falls to the Levites, or Levitical priests.[5] In the present context, the people must keep at a distance from it, because of its holiness, as they had once had to stay back from Mount Sinai when God came down upon it to make covenant with the people (Exod 19:21-24).

In religious terms, the ark is associated in Exodus-Deuteronomy with both the presence of God and the law given at Mount Sinai when Israel entered into covenant with him (Exod 25:10-22; Deut 10:1-5). The divine presence is a theme in both war and religion. Paramount here, it seems, is the connection between the ark and the law of Yahweh. When the ark crosses the Jordan, not only is it symbolic of Yahweh's victory over the peoples and gods of Canaan, but also of the connection between the land and the law. The occupation and tenure of the land will be in accordance with the law given in the making of the covenant.

In another echo of the Mount Sinai encounter (Exod 19:10-15, 22), the people are now commanded to "consecrate themselves" because of the holiness of the enterprise ahead (v. 5). In view of Exod 19:5-10, such consecration probably involved ritual washing and abstention from sexual intercourse, perhaps also from some foods (these preparations are echoed in 1 Sam 21:5; 2 Sam 11:11). The repetitions in v. 6 emphasize the solemnity of the ark's precedence.

3:7-13 Joshua is again likened to Moses (see on 1:1-5), and God prom-

---

5. The terms used for priests and Levites vary in the pentateuchal narrative. Broadly, the sections of the Pentateuch classed as "priestly" specify various roles within the priestly tribe, the tribe of Levi, as in Numbers 4. Deuteronomy speaks more generally of "the Levites," or "the priests the Levites," who appear to be the same (see Deut 31:9, 25). Joshua can both specify distinctions within the tribe (Josh 21:4) and adopt the more general usage (Josh 14:4). Here Joshua uses the term found in Deut 18:1.

ises him that his Moses-like authority will be seen in what is about to unfold. The event in prospect will be an act of faith, for the entry to the land has always been portrayed as such (Numbers 13–14; Deuteronomy 1). The exaltation of Joshua is not for his own sake, but so that Israel may know that God is carrying out his purposes through him. As the enterprise is one of faith, so Joshua's Mosaic role takes on prophetic tones when he declares the words of Yahweh (3:9). He then first commands the priests and second addresses all Israel, preparing them for the miraculous crossing of the Jordan, so similar to the crossing of the Reed Sea.

The priests' standing in the Jordan bearing the ark marks the river as the border of the land that God is about to give to Israel. Joshua commands the priests to stand in the river and at the same time addresses all Israel, proclaiming that he is about to dispossess the present inhabitants of the land. This, furthermore, will be a demonstration that he, Yahweh of Israel who has brought his people thus far, is truly the "living God" (אל חי/ʾēl ḥay). The term "el/El" used here can be both a generic ("god") and a proper name in Canaanite religion for the supreme deity.[6] It occurs in both senses in the Old Testament for the God of Israel, generically in, e.g., Exod 34:14 and in proper names such as El Shaddai (Gen 17:1; Exod 6:3). It can be difficult to tell the two types of use apart in some cases. Here "the living God" seems appropriate, the implication being that no other god can be called this.

The act of possessing is at the same time a dispossessing of the population of Canaan, a theme which has been building in the pentateuchal narrative since Exodus (Exod 3:8, 17; 13:5; 23:23; 34:11; Deut 20:17). These texts all name six nations, as do Josh 9:1; 11:3; 12:8. The seven nations mentioned here, adding the Girgashites (v. 10), are also named in Deut 7:1 and Josh 24:11. The terms Canaanite and Amorite can be used more generally to refer to the inhabitants of the whole land (Deut 1:7). The longer list specifies people groups more closely, and some can be linked with areas of the land (see Gen 34:2; Josh 9:7 for Hivites; Josh 15:63; 2 Sam 5:6 for Jebusites as inhabitants of Jerusalem). A number of them, notably Hittites, are thought to have origins in Anatolia (roughly modern Turkey), but little else is known of them.[7]

The act of dispossessing and putting in possession shows that the God of Israel is the God of creation and history, to whom all nations owe their life

---

6. Biblical forms such as El Elyon (God Most High) and El Shaddai (usually translated God Almighty) probably derive from the use of the name El for the high god in Canaan. One of these expressions, ʾēl ʿelyôn qōnēh šāmayim wāʾāreṣ (Gen 14:19), attaches to El Elyon the epithet "creator of heaven and earth" and has an attested Canaanite equivalent; see Cross, *Canaanite Myth and Hebrew Epic*, 15-16, 50-51, and 46-60 for a general discussion of El and Yahweh.

7. See Weinfeld, *Deuteronomy 1–11*, 363.

and well-being (cf. Deut 2:1-25; 32:8; Amos 9:7). It is a demonstration before the nations that he and not other gods have this kind of authority. The point is conveyed in the full expression "the ark of the covenant of the Lord of all the earth" (v. 11; cf. v. 13).

The command to select a man from each of the twelve tribes (v. 12) comes unexpectedly early in one sense, since their task of taking stones from the Jordan is not yet prescribed. In the context of the prophetic word about the miracle that is about to happen, it may signify that it is Israel as a whole that will have the title to the land, the twelve Israelites standing in contrast to the six nations about to be dispossessed.

The promised parting of the waters of the Jordan (v. 13) corresponds to Joshua's declaration in v. 10, "This is how you will know . . . ," and is the culmination of his speech in this chapter. By that sign the people would be assured that Yahweh was with them on their journey into this land occupied by others. The ark is called the "ark of the Lord," to focus on his action in the event (contrast "ark of the covenant" in vv. 8, 14); and Yahweh is once again qualified as "the Lord of all the earth."

3:14-17 The final paragraph tells how the promised sign is put into effect. The priests proceed ahead of the people as commanded (v. 6). The miraculous nature of the event is stressed by the fact that the Jordan was so full at the time of year (early harvest, after the winter's rains) that it overflowed its banks. (This point is slipped in parenthetically, v. 15a; for the time of year, see also 4:19; 5:10). The event was not merely an interruption in the slow flow of a half empty riverbed, but the halting of a river in flood, so that the waters coming down the valley stood in a heap (v. 16), and the echo of the miracle at the Reed Sea is unmistakable (cf. Exod 15:8, where the same word "heap" is used). And this happened as soon as the priests' feet touched the edge of the water. The perspective stretches several miles upriver to the place called Adam.[8]

The narrative finally returns to the people's crossing over towards Jericho (v. 16). The manner of the crossing is described, the priests in the center of the river while the people go on ahead (a suspension of the normal order of march in 3:3). It is emphasized that "the whole nation" (כל־הגוי/*kol-haggôy*) crosses. This focuses first on the unity of Israel; the word *gôy*, as applied to Israel in Joshua, occurs almost always in expressions stressing its wholeness (4:1; 5:6, 8). The word points secondly to Israel's status as one nation among (or over against) others (*gôyyīm*; Josh 12:23; 23:3, 4, 7, 9, 12, 13).

---

8. Cf. Hess, *Joshua*, 105, who locates Adam 18 miles north of Jericho, just south of the River Jabbok.

Joshua 4

4:1-9 In principle the story of the crossing has been told. However, this second part of the unit composed of chs. 3–4 takes it up from a different chronological point of view. The opening verse makes an express link with 3:17, with its perspective of a completed crossing. Yet immediately the lens appears to return to an earlier point. For the narrative now turns its attention to the stones set up in Jordan and at Gilgal to commemorate the event. And in order to do so it pans back to a point before the crossing, when the instructions about this are given (v. 5).

The selection of twelve men, one for each tribe, has been anticipated in 3:12 but comes here as God's command to Joshua (cf. the twelve spies in Deut 1:23). Their purpose is now explained, namely to take up stones from the Jordan to be set up in Gilgal. The theme of the stones is one of the complicated aspects of this narrative, for there appear to be two sets. The first, to which the narrative mainly refers, is taken out of the River Jordan (vv. 3-5) and set up on the Canaanite bank, deposited initially in the camp (vv. 3, 8), and eventually erected by Joshua in Gilgal (v. 20). The second, mentioned only in v. 9, is set up by Joshua in the river itself. This curious duplication has widely been seen as evidence of the complicated prehistory of the present text.[9]

The purpose of the stones is to be a "sign" (v. 6). This term (אוֹת/'ôt) refers in some texts to miraculous acts done by God (e.g., Deut 4:34, along with "wonders"), in others to prophetic signs, given as tokens of events that will surely follow (1 Sam 2:34; 2 Kgs 19:29; 20:8). In still others the "sign" is closer to a symbol, an object (or person) that connotes some deeper reality (Exod 12:13; Deut 6:8; Isa 8:18). Here it has elements of these latter two meanings. It is, of course, a memorial of something that has happened, and as such belongs squarely within the important Old Testament tradition of remembering as an act of worship and formation, as the formula about the questions of the children indicates (v. 6; see also Exod 12:26-27). At the same time it contains a promise, since it marks the claim to the land made in this formative moment by Yahweh.

The representative function of the twelve men is clear in v. 8, when the action with the stones is attributed to "the Israelites" and the twelve stones are expressly said to stand for the tribes. In this way attention is drawn again to the wholeness of Israel. Yet it is a wholeness that acknowledges the diversity of the people. The relationship between whole and part will become an important theme in the narrative of the distribution of land.

---

9. See Nelson, *Joshua*, 65.

The twelve stones placed in the river by Joshua (v. 9) have a different function from the stones set up at Gilgal. Here the middle of the river is significant in itself, as the place where the priests stood, on dry ground, while the tribes passed through (cf. 3:17; 4:10). It is possible that the stones are a platform for the priests to stand on.[10] However, they also serve the purpose of memorial.

4:10-13 The completion of the crossing is now announced again (cf. 3:17; 4:1), as a means of resuming the main line of the narrative. A note is added recalling the flow of authority from Yahweh to Moses to Joshua. The crossing has been done in obedience to Yahweh's command. And it has been done "quickly," conveying a sense that Israel is ready and willing (like the recurring narrative feature according to which Joshua and the people "rose early" for action). Finally, the priests, having waited for the people to cross, bear the ark to the other side. This anticipates vv. 16-18, but the function of the information at this point is to convey the manner in which the entire crossing was completed.

The nation is depicted as a military force ready for action (vv. 12-13). The tribes of Reuben, Gad, and the half-tribe of Manasseh are those who have already settled in lands awarded by Moses, but who are under an obligation to assist the remaining nine-and-a-half tribes to conquer the land west of the Jordan (see on 1:12-15). The mention of them here, therefore, is part of the portrayal of the people as a military force. The term used, "armed men," occurs most frequently in connection with Israel's march on the promised land. In Num 32:25-32 and Deut 3:18 its context, as here, is the obligation of the Transjordanians to participate in the battles ahead; and in Josh 6:7, 9, 13 it appears in the story of the fall of Jericho.

4:14 This verse harks back to 3:7, where Yahweh said to Joshua that he would begin to "make him great," a phrase used elsewhere of Abraham (Gen 12:2) and Solomon (1 Chr 29:25; 2 Chr 1:1). Joshua's authority in Israel is here virtually on a par with that of Moses (see also on 1:1-8).

4:15-19 The perspective returns to the point at which the priests emerge from the Jordan (see vv. 10-11). Here the new element is that they do so in response to the command of Joshua. The function of this passage is finally to round off the narrative of the crossing. As in the first portrayal of the event the miraculous aspect of it was stressed (3:15-16), so it is again, with the indication that the waters that had been held back suddenly poured downriver as soon as the priests set foot on the western bank (v. 18).

---

10. Hess, *Joshua*, 109; Nelson, *Joshua*, 69. Some argue that these stones are the same ones that are later set up in Gilgal, e.g., Hess; Howard, *Joshua*, 136-37. But this is not the most natural reading of the text.

The ark is here called by a new name (ארון העדות/'ărôn hā'ēdût) for the only time in the book (v. 16). This is the regular way of designating the ark in Exodus (Exod 25:22; 26:33-34). There the name is used because the 'ēdût, "testimony," is placed in the ark (Exod 25:16), and so the expression in our text is sometimes translated "ark of the testimony."[11] The name "testimony" puts a certain spin on the idea of God's commands, namely as a witness both to his making of the covenant with Israel and perhaps to his holy character. The word evidently refers to the laws given in the making of the covenant, as in Deut 10:1-5 (where the reference is expressly to the Ten Commandments). For this reason, to avoid confusion, other translations prefer "ark of the covenant" (NRSV), which is also used to translate the more usual phrase in Joshua 3–6, ארון הברית 'ărôn habbĕrît (e.g., 3:6, 8; cf. 4:18). (The term 'ēdût is used also in 2 Kgs 11:12 to refer to an emblem presented to the boy king Joash, perhaps referring to a copy of the "book of the law"; cf. Deut 17:18. NIV adopts this interpretation in 2 Kings 11, with "covenant," while ESV more cautiously has "testimony.")

The story of the crossing is rounded off (v. 19) with an indication of the date. We know already that the season is "harvest," referring to the earliest ripe growth of the year (3:15; cf. Lev 23:10). But now we are told that it is the "tenth day of the first month" (roughly March-April),[12] that is, the day on which preparations for the Passover begin (Exod 12:2-3) and just four days before the date of the Passover itself, which the people will in fact celebrate in Gilgal (5:10; cf. Exod 12:6-11; Lev 23:5). Since the whole narrative of the first entry to the land points towards this goal of Passover, it can be understood as a celebration of the passage from the barren wilderness, where they had depended on manna (5:12), to settled existence in fruitful land.

4:20-24 The event at the Jordan is placed finally in a context of memory and worship. The setting up of the stones in Gilgal is the occasion for anticipating the child's question to parents as to their meaning (v. 21; cf. vv. 6-7). This is also how the regular Passover celebration itself is initiated (Exod 12:26), the child's question having become a central part of the Passover liturgy to the present day. So the parallel between the crossing of the Jordan and the crossing of the Reed Sea (v. 23) includes the fact that they are memorialized in Israel's worship. The narrative has even been seen as based on a liturgy of Passover celebration at the sanctuary of Gilgal.[13]

---

11. NIV; ESV; Butler, *Joshua*, 38.
12. On the calendar in ancient Israel, see Clines, "New Year."
13. Kraus, "Gilgal"; Otto, *Das Mazzotfest in Gilgal*; see also Cross, *Canaanite Myth and Hebrew Epic*, 77-144.

Joshua 5:1-12

The crossing of the Jordan in Joshua forges strong links between Yahweh, Israel, and the land. Yahweh shows his power over the creation itself, the narrative having overtones of the primeval victory over the forces of chaos. At the same time he shows his power in history, since the victory is played out in historical time, as part of a military campaign. Israel is defined as a people entitled to this land, with its natural borders, by virtue of Yahweh's decision, and their relationship with him in covenant.

The tidy scheme is disturbed only by the fact that some of the tribes remain outside the land properly defined. In L. Daniel Hawk's words, "the nation and the promised land are not completely one."[14] This will prove an important factor in the theology of the book. The relationship between people and land is not so definite or immutable as Joshua is sometimes thought to be asserting, for example, when it is considered to be promoting the reform of King Josiah.[15]

Joshua 5

5:1-12 We are now told of three things that anticipate Israel's full and due possession of the land.

5:1 The first is a formulaic depiction of the fear of Israel's approach on the part of the Canaanite population. The population is made up of different groups, here as in other texts. The Amorites, "beyond the Jordan to the west" (NRSV), lived in the hill country in the central spine of the land, while the Canaanites were farther west, along the Mediterranean coast (cf. Num 13:29; Deut 1:7; Josh 10:5-6). The twofold division here aims to express the totality of the inhabitants, as does the expression "all the Amorite kings." The narrative of the nations' organized resistance to Israel often refers expressly to their kings (cf. 9:1; 10:1-6, 16-27; 11:1-2; 12).

The melting of the enemy's heart is a typical expression for the fear born of despair at certain defeat. It is used by Rahab, and elsewhere in Joshua (2:11; 7:5; see also Deut 1:28; 20:8; Isa 19:1). The fear is caused by the knowledge that Yahweh, the God of Israel, is coming against them. This was the fear also of Balak, king of Moab, who had hired the magician Balaam against Israel during their progress towards Canaan (Numbers 22). Rahab's confession indicates that the Canaanites had also been terrified by news of the crossing of the Reed Sea and Moses' victories over the Amorite kings Sihon and Og in

---

14. Hawk, *Joshua*, 61.
15. As in Coote, "The Book of Joshua," 599.

Transjordan (2:10). The miraculous crossing of the Jordan has had the effect of demonstrating the power and purpose of Yahweh to the nations.

5:2-9 The second episode is the circumcising of the men who had been born during the period of wilderness wandering, after the exodus from Egypt. This also anticipates the full possession of the land, because it puts into effect the mark of the covenant people, as it was given to Abraham (Gen 17:9-14).

The need for this mass circumcision arises because the people born during the wilderness had not been circumcised (vv. 5, 7).[16] The present text is the only place where this specific issue arises. It is in the context of the regularly repeated point that the generation that came out of Egypt perished in the wilderness, with the exception of only Joshua and Caleb (v. 6; cf. Num 14:26-35; Deut 1:34-40). That generation was prohibited from entering the land because of its unfaithfulness, even Moses being implicated in this. In this context their failure to circumcise their children born in the wilderness (v. 5) seems to correspond to that characterization.

In contrast, it is the generation born in the wilderness that is regarded as fit to enter the land. Joshua is associated with this generation also in Judg 2:6-10, where it is again portrayed as faithful. The performance of circumcision on its members is an act of obedience in fulfilment of the covenantal requirement of Gen 17:9-14. The action completes their readiness to become the people who rightly possess the land.

The symbolic function of the new generation's circumcision is now underlined. The passage of time for healing (v. 8) is followed by a declaration marking a decisive new phase following the time marked by "the disgrace of Egypt" (v. 9 NRSV). This odd phrase may refer to the failure to circumcise in the wilderness (see Gen 34:14 for a similar connection of thought). More likely, in my view, is a general reference to the Israelites' condition of slavery there. The "rolling away" of this disgrace is a play on the name Gilgal, the place at which the people entered the land. The present verses, therefore, focus on the decisive change that has been brought about by this people's crossing of the Jordan. They have passed from a condition of disgrace, and they bear once again in themselves the marks of their covenantal standing before God. This new status is symbolized by yet another memorial centered on Gilgal, the point of entry, in the etiological declaration of Yahweh concerning its name.

---

16. According to the LXX, some of those who had come out of Egypt had not been circumcised, and these are now included in Joshua's action. Nelson regards this as the earlier version of the story and thinks that it was revised by the tradition underlying MT; *Joshua*, 75-77. If this was indeed the original version, it has been completely submerged in MT.

Joshua 5:10-12

5:10-12 The third element in the preparation to move further into the land is a celebration of Passover. That a celebration of Passover should follow an act of circumcision is to be expected, since in the institution of Passover circumcision is a prerequisite of participating in the feast (Exod 12:44-48). The people having arrived at Gilgal on the tenth day of the first month (4:19), they now keep the Passover on the fourteenth day, according to Mosaic law (Exod 12:6; Lev 23:5). The narrative thus mirrors the regular progress of the feast as instituted, since there the tenth day is the point at which the lamb for the sacrifice is selected (Exod 12:3). After the Passover, they eat unleavened bread and parched grain. The logic of this is simply that these are natural foods for a people newly arrived, on the march, in a land which they have not had time to cultivate.[17] There is, nevertheless, an echo of the idea of firstfruits, which became a regular seasonal offering, but which are associated with the first entry to the land in texts that deal with them (Lev 23:10; Deut 26:1-2).[18]

When the text is read in the light of the institution of Passover and calendar texts concerning it and other feasts, the sequence of Passover–unleavened bread is inevitably heard in terms of the close connection between Passover and the solemn eating of unleavened bread in the days following (Exod 12:14-20; Unleavened Bread is itself regarded as a "feast" in Exod 23:15; Lev 23:6). The text in Joshua points to a close connection between the Passover and the eating of the unleavened bread, with its phrase "that very day" (v. 11), and this also gives the impression that the manna ceased immediately too (v. 12). The Hebrew text draws out the immediacy with which the unleavened bread was eaten with two expressions that are absent from the Greek text, namely "the day after the Passover" (v. 11) and "the day after [they ate]" (v. 12). It is possible that LXX is based on an older text and MT (Hebrew) has incorporated an expansion to make the event conform more clearly to the regulations for the feast.[19] The point should not be pressed too far, because the implication is present also in LXX, and in any case even MT does not spell out a full celebration as prescribed in the festal calendars.

The point of this passage is to emphasize again the new situation of Israel. Passover had marked their departure from Egypt, an event that set them apart from that nation; now again they are set apart, on the brink of a campaign against the peoples of the land they have entered.[20] The change from

---

17. See 1 Sam 17:17; 25:18 for roasted grain; and Howard, *Joshua*, 154.
18. Cf. Nelson, *Joshua*, 79.
19. Nelson, *Joshua*, 80.
20. Cf. Hawk, *Joshua*, 81.

manna, a food given daily by special means, to food produced by cultivation also marks the transition from wilderness, and the people's limbolike existence there, to cultivated land in which they will settle. This actual transition, which may in practice have been gradual, is compressed here for symbolic reasons, the symbolism being enhanced by the implicit allusion to the sequence of Passover–unleavened bread in the regular keeping of the feasts.

5:13-15 Attention now turns to Jericho. Joshua has an encounter with a man with a drawn sword, ready for war. This meeting is curiously detached from its context. Both the timing of it and the place are undetermined ("when Joshua was in Jericho"). "In Jericho" can hardly be taken at its face value, since, in the logic of the narrative, Joshua has not yet even approached it to give battle. It must be taken to mean "in the region of Jericho." By the same logic, the time between crossing the Jordan and besieging the city cannot have been long, and so the time of the meeting is specified in a sense by this circumstance. Even so, the detached form of the short section has the effect of pointing to another, unseen, dimension in the events that are about to unfold. It is as if Joshua is momentarily taken out of the normal process of rational planning to see where the real heart and cause of things lie.

The figure whom Joshua encounters is described initially simply as a man with a drawn sword. His appearance is so much like an ordinary soldier that Joshua asks him the natural question about which side he is on. Only when he answers with the startling "Neither!" (lit., "No!" or "Not so!")[21] and announces that he is the commander, or "prince," of Yahweh's army, does Joshua realize that he is in the presence of a supernatural being. He is not merely part of the Israelite army, but represents the mightier forces of God. Yahweh is understood here (as often in the Old Testament) as "Yahweh of Hosts" (familiarly, the Lord of Hosts), that is, "Yahweh of armies," to signify his command of greater power than any that lies at the disposal of human beings. People in desperate situations are sometimes granted a glimpse of this power (2 Kgs 6:16-17). In the visions of Daniel, we see that great issues on earth are fought over in wars in the heavenly realm (e.g., Dan 10:12-14).

The closest parallel to the phrase used here for the "commander [prince] of the Lord's army" is in Dan 8:11, where the tyrant Antiochus Epiphanes IV is said to have made himself as great as the "Prince of the host." In this case "the prince" seems to refer to Yahweh himself.[22] Also in Daniel, the archangel Michael is depicted as fighting in heaven against the power of

---

21. Some Hebrew manuscripts, supported by LXX, read "to him" instead of "no," based on a slightly different Hebrew reading. But MT should be preferred.

22. Here with Howard, *Joshua*, 157, n. 286.

Persia and is called "one of the chief princes" (Dan 10:13). Michael may offer a better analogy to the figure whom Joshua meets here.

Even so, Joshua's response to the disclosure of the man's identity is as if he was in the presence of God himself (v. 14). This is consistent with occasions when people are met by "the angel (lit., 'messenger') of Yahweh" and the appearance of the angel seems tantamount to an appearance of God (notice the reaction of Manoah after the visitation of "the angel of Yahweh": "We have seen God!"; Judg 13:21-22). The present figure is not called "the angel of Yahweh." Yet Joshua is told to remove his shoes since he is on holy ground, exactly as God instructed Moses when he met him in the burning bush before sending him to lead Israel out of Egypt (Exod 3:5).

Joshua asks for a word of command or guidance (v. 14), but is answered only by the word about holy ground. The appearance is different, therefore, from other incidents in which specific guidance is given (e.g., Judg 6:11-24). Such incidents are known in the ancient Near East also, where gods encourage kings to go to war with a promise of victory.[23] The effect of this encounter is to show Joshua that the issues that are about to be contended for are Yahweh's and that he will undertake for the outcome. The pointer to the presence and holiness of Yahweh is tantamount to an assurance of victory. Yet at the same time it shows that Joshua himself, in carrying out his mission, is only a servant of God.

Joshua 6

Joshua's taking of Jericho plays a unique role in the story. The importance of the city lies in its location, on an oasis at the southern end of the Jordan valley, also known as "the City of Palms" (Judg 3:13). Fed by the spring known today as 'Ain es-Sultan, it lies about ten miles north of the Dead Sea, four miles west of the River Jordan, and 800 feet below sea level. This location placed it on an important north-south trade route, as well as giving access into the hill country to the west, which would be the Israelites' next destination. In Joshua's day, Jericho had already enjoyed these natural benefits for six thousand years.

Jericho is essentially a border location. The deep Jordan valley and the river itself mark a natural boundary between east and west. In terms of Israel's tribal divisions, the city lay between north and south, being assigned to

---

23. See Nelson, *Joshua*, 81 and n. 16, who cites, e.g., the goddess Ishtar, sword in hand, appearing to the Assyrian king Ashurbanipal (*ANET*, 451).

Benjamin (18:21), but close to the northern territory of Ephraim (16:7). In the late monarchy it appears that Jericho was under the administration of Judah.[24] Jericho, therefore, was strategically located between both east and west and north and south. It often features in biblical narratives precisely because of its significance as a boundary, not only in the story of its destruction by Joshua, but elsewhere also (Judg 3:13; 2 Sam 10:5; 2 Kings 2).

In the logic of their march from the east into Canaan, the city was an inevitable first obstacle. While the River Jordan itself would form the eastern border of the land Israel was to occupy, Jericho represented the power to control it.

The interpretation of the present narrative has been beset by controversy about its historical plausibility. If the Israelites entered Canaan in the mid-thirteenth century, according to the conventional dating, this places the event in the period known to archaeology as Late Bronze Age (ca. 1550-1200 B.C.).[25] There is, however, no clear archaeological evidence that Jericho was occupied in that period, nor in the following Iron Age I. In particular, there were apparently no Late Bronze walls.[26] Not least for this reason, many commentators think that the story before us — about a collapse of walls — has no firm anchor in history.

Two issues here must be clearly distinguished. There is, first, the strictly historical question. This is in itself convoluted, since the nature of the archaeological evidence is contested. The best response to the argument that there was no LB city in Joshua's time is that settlements in the period often did not have walls of their own, though they might have reused walls from an earlier time.[27] In a further complication, remains from collapsed walls could have washed away by erosion, so that they are now beyond the reach of investigation of the site itself. In addition, there are fragmentary signs of occupation during early LB II, that is, late fifteenth century, and up to the late fourteenth century or early thirteenth century (ca. 1325 Kenyon; 1275, Bienkowski). This is too early for

---

24. Holland and Netzer, "Jericho," 737.

25. Bienkowski, *Jericho in the Late Bronze Age*, 9. See also Introduction above.

26. This has been widely accepted since the excavations of Kenyon, *Digging Up Jericho*; see Bienkowski, *Jericho in the Late Bronze Age*, 124-25. For Coogan, the lack of pottery from LB, and the fragmentary nature of the evidence in Iron Age I, can mean only that the site was uninhabited from about 1300 to 1000 B.C.; Coogan, "Archaeology and Biblical Studies." 21. He admits, however, that there are "some hints of occupation in the eleventh century." Bienkowski finds evidence of LB occupation, based on tomb and pottery evidence, up to about 1275; *Jericho in the Late Bronze Age*, 124-25, 155-56. But this was an unwalled settlement and apparently ceased for economic reasons, not military ones.

27. Mazar, "The Iron Age I," 283.

Joshua on most accounts.[28] However, considering the evidence as a whole, the Israeli archaeologist Amihai Mazar writes: "Undoubtedly, the biblical story of the battle of Jericho is legendary, but in this case archaeological evidence does not run directly counter to the biblical tale, as is asserted by some scholars."[29]

Mazar's comment raises the second important question about the story, namely its character as a piece of writing. Should it be read as ordinary history, or as edifying legend? In this regard, we are bound to make a judgment about the genre of the text, rather than begin with an *a priori* belief that historical issues are the central ones. As it would be mistaken to prejudge the nature of the biblical account on the basis of the archaeology, it will also be wrong to try to force the ambiguous archaeology to fit the biblical picture, without at least an attempt to understand the nature of the account and what it seeks to commit the reader to.

6:1-7 The story of the taking of Jericho continues directly from the crossing of the Jordan, as is indicated by the use here of the verb עבר/*ʿābar*, "cross over" (three times in vv. 7-8, sometimes translated "go forward"). The crossing and the taking are of a piece in the portrayal of the miraculous progress into the land. The scene is set in vv. 1-2. Jericho is a fortress, strongly barricaded against the Israelite siege. We recall the walled cities which the fearful Israelites under Moses thought they could never capture (Deut 1:28). Now defiant Jericho stands mutely opposed (6:1). But in the same breath the narrator conveys Yahweh's word of assurance: city, king, and army cannot withstand Israel, just as the formidable Amorite kings Og and Sihon could not (Num 21:21-32), nor Balak of Moab (Numbers 22–24; note the oracle of assurance in Num 21:34, like Josh 6:2). We know from the outset that this contest is a mismatch: Jericho will succumb, as surely as the waters of the Jordan yielded. And indeed, there is no account of battle in this chapter. Rather, this first conquest account displays theologically what is entailed in the conquest. The essential relationship between God, Israel, Canaanites, and land is portrayed in the story of Jericho.

The story therefore focuses on these relationships. Instead of battle we have an exhibition of Yahweh's command and Israel's performance. (There will be other battles, but this narrative establishes that Yahweh does not need the military might of Israel to secure victory.) The word of command is passed in due order from Yahweh to Joshua (vv. 2-5) and in turn from Joshua to priests (v. 6) and people (v. 7).

---

28. Kenyon, *Digging Up Jericho*, 260-62; Bienkowski, *Jericho in the Late Bronze Age*, see n. 26.

29. Mazar, "The Iron Age I," 283.

The action now commanded is both military and religious. The surrounding of the city, a regular military maneuvre, takes on here the aspect of a religious procession. The troops are not simply to invest Jericho, but march round it. The numbers six and seven make this act of siege highly formal, and have religious echoes (reminiscent of the six-plus-one days of creation, Gen 1:1–2:3). The sounding of "trumpets of rams' horns" (v. 4; two words, שׁופר/ šōpār and יובל/yôbēl, are used in a combined phrase) can be either military or religious (see 1 Sam 13:3, then 2 Sam 6:15), as can the "shout" (v. 5; see 1 Sam 4:5, then Ps 27:6; 47:5[MT 6]; 89:15[MT 16]).[30]

This military-religious portrayal is consistent with the underlying theology, that the entry of Israel to land is an act of God; the conquest is not only holy war, but also part of God's liberation of a people to be his own. This is perhaps best illustrated by the noun *yôbēl*, "ram's horn," which is also the word translated "Jubilee" in Leviticus 25; 27. At the Jubilee, first the trumpet *(šōpār)* is sounded (Lev 25:9), then the Jubilee *(yôbēl)* is proclaimed (25:10). Almost all the twenty-seven occurrences of *yôbēl* are in Leviticus 25; 27 and Joshua 6 (two others are at Exod 19:13; Num 36:4). This strongly suggests that the gift of land to Israel, following her liberation from slavery in Egypt, is a kind of Jubilee, a release from slavery into freedom, independence, and possession.[31]

6:8-14 The narrative now presents the actions of Israel in obedience to the commands in vv. 1-7. Priests and people obey the word of Joshua (vv. 8-9), with a new command entered in v. 10. The first two of the six days are recounted, in such a way as to show that the pattern was repeated on each of the six (v. 14b). The order of march is established: armed men, priests blowing trumpets, ark of the covenant, rearguard (vv. 8-9). The centrality of the ark in the procession is evident from v. 11, symbolizing the presence of Yahweh himself. The trumpets are sounded continuously (v. 9). The shout of triumph is carefully withheld until the day when Joshua commands it, that is, the seventh.

The style of the passage is as significant as its content. The regularity in the repeated events, the repetitive style with its insistent emphasis on the priests "going forward" and blowing the trumpets, the vivid use of participles to evoke the action as if in the present, the precision in the order of march, and the anticipation caused by the pointed withholding of the shout, build up a kind of dramatic tension, albeit a growing sense of the inevitability of the terrible fate awaiting the city.

---

30. The highly formalized account is clearer in the Hebrew MT than in the ancient Greek version (LXX), which Nelson thinks represents an older form of the story; Nelson, *Joshua*, 87-88.

31. Cf. Hawk, *Joshua*, 94-95.

Joshua 6:15-21

Finally, the seven-day structure of the event has unmistakable echoes of the creation account (Gen 1:1–2:3). This may point to a kind of completion: Israel's journey from Egypt to land is complete in the symbolic act of taking Jericho.[32] It may also indicate a connection between the "good" creation of Genesis 1 and the land Israel is about to enter. And there are sabbatical overtones: Israel is on the verge of entering its "rest" (see Deut 12:9-10 in this connection).

6:15-21 The action proceeds rapidly to the seventh day, on which the taking of Jericho will be completed. The people "got up early," a typical feature of the Joshua narrative, signifying willing obedience (cf. v. 12; also 3:1; 7:16; 8:10, 14). The word "seven" is repeated four times (cf. v. 4) and the special significance of this final day carefully marked out (v. 15b). Only when the city has been circled for the seventh time does Joshua give the awaited command: "Shout! For the Lord has given you the city!" (v. 16).

Joshua's words of command continue until v. 19, filling the gap between the command to shout and its performance with the explanation that Jericho is חרם/ḥērem, "devoted to destruction," and the special provision regarding Rahab, that she and her family should be spared. The theology of ḥērem is placed in the center of this part of the narrative. The noun appears four times in vv. 17-18. It refers both to the things which have been "devoted to the Lord" and the condition of being so devoted. Hence the whole camp of Israel might become ḥērem if any of the people tried to take the devoted things for themselves. Ḥērem denotes a condition of being put beyond normal use, of having entered the holy sphere, that of God himself. Objects, such as those enumerated in v. 19, may enter that sphere by being dedicated to the holy space of God's temple. As the entire city of Jericho was laid under ḥērem it followed that all such objects could find a home only in that sphere. (In v. 19 the word "sacred," קדש/qōdeš, is used for these objects.) For people, the consequence of being made ḥērem was death. In the logic of the book of Joshua, this death of all living creatures in Jericho is the terrible symbolism of Yahweh's ownership of the land and his intention to make it a place of his presence, together with a covenant people bound into a relationship of loyalty to him.

The concept of ḥērem was not confined to Israel. It was known also to Moab, and in the famous ninth-century Moabite Stone King Mesha of Moab boasts that he has made Israel ḥērem.[33] In the Old Testament story, the application of ḥērem is justified by the assertion that the peoples of Canaan were wicked and that in their destruction they fell under the judgment of God (Deut 9:5). The corollary of this is that if left alongside Israel they would lead

---

32. Cf. Hawk, *Joshua*, 98.
33. For this text, see Smelik, "The Inscription of King Mesha."

them into their idolatrous ways (Deut 20:16-18). This danger is reflected in our text with the warning that the people should not "covet" the holy things (v. 18).[34] This is exactly what Achan will later do, in the aftermath of the sack of Ai (Joshua 7; in 7:21, Achan confesses to having "coveted" the devoted things).

Rahab, however, is to be spared. It is an important feature of Joshua's account of the conquest that Israelites (such as Achan), indeed all Israel (v. 18), might be excluded from the possession of the land, in practice becoming ḥērem, while non-Israelites, even Canaanites who are in principle under the decree of destruction from the outset, might be spared. The case of Rahab is not accidental but expressly makes this point (v. 17). Rahab and her household avoid becoming ḥērem because she has in effect incorporated herself into Israel by accepting the Israelite spies (NRSV "messengers") into her home and protection and also making Yahweh her own God (cf. 2:11b). This mirror-imaging of Rahab, with her household, and Achan with his, places the idea of Israel as holy people beyond the realm of arbitrary election and religio-nationalism. The standard of being truly "Israel" in Joshua remains covenantal (see on 2:8-14, where Rahab, knowing the implications of ḥērem, appeals to ḥesed, the essential quality of covenant).

In this connection it is important to note that Christian commentators often look for interpretations of Joshua's ḥērem which avoid the plain sense of a command of God to destroy a population. The narrative can be made to represent the need for Israel to keep themselves absolutely from the worship of other gods and from immoral and idolatrous practices. On many accounts Joshua reflects the actual experience of worshippers of Yahweh who live alongside worshippers of other gods. The prophetic books' portrayal of mixed societies could support this view. And both Deuteronomy and Joshua acknowledge, when read carefully, that such mixing is a reality. Both the Rahab story and that of the Gibeonites (ch. 9) then function as explanations of the existence of a mixed population. The curious sequence in Deut 7:2-3 has a similar effect, when the unmitigated command to carry out ḥērem is followed up with a command not to make covenants or intermarry with the prohibited peoples. It seems that the latter has the mark of realism while the former is a kind of ideal.[35]

---

34. Following NRSV's "so as not to covet." MT has an occurrence of the verb "devote to destruction" here (adopted by NIV and, differently, ESV). However, this is likely to be a case of textual corruption. The LXX has instead the verb meaning "covet," which makes better sense, and NRSV follows this.

35. For metaphorical interpretations of ḥērem see Moberly, "Toward an Interpretation of the Shema," 133-37.

The climax of the account comes when the people obey Joshua's call to shout, the walls collapse, and the people rush into the city and carry out the destruction of all living beings (vv. 21-22). This is told briefly. There is apparently no struggle; the city falls as we knew it would, because it was decreed by Yahweh. The total silence about resistance on the part of the inhabitants emphasizes the impossibility of opposing his word and also demonstrates that he really is with Joshua (1:5). In Jericho, the destruction of life is total, in contrast to Ai (8:2, 27). This makes Jericho the most complete example of the *ḥērem* as it is prescribed in Deut 20:16-18.

6:22-25 Between the taking of the city and its final destruction Joshua has Rahab and family brought out to safety, in keeping with the spies' promise (2:14). This is done by the spies themselves, who could identify the house and people. It is only here that we have space to imagine the commotion of a city being ravaged and the urgency and difficulty of finding, separating, and extricating a single family from the ruins while sustaining the fierce attack. The city is burned as the last act in the process of destruction. And a coda to the action notes that the sparing of Rahab is the reason why certain Canaanites continue in the land alongside Israel "to this day" ("ever since," NRSV), an undetermined time after the events reported. It is significant that Rahab and family are taken to a place "outside the camp of Israel" (v. 23); how far they might be integrated into the community proper remains undecided here.

6:26-27 The destruction of Jericho is now declared to be permanent extinction. The land of Canaan has utterly changed its state, being henceforth the land of Israel; and the annihilation of Jericho testifies to this. Consequently, anyone who dared to rebuild it would be laid under a curse, and forfeit the foremost of blessings, descendants ("firstborn" and "youngest" in parallelism should perhaps be taken to mean all children). Jericho was apparently rebuilt during the reign of Ahab, by one Hiel, who did indeed fall victim to the curse pronounced here (1 Kgs 16:34). (It is possible that Hiel actually sacrificed his sons in a "foundation-sacrifice," thus inadvertently and ironically bringing the terms of the curse upon himself.)

The chapter ends by repeating that Yahweh was with Joshua. The "fame" that spread through the land will have been ominous for all who heard it.

We observed above that it is important to make a judgment about the genre of this narrative in order to know how it might relate to historical actuality. It has emerged, however, that such a judgment about Joshua 6 is difficult to make. It is evidently a theologized account. This does not mean that it tells us nothing about actual events; rather, it means that it is difficult to reconstruct a course of events in a realistic way on the basis of the narrative. The purpose of this narration of events in Israel's past can be expressed theologically: to demonstrate the relationships between God, Israel, Canaan, and land and the legitimacy of Israel's possession by virtue of God's victory. A comparison with Deut 7:2-3, furthermore, shows that the Old Testament writers knew of a distinction between a clean, rapid, and total conquest and a slower story of engagement and disengagement. The prominence of Rahab in chs. 2 and 6 gives further evidence that the narrative hints at this reality in Israel's history. The picture of the conquest of Jericho in ch. 6 forms a part, theologically, of the portrayal of total conquest in the book generally. But that is only one side of a carefully constructed and paradoxical picture. (The two sides of this picture are expressed most clearly in 11:21-23 and 13:1-7).

Joshua 7

7:1 The next thing we read after the account of Jericho is of Israel's trespass against the *ḥērem* ("the devoted things"). The first great test passed, it seems that a terrible obstacle now stands in the way of further progress. It is in line, incidentally, with a pattern established in the biblical story from the beginning: the sin of the first human beings leading to the flood; the idolatry of the Israelites at the inception of the Sinai covenant (Exodus 32). Now at the very point of salvation Israel "breaks faith" (NRSV), a strong word for sin, denoting purposeful rebellion and incurring the wrath of God (cf. 1 Chr 10:13-14). Now we wonder how the people can progress at all. That the issue of the *ḥērem* arises at this point shows how much it was the central concern of the preceding chapter.

It is important to notice that it is "the Israelites" who are said to have broken faith, even though the actual offense has been committed by one man, Achan. Achan's family line has the effect of showing his integral membership in the people of Israel. Achan has done precisely what was forbidden in 6:18, and so "brought disaster" on the camp of Israel, even making it liable to be *ḥērem* itself. (The verb "bring disaster," עכר/*'ākar*, resembles Achan's name). Israel itself now stands in danger of becoming like Jericho.

7:2-5 The reader knows that a huge obstacle stands in the way of Israel's progress, but Joshua does not, nor do the majority of Israelites, we presume. For their part, the march into the land continues. The direction taken, from Jericho to Ai, shows the people proceeding from border territory in the Jordan valley up into the central ridge, running north to south, that was the heart of the land. The names Beth-aven and Bethel are full of significance for

Israel. Bethel was the place where Jacob had his first encounter with God (Gen 28:10-17), and it later became the royal sanctuary of the northern kingdom of Israel and fell afoul of prophetic criticism (1 Kgs 12:25-33; Amos 4:4-5). Beth-aven means, lit., "house of wickedness," though this may be a deliberate recasting in the biblical tradition of a name that originally meant something more positive. In Hosea, Beth-aven has apparently come to refer to Bethel itself, the insult arising because of the worship of Jeroboam's images there (Hos 4:15; 5:8; 10:5).[36] However, in the present narrative, it stands simply for the heartland which in the logic of possession Israel must now penetrate.

The first attack on Ai is full of irony. The people are confident, perhaps imagining that this is what it is not to fear the enemy according to God's command (1:9). When spies reported to Moses on the former approach to the land, they told how good the land was and acknowledged that Yahweh was giving it (Deut 1:25). The casual report in this case does not stand well by comparison. Fresh now from the clean sweep at Jericho they feel they can handle opposition, with a hint of calculation which is disturbing.

The encounter is told quickly, Israel's three thousand easily repulsed by whatever force the people of Ai could muster. Israel's light losses somehow only add to the impression that this was barely a skirmish, and Israel's heroes had readily taken flight. Blithe confidence was not matched by performance. And while once the Canaanites' hearts melted in fear of Israel, now the boot is on the other foot (v. 5; cf. 2:9; 5:1)!

7:6-9 The scene that follows is one of those in which Israel and its leaders confront the terrible possibility that God may act in judgment on them, rather than continue with them into full possession of the land. Joshua and the elders adopt the marks of penitence and fall to prayer, as did Moses at Sinai when the people had made a golden calf (Exod 32:11-14) and as did Moses and Aaron together at the people's refusal of the spies' encouragement at the first approach (Num 14:5). Their long prostration ("till evening") before the ark, the symbol of God's presence, and the passion of the plea bespeak bewilderment, perhaps despair. Remarkably, Joshua himself expresses the sense of longing for return by the way they had come (v. 7b) that on previous occasions had been felt by the rebellious (Num 14:2-3; cf. Exod 17:3) and not uttered by the leaders. Indeed, Joshua had been one of the few who had tried to meet the pessimism with faithful exhortation, despite a serious threat to their lives (Num 14:6-10).[37] Now he seems tempted to give up. The appeal to Yahweh to act for the sake of

---

36. In Josh 7:2, the LXX omits "Beth-aven, east of," perhaps finding it confusing because of the identification of it with Bethel in Hosea.

37. Cf. Hawk, *Joshua*, 115.

his reputation is in line with the prayer of Moses (Exod 32:12). Moses had not on that occasion shown weakness in his own faith, though he was guilty elsewhere (Num 20:12). Joshua, the hero of the land-possession, now shows that he too has some of the infirmity common to humanity.

7:10-15 Joshua's fear that Israel might now suffer defeat by the Canaanites is well founded, but he has not seen the reason for it. This is now made abundantly clear in Yahweh's sharp response to his worship and that of the elders, which amounts to a rejection of it. In spite of their bowing before the ark, the symbol of Yahweh's presence, Yahweh refuses to be present to their worship, and it even seems offensive to him. The reason for Yahweh's anger is now expressed in the rapid-fire accusations that follow. The problem in general is that Israel has "sinned," indeed has "violated my covenant, which I commanded them to keep" (v. 11). The expression "violation of the covenant" means outright rejection of Yahweh, the act of sedition involved in worshipping other gods (Deut 17:2-7; cf. 13:6-18). Israel must utterly reject this (Deut 17:7b), since such sin amounts to a repudiation of the whole project of Yahweh's to bring them from slavery into freedom (Deut 13:5). These texts also display a sense of the danger of one person to the whole community (see in addition Deut 29:18).

This is just the scenario we now encounter. The particular offense is that Israel has offended against the *ḥērem*, the "devotion to destruction," through Achan's act of plunder. This act encompasses theft and deceit (v. 11), but above all it is in itself a direct rebellion against Yahweh. Achan's secretion of *ḥērem*, "devoted things," has in effect turned Israel into *ḥērem*, which had been the sentence on Jericho (note these two senses of the word in v. 12).

The sharpness in Yahweh's tone corresponds to this profound change in Israel's condition. The story of God's protecting, leading presence, symbolized by the ark of the covenant, is now at best on hold and in danger of going into reverse. The presence of *ḥērem* within Israel is the reason why it has suffered improbable defeat so soon after spectacular victory (v. 12a). However, the tone quickly changes again, so that the possibility of total loss is conditionalized ("I will not be with you anymore *unless*...," v. 12b). The situation can be saved if they rid themselves of that which has made them liable to destruction.

In preparation, the people must "sanctify," or "consecrate," themselves, as they had done just before crossing the Jordan; the stakes here are set as high as they were then (see on 3:5). What follows is an exhibition of Israel's ridding itself of that which would corrupt all. The layers of Israel's social structure, tribe, clan, household, head of house, are to be peeled away, "reversing the course by which the *ḥērem* contagion has spread throughout the entire na-

Joshua 7:16-21

tion,"[38] as Yahweh inexorably searches out the guilty and prescribes the penalty of death (vv. 14-15). The guilt of Israel is pinpointed to the one who has actually "violated the covenant" (cf. v. 11, where this is said of Israel as a whole). He is also said to have "done an outrageous thing (נבלה/*něbālâ*) in Israel" (NRSV; "shameful thing," RSV; "disgraceful thing," NIV). The term means something that undermines Israel's religious and social fabric (cf. Gen 34:7; Deut 22:21; Judg 19:23-24).

7:16-21 The prescribed action now quickly takes place, beginning with the usual formula in Joshua for decisiveness ("Joshua rose early in the morning," v. 16 NRSV). The zeroing in on Achan, through tribe of Judah, clan of Zerah, household of Zabdi, is on one level an insight into the organization of Israel, unified yet with a diversified authority structure. The cameo functions here to illustrate the responsibility at each level, down to the individual, for maintaining the welfare of the whole.

But the progressive identification of Achan is at the same time a discovery of the "devoted things," and the quest is heavy with symbolism. The contaminating goods are "hidden" within the community (7:21b) and must be brought to light and removed. The exchange between Joshua and Achan is designed to bring this out. Joshua's address to Achan as "my son" and his exhortation to "give glory to the Lord, the God of Israel" seem out of place in the circumstances. Achan's "sonship," or true belonging within Israel, has been called in question by his actions. And "giving glory to the Lord," that is, by confessing, is an act that will condemn him. Achan's ready confession (the Hebrew word can also connote praise or thanksgiving) suggests in addition a didactic and symbolic function of the conversation. The one who has deliberately hidden the "devoted things" is suddenly willing to expose all. The description of the goods stolen seems designed as a lesson to the reader or hearer in the powerful attraction of rich things and the dangers of coveting (as in the Tenth Commandment, Exod 20:17), that is, a passionate craving that can overwhelm the mind.

The deep concern of this narrative is the fear that the covenant community might become just like "Canaan," or those from whom they have first of all been radically distinguished. A number of features point to this. The consonants of Achan's name in Hebrew are also those of the word Canaan, so that he himself stands for a "Canaanite" threat within. And the repeated use of the word "take" in the story of his identification (vv. 16-18) echoes the "taking" of the Canaanite cities in war (Josh 6:20; 8:19). The removal from Israel of the "Canaanite" stolen goods, therefore, resembles the taking of the cities

---

38. Hawk, *Joshua*, 118.

by which the land ceased to be Canaanite and became Israelite.[39] The difference between this case and the conquest of cities is that this one represents the insidious danger from apostasy lurking unseen within the community.

7:22-26 The episode culminates in the discovery of the goods and the execution of Achan and all that belonged to him, including his family. In the presentation of the goods "before the Lord" it is noteworthy that "all the Israelites" are involved, for so the whole community participates in this excision of the root cause of the ill and is exonerated. The destruction of the goods finally implements the "devotion to destruction" of Jericho and all that was in it, which now also involves Achan.

The execution of Achan himself along with the destruction of the goods follows according to the logic of the story, but why does his family die with him? The usual answers are either that they stand or fall with him according to a belief in corporate solidarity in guilt, or that they are themselves guilty of the crime because they must have been party to the concealment and are therefore as much contaminated by the devoted goods as he is. The emphasis in the text, however, is that *everything that belonged to Achan* is destroyed. The rooting out of evil from Israel leaves nothing to chance.

The name of Achan is committed to perpetual memory by an association with the valley of Achor, "trouble," the names being similar. (In another moment of fundamental decision between two ways, the Canaanizing King Ahab accuses the prophet Elijah of being a "troubler" of Israel, only to be told by the prophet that it is he who is the "troubler"; 1 Kgs 18:17-18. In both cases this "trouble" is thoroughgoing and dangerous.) For Achan, the "troubling" is turned on him in his execution, which in the comprehensiveness of stoning then burning emphasizes the need for total extirpation of the contamination.

The incident is of such importance for Israel's future well-being that it is further memorialized by a raising of a heap of stones, an echo of the stones raised at the River Jordan. In an important sense this turning-point is a new "crossing" (as Achan had transgressed, i.e., "crossed," the covenant). Israel stands whole before Yahweh again, and the forward look into the land, rather than back beyond the Jordan (as in 7:7), can be resumed.

Joshua 8

8:1-2 Joshua and Israel now proceed against Ai at God's command, the crucial factor that was lacking in their first abortive attempt (7:2-5). The words

---

39. See also Hawk, *Joshua*, 119-20.

"Do not be afraid; do not be discouraged" recall Deut 1:21, where they also herald the beginning of a new phase in the narrative of land-possession. With the march on Ai, the sweep into the land takes a significant second step following the taking of Jericho. Ai was, in itself, an unexceptional place. Its name means "the ruin," as does et-Tell, the modern name of the site with which it is normally identified.[40] It is surprising, perhaps, that the account of Israel's penetration into the central highlands is represented by a battle for this nonentity and that there is no separate account of a battle for the far more important Bethel, or indeed other key sites such as Shiloh or Shechem. Israel's possession of these places is simply taken as read in the subsequent narrative (12:16; 18:1; 20:7; 24:1). Bethel is closely associated with Ai in the present account (esp. in v. 17), and its fall may be implicit in it. In any case, the battle for Ai does duty for Israel's advance into the central highlands and control of the area, as is clear from the sequel in 8:30-35, in which Joshua is able to proceed to Mounts Ebal and Gerizim, close to Shechem, and stake a symbolic claim there to possession of the whole land.

Ai is to be treated like Jericho, that is, "devoted to destruction" (cf. v. 26), except that on this occasion Israel may take plunder. The law concerning war within the promised land itself (Deut 20:16-18) requires the killing of "anything that breathes." This logic is applied in the case of Jericho and also underlies the command concerning the Amalekites in 1 Sam 15:3, where Saul's sparing of livestock is taken as an infringement of it (1 Sam 15:9, 14). The permission to take booty at Ai, therefore, seems to relax the usual stringency of the *ḥērem*. No reason is given for this. Perhaps the point about holding back nothing from God has been sufficiently demonstrated through Achan. The permission now to take booty is somewhat ironic after Achan's punishment for doing that very thing. But the crucial factor here as elsewhere is the express command of Yahweh.

8:3-29 The story of the taking of Ai differs enormously from that of Jericho, for whereas in that case the action of Yahweh is in the forefront, here Joshua's resourceful military strategy is of the essence. Different from the first failed attack are the careful preparation and the deployment of a formidable force (vv. 3-4; contrast 7:3-5). The pretence of flight cunningly mimics the for-

---

40. The story of Ai presents problems historically and archaeologically, as et-Tell was uninhabited for centuries up to about 1200 B.C., and therefore at the time of Joshua (ca. 1250). Proposed solutions are (a) that Ai was closely connected with Bethel, as a kind of military outpost, or (b) that the usual archaeological identifications of both Bethel (Beitin) and Ai are erroneous; Livingston, "Location of Biblical Bethel Reconsidered." The former suffers from the portrayal of Ai as an independent city with its own king besides the king of Bethel (8:1; 12:9, 16). The latter has found some support but also criticism and is at best inconclusive.

mer defeat, the forces of Ai being drawn out of their ground in anticipated repeat of their recent triumph. Events unfold, therefore, just as Joshua has calculated (8:6). Curiously, the debacle that resulted from that disobedience contributes to this success: the failure there and the success here are attributable on one level to the respective responses to Yahweh, while on another there is an element of mere experience. Both these levels are operative in the account.

The strategy itself is rather simple. An ambush is laid at night to the west of Ai, on the Bethel side, while the main force gathers to the north at daybreak, in full view of the city, having approached from the east (the "wilderness" or Arabah, vv. 14-15, i.e., the direction of Jericho). The king of Ai, sensing easy victory, comes quickly out to face the attacker. As Israel appears to flee, Joshua stretches out his sword towards Ai, in a sign that it is Yahweh who reigns over the events (as Moses extended his staff at the crossing of the Reed Sea, Exod 14:16, 21, 26-27). At this, the ambush rushes forward to take the city (v. 19). The men of Ai, seeing their city destroyed, are utterly dispirited and caught between two Israelite phalanxes are unable to offer resistance. Their transformation from confident attacker to helpless victim mirrors Israel's former experience, in a turning of the tables that is a feature of the story of the possession of the land (cf. Deut 1:19–3:17). Their helplessness is well expressed in v. 20: "They had no power (lit., 'hands') to flee this way or that" (NRSV). The sudden loss of courage and initiative at the realization that they have been outmaneuvered rings true psychologically. (For a similar story, see Judg 20:36-48.) But the true source of the victory is indicated by Joshua's sword, which remains extended until the victory is secure (v. 26). The story shows how success depends, not on superior numbers, but on obedience to Yahweh, and perhaps also on good leadership.

For all the vividness of the account, the relationship between Ai and Bethel remains hard to understand. Why do we suddenly find, in v. 17, that not only the forces of Ai but also of Bethel have come out against Israel, even though both the Israelite strategy and the response to it have hitherto focused exclusively on Ai? Moreover, Bethel is not mentioned again in the account, and when the numbers of the fallen are given (8:25) they are again limited to "the people of Ai." One answer is suggested by LXX, which has no reference to Bethel in 8:17. If this is closer to the original text, then Bethel's role in the story is simply a reference point, serving to locate the less well-known Ai. However, it is likely that the story of the taking of Ai gave rise to the question how Bethel itself fell, since there is no other account of this, and especially as the campaign against Ai involved a maneuver right in the face of Bethel. MT in 8:17 may be an expansion of the original text, representing the understanding that Bethel also fell at this time. In any case, it is in line with the function of the account in the context of the wider narrative of Joshua's advance into the land, namely that the taking of Ai is symbolic of what would have had to be a more extensive campaign than is actually described.

The defeat of Ai is memorialized both by the heap of stones that is all that is left of the city itself, and which perhaps symbolizes the destruction of the Canaanite centers of power and culture, and also by a heap of stones at the spot where the king of Ai was executed (8:28-29). The phrase "to this day" appears in both these cases, to highlight the enduring importance of the events. The separation of the king of the city for exemplary execution adds further force to the symbolism. Israel is not only establishing its and Yahweh's superior strength, but displacing a whole cultural-religious system typified by its kings (as also emerges graphically in 12:7-24).

8:30-35 The central highlands secured, Joshua can lead Israel to the region around Shechem, in order to lay claim formally to the whole land for Yahweh. The importance of the ceremony that is now described may be gauged from the fact that it is prepared for at two key points in the structure of Deuteronomy, just before and just after the long section of laws (Deuteronomy 12–26), namely at Deut 11:26-32 and Deuteronomy 27. The first of these commands the Israelites, when they cross the Jordan, to "proclaim on Mount Gerizim the blessings, and on Mount Ebal the curses" (Deut 11:29), the blessing and the curse being associated respectively with the obeying and disobeying of the commandments of the covenant. These mountains are "in the land of the Canaanites who live in the Arabah, opposite Gilgal, beside the oak of Moreh" (Deut 11:30 NRSV). Thus the ceremony of blessing and curse is set in the context of the entry to the land that the book of Joshua now describes. The centrality of the region around Shechem is important in this respect, occupying a position close to the geographical middle of the land. It is the place at which Joshua will later renew the covenant with Israel (Joshua 24). The positioning of the present ceremony here is significant, therefore, because Mounts Gerizim and Ebal have a claim geographically to be a central place in the whole land. In the logic of Deuteronomy-Joshua too, Shechem has "centrality" in a theological sense, since the repeated instructions in the law code to "seek the place the Lord your God will choose" (Deut 12:5, etc.) are framed precisely by Deut 11:26-32 and Deuteronomy 27.[41]

In Deuteronomy 27, the connection between crossing the Jordan and

---

41. The association between "chosen place" and Shechem was made by Wenham in his thesis "The Structure and Date of Deuteronomy." It has recently been argued again, with emphasis on Mount Ebal, by Richter, *The Deuteronomistic History and the Name Theology*.

proceeding to Mounts Gerizim and Ebal for the blessing and the curse is reiterated (Deut 27:2, 4, 12-13), but now it is further specified that "the words of the law," that is, the laws that Moses has just proclaimed, should be inscribed on a pile of stones covered with plaster (27:2-3). The present text (8:31) explicitly takes its cue from those in Deuteronomy. The stones on which the laws are now written could be the same stones as those used for the altar or a separate structure, though the latter is preferable because of the evident dependence on the Deuteronomic text, where they are clearly separate.[42] Both the altar and the inscription testify to a claim that is now made on the part of Yahweh to ownership of the land. The altar, modelled on the prescription in Exod 20:25, proclaims that only Yahweh is to be worshipped in this land. And the laws, publicly displayed, establish that his writ runs in it. The people that possesses this land must be true to its covenant with Yahweh.

The ceremony itself has two parts. First, the newly built altar is used for sacrifice (v. 31), as at the moment when Israel under Moses entered into covenant with Yahweh at Mount Sinai, where too the giving of laws was ratified by sacrifice (Exod 24:3-8). Then, on behalf of all Israel, Joshua writes the laws on the stones. The laws are identified as "a copy of the law of Moses," establishing that it is the laws given by Yahweh through Moses that are now inscribed, laws which are known in the book of Deuteronomy as "this Book of the Law" (Deut 28:58, 61; 29:20-21; 31:26) and in one place as "a copy of this law" (Deut 17:18, referring to a copy which the king should make for himself; this is the closest expression to the one used here). The phrase "a copy of the law of Moses, *which he had written*" (NRSV) could refer to a copy written by Moses himself or to one written by Joshua (v. 32). The ambiguity may be deliberate, since in important respects Joshua continues the work of Moses (see on Joshua 1). The essential thing, however, is that it is the law given to Moses that is perpetuated and that now takes its place formally in the life of Israel.

The law is valid not only for the whole land but also for the whole people. Israel as a totality emerges strongly from the way in which the ceremony is portrayed. In this respect, the present text has a distinctive angle when compared with Deuteronomy 27, the text that prescribes this ceremony. In that place the tribes of Israel line up on Mounts Ebal and Gerizim for the solemn declaration of the blessings and curses by the Levites (though only curses are actually declaimed; Deut 27:12-13, 14-26). Here "all Israel, aliens and

---

42. It is possible to read "the stones" in 30:32 simply as "stones" (with NIV, contrast NRSV), the definite article referring not to the stones of the altar just mentioned but, in good Hebrew idiom, to the stones in question, i.e., those on which Joshua now wrote the words of the law.

citizens alike, with their elders, officials and judges" take their positions, half of them facing each mountain, for the blessing by the "levitical priests" (8:33). Then Joshua himself reads the "words of the law" (v. 34).

The reason for the difference from Deuteronomy 27 is that the single event anticipated in that text has been combined with the sort of public reading of the law intended to be performed regularly in Israel according to Deut 31:9-12.[43] The most important echo of that text is the designation of Israel as "assembly" (קהל/qāhāl, v. 35), one of the formal terms for the people gathered together on solemn occasions in worship and allegiance to Yahweh (cf. Deut 5:22; 9:10, where the "assembly" at Sinai itself is meant. In Deut 31:12 a verbal form of the same term is used; cf. Josh 18:1; 22:12). A further echo of Deuteronomy 31 is the enumeration of the varied membership of the people: "aliens and citizens alike" (v. 33), "the women and children, and the aliens who lived among them" (v. 35; cf. Deut 31:12; also 29:10-11).[44] The Israelite assembly is constitutional, the roles of elders and other officials being expressly mentioned alongside Joshua (8:33). That is, it is not a "monarchical" polity, with Joshua as Israelite "king" in place of the expelled Canaanite kings. A new kind of people now has possession of Canaan.

After the capture of Ai, Israel has established itself "across the Jordan," and so has been able to take possession of the land at least symbolically (though not yet fully) by carrying out the prescribed ceremony at Mounts Ebal and Gerizim. The claim of Yahweh as the true owner and ruler of this land has been staked by a people that owes him allegiance. It remains for this vision to be worked out in what lies ahead.

Joshua 9

9:1-2 The erection of the altar on Mount Ebal lays claim to Yahweh's possession of the whole land, and the narrative recognizes this by telling immediately of the reaction of all the kings of Canaan throughout the land to defend themselves against Israel. The notice in these verses is somewhat stylized, picturing the hostility of all the Canaanites to Israel in principle. It is not followed by an account of action by an actual alliance of all the Canaanite kings. In practice the events that follow — the Gibeonites' covenant with Joshua and

---

43. Cf. Nelson, *Joshua*, 118.
44. This last text also includes "those who cut your wood and those who draw your water," a phrase which will be applied to the Gibeonites in Josh 9:21. They may be omitted in Josh 8:35 in anticipation of the story in Joshua 9.

the consequent attack on them by an alliance of southern kings — could have been occasioned either by the erecting of the altar at Shechem or by the attack on Ai or both. The progress of Israel unfolds locally first. Even so, these verses portray the ultimate issue: that Israel lays claim to the whole land and is therefore in conflict with all its peoples.

9:3-15 Whereas all the peoples of the land are said to have allied themselves to fight against Joshua, we now find that one group in particular took the very opposite course. Gibeon lay not far from Ai, between that city and Jerusalem. Its inhabitants, called "Hivites" (cf. v. 1), "heard" of Joshua's progress just as the kings of other cities did; they, however, decide not to resist, but rather to attempt to become assimilated with Israel.

The narrative of their action assumes that they know a great deal about Israel, its God, and his law. In pretending not to be indigenous but to have recently arrived from "a distant country," they know not only that Israel is obliged by Yahweh's command to destroy the indigenous peoples, making no covenant with them (Deut 7:2), but also that Israel's law concerning warfare makes a distinction between peoples of the land itself and those who live beyond its borders (Deut 20:10-15; contrast vv. 16-18). In the event of war against a city outside the land, terms of peace may be offered and its people permitted to "serve" Israel by doing forced labor (vv. 10-11). In effect Gibeon succeeds in having itself treated as a city outside the land, even though it is well within its borders.

The Gibeonites are persuasive. They take pains to look like bedraggled, hungry travellers; they go to Joshua at Gilgal rather than wait for him to come to Gibeon, for then their ruse would have been impossible; they declare that they have come because of what they have heard of Yahweh's victories over Egypt and the kings of Transjordan; they cast themselves in the role of "servants" to Joshua and Israel, and they ask repeatedly that Joshua make a "covenant" with them (ברית/bĕrît; NIV, NRSV "treaty"). Perhaps they have heard not only of Israelite victories, but also of how they spared Rahab and her family, swearing an oath to her that they should be allowed to live alongside Israel in perpetuity (2:12-14; 6:22-25). This Israel might not be as rigorous as it seems.

Israel is indeed faced with a dilemma. How do they know if these travellers are what they seem? Joshua expresses doubts at the outset (v. 8), and this elicits the story of how the Gibeonites' "elders and all those living in their country" had commissioned their trip, having heard of the greatness of Yahweh (vv. 8-13). At this, Israel's leaders immediately accept them, by eating with them,[45] and Joshua formally makes peace by means of the covenant or

---

45. They might alternatively be testing the travellers' claim about the food, though this

treaty that they had sought at the beginning (vv. 14-15; cf. Deut 20:10). The firm commitment of Israel to Gibeon is stressed by the accumulation of terms: treaty/covenant, peace, and oath (to make "peace" is closely analogous to making a covenant[46]). Israel's acceptance of the Gibeonites' self-portrayal and their recourse to this solemnly binding agreement come surprisingly quickly, notwithstanding initial doubts. Some inquiry might have been expected. What "distant country" had these people come from? Why would they put themselves in this position of danger when there was no strategic need to do so? The hastiness of their response is signalled with the note that the Israelite negotiators "did not inquire of the Lord" (v. 14). A notable feature of the exchange is the untidy changes of subject on the Israelite side that run through the encounter: the Israelites (lit., "man of Israel," v. 7), "the men" (v. 14), the "leaders of the assembly" (v. 15b), and Joshua himself.[47] Who is in charge? While "the men" eat with the Gibeonites and do not inquire of the Lord (v. 14), it is Joshua who makes peace (v. 15). Have certain representatives of Israel preempted Joshua, and is he thus exonerated from blame for this capitulation?[48] Yet the effect of the alternation of agents in the narration is scarcely to protect Joshua from blame, but rather to signify a certain division and lack of purposeful leadership on the Israelite side, a division which will erupt a little later (v. 18). Joshua himself hardly follows up the Israelites' hesitant querying of the travellers' story (v. 7). His own question to the travellers (v. 8) seeks to elicit more than they have already offered, but though their rejoinder does nothing to identify them further, he signs on the dotted line of the agreement without more ado (v. 15). So he too has nowhere to hide. As Hawk asks, has Israel been "bamboozled?"[49]

---

seems unlikely since the note that they ate it is paralleled by the information that they did not inquire of Yahweh. Nelson accepts the "testing" option, but thinks that "at the same time they may be participating in a covenant-making meal or taking on a responsibility to protect those with whom they have eaten"; *Joshua*, 130.

46. The Hebrew שלום/*šālôm*, "peace," is akin to the Akkadian *šulmu*, which is often used for the peace imposed on a subject people after war. "Peace" as a settlement with terms is also the concept in Deut 20:10-11.

47. The uncertainties as to who speaks for Israel are reflected at the textual level. "Man of Israel" (v. 7) is supplied with a plural verb in MT (though smoothed to a singular elsewhere, e.g., Qumran); the reference in any case must be to a plurality. "The men" (v. 14) is read as "the leaders" in LXX (followed by NRSV, but contrast RSV), the two terms being capable of confusion in the Hebrew consonantal text by the transposition of a single letter.

48. As some have it, the redaction of the chapter aims to exempt Joshua from responsibility for the failure to "inquire"; for an account of the redactional history of ch. 9, see Nelson, *Joshua*, 123-29.

49. Hawk, *Joshua*, 143.

9:16-27 The Gibeonites' subterfuge is inevitably discovered (v. 16), showing why they had been so anxious to conclude the affair in haste. And the Israelites are now faced with the acute dilemma which is at the heart of the story. They march to the Gibeonite cities, which we now find are four in number, in an action resembling the military march that might have been expected according to the terms of the "ban of destruction" (v. 17), but which cannot accomplish that aim. The dilemma is expressed in the dissension that now arises within Israel, the Israelites' dissatisfaction caused presumably by the restraint on their forward momentum following victories at Jericho and Ai. They "murmur" against the leaders, as the former generation had "murmured" against Moses in the wilderness,[50] whether because of this impediment to fulfilment of the covenant command, because of fear of a fifth column within, or because of the lost prospect of booty and land. The "leaders" respond by recalling the solemn oath made to the Gibeonites, which could not be broken (v. 20). This shows the extreme difficulty of the situation, for they are forced either to break the fundamental terms of the mandate to occupy the land by letting these inhabitants live or to break an oath made before Yahweh, by which they were equally bound. They resolve the issue by declaring that these residents of the land should remain, albeit in the status of servants to Israel, an ironic echo of their self-introduction in v. 8 (v. 21). Yet there is a sense that this is an imperfect resolution, brought about by Israel's own false step at the outset.

The matter comes to its conclusion as Joshua now steps forward to address the Gibeonites. His opening question (v. 22) does not so much require an answer (they did it to protect themselves, as anyone might) as describe the situation arising from their ruse. The Gibeonites are among Israel only because their deceit obscured the real relationship between them, and not by any fundamental right. Whether because of the deceit or because their presence is in principle offensive, they are now "accursed." The curse on them takes a particular form, namely their enslavement to Israel.[51] Their status as servants of Israel is further confirmed, with the addition that some of them would be assigned in perpetuity to the service of the Israelite sanctuary (v. 23; v. 27 seems to combine the idea that they were enslaved to the Israelites in general with that of their bondage to the sanctuary in particular). Those who were subject to the "holiness" command of the "ban" are now made to serve the holiness of Yahweh in this different way.

---

50. Cf. Exod 16:2, 7; cf. Hawk, *Joshua*, 145.

51. Curses in the Old Testament typically have specific content, as have their counterparts in blessing; cf. Gen 4:11-12; 9:25-27.

Joshua 9:16-27

The Gibeonites now give an alternative account of themselves to the one they had offered at Gilgal (vv. 24-25). They express their fear of the advancing Israelites, just as first the Moabites (Num 22:3) then Rahab had done, borrowing the language of Israel when they speak of Yahweh's promise and command to Moses, to possess the land by destroying its inhabitants. There is no reason to doubt them when they speak in this way, and their final word is one of acquiescence (v. 25).

The story of the Israelites' oath and treaty with the Gibeonites, like that of their oath to Rahab, occupies an important place in the story and theology of Joshua. In a narrative of the occupation of land by a people marked by their ethnicity and their religious allegiance, at the expense of other peoples who worshipped other gods, a considerable enclave of non-Israelites is permitted to live alongside the incomers in the heart of the land. It cannot be lost on the reader that this story comes as the immediate sequel to that of Achan, the Israelite who with his family was excised from the congregation. Although they have been enslaved as the price of their "peace" with Israel, they have nevertheless become embedded in Israel, indeed hardly distinguishable from it, as the sequel will show (ch. 10). The tension between a rigorous concept of the people Israel, descended from Abraham, Isaac, and Jacob and incomers to this given land, and a more pragmatic concept, in which Israel also embraces Rahab and Gibeon, marks the book of Joshua, just like that other tension, between total victory and partial possession. The story evokes the political realities that attend the vocation to be Israel. How can Israel keep its identity in an objective, visible sense, when it lives in reality within an ethnic and religious mix? The dilemma of Joshua and the Israelites, forced to choose between a fundamental commitment to Yahweh and an equally binding commitment arising from their own imperfect perception of similarity and difference, may be extrapolated from the unique encounter in the story to the regularities of life in the land.[52] That dilemma may be judged from one perspective as a failure, a problem of their own making, even anticipating Joshua's cry later at Shechem: "You are not able to serve the Lord!" (24:19) — though Joshua himself is implicated here. From another, it is a realistic reckoning that Israel must pursue its vocation in the midst of the imperfections of life, including the consequences of disobedience and compromise.

---

52. Hawk comments that the Gibeonites are in some important respects like Israel and unlike others in Canaan, namely in that they apparently have no king, decisions are made by their elders together with the whole people, and they act in a unified way. In some respects they even outdo Israel in what should be characteristic of the latter; Hawk, *Joshua*, 138-39, 149.

Joshua 10

10:1-5 The episode of the alliance between Israel and Gibeon is immediately followed by one which features another alliance. The calling of this alliance, by the king of Jerusalem, is sparked by the Gibeonite one, because the falling of Gibeon into Israelite hands now enhances the threat that Joshua and Israel is perceived to represent to the other powers in the region. It emerges that Gibeon is regarded as a major center of power (v. 2), and the reader senses the heightened alarm among the allied leaders, as the new development shifts the balance of power in the area to their disadvantage. A defensive reaction to Israel among the "kings" of Canaan was signalled in 9:1. This indeed was the context in which Gibeon, against the trend, sought a coexistence treaty with Israel. Now, however, the resistance movement comes to fruition in a specific military initiative of the king of Jerusalem, Adonizedek.[53]

Adonizedek is said to have "heard" of Joshua's victories at Ai and Jericho (v. 1). The motif of "hearing" thus continues (as in 9:1), not offering new information to the reader, but reiterating the irresistible advance of Israel and the alarm caused by it. What is new in Adonizedek's plan is this consortium of kings. The king of Jericho had played a part in the depiction of the conflict between that city and Israel (2:2-3; 6:2). The king of Ai had led his army, and Joshua had marked victory there by the public exposure of his body (8:14, 29). Furthermore, Rahab's memory of Israel's victories up to that point specified the kings Sihon and Og, whom Israel had met in Transjordan (2:10). It was an oddity of Gibeon that it was not led by a king (though it was like "one of the royal cities"[54]). With Adonizedek's alliance of city-states in the region south of Jerusalem, kings find new prominence in the narrative, as the real centers of power and those who are directly threatened by the new arrival in their region. Israel under Joshua is no respecter of the power of tyrants, and this defensive alliance is at the same time a response of forces of reaction.

It is striking, of course, that the alliance is led by the king of Jerusalem. The episode puts at the center of resistance to Israel the very city that will in due course be the capital of King David, the location of King Solomon's temple, and Yahweh's "dwelling" and "resting place" (Ps 132:13-14). Adonizedek's very name, meaning "the Lord is righteousness," bears an irony. The association of Jerusalem with צדק/ṣedeq ("righteousness" — often written "zedek") is apparently ancient, for it was from Salem (Jerusalem; cf. Ps. 76:2) that the

---

53. He is called Adonibezek in the LXX of this passage, and also in Judg 1:5-7.

54. The phrase puts Gibeon on a footing with the more powerful royal city-states, while acknowledging that it did not have a king itself; cf. Butler, *Joshua*, 114.

mysterious priest-king Melchizedek had once blessed Abraham (Gen 14:18-20).[55] The assertion contained in the name Adonizedek is ultimately true of Yahweh according to the narrative, and that narrative is leading us to a time when Yahweh would be recognized as God in Jerusalem and when he would call kings to act righteously there (cf. 2 Sam 8:15). Adonizedek, therefore, points to a goal of the story well beyond himself, while in the meantime he stands in defiant opposition to it. The irony points up well the nature of the conflict: who has the right to claim the mantle of righteousness, and who rules truly in the land?

10:6-15   The alliance aims directly at Gibeon, since it is Gibeon's action that has destabilized the region and so threatens to make its neighbors' positions untenable. Possibly, this was exactly what Gibeon had anticipated. In any case, its leaders hurry now to invoke the terms of its alliance with Israel, for that alliance had gone much further than simply sparing the Gibeonite cities. Rather, in common with ancient Near Eastern vassal-treaties generally, it had committed Israel to act against the enemies of its "servants" the Gibeonites (v. 6) as if they were the enemies of Israel itself. In fact, they were indeed Israel's enemies, and the assault on Gibeon thus becomes the occasion of the next stage in Joshua's war on the nations of the land. Having taken the central part of the land, the area encompassing Bethel, Ai, and Shechem, Israel now turns its attention to the south, the region that would in future roughly correspond to the territory of Judah.

Joshua and the Israelites come quickly from Gilgal, where they had their base camp since the crossing of the Jordan. Yahweh reiterates his fundamental challenge and commitment: that they should not fear and that he has already given the enemy into Israel's hand (v. 8; cf. 1:5-9). Joshua's haste (an all-night march) is matched by Yahweh's decisive intervention, throwing the enemy into confusion, in a clear echo of his action against Egypt at the crossing of the Red Sea (Exod 14:24-25), and enabling Joshua to prevail (see also God's promise in Exod 23:27). The victory over the alliance is swift and complete, dispensing with stories of strategy and reverse as at Ai. It becomes instead a demonstration of the irresistibility of Joshua's Israel, backed by the supreme power and resolution of Yahweh. The supernatural aspect of the victory is stressed by the role played by the extraordinary hailstorm, which claimed more of the enemy than the military might of Israel (v. 11).

---

55. The names Melchizedek and Adonizedek, therefore, are closely related. The former means "the king is righteousness." Both the names convey that the *god* worshipped at Jerusalem is righteousness. In Genesis 14, that god is El Elyon ("God Most High"), who may have been worshipped by that name before Israel's time, but who is later identified with Yahweh (cf. e.g., Ps. 46:4; 47:2).

The centerpiece of the story is the strange event that accompanied the battle: the sun and moon standing still while the victory was completed (vv. 12-14). This is curious in a number of ways. First, it is commemorated in a fragment of poetry, which, as the only such case in the book, heightens the sense that the event was unique. The poetic utterance is attributed to the "book of Jashar" ("the upright one"), which is cited also in 2 Sam 1:18, where it is said to contain David's lament for Saul and Jonathan. Nothing else is known of this ancient record, but it is one pointer to the sources available to the biblical writers.

Second, it is Joshua who initiates the event, by "speaking" to Yahweh in a way that more typically refers to Yahweh's own commanding speech (v. 12) and proceeding to command the sun and moon to stop in their tracks.[56] It is this role of Joshua in relation to Yahweh that is specified as the really remarkable thing about the event (v. 14), namely that Yahweh "listened" to the voice of a human, where "listened" is a word that often connotes obedience. The strange happening at Gibeon gives Joshua an extraordinary authority. It is Joshua and Yahweh together, apparently, who bring about the decisive outcome of the day.

Unusual astronomical events are recorded elsewhere in the Old Testament as signs of Yahweh's special action (cf. Isa 38:8; Hab 3:11). This one is so spectacular that it challenges the imagination, and has led some to propose readings of the text different from the traditional one, and contrary to the explanation in v. 13b. But however one visualizes the event, the point is to assert the concordance between the forces of nature under God and the human capacities of Joshua and Israel.[57]

10:16-27 The fate of the five kings is told separately from that of their

---

56. See Hawk, *Joshua*, 152-53.

57. See Nelson, *Joshua*, 141-45, for further discussion. The verb used in v. 12b in the address to the sun, and by extension the moon, is דוֹם/*dôm*, from דמם/*dmm*, which normally means "be silent," "be silenced." This could be understood to mean "be stunned into immobility." In v. 13a, the same verb occurs to describe what the sun did, and here it is in parallel with עמד/*'āmad*, which is used for the moon and which usually means "stand" or "come to a standstill." The explanation of the event in v. 13b then uses the verb עמד/*'āmad* for the sun, which clearly reads both verbs in vv. 12b-13a as "come to a standstill." The somewhat unusual use of the verb דמם/*dmm* in v. 12b, however, together with the absence of a reference to the moon in v. 13b, has led some commentators to think that the explanation in v. 13b misunderstands the original poetic lines and to speculate otherwise on the nature of the event. Suggestions for that original meaning include a prayer that the sun and moon might darken, or that the sun might not rise, or that sun and moon might be appalled at what they were about to witness. For these and other interpretations see Nelson, *Joshua*, 142-45. See also Stephen Williams's comments on the passage below, in the section entitled "God of Miracle and Mystery."

armies, the action of this section overlapping with that of the previous. (While the first account of the victory ends with Joshua and Israel returning to the camp at Gilgal, v. 15, this account tells of a return to the camp at Makkedah where the kings were discovered, v. 21. This was presumably a field camp, as distinct from the permanent base at Gilgal.[58]) Watching over the battle, perhaps from a safe position, they flee together when it is clear that all is lost. Proud leaders of a seemingly powerful alliance, they become humiliated prey, hiding in a cave. The hopelessness of their position is clear from the ease with which they are discovered. The hiding place becomes first their prison and soon their tomb. Their isolation from the action expresses the actual impotence of this power that would resist the divine purpose, and underlines the inevitable defeat of their armies. Joshua can safely leave them under guard while the action in the field is pursued to its conclusion. A remnant of the alliance forces escapes to their cities, awaiting the Israelite action against the cities themselves (v. 20).

The execution of the kings becomes an object lesson to Israel, that Yahweh has indeed given their enemies over to them and that therefore they have no grounds for fear. This has been the chief moral issue confronting the people since Moses' exhortation at Horeb and Israel's first fateful failure in that respect (Deut 1:21, 26-40). And even yet, with Jericho and Ai in ruins, Joshua thinks it necessary to insist on the point. The leaders ceremonially put their feet on the kings' necks, in figurative display of the impotence of the proud (a major theme of the prophet Isaiah, e.g., Isa 2:9-21). They are then executed, and hung in humiliating exposure, according to the fate set by the law of Deuteronomy for the criminal condemned to death (Deut 21:22-23). The same law determined the limit set on such exposure, and so the bodies are taken down at sunset and sealed in the cave which they had hoped would be a lifeline. Their burial there is marked by yet more stones of remembrance, another lasting memorial to Yahweh's possession of this land.

10:28-39 Following the execution of the five kings, Joshua turns his attention to the cities themselves and others in the region. In fact his action against the cities of the southern alliance is the beginning of a narrative of conquest that continues with an account of the defeat of another alliance of kings in the north (ch. 11) and thus of the entire land. As in the battle with the five kings, the accounts emphasize the swiftness and totality of the victories. As K. Lawson Younger has shown, they fall formally within a pattern familiar

---

58. The words "to the camp" are missing from LXX. As Butler points out, this is "a regular LXX feature by which the camp is never located outside Gilgal (cf. 8:13; 18:9)," *Joshua*, 110. The words are likely to be original.

in ancient conquest accounts, with a tendency to hyperbole and an intention to demonstrate the superiority of the victor.[59] Joshua's conquest accounts have the theological purpose of declaring the irresistibility of Yahweh in his resolve to overcome the nations of Canaan.

The accounts recall Moses' victories over the Transjordanian kings Sihon and Og, as reported in Deut 2:26–3:11.[60] Yahweh gives the enemy city over to Israel, who fall upon it and utterly destroy it in accordance with the requirement of חרם/*ḥērem* ("devotion to destruction"), leaving none remaining (Deut 2:33-34; 3:3-6). The language of the *ḥērem* is used expressly of Makkedah, Eglon, Hebron, and Debir (vv. 28, 35, 37, 39), and this is the logic of the whole account. It is not used of Libnah or Lachish, though their fate is the same and so the concept is presumably to be applied there too. (Gezer is treated slightly differently, with no account of the city itself being destroyed.) There is a strong sense of a single unified action unfolding. Og of Bashan was destroyed just like Sihon of Heshbon (Deut 3:6); so now Makkedah and Libnah are destroyed just like Jericho (Josh 10:28, 30), Lachish just like Libnah (10:32), Eglon like Lachish (v. 35), Hebron like Eglon (v. 37), Debir like Hebron and Libnah (v. 39).

The cities named in the account do not correspond exactly to those that formed the alliance under Adonizedek. Jerusalem and Jarmuth are missing, and Makkedah, Libnah, and Debir are new. Jerusalem and Jarmuth are listed in 12:10-11, along with several of those in the present account, as kings whom Joshua defeated and whose lands he turned over to Israel (12:7-8). Jarmuth later appears as a city allocated to Judah (15:35). The fate of Jerusalem (Jebus) is more complicated. It is said to have been taken by the forces of Judah in Judg 1:8, yet in the same chapter we find that the *Benjaminites* were unable to drive out its Jebusite inhabitants. And Josh 15:63 agrees with this, though here it is Judah and not Benjamin that is said to have failed. That Jerusalem was not taken either by Joshua or the generation after him is confirmed by the record that the city finally fell only to David (2 Sam 5:5-16). Behind the varied traditions in Joshua and Judges lies a story, presumably, in which Jerusalem was not only contested over generations between Israelites and Canaanites, but even between the tribes of Judah and Benjamin. The latter point is also implied by the course of the eventual civil war between David and Saul, where David can enter Jerusalem only after victory over the northern tribes including Saul's Benjamin.

---

59. Younger, *Ancient Conquest Accounts*.
60. For a full account of the similarities between Josh 10:28–11:23 and the defeats of Sihon and Og, see Hawk, *Joshua*, 159-67. The similarities extend to the vocabulary used, such as the verb נכה/*nkh*, "smite" or "strike."

The present passage, therefore, leaves certain gaps which we are obliged to fill as best we can. Gezer is another case in point. While its king is defeated in Joshua's action, the city is not said to be taken here. It appears as a city on the boundary of territory allocated to the descendants of Joseph (16:3), but the Joseph tribes of Ephraim and Manasseh were unable to drive out its inhabitants (16:10). It appears again as a Levitical city in 21:21, but later is in territory that figures in David's conflict with the Philistines (2 Sam 5:25); and even when Solomon reigns over the united kingdom at its full extent, Gezer is said to have been gifted to him by the Egyptian pharaoh, who had taken it from its Canaanite population and given it to Solomon as dowry in Solomon's marriage to his daughter (1 Kgs 9:15-16). Gezer, it seems, occupying a key position between coastal plain and hill country, was always disputed territory. Finally, it should be noted that both Hebron and Debir reappear in Judg 1:9-15, where they are said to have been taken by the tribe of Judah after Joshua's death.

The gaps confirm that the present account is somewhat stylized and serves the theological purpose of declaring Yahweh's total victory and Israel's outright possession. This purpose will be pursued in ch. 11.

10:40-43 The coda to the narrative of the war with the southern alliance reaffirms its principal themes. The "whole land" means here the southern region in its entirety, as described according to its parts in v. 40. Once again it is noted that it was the Canaanite *kings* who were the enemy, and that the whole area was subjected to the "devotion of destruction." The extent of the land taken is measured from Kadesh-barnea, which was the camp of Israel at the northern Sinai edge prior to its march towards the land. Joshua's action is thus put on a broad canvas which comprises also Moses' victories in Transjordan.[61] The unity of Moses' and Joshua's campaigns is signalled once again by this notice. The swiftness of the victories is also restated, being a consequence of the fundamental factor that Yahweh fought for Israel (v. 42). The return of Joshua and Israel to the camp at Gilgal indicates that this phase of the campaign is settled and over.

The picture of total victory, however, is only one side of the theological view of the conquest in Joshua, as will emerge in due course, from ch. 13. Some of the "gaps" in the narrative serve, not just to remind us that the historical actuality was probably less tidy than a superficial reading of the account appears, but to remind the reader of the complicating issues that have already been aired. Gibeon (v. 41) is such a reminder.

---

61. Goshen, however, is apparently an area in the southern part of the land, and not the place in Egypt where Jacob's family had once settled (cf. 11:16).

Joshua 11

11:1-5 The news of Israel's victories continues to travel and now reaches the king of Hazor, one of the largest and most significant city-states in the northern part of the land, commanding an important north-south trade route.[62] So it is not surprising that its king should take the lead in mounting a defensive war against advancing Israel. The other geographical locations are only partly known, but they are clearly meant to cover the northern part of the land comprehensively. Madon (v. 1) may be the same place as Merom (v. 7).[63] Kinnereth (or Chinneroth) is the Sea of Galilee, and the Arabah to the south of it means the northern part of the Jordan Valley. Hermon designates the mountainous territory in the far north, on the modern borders of Israel, Lebanon, and Syria. Naphoth-dor to the west suggests an extension as far as the Mediterranean Sea. The portrayal of northern Israel includes not only place names but also six peoples, corresponding to the description of the population of the land in the programmatic text of conquest in Exod 23:23.[64]

The king of Hazor thus assembles a powerful alliance, echoing the southern alliance that Joshua and Israel have just defeated. The accent is on the exceptional size and might of the army that gathers at Merom (v. 4). With horses and chariots, in contrast to the forces that met Israel in the southern hill country, they are fully equipped for war. The opening verses of the chapter, therefore, deliberately characterize the enemy as extremely formidable. The impression of a great showdown is heightened by the fact that the battle lines opposing Israel precisely represent the population that they have a warrant to destroy and drive out. This superior and highly organized force represents the full might of opposition to the purpose of Yahweh for the land and his people.

11:6-15 The portrayal of the might of the enemy, however, is followed immediately by Yahweh's encouragement "not to fear." Israel had faced overwhelming odds before and been exhorted with the same words (Deut 1:21). Their experience in the long years prior to Jericho had been that the power of the opposition was not the decisive factor, but rather that Yahweh was with them. They had learned both through failure to believe this, then through believing it. The word is spoken directly to Joshua and echoes the same encour-

---

62. Cf. Hess, *Joshua*, 212-13.

63. The possibility of confusion between the names rests on the similarity of the letters "d" and "r" in Hebrew, and of the alteration of "on" and "om" endings in certain place names; see Hess, *Joshua*, 208 and n. Hess suggests that Madon, or Merom, may be identified with Tel Qarnei Hittin ("the horns of Hittin"), which lies above Tiberias, overlooking the Sea of Galilee.

64. Deut 7:1 has one extra, the Girgashites.

agement given to him at the outset of his commission to take the land for Israel (Josh 1:6-9). His response is to obey the divine word. And the result is swift success. Here as in the case of the southern alliance little time is spent on describing the course of the battle. Rather, the victory is rapid and total. The symbols of great military strength are disabled and destroyed (v. 9b). The narrative aims simply to make the point that Yahweh could be trusted and that obedience leads to the promised outcome (v. 9a). The might of the enemy forces was played up only for the purpose of showing that no enemy, however great, could withstand the purpose of Yahweh. It is a story that is repeated elsewhere in the Old Testament. The giant Goliath is no match for young David, because David acts out of faith in Yahweh.

Having won in the field, Joshua turns to the cities themselves, where the power and wealth of the enemy are situated. Hazor, the first among the alliance, is first to undergo the "devotion to destruction," told in the usual formulaic way. Its preeminence among the victims of Yahweh's wrath on this occasion is further signalled by the fact that it alone is burned (v. 13), like Jericho and Ai before it (6:24; 8:28). The "devotion to destruction" could apparently admit of variations of rigor. (The permission in this case to take spoil, as at Ai but in contrast to Jericho, is another instance of such variation; cf. 6:21; 8:27.) The other cities of the alliance, unnamed, then share the same fate. And as in the case of the king of Jerusalem and his confederates, so the execution of the kings of those cities is singled out for special mention (v. 12), to stress that it is not only the cities that are destroyed, but the whole system of power which they represent.

Joshua's acts are now put in line with those of Moses. He acts not only in direct obedience to Yahweh, but also within the chain of command and obedience that went back to the original commission of Moses to lead and equip the people for their future lives (vv. 12b, 15). Joshua's victories have already been shown to be in continuity with the work of conquest begun by Moses east of the Jordan. Now in this way too, the unity of the combined actions of Moses and Joshua is accentuated. The whole life of Israel, from Egypt to Canaan, has been all along the gift of Yahweh and subject to his guidance and control. Moses also recalls, of course, the obligation on Israel to keep the covenant originated at Sinai when they take possession of their gifted land.

11:16-23 The final section of the chapter looks back at both the northern and southern campaigns, whose result is that Joshua has taken "this entire land," from the Negeb in the far south to Hermon in the far north (vv. 16-17). Once again the execution of kings is singled out, to show that the conquest entails that a whole new order, religious and political, will henceforth prevail in this land. It is intriguing to read that no nation "made peace" with Israel;

that is, none attempted to make a peace treaty with them (v. 19 NRSV; so NIV). This puts a particular angle on the conflict, which may not seem logically consonant with the fact that Israel was under covenantal obligation to destroy all the nations in any case. Yet it makes the important point that the peoples of the land met Israel with hostile intent, and this serves to explain why the issue of showing mercy to them did not arise (v. 20). Indeed, Yahweh had "hardened their hearts," as he had done in the case of Pharaoh in Egypt. His purpose would prevail; but the conflicts involved were not arbitrarily chosen or pursued. The confrontations in both Egypt and Canaan were real clashes of culture, religion, politics, and morality. Joshua is said to have made war on these nations for "a long time" (v. 18). This sits a little oddly with the narratives of swift victory. However, it may be taken as a symptom both of their outright opposition and his resolution.

Only Gibeon is excepted from the totalizing picture. This city had indeed made a peace treaty with Israel. Nor was its exemption from destruction a case of mercy; on the contrary, it was portrayed as a consequence of trickery, so that the presence of the Hivites of Gibeon among Israel constitutes a troubling exception to the picture of the eradication of all elements hostile to Yahweh's rule in the land. The totality of that eradication takes its rationale from the possibility that Israel may be seduced away from Yahweh (Deut 7:4). And because of Gibeon, this rationale is compromised.

The coda to the account (vv. 21-23) adds little to the picture. It returns to the notion of "Anakim," renowned gigantic ancient warriors who had been a major cause of Israel's first terror when their spies went from Kadesh-barnea to view the land (Deut 1:28). These are now included in the resumptive account of victory. How they relate to other inhabitants of the southern region is not said, nor when Joshua's actions against them took place in relation to his war with the southern alliance. The notice evidently intends to correspond to that first fearful vision of Israel, and thus becomes part of the story of the conquest of every foe, even unnatural ones. Yet there is some ambivalence in the allusion, since it is the occasion for the information that some "Anakim" were in fact left, namely in cities that would become notorious as Philistine strongholds. For this reason the story of the conquest ends on a slightly uncertain note. On one hand it affirms that Yahweh's promise has been fully kept, and Israel has come into possession of the land promised to them. Yet on the other a pointer is given to the difficulty the people will experience in fully realizing the fruits of that promise, a difficulty that will be illustrated in the narrative that stretches well beyond the book of Joshua.

Joshua 12

This chapter continues to look back on the conquest, taking its cue from the closing verses of the previous chapter. Its theme, again, is the totality of the conquest. Its special angle, however, is to reiterate and document the continuity of Moses' victories east of the Jordan and Joshua's victories in the land west of the Jordan. The unity of Moses' and Joshua's work of causing the tribes to inherit is thus emphasized, as is the unity of the land east and west of the Jordan (vv. 1-6, 7-24, respectively). These themes have been signalled already in the narrative. The defeats of Sihon and Og were cited by both Rahab and the Gibeonites as evidence of Yahweh's determination to give the whole land to Israel (2:10; 9:10). And we recall that the language in which the northern and southern campaigns are couched is reminiscent of the account of the Transjordanian successes in Deut 2:24–3:11.

The present chapter therefore not only resumes the victories of Joshua and Moses, but insists that together they form a single action of Yahweh in fulfilment of his promise to gift the land of Canaan to Israel. It also has the effect of determining that the two areas, east and west of the Jordan, together form the full extent of the given land. Transjordan is not secondary to the western territory in this respect, a point of view particularly espoused by Deuteronomy and Joshua.[65] The unity and common destiny of the tribes that settled east and west is the particular concern of Joshua 22.

The pervading theme of the present chapter is the rule that was exercised by the kings of Transjordan and Canaan. Both parts of the chapter begin, "These are the kings of the land. . . ." Both Sihon and Og are said to have "dwelt" in their capitals (vv. 2, 4), a term which has connotations of enthronement in the case of kings; and they "ruled" over their lands (vv. 3, 5; NIV combines both as "reigned"). The array of conquered cities in vv. 7-24 is really a list of kings, strikingly laid out in list form in some translations (NIV, NRSV). A whole world of powers is unfolded here. It is a kind of power that echoes in a minor way the pretensions of the Egyptian pharaoh; that is, their claim to rule this land is found to be falsely based by virtue of the very fact that they are disqualified and overcome by the power of Yahweh, who rules by right. There is in addition, as Hawk argues, a contrast between the plurality of Canaan and the unity of Israel.[66] Plurality in this case may be seen as a function of division and self-interested

---

65. The unity of east and west is less clear in Numbers 32, where "this land," referring to Transjordan (v. 5), seems to contrast with "the land the Lord has given them" in v. 7.

66. Hawk, *Joshua*, 176.

power, while Israel's unity bespeaks obedience to the freedom-bringing word of Yahweh.

The record of defeated kings in vv. 9-24 follows more or less the order of events in the narrative of conquest, beginning with Jericho and Ai and continuing according to the campaigns related in chs. 10–11, that is, proceeding from south to north. Compared with those accounts there are some new entries here (Geder, Hormah, Arad, Adullam, Tappuah, Hepher, Aphek, Lasharon, Taanach, Megiddo, Kedesh, Jokneam, Tirzah). The impression this gives is of a massive war carried out throughout the land, going beyond the scope of the narratives in the book and helping to suggest the totality of victory. The summation, "thirty-one kings in all" (v. 24), underlines the point.

Joshua 13

Once in the land, the task of Joshua was to establish Israel in its inheritance, allocating territory tribe by tribe, in accordance with God's command to him in 1:6. The story of how this was done now occupies most of the remainder of the book, up to ch. 21. Joshua himself is depicted as old, recalling the note in 11:18 that he had made war on the kings of Canaan for "a long time." Indeed, he is close to the point at which he will call Israel together for a last time and charge them to keep faithful to the covenant with Yahweh after he has gone (cf. 23:1-3).[67] Yet his work is not yet complete.

13:1-7 Now that it comes to the distribution of the land, we encounter a new and surprising perspective on Joshua's achievement. For we now discover that, at this late stage in Joshua's life, much land remains to be taken (v. 1). The present chapter, in fact, faces two ways: forward into the narrative of distribution and backward, by way of reflection and comment on the story of conquest so far. And in the latter respect, ch. 13 stands in striking contrast to chs. 10–12. In that extended sequence, emphasis was laid on the totality of the control established by Joshua and Israel over the whole land. Chapter 12 in particular had affirmed the far reach of Joshua's victories. The accounts of victory had been a kind of gazette, building up a picture of the new domains of Israel. The accounts of distribution will have their gazettelike quality too. Yet now the territorial descriptions will routinely show that parts of the land in every tribal area have not yet been fully controlled by Israel.

---

67. There are two accounts of covenant ceremonies in chs. 23, 24. See below on these chapters for the relationship between them.

Joshua 13:8-13

The structure of ch. 13 is similar to ch. 12 in that it deals separately with the areas to the west and east of the River Jordan, respectively. The main interest of the chapter lies with the eastern part of the land (vv. 8-33). But it opens in vv. 1-7 with a preliminary command to divide the land west of the Jordan for the nine-and-a-half tribes (v. 7). The arithmetic of the nine-and-a-half arises from the settling of two-and-a-half in Transjordan, namely Reuben, Gad, and the half-tribe of Manasseh. Manasseh had subdivided into two separate parts, which settled east and west, respectively. Levi is left out of the count, since it received no land-inheritance. The number twelve was maintained by the division of Joseph into Ephraim and Manasseh, the two sons of Joseph who had received a special blessing from Jacob (Gen 48:8-22).

There had been hints in the preceding narrative of total conquest that parts of the land had not been wholly subdued. One such part was the Philistine territory (11:22). Now the Philistine region as a whole, with its five cities and rulers[68] lying along the Mediterranean west of Judah, emerges as unconquered (vv. 2-3). Along with the Philistines in this region are mentioned the Geshurites, who can hardly be the same as the northern Transjordanians of the same name (in 12:5; 13:11),[69] and the Avvim, who are associated with the Philistine area in Deut 2:23. The seacoast to the north towards Lebanon is similarly untouched (vv. 4-5a), and also areas in the far north, including Lebanon itself and the region around Hermon (vv. 5b-6). (The northern limit of conquest had also been noted at 11:17.)

Along with the acknowledgment of land as yet unsubdued comes a renewed pledge of Yahweh that he will drive out these peoples (v. 6). In the meantime, Joshua is to fulfil his commission to cause the people to inherit and divide the land according to its full, ideal boundaries (v. 7).

13:8-13 The territory allotted to the two-and-a-half Transjordanian tribes is now specified,[70] first globally (vv. 8-13), then by individual tribes (vv. 15-31), with a parenthesis concerning the Levites in v. 14.

The description of the territory (vv. 8-13) corresponds to that which is given in 12:1-6, where it was recorded as the realms of the defeated Amorite

---

68. The term in this case is not "king" (מלך/*melek*), but a special term used for Philistine rulers (סרן/*seren*; also in Judg 3:3 and frequently in Judges 16; 1 Samuel 6).

69. Cf. Butler, *Joshua*, 148.

70. A textual problem at the beginning of v. 8 is noticed by most translations, which usually supply a phrase like "With the other half of the tribe of Manasseh" (RSV), though Hebrew only has a cryptic "With it." It is likely that the usual restoration corresponds to what was originally meant and that our Hebrew text (MT) lost the missing words due to a scribal error. See, however, Hawk, *Joshua*, 185-88, who thinks the curious form in MT draws attention to a disunity in Israel symptomized by this geographical division of the tribe of Manasseh.

kings Sihon and Og.[71] It stretched from the valley of the River Arnon, an eastern tributary of the Jordan, as far north as Mount Hermon and to specified places eastward. Hermon thus appears in the descriptions of land both west and east of Jordan, it being an extensive region in which the two territories converge and from which the Jordan itself takes its source. The passage ends by recalling that it was Moses who had taken these lands, but also with the concession that the Israelites had not at that time succeeded in expelling their populations completely (vv. 12b-13).

13:14 The tribe of Levi was the priestly tribe and as such belonged both to the divine service and to Israel as a whole in a way that no other tribe did. Their special position was marked by the fact that they did not receive a tribal territory, but rather entitlements arising from their service in worship and cities with surrounding land in each of the other tribes' allocations (these are catalogued separately in ch. 21). While the other tribes received an "inheritance" in land, the Levites' inheritance consisted of Israel's "offerings by fire,"[72] a term which can apply to a range of types of sacrifice,[72] but occurs also elsewhere in relation to priestly perquisites (cf. Deut 18:1; Lev 2:3).

13:15-33 The territory of Reuben (vv. 15-23) occupied roughly the southern part of the Transjordanian lands. Reuben's occupation of its land is depicted as complete and successful with the elimination of elements that might have led astray to false worship. The references to Balaam and the Midianites recall a sequence in the book of Numbers, in which Balaam was hired by King Balak of Moab to frustrate Israel's advance towards the land (Numbers 22–24) and the Midianites then became the cause of an episode of apostasy (Numbers 25).

The areas occupied by Gad and half-Manasseh, respectively (vv. 24-31), are described in a generally south-north direction. Hawk points out a tendency here towards vagueness in the descriptions, with less clear boundaries and a repetition of the word "half" in the case of Manasseh possibly signalling incompleteness.[73]

The record ends with a further notice that it was Moses who enabled Is-

---

71. King Og is here said to be a lone survivor of the Rephaim, a people elsewhere counted among the ancient inhabitants of the promised land east of the Jordan and remembered as gigantic warriors like the Anakim (Gen 15:20; Deut 2:11, 20; 3:13). In Deut 3:11 Og's own extraordinary physical stature is memorialized in a note about the size of his iron bedstead, said to be found in the city of Rabbah.

72. This is clear from its frequent use in Leviticus 1-7, where it is a category that can correspond to burnt offerings (wholly consumed on the altar) as well as other blood sacrifices and grain offerings where parts of the sacrifice fall to the priests (see Lev 2:1-2; Num 15:8-10).

73. Hawk, *Joshua*, 188-90.

rael to "inherit" this part of their land and another reminder that Levi's inheritance was different (vv. 32-33).

This chapter begins to convey the extent of Israel's occupation in detail. Paradoxically, it thus serves to enter a claim for Israel's right of ownership throughout the borders established for it by Yahweh, yet at the same time it acknowledges the imperfection of its occupancy, in a tendency that will become increasingly evident to the reader as the story progresses. The ironic character of this counterpoint of possession and nonpossession has been found to be an important aspect of the message of the book by a number of interpreters.[74]

Joshua 14

14:1-5 The story of the tribes taking possession of the land west of the Jordan now begins in earnest. The theme is set by the double use of the verb נחל/*nḥl*, "inherit," in v. 1, lit.: "These are what the Israelites *inherited* . . . Eleazar, Joshua and the heads of the tribal families *made them inherit*."[75] Joshua's commission from Yahweh in 1:6 is thus about to be accomplished. The possession of the western lands is first spliced once more with that of the east, and so the authority of Moses is invoked again as the presiding genius over the whole venture. In that connection the broad canvas of territorial possession is again displayed: the two-and-a-half tribes having land to the east, together with the explanation regarding the division of Joseph into two and the concession of cities and grazing lands to the Levites rather than a single unified territory (as observed above on ch. 13). The distribution of land will proceed by lot (v. 2), forestalling internal conflict and emphasizing the nature of this acquisition of land as divine gift. The procedure is presided over by Joshua in conjunction with the priest Eleazar and leading representatives of the tribes, following instructions given beforehand by Yahweh through Moses (Num 34:16-29). The presence of Eleazar would serve to symbolize the hand of God in the events. And the tribal representation guaranteed that the act of distribution was at the same time performed, witnessed, and accepted by all Israel in unison.

14:6-12 The tribe of Judah will be the first to take their possession, the narrative continuing through the long ch. 15. For this purpose the tribe as a whole appears before Joshua at Gilgal (v. 6a). However, before the expected

---

74. A seminal work in this regard was that of Polzin, *Moses and the Deuteronomist*. Hawk, cited several times so far in our treatment, has made a further substantial contribution to this perspective on the book.

75. The repetition of the verb is obscured in many translations for the sake of euphony. Thus NIV has "allotted" for the second occurrence of the verb, while NRSV has "distributed."

continuation in 15:1, the allocation to Judah is prefaced by the special arrangements made for Caleb, son of Jephunneh the Kenizzite. Along with Joshua himself, Caleb had been one of the two original spies of the land who had urged Israel to take courage and go straight into the promised land, in contrast to the majority who had offered a counsel of fear (Num 13:25-33). The consequences of that decision, in long delay in the limbo of Kadesh-barnea, loom large in the memory of Israel as recorded in Numbers 14 and Deuteronomy 1. At the present juncture, Israel bids fair to win at last the prize long withheld. Yet it is already clear that struggles lie ahead. The focus on Caleb at this point, therefore, does more than simply recall the special promise made to him by Moses (v. 9; cf. Deut 1:36); it recalls the fundamental issue that faces Israel as it embarks upon this new phase of its mission and places at the beginning of it the most outstanding example of the courage and faithfulness required in the task that lies ahead. The allocation to Caleb will appear again as part of the account of the allocation to Judah (15:13-19). But its special significance is highlighted here.

The incident stresses the exemplary character of the man. Though told by himself, his story chimes with what we have already learned of him. There is a contrast between his "heart," fully obedient and courageous, and the "heart" of the people which melted at the news of the fearsome opposition (vv. 7-8). The word for heart (לֵב/lēb or לֵבָב/lēbāb) even makes an echo with Caleb's name, which, though literally meaning "dog," thus becomes in itself a pointer to the kind of "heart" approved by God.[76]

Caleb's exemplary role extends to his continued vigor even in his old age, in which he resembles Moses himself (vv. 10-11; cf. Deut 34:7). A young man of forty at the time of the first exploration of the land, his advanced age of eighty-five gives notice of the time that has passed since — the forty years of living in the wilderness, plus an additional five representing (we infer) the length of time spent engaging the Canaanites to this point. But it does more than this, for it allows a reflection on the relationship between that time and this. Caleb is now as he was then, both strong and ready for action in the service of Yahweh; as Yahweh spoke then, so now is the time of fulfilment. The faithfulness of Yahweh is met here by the consistency and ready courage of one of his covenant people. Caleb does not regard the gift as a thing done once for all in the past; rather, he takes it as a new challenge, knowing that it

---

76. The word "dog" is usually a name of abuse or dishonor in the Old Testament. There may then be ironic undertones in the way in which the name functions in the narrative: one who is on the surface "dog" is in reality all "heart." (These and other echoes were penetratingly explored by Pennant in "The Significance of Rootplay, Leading Words and Thematic Links in the Book of Judges.")

Joshua 14:13-15

can only be accomplished by his resolute faith and the Lord going with him even yet (v. 12).[77]

14:13-15 The episode closes with the allocation of Hebron to Caleb. Hebron, in the deep south of Judah, had significance already in Israel because of its ancient association with Abraham (Gen 13:18). It would later be for a time the first capital of King David (2 Sam 5:1-5). Here it is remembered by its former name of Kiriath-arba, "city of Arba," Arba himself reputed to be the greatest of the Anakim (in 15:13 he is said to have been the father of Anak). Caleb's possession therefore corresponds perfectly to his illustrious reputation as the one who showed no fear of the giants in the land.

It remains to notice Caleb's origin, through his father Jephunneh, as a "Kenizzite." Jephunneh is the only named Kenizzite in the Old Testament and is mentioned only in connection with Caleb (cf. Num 32:12). The only other occurrence of the term is in Gen 15:19, where Kenizzites are listed along with Canaanites and others as inhabitants of the land that Yahweh plans to give to Israel. It is strange, therefore, that this model of Israelite faithfulness should have a lineage from among the dispossessed, rather than the Israelite heirs to the land. This hero narrative, therefore, setting up a model for Israelites to emulate, has surprising echoes of the insider-outsider motif that we have traced from Rahab through Achan to Gibeon. Caleb overcomes his dubious ancestry to take his place as model Israelite by virtue of his faith in Yahweh. This eclipsing of an original handicap corresponds to the eclipsing of a "dog" by one who is "all heart."

Joshua 15

This long chapter continues the account of the allocation of land to Judah, following 14:6a. It describes Judah's boundaries (vv. 1-12), tells a story about Caleb's acquisition of his property (vv. 13-19), and finally lists Judah's territory by city (vv. 20-63).

15:1-12 Judah's territory covers a large area in the south of the land. Its southern boundary corresponds to the southern boundary of all Israel as delimited in Num 34:2-5. The present description, therefore, is not merely pragmatic, but expresses the forward movement of the divine purpose. This border[78] runs from the southern end of the Dead Sea, touching Kadesh-

---

77. Note the fourfold "now" (Hebrew עתה/'attâ) in vv. 10-12, setting up this tension between past fact and present reality; cf. Hawk, *Joshua*, 197.

78. It was in reality probably a series of outposts rather than a border in the strict sense.

barnea on the edge of the Sinai desert, where the people had stayed for so many years, and reaching to the Mediterranean at the Wadi of Egypt (the Wadi el-Arish), situated between Gaza and the Nile Delta. Eastern and western limits are marked by the Dead Sea and the Mediterranean, respectively. The northern boundary is elaborated in most detail (vv. 5b-12), no doubt because it is only on this side that Judah is marked off from another territory, Benjamin (cf. 18:15-19). It skirts Jerusalem to the south, reflecting the fact that that city could not yet be taken (v. 63).

Many of the places named here are not known, but some are familiar.[79] On its eastern side Judah touches places that were important at Israel's entry to the land (v. 7). The valley of Achor led into the interior from Jericho and is later remembered by the prophet Hosea as "a door of hope," when he speaks of renewed possession after a period of exile (Hos 2:15). Gilgal was the location of the first Passover in the land (5:10) and of Joshua's camp during the battles that followed (10:6), but would in time be criticized by Amos for the false worship conducted there (Amos 4:4). Jebus (v. 8) is the ancient Canaanite name for Jerusalem (the identification is made here for the benefit of the book's first readers). The valley of Hinnom marks the edge of Jerusalem to its south and west. The Judahites would later make it a place of human sacrifice and suffer judgment accordingly (Jer 7:31-34). The boundary continues westward through Philistine country (vv. 10-11) and on to the Mediterranean Sea.

Judah's territory is well-defined and the description of it pregnant with possibilities. The place of promise is mapped out in detail offering space and resources for life. Yet there are hints and foreshadowings of the dangers ahead. Places received as gift may become temptations to idolatry. The way of possession can also become a way of exile. Boundaries may signal conflict, such as would arise between Judah and Benjamin in the days of David and Saul (2 Sam 2–4). The Philistine territory around Timnah (Judg 14:5) would be contested anew in the days of Samson. Latent in Hinnom are all the possibilities of apostasy and judgment.[80] And Jerusalem remains unpossessed, by either Judah or Benjamin, and somewhat alien.

15:13-19 The topographical record is followed by a colorful narrative, which develops the story of Caleb's special inheritance around Hebron (see 14:6-15). According to 10:36-39 both Hebron and Debir fell to Joshua follow-

---

79. Hess provides identifications with modern sites as far as possible, though there are numerous gaps; *Joshua,* 249-55.

80. The valley of Hinnom (v. 8), הנם גי/*gê hinnōm,* becomes in Greek *Gehenna,* or a name for hell (Matt 5:22, 29-30; 2 Esd. 2:29), on account of its use for human sacrifice.

ing his campaign against the southern alliance of kings led by Adonizedek of Jerusalem. This is reflected in the concept that these places are in the gift of Joshua and in his allocation of them to Caleb. Yet Caleb still has to take them and does so in actions which the narrative makes no attempt to connect with the former account. The relationship between these two accounts of the conquest of Hebron and Debir corresponds to the wider picture in Joshua of a complete conquest on one hand and the need for ongoing action on the other.

The story of Caleb's gift of his daughter Achsah in marriage to his brother Othniel[81] offers an insight into practical issues concerning both marriage and land possession. The field that Othniel is entitled to request, and the springs which Achsah herself requests of her father, amount to a dowry. The request for springs is especially significant in view of the dry climate of the Negeb, to which Achsah alludes. Legally acknowledged rights to water are essential in such situations, and the present narrative demonstrates the need for such acknowledgment to be publicly preserved. The little episode makes a good foil to the more factual information preceding, and is an instance of the faithfulness of Yahweh in providing the means of life for ordinary Israelites in the land.

15:20-63 The allocation to Judah continues with a further list, not now of boundaries, but of cities within the boundaries. Their distribution accords with the extent of the land outlined early in the chapter and falls into four broad districts proceeding from the south (vv. 21-32), to the western lowland, or Shephelah, and on to the Philistine region on the Mediterranean (vv. 33-47), the central hill country up to the border with Benjamin (vv. 48-60), and the eastern part towards Jericho and the Dead Sea (vv. 61-62). There is an additional division based on groups of cities "and their villages" (vv. 32, 36, etc.), which can be counted as a twelvefold division,[82] possibly representing an administrative plan.[83]

The list of cities poses certain historical questions. There is overlap with cities attributed to Simeon in 19:2-8, which here are part of Judah's southernmost territory (see esp. 15:26-32). Apparently Simeon ceased at an early stage to possess a territory of its own, but was absorbed into Judah. This process is only obliquely visible in the texts, and the overlap between chs. 15 and 19 sug-

---

81. The same Othniel would distinguish himself as the first of the "deliverers" of Israel who are the subject of the book of Judges (Judg 3:9-11).

82. See Butler, *Joshua*, 183. This count involves taking vv. 45-47 as a single grouping, though the pattern breaks slightly there, and also counting a half-verse (v. 59a) that appears only in LXX.

83. So Soggin, *Joshua*, 176-80.

gests that the lists before us do not come in their entirety from a single time. There are other overlaps involving Judah, with both Benjamin and Dan.[84] This too suggests changing boundaries over time, and once again that the lists reflect realities at different periods.[85] On archaeological and other grounds, it seems that some of the places named are unlikely to have been inhabited by Israelites until a rather later period than Joshua.[86] The text as we have it, therefore, appears to have undergone expansion and alteration over the time of Israel's life in the land.

It has, however, clear theological purposes. The priority of Judah corresponds to its priority elsewhere in the biblical record, notably in Judg 1:1-2, where Yahweh appoints this tribe to "go up first" against the Canaanites.[87] It will in due course be the tribe of David, Jerusalem, and the temple and as the kingdom of Judah will endure longer than the remainder of Israel and even form the basis of the people who occupy the land again after the Babylonian exile. The significance of this tribe in what lies ahead for Israel is anticipated here.

The outlook of the chapter reflects both Yahweh's faithfulness in keeping promises and the challenge that lies ahead for the people. The territory of Judah is described as its "lot," in a somewhat unusual use of the term (15:1), intended to recall that Judah will occupy its land entirely as a consequence of the power, command, and gift of God. The careful delineation of boundaries and cities denotes God's careful ordering of the whole process of possession. The gift of land now takes on its specific content and contours. There will be many like Achsah who will have reason to recall God's gift when they draw water in security from their wells.

---

84. The cities of Kiriath-jearim and Beth-arabah are common to Judah and Benjamin, while Eshtaol and Zorah are assigned to both Judah and Dan (see further Hess, *Joshua*, 246-47).

85. The same may be suggested by variations in the lists in different Old Testament texts. There are a large number of differences especially between MT (the standard Hebrew text) and the Greek LXX, which dates from the third century B.C. These are fully documented by de Vos, *Das Los Judas*, 15-86. However, many of the LXX's variations may be attributable to unfamiliarity with names from a much older text (de Vos, 87).

86. Cf. Hess, *Joshua*, 246-47, who points to the united monarchy (David-Solomon) and the eighth century respectively for two sections of the record, though he distinguishes between the extent of Joshua's settlement and what can be known archaeologically of the particular sites listed (249). De Vos points to the tenth and eighth centuries for parts of the boundary list; *Das Los Judas*, 340.

87. The eldest son of Jacob, Reuben, loses his natural right as firstborn, according to the Blessing of Jacob (Gen 49:4), because he slept with his father's concubine Bilhah (Gen 35:22). Simeon and Levi also forfeited potential claims because of their violence in the conflict with Shechem following the rape of their sister Dinah there (Genesis 34; 49:5-7). This left Judah, as the fourth son of Leah (Gen 29:31-35), next in line to the seniority.

Yet Jerusalem has not been taken (v. 63). Curiously, the city *is* said to have been taken by Judah in Judg 1:8. In Josh 18:28, furthermore, it is assigned to Benjamin, who in turn could not drive out the Jebusites, according to Judg 1:21. So here as in other cases the actual historical events seem to have been more untidy than the text before us discloses. As we have seen, the lists of cities hitherto in the present chapter pass over historical vicissitudes and portray a territory of Judah as if complete in spite of actual gaps. In the case of Jerusalem the passing over of some of the history evidently makes the opposite point: that of all the places Judah may have tried to take it could not take Jerusalem. The notice of this is highly significant in view of the later importance of this city of throne and temple. In the biblical narrative, the final possession of Jerusalem was the accomplishment of David (2 Sam 5:6-10), to whom will be attributed "rest from all his enemies" (2 Sam 7:1), rather as it was said of Joshua (Josh 11:23). So the nonpossession of Jerusalem at this stage is part of that carefully constructed two-sided picture in the book, in which the land is in principle subdued and gifted, but in practice it remains to be fully realized.

Joshua 16–17

16:1-10 The account of the distribution turns next to Joseph, outstandingly important because of its great numbers and because it formed in effect the backbone of the northern part of Israel. The structure of this section is governed by the division of Joseph into two tribes, Ephraim and Manasseh. These were Joseph's sons whom Jacob had adopted as his own and blessed on a par with the others (Gen 48:5-6, 8-14), Ephraim, the younger, being given the priority (48:17-20).[88] The present narrative gives its own reason for the double lot granted to Joseph, namely in their great numbers alone, and this at the close of the section (17:14-18). The prominence of Joseph in the account of the distribution no doubt reflects the historical importance of the tribe, as well as complicated internal border relations between its two constituent parts. The basis of distribution is again by lot (גורל/*gôrāl*, 16:1; 17:1), as in the case of Judah (15:1), though this is frequently obscured in translations.[89] The actual taking of lots is not described but must be assumed.

The narrative opens (vv. 2-3) with a description of the southern border

---

88. Jacob may have had in mind that he himself had received the blessing of the firstborn from his father Isaac in place of Esau (Genesis 27).

89. The term "allotment" (RSV, NRSV, ESV, NIV) no doubt intends to hint at "lot." The RSV "family" has "lot" in 15:1 but "allotment" in 16:1; 17:1, while NIV has "allotment" in all three texts.

of Joseph, which is also the southern border of Ephraim. Beginning at Jericho, it follows the road to Bethel,[90] once taken by the advancing Israelites, corresponding in part to the northern limit of Benjamin as in 18:12-13, and continues via Gezer in the lowlands to the Mediterranean. As in the case of Judah, some of the places named are laden with significance. Bethel would become one of the shrines of King Jeroboam in his secession from Jerusalem and the temple (1 Kings 12) and associated with false worship in the preaching of Amos (Amos 4:4). Gezer, an important outpost in the western lowlands guarding access to the hill country, was not securely Israelite until Solomon's time, and then was only granted to Solomon as dowry in the marriage of Solomon to the pharaoh's daughter (1 Kgs 9:16).

The Ephraimite border is described more carefully on the northern and eastern sides (vv. 5-9), spanning the width of the land from Mediterranean to Jordan, and here its territory is marked off from that of Manasseh. A number of the cities listed have been identified with archaeological sites.[91] The line dividing Ephraim from Manasseh seems untidy in places, with some Ephraimite cities and villages located apparently as enclaves within Manassite territory (v. 9). This presumably reflects historical realities and may have been contentious. It would certainly have been significant in relation to property rights such as might have arisen in cases of intermarriage. A further unclarity in tracing the boundaries of Ephraim concerns the land originally given to Dan, which included a region by the Mediterranean Sea in the vicinity of Joppa (19:46). This raises a question about the precise way in which Ephraim's allotment goes "to the sea" (vv. 6, 8). The present text does not pay attention to Dan's claim in this area and may ignore it in view of Dan's eventual inability to hold it (19:47).

The closing note on Ephraimite territory tells that it was not entirely held, because the tribe could not drive out Canaanites from Gezer, but put them to forced labor. This has echoes of the Gibeonite compromise (ch. 9). No explanation is offered here, as it was there. But once again we have an impression that the land is not perfectly occupied by Israel.

17:1-6 The allocation to Manasseh opens (vv. 1-2) with remarks about the Manassite tribe as a whole, including elements in Transjordan where half the tribe has already settled (Gilead and Bashan). The notice in these verses has the character of genealogy, unusual in these predominantly topographical texts (cf. Num 26:29-34). In Machir and Gilead we see personal names becoming interchangeable with place names, as is illustrated and confirmed in Judg 5:14, 17.

---

90. Bethel and Luz are distinguished here, though they are identified with each other in 18:13; cf. Judg 1:23; Gen 28:19.

91. Hess provides the identifications, some tentative; *Joshua*, 256-57.

The relationship between place and family is not accidental. The Israelite occupation of land is regularly called "inheritance" in Joshua (as in Numbers and Deuteronomy). However, inheritance by its nature does not stop at a single point, but is an ongoing issue for tribe, family, and clan. The opening verses on Manasseh lead appropriately into the narrative about a certain family of Manassites, namely Mahlah, Noah, Hoglah, Milcah, and Tirzah, the daughters of Zelophehad. Their claim to inheritance rights was previously established by appeal to Moses (Numbers 27, 36), being a case in which the father had no sons, only daughters. The ground of their appeal was that, if they could not participate in the inheritance of land in Israel, the name of their father, who had died in the wilderness, would be lost to his "family" (Num 27:4)[92] Moses, in granting the women's petition, made it a perpetual rule in Israel that in the event of no male children inheritance may pass to daughters, with the proviso — on appeal by tribal leaders — that the daughters should marry within the tribe (Num 27:8-11; 36:2-9). Joshua, along with Eleazar and the tribal leaders, now confirms the former decision of Moses. The case has more to do with the need to secure tribal holdings than with the rights and status of women as such. The story, therefore, serves not only to inform and authorize practice, but also hints at some of the most pressing issues that would face Israel through its generations. The untidy borders between Ephraim and Manasseh gave another insight into this. Intertribal tensions emerge in a number of places in the Old Testament, most importantly between northern and southern divisions (especially Judah and Benjamin), but not exclusively. (Simeon and Dan will shed further light on this, below.) Such "fraternal" tensions are perhaps not unexpected in view of the fraught relations between the sons of Jacob recorded in Genesis (Genesis 37–50). They pose a deep question about fundamental unity and identity among the Israelites.

Old Testament texts do not give a full picture of women's property rights, with some texts implying their dependence on male relatives (e.g., Deut 25:5-10; Ruth), while others, however, suggest that women could be fully independent economically.[93]

17:7-13 There follows the expected description of the territory of Manasseh west of the Jordan.[94] The interpenetration of Ephraim and Manas-

---

92. The term used is משפחה/*mišpāḥâ*, which designates a middle level of familial organization between "the father's house" and the tribe. The *mišpāḥâ* in Israel had both genealogical and topographical connotations.

93. Deut 15:12-18, a law of slave release, is a case in point because of its assumption that a woman could both lose her economic independence through misfortune and regain it upon the kind of release legislated there.

94. See Hess, *Joshua*, 260, for identifications.

seh, noticed above, is apparent here also (vv. 8-10), and Manasseh had porous borders too with Issachar and Asher (v. 11). Finally, the possession is again incomplete in the sense that Canaanites remain alongside Israelites in the land, albeit eventually put to forced labor (vv. 12-13).

17:14-18 The demand of Joseph for extra land follows unexpectedly on the narrative of distribution which was already based on the knowledge that Joseph has two large subdivisions and is not even contained on one side of the Jordan. The passage is perhaps best understood as affording a further insight into the relative power of Joseph within Israel, which is attributed here to its blessing by the Lord (17:14). The claim to special blessing rings true, because not only did Ephraim and Manasseh receive their own blessings from Jacob, but Jacob's final blessing of Joseph as a whole seemed to promise richer blessing for that tribe than for any other (Gen 49:22-26). The charge to make the forested hill country habitable by clearing it no doubt represented a necessity that faced the incoming Israelites. It is somewhat ironic, since while it becomes a way in which this major part of Israel is able to enter upon its inheritance, the need arises because Joseph is unable to dislodge powerful Canaanite peoples from the level areas where their chariots gave them military superiority. These same areas were also the richest and most fertile. The failure to conquer the Canaanites appears more serious than ever in the case of Joseph, and this sits oddly with their portrayal as the largest and most blessed of the Israelite tribes.

Joshua 18:1–19:51

The following two chapters complete the allocation of land to the tribes of Israel. With territory apportioned already to four tribes, Reuben, Gad, Judah, and Joseph (comprising Ephraim and Manasseh), and Levi excluded from the distribution process, seven tribes remain to receive their share in the inheritance of Israel.

18:1 This opening verse is one of the most theologically pregnant in the book of Joshua. The setting up of the tent of meeting at Shiloh clearly marks a significant step in the progress of Israel towards fulfilling its destiny in the promised land. It is the first reference to the tent of meeting in Joshua, though the closely associated ark of the covenant was prominent in the narratives of entry to the land (Joshua 3–4).[95] It is also the first time that Shiloh has

---

95. The ark was to be placed within the "tent," also known as the "tabernacle" in the Priestly narratives of Exodus; see Exod 40:2-3.

appeared as a place of special significance. The conjunction of the two, however, now focuses attention on the nature of Israel as a worshipping community in covenantal relationship with Yahweh.

The tent of meeting is the place where God undertakes to "meet" Israel in its worship throughout the generations (Exod 29:42-43), this place being symbolic of the covenantal relationship between them. The covenantal relationship is expressed in immediate connection with God's promise to dwell among his people.[96] The assembly at Shiloh, therefore, affirms that the presence of God with Israel in covenantal relationship has now been realized in the land.

The formal gathering of Israel before God at Shiloh is indicated by two terms in the first three words of v. 1. The first is the verb "assembled" (ויקהלו/ *wayyiqqāhălû*; NIV "gathered"), which corresponds to the noun קהל/*qāhāl*, "assembly," used of the solemn congregation of Israel before Yahweh at Sinai and subsequently at the central place of worship at the great annual feasts (Deut 5:22; 9:10; 23:1-3; 31:30). The second, "congregation of Israel" (עדת בני־ישראל/*'ădat bĕnê yiśrā'ēl*; NIV "assembly"), is closely analogous to *qāhāl*.[97] Furthermore, the verb underlying "set up" (שכן/*škn*) is a key term in the expression of God's dwelling-presence.[98]

The location of this solemn assembly at Shiloh is also significant. Shiloh is the first location in the biblical narrative to fulfil expressly the criteria for the place that Yahweh would choose as the central place of worship for all Israel after their arrival in the promised land. The formulaic expression for such a place is found first in Deut 12:5, where the place is unnamed. The command is therefore capable of being fulfilled in a number of places over time. In due course Jerusalem would take on the mantle.[99] But the book of Joshua, and the present section in particular, makes it clear that Shiloh takes the role initially.[100] The chosen place signifies not only

---

96. See Exod 29:45, where the promise to dwell among them is accompanied by the assertion: "I will be their God"; and also Lev 26:11-12, where again the divine dwelling occurs along with the covenantal formula, which is fuller in this case: "I will be your God, and you will be my people."

97. The latter, עדת/*'ădat*, or עדה/*'ēdâ* in its absolute form, is more common in the Priestly literature, e.g., in Exod 16:10; 17:1; Num 16:2.

98. See again Exod 29:45, where the verb "[and] I will dwell" is ושכנתי/*wĕšākantî*. The same verb underlies the later Jewish concept of the Shekinah, the glory-presence of God.

99. A text such as 2 Kgs 21:4 makes an explicit link between the Deuteronomic promise and Jerusalem as the chosen place.

100. Shiloh appears as the worship center for all Israel in the opening chapters of 1 Samuel, with Eli as priest and the young Samuel in training for his leadership role in Israel. Jer 7:12 also asserts that Shiloh was the first place to correspond to the criteria set down in Deut 12:5.

Yahweh's presence to Israel in worship, but also his ownership of the land that Israel is "inheriting."[101]

The present verse has a function, therefore, in the whole narrative from Exodus to Kings in its affirmation that under Joshua the people of Israel have entered upon the benefits of their relationship with Yahweh, promised since Sinai. Israel is in its land; they have sought and found the place which would symbolize Yahweh's ownership of the land and his presence to them for worship and inquiry. The point is reinforced by the structure of chs. 18–19 together. This clearly defined unit, with its subject matter in the allocation of land to the remaining seven tribes, is framed by the reference to the assembly of all Israel before the Lord at the tent of meeting set up at Shiloh (cf. 19:51).

This high point in the drama of Israel's progress has even more profound echoes, for it contains a reminiscence of the creation command to the first humans to "subdue the earth" (Gen 1:28). This is because the phrase "the *land* lay *subdued* before them" (NRSV) uses precisely the same terms as in the creation command.[102] Israel's possession of Canaan, therefore, together with its presence before God in worship, has a significance far beyond itself, for it stands as a symbol and promise of the human fulfilment of its mandate to "subdue the earth," namely to bring it to that ordering and completion that God's creative purpose intended for it. The command to "subdue the earth" is no permission to strip and exploit it. However, the task of bringing order entails confrontation with forces of disorder, as is instantiated in the war narratives of Joshua as a whole.

18:2-10 The remaining tribes are now charged by Joshua to take possession of the land not yet "inherited" (v. 3). In this way, the exhortation of Israel to enter into their inheritance as a matter of obedience is maintained, though predicated on God's prior gift. The distribution is to be prefaced by a new survey of the land to be taken and a division of it into seven portions (vv. 4-5), the land already assigned being once more carefully excluded. There is a new attention here to the means of the allocation, not only in the survey, but in the procedure of casting lots "in the presence of the Lord our God." This last feature is no doubt occasioned by the fact that Joshua and Israel are now gathered at the tent of meeting, the place where God may henceforth be formally consulted. The lot-taking thus gains a higher profile here as a mark of

---

101. The latter point is supported by the idea of "placing the name," an integral part of the "chosen place" formula (Deut 12:5), as has been well demonstrated by Richter, *The Deuteronomistic History and the Name Theology*.

102. The noun ארץ/'ereṣ, may mean "earth" or "land" according to context. The verb "subdue" is כבש/kbš, which elsewhere means to subdue forcibly (Jer 34:16; Neh 5:5; Esth 7:8; 1 Chr 22:18).

God's prerogative in the gift of land down to its last details. The procedure and the location of it are repeated in v. 10 to reinforce their importance.

18:11-28 Benjamin's territory lies between Judah to the south and Joseph (specifically Ephraim) to the north. It forms a narrow east-west band stretching from the River Jordan north of the Dead Sea to a point in the hill country west of Jerusalem. Its southern boundary corresponds to Judah's northern boundary, as we have seen (cf. 15:5-12), and thus takes in Jerusalem (v. 28). The western boundary appears to take account of the original territory of Dan, which included western approaches to the central hill country through such places as Beth-shemesh, Timnah, and Aijalon (19:41-43). (This is in contrast to the boundary description of Ephraim, which, as we saw, ignored Dan's original claim.) Benjamin's territorial allocation is completed with a list of cities with their villages, following the pattern of Judah (18:21-28; cf. 15:20-63).

19:1-9 The most striking thing about the allocation to Simeon is that it is located entirely within the territory of Judah, a point that is made both at the beginning and the end of the section. More importantly, there is no boundary description, so Simeon's holding is not even a clearly defined enclave. The allocation to Simeon seems in practice to be no actual territory at all, and their case to be no different from that of the Levites, who are expressly said to have no tribal territory but only cities within other tribal lands, since Yahweh himself would be their "inheritance" — except that in Simeon's case no such rationale is attached, and therefore no built-in protection for the future. (This commonality in the destiny of Simeon and Levi recalls the prediction of Jacob in his "blessing," namely that these two tribes would be "dispersed in Israel," in consequence of their undue violence in the revenge taken for Dinah; Gen 49:7; cf. 34:25-31.) The insecurity of Simeon's position is further highlighted by the fact that there is overlap between the cities attributed to it and those allotted to Judah in its southernmost region (esp. in 15:26-29). The record strongly hints that in time Simeon would simply be absorbed by its larger and more powerful neighbor. Curiously, the location of Simeon's land within Judah's is explained by the fact that Judah's territory was too large for it, in contrast to Joseph's claim that its portion was too small (19:9). Its encroachment upon Simeon, already suggested in the overlapping city lists, shows that this was not Judah's permanent view.

19:10-39 The allocations to Zebulun, Issachar, Asher, and Naphtali fall in the northernmost part of the land, to the north of Manasseh, occupying the area between the River Jordan from its source in Mount Hermon to a point south of the Sea of Galilee in the east to the Mediterranean in the west. It includes the fertile valley of Jezreel (Issachar), the area known later as Galilee (roughly Naphtali), and the Carmel range lying by the coast (Asher). Here again the material is mixed and in places the boundaries are difficult to draw. Issachar's description, for example, is essentially just a list of cities.[103]

19:40-48 The case of Dan is particularly strange. It is grouped here with the northern tribes presumably because it finally settles in the region of Leshem, under the slopes of Hermon at the source of the Jordan (close to the New Testament's Caesarea Philippi). The territory assigned to it, however, lies west of Benjamin, stretching through the lowlands (Shephelah) to the Mediterranean at Joppa, with Judah to the south and Ephraim to the east and north. The hypothetical nature of this allotment to Dan was already noticeable in the Ephraimite allocation, which took no account of its claim to part of the Mediterranean coast. And now this account of its "inheritance" becomes an account of its actual settlement in a completely different part of the land. Dan's loss of the land to which it was entitled by lot (and thus divine decision) is not described or explained, but simply related as a fact, and the reader infers that it was not able to hold the territory in the face of resistance from its existing occupants. This corresponds to the impression given in the allocations to Ephraim and Manasseh, that the large coastal plain that in theory fell to the Israelite tribes was in fact off-limits because of the strength of the Canaanite populations there (17:16).

The story of Dan's failure to possess its proper inheritance is told at greater length in Judges 18. This finds the Danites initially in the area of Zorah and Eshtaol, cities allocated to them in Joshua account (19:41), yet we read that Dan was "seeking for itself an inheritance (נחלה/*naḥălâ*) to dwell in; for until then no inheritance among the tribes of Israel had fallen to them" (Judg 18:1 RSV). Then, in what seems a parody of the occupation of the land by Israel as a whole, they spy out a new territory for themselves (Judg 18:2), the spies bring back a report of Leshem/Laish that it is a good land that "God has put into your hands" (18:10), and in due course they put the people to death with the sword and burn the city (v. 27). While the story mimics the duly authorized conquest of the promised land, it also makes clear that this action was illegitimate. There is no word from God to take Laish, much less subject the city and people to complete destruction (in spite of the spies' claim that God has given it to them). And the people of Laish were "peaceful and unsuspecting" (v. 27), a point not made about other Canaanite peoples that Israel had legitimately displaced, suggesting that these were not people intended for

---

103. For other difficulties in determining the boundaries of these northern tribes, see Hawk, *Joshua*, 219. One curious anomaly is that Naphtali's territory is said to touch that of Judah "on the east at the Jordan" (19:34 NRSV), but Judah lies a long way to the south.

the "ban." The impression of illegitimacy is further corroborated by the fact that the Danites set up a place of worship for themselves, again without due authorization, with idolatrous connotations (the "graven image," 18:30-31 RSV), and indeed by theft and abduction (18:14-20). The renaming of Laish as Dan, after their ancestor, thus rings hollow as a true claim to a tribal inheritance (18:29).

The Joshua narrative lacks the express ironies of the Judges account, yet it poses the same question. How can it be said of this territory which is expressly not the one allocated to them as their inheritance by lot that it is "the inheritance of the tribe of Dan" (v. 48)? The case of Dan posits a sharp discrepancy between the notion of legitimate possession and the actuality of Israel's occupation.

19:49-51 With all the lots cast for the remaining territory, the task of Joshua in supervising the Israelites' inheritance of their respective territories is complete. Like Caleb, the other hero of the conquest, he is now given an "inheritance" of his own within that of Ephraim (19:49-50). The present section closes with a notice that harks back to the beginning of the narrative of the distribution (14:1), naming again Joshua, Eleazar, and the tribal leaders as those responsible, reiterating the location of the final actions at Shiloh, and declaring that the division of the land is complete.

The overall picture in Joshua 18–19 is somewhat mixed. Formally, it tells how the process of land division was completed. The location of this process at Shiloh also points to the fulfilment of the mission of Israel to possess the land entirely and to secure it as the place in which Yahweh alone is worshipped by his chosen people. Formally too the narrative from ch. 14 has described systematically how each tribe would come into its own legitimate possession of an inheritance within the whole. Yet just as there was a disjunction between the concept of total conquest in chs 10-12 and the picture of "much land still to be taken" in 13:1, so there is a discrepancy between the formal portrayal of the land distribution and realities "on the ground."

In general, the expectation of a systematic and rational division of the territory into eleven coherent sections (Levi being excluded) is disappointed. In a number of cases the data given are insufficient to permit the drawing of boundaries; the material itself is disparate, at times describing boundaries, at times merely listing cities, and incorporating narrative fragments; the lines between tribal allotments are not clear; silences about cities within territories bespeak large areas of nonpossession; failure to dislodge existing populations is candidly acknowledged in several cases. Simeon and Dan are the extreme cases of failure to obtain a foothold in the land. But Joseph's necessary resort to deforestation in the hill country plainly reflects the failure of both Ephraim and Manasseh to secure large parts of the areas that fell to them in theory. The division between Ephraim and Manasseh in itself seems somewhat anomalous: are they fully separate, and if so why do they still appear at times as "Joseph"? This indeterminacy seems to be symbolized by the fact that each possesses cities in the territory of the other. Not only is the status of Manasseh as a full tribe questionable, but it is further subdivided between two parts, east and west of the Jordan, respectively. Indeed, the Transjordanian settlement, which seemed to preempt the entry to the land proper, and the distribution in it by lot is itself a disturbing factor in the total picture, as will shortly become starkly evident in Joshua 22. Not the least question is why Judah and Joseph between them receive an overwhelmingly large proportion of the total land area.

In sum, the detailed descriptions have the effect of calling into question the text's basic predicate of a rational, complete distribution of an entirely subdued land, thus in tension with what we expect at the outset. How may this be explained? In one respect, the detailed accounts may simply be said to reflect developments in historical actuality, the data consisting of various kinds of material from different times and places. It is clear that some kind of historical retrospect is implied at least in the case of Dan, as also in the formulaic notes that certain tribes could not drive out the existing populations "to this day" (15:63; 16:10). The acute consciousness that Jerusalem remains unsecured seems to imply a concern for this city which no doubt comes from a later time than Joshua.

Seen from another perspective, the incomplete possession may be implicitly laid at the door of the Israelites by way of censure. The land has been completely and unconditionally bestowed upon Israel by Yahweh: how is it then that it has not in practice been occupied? This is a central question that the book of Joshua poses throughout.

Joshua 20–21

20:1-6 Following the allocation of land to the tribes, attention turns to a number of matters that arise in connection with regular life in the land, namely the appointment of "cities of refuge" (ch. 20), Levitical cities (ch. 21), and the position of the Transjordanian tribes in relation to the central place of worship (ch. 22).

The need for cities of refuge, or asylum, has already been signalled in the narrative of Moses and Israel, in Num 35:9-28; Deut 4:41-43; 19:1-10, and is evidently an important corollary of the concept of a territorial division of land among the tribes. The provision of such cities aims to establish due process in cases of homicide which are not deliberate murder. It aims to set limits on the traditional tribal-familial way of settling the felt need for requital in such cases. The "avenger of blood" would have been a close relative of the victim, appointed by the family to exact blood for blood in response to the killing. The term "avenger" is גאל/*gōʾēl*, which is elsewhere translated as "kinsman-redeemer" (Ruth 2:20). In both contexts it expresses the strong bond that existed among extended family in ancient Israel and the will to preserve its integrity.

The reception of a refugee from the avenger of blood is not in itself a decision regarding his innocence, although it is close to a presumption of innocence until proved guilty. The refugee, arriving at the city gates, makes his initial representation to the elders (lit., "speaks his words," v. 4), perhaps simply asking to be received under the terms of asylum. The city authorities are obliged to take him in, with an implication that this involves provision for his ordinary life ("give him a place") and possibly for a considerable time. The intention is that in due course there should be a proper inquiry and hearing, with the ultimate aim that, innocence being established, the refugee should be able to return to his home city (v. 6). The implication is that his pursuer will now be permanently prohibited from exacting vengeance.

The provision for a proper hearing is expressed in the words "until he stands before the congregation for a verdict" (משפט/*mišpāṭ*, "judgment"; v. 6; cf. Num 35:12). The "congregation" is the assembly of Israel gathered as the people of God (cf. 18:1). Presumably this would happen in some representative way, with a court consisting perhaps of elders from the city of refuge, Levites (since all these cities of refuge are also listed among the Levitical cities in Joshua 21; cf. Num 35:6), and representatives from cities of the victim and accused. In fact nothing about such representation is said, nor about the process itself, which may or may not have happened within the city of refuge. General rules about inquiry and evidence are given in Deuteronomy, which highlight the importance of safe testimony and thorough investigation (Deut 19:15-21; cf. 17:4, 6-7), and such principles may be supposed to be mandatory in the sort of inquiry enjoined in these cases. The outcome would not necessarily be favorable to the refugee, as is clear from Deut 19:11-13 (where the due inquiry is not mentioned but is presumably implied).

Acquittal too would not necessarily defuse the situation immediately for the accused. This point is made by the phrase "until the death of the high priest who is serving at that time" (v. 6), which sits oddly with the preceding phrase ("until he has stood trial before the assembly"). The text echoes the fuller explanation in Numbers, where acquittal results in the refugee's restoration first of all to the city of refuge to which he had fled, where he must live "until the death of the high priest" (Num 35:25). During this time he steps outside the city at his peril, for the avenger of blood will be able to exact the old-style vengeance with impunity (Num 35:26-27). The limitation concerning the death of the high priest may suggest a kind of atoning function, based on the notional possibility that the refugee was in fact guilty, even if not found to have been so. To release him back into ordinary life would then have the effect of "polluting" the land in ritual terms, and bringing guilt on the whole people. (A similar concept underlies the ritual for the unknown homicide in Deut 21:1-9.) Alternatively the limitation may simply establish a lapse of time, in recognition of the actual tension that must have existed in a society in transition from old tribal means of exacting justice to properly representative due process. We have no records that tell us of an "avenger of blood" who either respected or flouted the provisions made here.

In the context of Joshua, the provision of cities of refuge marks an important step in the conceptualizing of Israel as a nation in its land. The land has been apportioned according to tribes, but the people remains in principle one. The realm of justice is an important area within which this must be recognized. Justice is not something that can be prosecuted locally, especially by those with a strong emotive investment in the case. Rather it belongs to the community as a whole and indeed the community understood and constituted as the "congregation" of Yahweh. It is his justice that must prevail in the land, and by duly established means that safeguard its prosecution.

20:7-9 Three cities are now named, situated in the northern, central, and southern regions of the land west of the Jordan (v. 7), and three more in Transjordan, one in each tribal territory there. The latter were already set apart by Moses (Deut 4:41-43). The three new ones are appointed in fulfilment of the command in Deut 19:7. Curiously, there is no reference to the additional three which might be chosen when the land was fully possessed (Deut 19:8). This may be an unimportant omission; or it may be one of those features of Joshua which suggest that the picture of total possession is superficial, and chiming rather with the perspective that "much land remains to be possessed" (13:1). Joshua also adds to Deuteronomy that the provision of asylum rights should extend to the "stranger" (the "resident alien," גֵּר/gēr, v. 9). This reflects a movement towards an inclusive, nonnational concept of citizenship (cf. 8:33; Exod 12:48-49).

21:1-42 The allocation of cities for the Levites accords with the principle already established that the tribe of Levi would not have a territorial inheritance as such on account of their priestly vocation (13:14; 14:4; cf. Deut 10:8-9; 18:1-2). In one expression of their position, Yahweh himself was said to be their "inheritance." This no doubt has the connotation of a special spiritual blessing, consisting in the vocation to spend their lives in close attention to worship. But it also carries with it material entitlements, not only in specially designated shares of offerings brought in worship (Deut 18:3-5; Num 18:8-24), but also in cities with surrounding land on which they could raise cattle as their own property. (The extent of their lands is specified in Num 35:2-5.) The allocation of cities to Levi now comes as an integral part of the distribution of land to the tribes. It has the effect of limiting the possession of the eleven tribes, yet also of placing among them those who symbolized, by virtue of their vocation, the devotion of Israel to Yahweh.

The allocation follows the threefold division of the tribe of Levi according to Levi's three sons, Kohath, Gershom, and Merari. This is specified in the first general statement of the distribution (vv. 4-8), then in the more detailed list (vv. 9-40). A further distinction operates here, namely between the descendants of Aaron, Moses' brother, and other Levites, a distinction between higher and lower priestly officials that is set out in Numbers 3–4 and that derives from the fact that Aaron was the first priest of Israel according to Exodus 28–29. The precedence of Aaron's line is also visible both in the general description of the distribution and in the detailed one. Aaron belonged to the line of Kohath, though of course not all Kohathites did. Aaron's line is therefore distinguished not only from descendants of Gershom and Merari, but also from other Kohathites.

Aaron's descendants receive their cities in the territories of Judah, Simeon, and Benjamin (v. 4), enumerated in vv. 9-19. These are the "southern" tribes. The coalescence of Judah and Simeon is evident from v. 9, so that "Judah and Simeon" is in effect Judah. Benjamin, Judah's neighbor to the north, has a special affinity with Judah because it is along the border between them that Jerusalem lies. Jerusalem is not mentioned here, yet is conspicuous by its absence, being the city in which the Aaronite priesthood would in time officiate. At this stage, we recall, it has been notionally assigned to Benjamin, yet it has not yet fallen into Israelite hands (18:28; but cf. 15:63).

It is curious to find Hebron featuring prominently among the cities given to the Aaronites (21:11-13), since we have previously read how that city has already been granted to Caleb (indeed, the information is given twice and at some length, 14:13-15; 15:13-19). The difficulty receives some acknowledgment in 21:12, which says that Caleb actually received only the city's "fields and villages." This hardly resolves the tension, since the Levitical cities came with considerable areas of surrounding land, as we have observed. And in any case the stories of Caleb's conquest and legitimate possession of Hebron do not naturally support the qualification entered here. The reader is left wondering in what way Caleb may be said to have received Hebron as his "inheritance" (14:13-14). The dissonant information about Hebron points up a possible conflict arising in general from these extensive Levitical possessions within tribal territories. Hawk finds a discrepancy here with the prevailing assumptions of the narratives of distribution, namely that there is a tight connection between conquest, land division, "inheritance" and actual possession.[104] Caleb has "inherited" and conquered, but he seems not to possess.

21:43-45 The section closes with one of the book's most comprehensive statements about the completeness of the conquest and possession (the word כל/*kōl,* meaning "all," "every," "whole," occurs six times). It uses language which reminds us of the opening passages of Deuteronomy (Deut 1:8) and Joshua (1:2-6) and so gives the impression that the promises and commands regarding God's gift of the land and Israel's occupation of it have been completely fulfilled. The passage corresponds also to 11:23, another statement of sweeping success. We know by now, however, that the possession of the land as described in the tribal allocations is far from complete, that Canaanite enclaves remain, that in some cases the existing populations have proved stronger than Israel, that Dan was unable to hold his territory and was forced north where he took land not given by lot and with illegitimate violence, that the boundaries between tribal allotments have at times been difficult to draw, and that land once given may not have remained in its original Israelite hands. The reader is faced with the question whether these tensions are part of a deliberate portrayal by the author. The discrepancy between the perspective of total conquest by virtue of God's gift and that of untidy, incomplete possession is such that it is most easily read as a feature intended to catch the reader's eye. It may be a device to convey the message that reality is far from ideal and that the call to live before Yahweh will have to be played out in a plural situation of conflicted loyalties.

Joshua 22

22:1-9 The focus now turns to another disturbing factor in the concept of a united people in a united land, namely the settlement of some of the tribes — one no more than a "half-tribe" — east of the Jordan. In the story of settlement there has always been something anomalous about this. The request of Reuben, Gad, and half-Manasseh to settle there, following the conquest of the Amorite kings Sihon and Og, in a sense preempts the occupation and settle-

---

104. Hawk, *Joshua,* 223.

ment of the land proper. Whereas the other tribes await the completion of the conquest and then submit to the authorized process of allocation under Joshua and Eleazar (Num 34:16-29), these tribes requested special leave of Moses to settle before the conquest was complete (Num 32:1-5). While the permission was granted, it was necessarily accompanied by particular obligations laid on the Transjordanians to participate fully in the possession of Canaan and thus affirm their membership within a united Israel (cf. 1:12-18; Deut 3:18-20). In the account of their request in Numbers, Moses' initial response has a note of censure, implying that their plan detracts in some measure from the great project to take the land, somewhat analogous to the first refusal of the people to go into the land following the advice of the majority of the spies. The Transjordanians' request might have the same effect, of discouraging the remainder of Israel, or even destroying them, if discouragement turned to apostasy (Num 32:6-15; note v. 15c). There is also a hint in the language of Numbers that the "land" occupied by the Transjordanians is distinct from the "land" promised to Israel (Num 32:21-22), and this is echoed here in the contrast between "the land of Canaan" and "the land of Gilead" (Josh 22:9 NRSV).

Joshua now looks back on the occupation (thus assuming the complete conquest perspective of 21:43-45) and declares that the Transjordanians have fulfilled their obligation to participate in the military action (vv. 2-4a). He then charges them to remain wholly faithful to Yahweh, in terms of commandment-keeping and wholehearted devotion characteristic of Deuteronomy (v. 5; cf. Deut 6:4-5; 10:20; 11:22). The two-and-a-half tribes then leave the people assembled at Shiloh, to their own land, charged with remaining part of Yahweh's people, yet with a strong sense of separation and farewell (vv. 6, 9).

22:10-20 The underlying doubts about the unity of Israel occasioned by the Transjordanian independent-mindedness immediately blows up into a rift and potential civil war, because they build an altar at the River Jordan. The significance of the Jordan as boundary is embedded in the Joshua narrative, since the crossing of it was the necessary prelude to the first steps of conquest and was manifestly similar to that other defining moment in Israel's life, the crossing of the Red Sea (3:14-17; cf. Exod 14:21-25). The dubious status of the land beyond the Jordan is now emphasized again when the description of the altar's location refers to "the Israelite side" (v. 11). Exactly where the altar was placed in relation to the river is tantalizingly difficult to determine. Curiously, the accumulation of data purporting to fix the spot seems to have the opposite effect, leaving no clarity at all.[105] For Hawk the confusion ex-

---

105. This is often pointed out. Nelson translates the last phrase of v. 11 "on the Israelite side," in common with NRSV, ESV, NIV, NJB, but notes that the text may be translated alterna-

tends to the question what "the Israelite side" actually is,[106] the effect being to accentuate the point at issue: what are the true boundaries of Israel and who really belongs? When "the people of Israel" hear of it they gather at Shiloh to make war, thus setting up stark oppositions: the people of Israel, defined as "the congregation" and thus the very definition of united Israel, ranged against the Transjordanian outsiders; the symbolic unifying center of Shiloh against the altar at the Jordan, a challenge that goes to the heart of Israel's identity and loyalty to Yahweh; and the "land of Canaan" against "the land of Gilead" (cf. vv. 13, 15).

The next development is a high-level delegation to the Transjordanians, consisting of senior tribal leaders with Phinehas, son of Eleazar, at their head (vv. 13-15). The delegation's opening accusation uses the most severe language to denote apostasy and rebellion (v. 16).[107] They invoke the rebellion at Peor (vv. 17-18), which brought dire punishment on Israel, only mitigated by the zealous action of Phinehas (Num 25:1-9) — now, ominously, the leader of the present investigation — and also the sacrilege of Achan, which brought upon him and his family the full force of the *ḥērem* and thus avoided a terrible calamity for all Israel (v. 20). They address the underlying issue, whether the land beyond the Jordan is fully "Israel," using the language of ritual purity ("if the land you possess is defiled," v. 19), and offering a remedy for that problem, namely that they reverse their original decision and come over into "the Lord's land, where the Lord's tabernacle stands."

22:21-34 The Transjordanians respond to the Israelites by refuting the premise of the whole inquiry. The "altar" at the Jordan was not, after all, an altar for sacrifice, but only a kind of replica altar, intended as a witness to the true altar in the tabernacle at Shiloh. Therefore it signifies, not rebellion, but its opposite, the absolute loyalty of the two-and-a-half tribes to Yahweh and their integrity within Israel. They do so in strongly confessional language, beginning with the attribution of a series of divine names to the God of Israel: אל אלהים יהוה/*'ēl 'ĕlōhîm yhwh* [Yahweh], which they then repeat (v. 22). This conjunction of names for God also occurs in Ps 50:1, and so in the con-

---

tively to mean "across from the Israelites," as preferred by REB, NAB, JPSV; Nelson, *Joshua*, 246. Hawk comments: "With every clarifying note, the location of the altar becomes increasingly obscure!"; *Joshua*, 237.

106. Hawk, *Joshua*, 237-38.

107. מעל/*ma'al*, "treachery" (NRSV), or breach of faith, is used in this chapter for Achan's sin (v. 20; cf. 7:1) and elsewhere for the apostasy of King Saul (1 Chr 10:13); it may also be translated "sacrilege"; Nelson, *Joshua*, 244, 246, citing Milgrom, *Leviticus 1–16*, 345-56. "Turning away," שוב/*šûb*, is the opposite of "repentance" (same verb), and the root is much used for "backsliding" to other gods in Jeremiah (see Jer 3:12, 14).

text of the worship of Yahweh in the temple. The first two terms may both be simply translated "God." The former, 'ēl, is frequently compounded, especially in Genesis, with epithets, in forms such as El Shaddai, and falls between a proper name for God (as in Canaan, where the High God was El) and a generic, "god." The series of names, proclaimed here by the Transjordanians, is a strong statement that Yahweh is indeed the only true God and even takes the form of an act of worship. It is therefore a powerful rebuttal of the accusation of Phinehas.

The Transjordanians further argue that their replica altar was not for the purpose of sacrifice. The conceptual background to this is the premise that there would only be one true place of worship for Israel after the occupation of the land and only one place of legitimate sacrifice. The base text for this conception is Deuteronomy 12, which, especially in v. 5, is most naturally taken to prescribe this exclusive right for the central sanctuary. In the logic of Joshua, Shiloh is the first place that answers to the criteria of that command, marked as such by the presence of the tabernacle. This lies behind the Transjordanians' protest in v. 23. They then offer a positive defense, that they erected the replica altar as a memorial to their loyalty to Yahweh and Israel, in view of the possibility that passing time would efface the memory that they were fully Israelite by decree of Yahweh, confirmed by Moses. In time, the Jordan could assert itself as the great symbol of division it was and the Transjordanians would lose their Israelite identity (vv. 24-28). The Transjordanians thus appeal effectively to a theme of memory and perpetuation, resonating with a concern of Deuteronomy, that the faith should be diligently passed from generation to generation (Deut 6:1-9).

With this explanation, the delegates are satisfied. The danger of divine wrath on Israel because of apostasy is allayed, the unity of Israel is reasserted, talk of war ceases, and the loyalty of all Israel to Yahweh their God is reaffirmed (vv. 30-34).

Joshua 23

23:1-8 The book of Joshua closes with two ceremonies, a farewell address of Joshua near the end of his life (ch. 23) and a covenant renewal at Shechem, in which all Israel reaffirms its commitment to Yahweh (ch. 24). These have features in common, yet are formally distinct.

The farewell address is reminiscent of other scenes in which a leader gives a charge or a blessing near the end of his life. Moses left Israel both a Song of Witness (Deuteronomy 32), effectively a charge to keep the covenant, and a Blessing (Deuteronomy 33). The dying King David would in due course charge his son and successor Solomon to remain faithful to the covenant and laws of Yahweh, in language that has particular echoes of Joshua here (1 Kgs 2:2-4). Those who follow him in leadership will have a particular responsibility to ensure that what has begun may be sustained.

The setting of the address in relation to the events of the book is not precisely specified (v. 1). Its perspective is similar to that in 13:1. In that place too Joshua is old, and there has been an account of the conquest of the land (11:21-23; 12), yet, paradoxically, there remained much land still to subdue. This same tension pervades the farewell address. Yahweh has given "rest" to Israel (v. 1); his fighting on their behalf is spoken of as something completed in the past (v. 3). Yet immediately attention shifts to "the nations that remain" (vv. 4-5) and an overcoming of them that has still to be accomplished (v. 5). This double focus is potentially bewildering, yet it is not new in Joshua; indeed it may be said to lie at the heart of the book.

The fact that victory is not complete becomes an occasion for renewed exhortation to the people to remain faithful to the covenant. In a sense their situation is not essentially different from what it was at the beginning: they are obliged to keep covenant with Yahweh, the task of possession lies before them, and they are assured that Yahweh will enable them to enter into their full inheritance. The language of the exhortation is very familiar (vv. 6-8). Joshua himself, on the death of Moses and at the beginning of his commission, had been charged to keep the commands written in "the book of the law"[108] and not to deviate from it either to right or left (1:7), so he now lays the same obligation upon Israel (23:6; cf. also Deut 5:32). Most urgently, this will mean keeping entirely separate from the peoples of the land who do not worship Yahweh, also a key concern of Deuteronomy (v. 7; cf. Deut 7:1-5), and holding steadfastly to him (v. 8; cf. Deut 10:20).

23:9-13 The structure of Joshua's charge in these verses is similar to the preceding. Once again he points to the acts of God as already accomplished, especially recalling how the inhabitants of the land had seemed invincible to the Israelites as they approached the land. In v. 9, then, there is a retrospect on the people's first failure of faith, which had resulted in the long delay in the fulfilment of the promise, as well as a memory of how Yahweh had easily overcome those formidable obstacles (Deut 1:19-46; Joshua 1–12). As he has done, so he can continue to do, and they too can have victory in his strength (v. 10; cf. Deut 32:30).

This postulate of Yahweh's supreme strength, and therefore Israel's ca-

---

108. See above on Josh 1:7.

pacity for victory, then leads again to exhortation to be faithful to Yahweh. This is now accompanied by a solemn warning that if they compromise through intermarriage, and therefore turn to other gods, their compromises will become the means of their own undoing and they will ultimately lose the land and the life it gave. What they had once feared could happen because of the power of the enemy would eventually come to pass because of their own inconstancy.

23:14-16 The farewell address gains intensity as Joshua's mind is concentrated by his own imminent death. The message of these verses is again similar to the preceding. Frequent repetition of the word "all" helps convey this intensity: all Israel ("all of you," v. 14 NRSV) know that God had kept all his promises; yet "all the good" will give way to "all the evil" (v. 15), if they prove unfaithful. The stark choice before Israel is stressed by the stark language: all or nothing; "good" or "evil"; long, full life in the land or loss of land and death. Everything that has been gained stands to be lost. At the beginning of the book, Israel stood outside the land and had before them every opportunity for life. At the end, they stand within it, still with all those opportunities, yet also facing the possibility of losing everything.

Joshua 24

24:1-13 The book of Joshua closes with a great covenantal ceremony. Whereas Joshua's farewell speech (ch. 23) was not specifically located, the scene is now set in Shechem. This is somewhat unexpected in view of the prominence of Shiloh in the preceding chapters, yet Shechem has its own deep resonances. Situated in the heart of the country, in the uplands of Ephraim (21:21), its status as a place of the covenant is well established in the Old Testament. Deuteronomy specified it, more precisely the mountains Ebal and Gerizim in its immediate vicinity, as the place where the tribes should go for the purpose of covenant renewal upon their entry to the land (Deut 11:29; 27:4, 11-14), and Israel's response to this command has already been recorded in Josh 8:30-35. The book of Judges also knows of an ancient association of Shechem and covenant (Judg 9:46).[109]

---

[109]. The divine name El-berith is "God of the covenant." In the Judges narrative this could be an echo of Israel's covenant with Yahweh there (since the name El is applied to Yahweh frequently in the Old Testament, especially in Genesis), or it could represent a Canaanite, or Canaanizing, form of religion, perhaps mixed syncretistically with the worship of Yahweh. The expression is perhaps pointedly imprecise, corresponding to the uncertain nature of the Shechemites' loyalties.

The chosen setting corresponds to a widening of the angle, as Joshua calls Israel to consider itself and its destiny in the light of its whole history with Yahweh up to this point. Joshua, uttering God's words in the manner of a prophet ("Thus says the Lord," v. 2), begins the review with Abraham, recalling that he had lived "beyond the River" (Euphrates) and had worshipped other gods. This is the implication of the Genesis account until the moment when Abraham encounters Yahweh (Gen 11:31–12:3). Joshua makes this point about Israel's prehistory in order to remind them that their origins outside the land in polytheistic worship had been expressly left behind, their presence as the people of Yahweh in Canaan being the goal and purpose of the long and patient acts of God. The speech goes on to recall how God led Abraham into Canaan and promised him numerous offspring (v. 3; cf. Gen 12:1-3; 15:1-6); the passing of the promise from Abraham to the line of Jacob, while Esau was assigned Edom, outside the promised land (Genesis 25–33); and the descent of Jacob's family into Egypt (Genesis 37–50). This was the prelude for the great deliverance from slavery there that would follow in due course (vv. 6-7; cf. Exodus 1–15). The story moves into Numbers, with the memory of God's victories over the Amorite kings Sihon and Og (v. 8; cf. Num 21:21-35) and the resistance to Israel mounted by Balak king of Moab and his failed attempt to use the power of Balaam's magic to thwart their progress (vv. 9-10; cf. Numbers 22–24). There is then a summary reprise of the action of Joshua itself, with the fall of Jericho highlighted as the symbol of Yahweh's victories (v. 11). The list of Canaanite peoples is formulaic (cf. Deut 7:1). Here Jericho is said to have offered a fight, somewhat in contrast to Joshua 6, but in line with the catalogue of futile resistance to Israel's advance under God. The decisive role of God in the events is then reemphasized, together with his gift of the land and Israel's own helplessness to secure its own life (vv. 11-12; cf. Deut 6:10-13).

The rehearsal of key events in the past relationship between Yahweh and Israel is typical of covenantal transactions in the Old Testament (cf. Exod 19:4-6; Deuteronomy 1–3), and behind this pattern lies the treaty tradition of the ancient Near East. It functions rhetorically to remind Israel of its absolute debt to Yahweh, as the foundation for the exhortation which now ensues.

24:14-15 The radical choice which faces Israel is now starkly expressed, and the purpose of the memory of Abraham becomes clear. In Egypt too Israel is said to have worshipped other gods (v. 14). This is not expressly said in Exodus, though may be traced in the people's reluctance to follow Moses through the wilderness. The detail fits with the rhetorical intention to portray Israel's present choice as starkly as possible: there must be no compromise or turning back. The issue is clear: Will Israel remain distinctive from the world around it and faithful to Yahweh alone, or will it succumb to the pressures of conformity and idolatry? It is a challenge that will resound through the pages of Israel's story, with particular hints of Elijah's challenge on Mount Carmel at a point when Israel had fallen under the powerful influence of Baal and the prophets of the Phoenician Jezebel (1 Kgs 18:21). Joshua himself, hardly waiting for Israel's answer, makes his own affirmation: he at least, and his "household," will follow Yahweh (v. 15). This famous declaration is highly suggestive. Joshua's leadership in Israel is nearing its end. He has received his inheritance in Timnath-serah (19:50), to which he will presumably shortly retire, taking his place as an ordinary Israelite among many others. His oath of loyalty to Yahweh becomes exemplary for all the "houses" of Israel. It shows that if Israel is to be faithful to Yahweh it will be up to all Israelites, individuals and families, to take the covenantal obligations directly upon themselves. At the same time, there is perhaps a hint of what might equally well ensue, that is, a divided Israel, in which some "houses" have opted for Yahweh while others have chosen the other path.

24:16-28 The people respond with an affirmation that they will indeed remain faithful to Yahweh, borrowing the retrospective method of Joshua's speech in order to lend weight to their assertion (vv. 16-18). If we expected Joshua to welcome this, his response is astonishing, with its fierce assertion that they "are not able to serve the Lord" (v. 19). It is difficult to take this categorically, since it would then seem to mock and invalidate the very assumptions on which the covenant is based, and the whole purpose of this particular ceremony. The concept corresponds to other strong statements that put in question Israel's capacity to keep the covenant (cf. Deut 9:4-6). But these are best taken as sharp rhetorical devices, intended to produce the desired response. They might equally be taken as prophetic, since Joshua speaks here with the voice of a prophet. In either case, Joshua's uncompromising statement is immediately followed by an "if" (v. 20). And the outcome of his challenge is that the people assert once more that they will keep the faith (v. 21), this time with a solemn oath, reminiscent of the "book of the law" and the Song of Moses which would stand as a witness against Israel in the event of their apostasy (v. 22; cf. Deut 31:24-29; Moses' premonition of Israel's waywardness, 31:29, corresponds somewhat to Joshua's statement here in v. 19).

In a yet further exchange between them, Joshua now refers to "foreign gods" which he envisages them harboring even as they speak (v. 23). This too is surprising, since there has been no prior indication of idolatry among the people who have participated in the war for the land and the distribution of territory. Elsewhere, Joshua's generation is remembered as faithful (v. 31; Judg 2:7). But Joshua may be speaking rhetorically and prophetically here too, vividly portraying the kind of double-mindedness which could and will become a temptation in the pressured situation in Canaan. In this way Joshua's final exhortation to Israel parallels the narrative, which has regularly posed Israel's position as paradoxical, possessing yet not possessing, the land given yet not fully taken. This covenant renewal leaves no room for complacency; the people of God is compelled to face its own serious weaknesses in the moment of solemn affirmation. The shades of the golden calf apostasy (Exodus 32), committed at the very moment when Moses was concluding the Sinai covenant with God on Mount Sinai, hover in the background.

The ceremony comes to a climax with Joshua making a covenant with (or "on behalf of"[110]) the people. He then established it as "a statute and ordinance," or a "fixed rule."[111] And he writes words in "the book of the law of God," evoking "the book of the law" which became the deposit of Moses' commands in Deuteronomy (Deut 31:26).[112] Here, the specific focus is on loyalty to Yahweh, rather than on the laws as such.[113] Finally, Joshua sets up a stone of witness, in keeping with other stones of witness in the book (4:1-8; 22:26-28) and the strong emphasis on the need for Israel to remember who they are, where they have come from, and what their destiny is, an emphasis that is maintained throughout the present chapter.

24:29-33 Joshua's death is reminiscent of Joseph's in Egypt (both died at 110 years old; cf. Gen 50:22). The parallel with Joseph serves as a signal that Israel's present position in Canaan is the culmination of a long history begun in divine promise ages ago. The same link is explicitly established in v. 32, with the bringing of Joseph's bones to Canaan for burial, in fulfilment of Joseph's own command (Gen 50:25). The burial place at Shechem touches another nerve in the ancient history, with an allusion to the conflict between Jacob's sons and the family of Hamor at that place, the encounter which had resulted in Simeon and Levi being condemned to be "dispersed in Israel" (Gen 34; 49:5-7). This final procession from Egypt to Canaan puts a finish to the whole story of exodus, wandering, and entry upon the inheritance.

---

110. Nelson, *Joshua*, 276-77.

111. The phrase חק ומשפט/*ḥōq ûmišpāṭ* is similar to the plural form used frequently in Deuteronomy for the laws of Moses. And a number of English translations take it as if it was expressing the same thing (e.g., "statutes and ordinances," RSV, NRSV; "decrees and laws," NIV). It is preferable to take it as the confirmation of a thing done once for all, hence "fixed rule" (with Nelson, *Joshua*, 277; and cf. 1 Sam 30:25).

112. It is not clear how Joshua's book relates to that of Moses. Some think that Joshua had his own copy of "the book of the law," on analogy with the king according to the Deuteronomic law (Deut 17:18). Nelson points to 1:8; 8:32 as evidence for Joshua having such a copy (*Joshua*, 277). The main point, however, is to evoke the obligation on Israel to maintain the obligations accepted under Moses.

113. Cf. Hawk, *Joshua*, 277-78.

Joshua himself is buried at Timnath-serah, with little fanfare. Having carried out his appointed duty of leading Israel into Canaan, he goes to his own allotted place in the land, according to the destiny of Israelites generally, dies and is buried there, and leaves no successor. The great leader of Israel becomes a symbol of humility and the egalitarianism that has pervaded the Mosaic laws, especially in Deuteronomy. His burial notice is joined by that of Eleazar, who had officiated with Joshua in the allocation of the land.

The ending of the book of Joshua is both a strong culmination and highly expectant. Not only the end of Joshua, its allusions to Genesis signal that it is a conclusion to the books Genesis-Joshua. We saw echoes of the creation in the settlement of Israel in Canaan when Israel stood at Shiloh before the tent of meeting, and the end of the book also suggests that the story that began with creation has reached a point of at least relative consummation in Israel's act of commitment at Shechem. Joshua is dead, but it is not a case of "long live the king." The succession to Moses and Joshua together will not devolve on an individual, or not yet. Rather it will consist in the whole people of Israel, both in its rank and file and in its solemn "assembly," willingly submitting itself to the covenant and its stipulations in the Torah. To that end they must put in place duly authorized institutions to manage and uphold the Torah (as laid out in Deut 16:18–18:22). It is no longer a time for a great leader; it is time for Israel to enter into its destiny of becoming in reality a people of Yahweh, forming a society framed by the Torah in its core. The story of how they fared is not told in Joshua, but in the books that follow it.

Theological Horizons of Joshua

Theology in the Book of Joshua

Stephen Williams

The Question of the Land

Possession and Loss

When we open the book of Joshua, we meet a people poised to go to war in order to take land. It is so positioned not only in God's name and with God's permission, but by God's command. How are we to read and understand this? We view Joshua today against the background of the incessant strife of nations and peoples over land, and particularly the conflict raging in the Middle East between Arabs and Israelis. Christians read the account in the context of the canonical Scriptures of their Old and New Testaments. It is an exercise which takes us to the very heart of those Scriptures. For the question of land dominates the Hebrew Bible, and what is spoken, unspoken, or implied by words and silences in the New Testament on the subject of the land tells us a lot about the relationship between the two Testaments.

Joshua succeeded Moses in leadership, fulfilling his commission to conduct the people of Israel into the land of Canaan. The second half of the book of Joshua chronicles in detail the distribution of territories among the tribes. When God first appears to Moses, it is with an announcement that he will bring the people of Israel into "a good and spacious land . . . flowing with milk and honey" (Exod 3:8). This announcement is preceded by God's self-description as the "God of Abraham, Isaac, and Jacob." a family whose story dominates Genesis and whose history is set in motion by God's declaration to Abraham that he would give the land of Canaan to his descendants and bless the wider nations of humankind through them (Gen 12:1-7). It is given as an everlasting possession (13:15; 17:8). Indeed, Abraham is apparently brought out of Ur specifically in order to receive it (Gen 15:7). Over the course of the

Pentateuch, its boundaries are described sometimes in more general, sometimes in more detailed, terms and we cannot extract from the Hexateuch a single territorially precise account.[1] Yet they are sufficiently precise for Joshua, as we encounter him, to have a clear and definite mandate, and the book is massively interested in territorial detail. Joshua 21:43-45 forms a kind of climax to a narrative that begins in Gen 12:1.

God's promise is reiterated all the way through to Deuteronomy; its terms are strong, embracing covenant and oath, and Isaac and Jacob are named along with Abraham. But another feature insinuates itself into the account with increasing prominence. In the intense, strident, concentrated and reiterated terms which characterise Deuteronomy, the people is reminded that God's covenant has a correlative requirement attached to it, though the exact relation between "covenant" and "requirement" may not be easy to specify and the narrative has introduced us to both an Abrahamic and a Sinaitic covenant. As the people approach the solemn moment when God will speak from Mount Sinai, it is told that "if you obey me fully and keep my covenant, then out of all nations you will be my treasured possession" (Exod 19:5). Accordingly, the people makes a solemn promise to obey what is read in a "book of the covenant" (24:7). Its immediate and drastic failure to deliver on its commitment, in the incident of the golden calf, brings to light a divine radicalism that accompanies divine promise. God threatens to destroy the people and, instead, make Moses into a great nation (32:10). Moses was later to remind the people of God's offer (Deut 9:14). This does not mean that the covenant was about to be broken from God's side: Moses was of the house of Levi and therefore a descendant of Jacob and of Abraham. But it looks as though intended beneficiaries could be cut out. Promise and command are linked in the Sinaitic covenant as is indicated by the fact that the Ten Commandments are called the "words of the covenant" (Exod 34:28). Deuteronomy, in particular, hammers home the connection between holding the land of promise and adhering to the law of the God who promised it. But long before we arrive at Exodus and Sinai, Abraham has been told to "keep the covenant" (Gen 17:9); his obedience plays a role in securing the blessing of his descendants (22:18), and Isaac is reminded of the connection between promise and obedience (26:4-5). However they differ, the covenant with Abraham and the covenant at Sinai both draw attention to the importance of obedience.

As we approach the book of Joshua, whose narrative studiously adver-

---

1. Genesis-Joshua has sometimes been treated as a unity and designated the "Hexateuch," but in using that word I make no assumptions about the composition or tradition-history of these books.

tises its connection with the immediately preceding book of Deuteronomy, we find promise and precariousness sitting side by side. It is God's secure word that the land will be possessed; he apparently both intends and instructs the Israelites to live long there, retaining possession. Disobedience, however, will bring disaster, leading the Israelites to a destruction already tasted by other nations (Deut 8:20). God is apparently committed only to the restoration of a remnant from among those driven out into the nations if and when disobedience occurs. Even then, restoration will not be independent of seeking God with heart and soul (Deut 4:26-31). The divine declaration of what *would* happen should the Israelites call upon God in the future blends into the declaration *that* certain things will take place. Deuteronomy ends on a predictive note (28:15-68; 30:1-10; 31:21).[2]

Is the promise of perpetual possession of the land regarded in the book of Joshua as conditional on the obedience of the people? Joshua is well aware that the fate of his fellow Israelites is in the balance and that it is extremely perilous to presume on promise. He was a close associate of Moses in the book of Exodus, and when Moses ascended Sinai to procure the stone tablets, Joshua was on the scene (Exod 24:13). When Moses is alerted by God to the apostasy of the golden calf — the event which led to a threat of destruction and an offer to transfer the privilege of nationhood to Moses' descendants — Joshua is his companion and observes with him the riotous scene. He knows about the radically fickle ways of the people and what God will accordingly contemplate. Later, when God foretells Israel's rebellion, he tells Moses to summon Joshua so that he also should hear of it (Deut 31:14). After decades of knowledge and experience, when Joshua delivers his final speech to the people, at the end of his days, he issues a warning on his own account: "If you forsake the Lord and serve foreign gods, he will turn and bring disaster on you and make an end of you, after he has been good to you" (Josh 24:20).

Questions about the terms of the covenant and the tenure of the land, what is irrevocably promised and what is subject to change, are sometimes discussed in terms of the "unconditional" and "conditional" or distinctions between a covenant with "conditions" and one with "requirements." This may be legitimate, although there is a danger of imposing on the Hebrew Scriptures alien, oversystematized or excessively abstract forms of thought and unwittingly distorting the picture.[3] But even when we try to avoid the risk by at-

---

2. I am following the canonical narrative here without attending to the question of the relation of documentary dating to the prediction embodied in the text. This is the general approach adopted in these essays.

3. Prominent amongst contemporary theologians who have treated covenant systemati-

tending closely to the differing inflections and contents of biblical language spread over the canonical books, the canonical narrative itself suggests that it is the course of future history, rather than semantic analysis, that will show how promise, command, and obedience are related. It is history as interpreted in Scripture that reveals the meaning of promise. The occupation of the land as recorded in the book of Joshua, however incomplete it is, is one of the twin peaks of the story that stretches from the beginning of the book right through to the accounts in Kings and Chronicles (the Davidic establishment being the other). The story itself runs a sad course. The establishment of the Davidic monarchy portends not only short-term security for the land but also the benediction of a glorious and perpetual royal succession. In broad accordance with the pattern that we have noted, David's speech in the opening chapters of 1 Kings also expresses the conviction that promise is correlated with obedience (1 Kgs 2:4). It is not only the future of the land that is now at stake; it is the Davidic dynasty as well.[4] What eventuates is therefore doubly grim — triply, because the fate of temple is also implicated. Israel and Judah separate, but alike share the fate of exile. Towards the end of 2 Kings, we read the chilling words that "in the end he [God] thrust them [Jerusalem and Judah] from his presence" (2 Kgs 24:20).[5]

Although some exiles return, these are only from among the people deported from the southern kingdom of Judah. Ezra reestablishes the temple in the land and Nehemiah concentrates on the physical security of Jerusalem. The prospect of a newly sanctified land, indwelt by temple and Torah, seems capable of realization. This is what the postexilic leadership wants, and this is entirely consistent, as far as it goes, with the aspirations set forth in Deuteronomy and Joshua. Yet the prophetic writings of the Old Testament close with the portentous suggestion that things are as precarious as ever and that history may repeat itself as far as is possible under changed conditions. The book of Malachi in the Hebrew Bible ends with reference to the land: "See, I will

---

cally, attempting to root his theology in Old Testament exegesis, is Michael Horton. For a general introduction to his more detailed studies, see his *God of Promise*. Among those who regard the "conditional"/"unconditional" distinction as unhelpful, see Brueggemann, *Theology of the Old Testament*, 419-21.

4. For a similar balance of promise and warning in the books of Chronicles, see, e.g., 1 Chr 17:17-27; 22:13; 2 Chr 6:16.

5. Cf. 2 Kgs 17:7-23. Another reason why the question of what is promised in perpetuity cannot be answered simply by scrutinizing the way in which the language and concepts work in the passages specifically treating land or covenant is that other data is relevant. See, e.g., the way in which the story tells the fate of the promise to Eli (1 Sam. 2:27-36). On this, see McConville, *God and Earthly Power*, ch. 8.

send you the prophet Elijah before that great and dreadful day of the Lord comes. He will turn the hearts of the fathers to their children, and the hearts of the children to their fathers; or else I will come and strike the land with a curse" (Mal 4:5-6). Is it because these words are so ominous that, in the Septuagint, the order of the last three verses is reversed, so that Malachi brings prophecy to its conclusion with an exhortation to remember the laws of Moses and not with the prospect of a great and dreadful day? The Hebrew ends with the ominous word translated above as "curse," but more strictly "ban" — the very word used in Deuteronomy and Joshua to designate what is devoted to destruction when the Israelites go about the business of war in Canaan. Joshua begins the "Prophetic" division of the Hebrew Bible which ends with Malachi. (In the Hebrew Bible, Malachi is succeeded by the division usually termed "Writings," but in the Christian Old Testament those writings are all inserted somewhere between Joshua and Malachi.)

Centuries later, the cry of prophecy cleaves through the Judean wilderness when a figure apparelled like Elijah and known to us as John the Baptist summons the people of Israel to repentance. By then, after a history of fluctuating fortunes, the people and the temple were in the land, but the people were not its free possessors, having been integrated into the Roman Empire, set under Roman governorship and paying taxes to their rulers. It has been argued that this was in fact an experience of exile.[6] The Torah does not hold political sway in the land. Now the prophetic summons to repentance is focused, in the person of John the Baptist, on the need to prepare the way for the Messiah of Israel. Jesus, believed by Christians to fulfill that role, ministered in the land of promise. He was crucified in Jerusalem, city of David. The temple was destroyed within about a generation of his death, inaugurating a new stage in the history of the Jewish people, with a devastating sequence in the following century, a stage which lasted through protracted centuries until the formation of the state of Israel in 1948 ushered in a new phase in the political history of international Jewry.

The New Testament and the Land

The New Testament is a witness to Jesus Christ and connects him with a new covenant, but there is a conspicuous and eloquent silence on the matter of the land. Ezekiel was the prophet of a renewed covenant, a "covenant of peace"

---

6. So N. T. Wright, *The New Testament and the People of God;* and *Jesus and the Victory of God.*

(Ezek 34:25; 37:26), and his prophecy culminated in a specific description of future land allocation more reminiscent of the territorial distributions recorded in the second half of the book of Joshua than any other portion of the Hebrew Bible outside the Pentateuch (Ezek 47:13–48:29). Yet it is Jeremiah's formulation of a "new" covenant that is quoted twice in the letter to the Hebrews, which is by far the most direct and explicit of the New Testament writings in its focused treatment of covenant (Jer 8:8-12; 10:16-17), although "new covenant" language is vitally present in Luke's account of the last supper (Luke 22:20).[7] The same letter contains one of the two New Testament references to the person of Joshua.[8] The story of exodus, wilderness, and entry into the promised land serves Christian believers as in some respects a type of their own story; it prefigures what is to come, and what is to come has now come in Jesus Christ, so a new covenant replaces the old. As interpreted in the book of Hebrews, this new covenant reorients hope by dissociating it from connection with the specific territory of Canaan. Joshua had not given the people rest (Heb 4:8). If he had, there would have been no more promise to be fulfilled. However, there was a promise then, and there is a fulfilment now, yet in such a way that Joshua's territorial concerns have apparently had their day. The promised land seems to have disappeared from God's agenda. For what we possess in the new covenant is forgiveness through the sacrificial death and high priestly ministry of Jesus Christ, founder of "a kingdom that cannot be shaken" (Heb 12:28). Hope remains and the wilderness experience serves to describe the ongoing experience of the Christian church, yet the hope is disconnected from association with a particular physical land of promise. The famous exposition in Hebrews 11 and the exhortation to suffer in light of the fact that we have no enduring city (13:14) establish clear metaphorical water between Joshua's possession of land and the Christian's possession of the kingdom.

Although the book of Hebrews is distinctive, it is remarkably representative of the New Testament as far as the question of land is concerned. On its surface, the New Testament witness is surprisingly uninterested in the question of the promised land.[9] Christology accounts for this. Old Testament prophecies have been, are being, or will be fulfilled through Jesus Christ.

---

7. It is also found in some manuscripts of Matthew (26:28) and Mark (14:24).

8. The other is in Acts 7:45.

9. See Davies, *The Gospel and the Land*. Davies also wrote a useful short account of "Jerusalem and the Land in the Christian Tradition." Brueggemann, in *The Land*, strives hard, but not very convincingly, to modify Davies's conclusions (ch. 10). For a fairly recent conspectus which usually takes the same sort of general line as I take here, see Johnston and Walker, *The Land of Promise*.

What is accomplished in and promised through Christ determines the nature of religious hope and casts new light on the trajectory of history and promise described in the Old Testament. Christ and his kingdom constitute the Christian's inheritance, hope, and goal, and the kingdom is not particularly identified with the turf that is the land of Israel. Is this what is sometimes termed "supersessionism," the belief that the promises to Israel have been redirected towards the church and so redefined within it that the significance of the land and the ethnic people of Israel is terminated?[10] If so, does it involve reading Joshua against its grain, detaching its meaning and significance from a pentateuchal, historical, or prophetic context that contains far-reaching and immutable promises to Abraham and his descendants?

In pondering the significance of and relationship between the promise to Abraham and the giving of the law, Paul addressed a cognate question. He was a Benjaminite, "Hebrew of Hebrews," Israelite Pharisee, descendant of Abraham (2 Cor 11:22; Phil 3:5). What is the religious significance of the lineage? In his Letter to the Romans, Paul argued that Abraham is the father of Jew and Gentile alike for he exemplifies that faith which justifies Jew and Gentile alike before God (Rom 4:16). More than exemplification is involved. He is promised that he will be the father of many nations, and the promise is described strikingly: Abraham will be "heir of the world" (4:13).[11] Abraham receives the promises on behalf of the world and the world is promised to him. In the Letter to the Galatians, Paul quotes the promise reiterated in Genesis that all nations would be blessed through Abraham. The blessing comes through and with faith. But, more than this, the promise made and inheritance given to Abraham and his seed apply primarily to Jesus Christ (Gal 3:16). There is not a word here about land, and the silence is significant. It is true that the omission of specific reference to land need not always entail that it is completely out of mind. When Paul enumerates the explicit privileges of Israel in Rom 9:4, there is a striking lack of reference to land, but it may be that the idea is subsumed under "covenant," "promise," and especially "temple" in that text.[12] What is important is that a positive theological perspective accounts for the New Testament silence on the land: Christ is the promised inheritance.

But this is not a case of the church superseding Israel or a case of Christians succeeding Jews. Jesus was a Jew; his twelve disciples were Jews; Paul was

---

10. Soulen has distinguished different types of supersessionism; *The God of Israel and Christian Theology.* McDermott, "The Land," provides a brief introduction to this and to the complex variety of attitudes that surround the question of the land today.

11. Cranfield connects this with 1 Cor 3:21-23 in *Commentary on Romans*, 1:240.

12. Cf. the use of the evidence from Maccabees in Davies, *The Gospel and the Land*, 90-95.

a Jew. Christianity is the outcome of an inner-Jewish split and dissent over the significance of Jesus. Israel has come to a fork on the road. Paul is among the Israelites who have taken one route; Israelites who reject the faith of the fledgling Christian church take another. If Gentile Christians boast that the favor of God has been transferred from Jews to Gentiles, Paul has at least four immediate responses (Rom 11:13-24). First, Gentiles are not self-standing; they are grafted on to the root which supports them, Israel.[13] Second, they are not secure; they can be detached from the root just as unbelieving Israel could be detached from the root. Third, God can reattach unbelieving Israel to the root, so that believing Jews, believing Gentiles, and hitherto-unbelieving Jews can form the tree. Fourth, if and when that happens, it can be described in terms of Jews being "grafted into their own olive tree" whereas Gentiles do not have their own olive tree.

The physical soil of Palestine, on which Jesus lived, along which he traipsed, and in which he ministered, was the very land where people "living in darkness have seen a great light" (Matt 4:16, quoting Isa 9:1-2). The instructive words of the Messiah, the fully sanctified life, the redeeming cross, and the saving resurrection all took place in and through the physical body of Jesus in the physical land promised to Abraham and his descendants. It was in Jerusalem that the promised Spirit came; it was from Jerusalem that the word and salvation of the Lord went forth to all the ends of the earth. In this respect, Paul and others assume the unsubstitutable instrumentality of the promised land in the fulfilment of God's purposes. They do so not by seeking first to impose a spiritual meaning on Old Testament texts that is alien to those texts, but by interpreting them in light of the events surrounding Jesus.[14] If, within the covers of the Old Testament, it is the course of history that sheds light on the meaning and significance of the promises, interpreted history remains the hermeneutical principle deployed in the New Testament for understanding the significance of Abraham, promise, and land. The scope of the blessing that God had in store for Abraham was extremely wide from the outset: "All peoples on earth will be blessed through you" (Gen 12:3); "I will make nations of you, and kings will come from you" (17:6); "through your offspring all nations on earth will be blessed" (22:18). The prophets lift up their eyes in the hope that the earth, as Habakkuk puts it, will be "filled with

---

13. I have deliberately used the cryptic "Israel" because what Paul means by "root" has been variously understood. I take "Israel" to be one way or another comprehended within the reference, whether patriarchs or Christ or anything different is more specifically in Paul's mind.

14. Davies makes this point forcefully; he is not "succumbing to an otherworldly hermeneutic" (Brueggemann, *The Land*, 167) but tracking the christological hermeneutic of the New Testament, grounded in this-worldly events.

the knowledge of the glory of the Lord, as the waters cover the sea" (Hab 2:14; cf. Isa 11:9). Israel's vocation, represented in the figure of the servant, is to be a light for the Gentiles (Isa 42:6; 49:6). Deuteronomy already views possession of land in a rather similar light (Deut 4:6-8). If the New Testament authors were persuaded that Jesus was the Messiah of Israel, risen from the dead, it would have been impossibly perverse for them to read their Scriptures in any other light. The history of fulfilment interprets the meaning of promise. And we might add that, while history rolls on towards the eschaton, there is meaning in Christianity that is yet to be disclosed and understood.

Back to the Land?

Let us return to Joshua. We shall have occasion in other essays to revert to the question of reading the book against its grain, translating Joshua into an alien sphere. What the New Testament invites us to do is to read Joshua against the background of God's fundamental purposes in creation, which entails reading it in terms of the first as well as the last book of the Pentateuch. But that is only an invitation reissued, for, as the exegetical portion of our commentary has shown, it should be so read independently of any New Testament direction. Genesis knits the story of Abraham together with the text of the first eleven chapters. The Hebrew word for "land" in Gen 12:1 is the same as the word for "earth" in Gen 1:1, and attention is frequently drawn to the relevant literary connections.[15] In Genesis, the call of Abram to head towards a particular land is God's response to the crisis of the whole earth. Eden, the original paradise, became the earthly scene of the human fall, corruption, and explusion. Canaan, the land of Sodom and Gomorrah, is a particularly defiled land, according to the tale told from Genesis 13 onwards, the trouble going back to an incident recorded in Gen 9:18-27. On account of the sin of Ham, his son, against him, Noah cursed Canaan, son of Ham, and his descendants. The land of Canaan is not just destined by God to be a possession for the Israelites; it is destined to become the scene of corruption reversed and the place where God's universal holiness shines forth. Dispossession of the land is obviously not *per se* a sign of grace manifested towards Canaanites, and Israel's possession of the land is not *per se* a sufficient sign of grace towards the world. Only when Abraham is viewed as God's means of blessing people beyond the boundaries of Israel do we begin to understand why Israel is given boundaries, i.e., land. In Christian perspective, the dispensation in

---

15. See, e.g., McKeown, "The Theme of Land."

which a promised land is given to Israel radically gives way to a new one when Jesus dies and rises again, for the universal purposes of God in creation now flow through Jesus Christ, through whom all things were created. The promised land becomes the site from which blessing flows to all nations for the renewal of creation, the place to which all eyes must look and from which mission goes forth, proclaiming that the exalted Lord privileges no land, language, or temple to the exclusion of others.

Prophetic hope for the postexilic future of Israel can be couched in terms of the restoration of and to the land, but Ezek 47:13–48:29 is both instructive and intriguing in this connection. A comparison of the accounts of the boundaries of the promised land in Joshua and Ezekiel (and Numbers 34) does not just reveal divergence in geographical detail. For Ezekiel does not even aim to produce "a literary photograph of the land of Israel but ... a cartographic painting by an artist with a particular theological agenda."[16] Ezekiel's concrete references to the land west of the Jordan should not mislead us into the ready supposition that he is assuming literal fulfilment or, to be more precise, that he is assuming fulfilment in the literal form in which he sets forth his prophecy. Old Testament prophecy defines and redefines the hope of Israel in a variety of ways and in a variety of circumstances, but even if land features strongly and centrally in most representations, the closing chapters of Ezekiel force us to inquire into the relation of the literal and symbolic in eschatological prophecy even when it comes to the most concrete imaginable descriptions. In that last respect, Ezekiel is unparalleled.

Even an urbanized, mobile Christian Gentile reading the Bible in his or her native tongue can feel something of the tremendous force of Ezekiel's portrayal in all its concrete detail.[17] How much more, then, the Jew! It is tempting to argue about the significance of the land by debating what is a true and a false proposition, warranted or unwarranted hermeneutics. But it "is in the Haggadah and the liturgy that the full force of sentiment for the land is to be felt. It cannot properly be seen except through Jewish eyes, nor felt except through Jewish words."[18] Correspondingly, the force of the Christian understanding of the land cannot be grasped simply in terms of true or false propositions, warranted or unwarranted hermeneutics. It is the profound, revolutionary, and transformative impact of Jesus, believed to be Messiah and son of God, that explains the force of Christian conviction about the land.

---

16. Block, *The Book of Ezekiel, Chapters 25–48*, 723. See the whole discussion on 722-24.

17. Barr might have greeted this sentence with incredulity: see the reference to the closing chapters of Ezekiel in *The Concept of Biblical Theology*, 166.

18. Davies, *The Gospel and the Land*, 74. The Haggadah here refers to the literature of Rabbinic Judaism that includes the "liturgical" ritual order for the Passover meal.

Yet, the relative silence of the New Testament on the land in the wake of its theologically developed understanding of the status of Jew and Gentile in Christ does not entail that territorial Israel — however we define it with geographical precision — cannot possibly have theological significance for the future. In Romans 9–11, Paul provides us with a studied and passionate account of the relation of Israel to church. The shadow of tragedy engulfs a discourse which ends in doxology, for Israelite unbelief has led to the rejection of the Messiah. But this is not the last word. "All Israel" is eventually saved (Rom 11:26). What does this mean? It is a matter of dispute. It is often interpreted as the expression of a conviction that there will be a significant conversion of Jews to Christ in the future. Let us, for the sake of argument, grant the plausibility of that interpretation. It remains that nothing is said about the occupation by Israel of the promised land. Nation, people, and territory are not specifically interconnected here. Yet even the lack of definite connection does not entail that there can be no connection. Silence may signify to us that the question of land is an open, not a closed, one. The possibility should not be ruled out that ancient land may yet be the site of peculiar blessing for a people that stands in some ethnic continuity with the ancient people of Israel. The complexity of the issues involved in a putative dissociation of "people" from "land" in Pauline eschatological thought, even if we insist on the absence of reference to land, should not be underestimated.

This conclusion appears to do justice both to the New Testament approach to prophetic eschatology and to our earlier remarks that it is the course of history that will reveal the nature of promise. If we should not assume, on the basis of the Pentateuch, that the Jewish people can claim Israel today as a land that is rightfully theirs (even after working out what territory should exactly constitute the "land of Israel") we cannot preclude the possibility that God will in fact return the land in some form to some form of the people and that this will be historically and religiously momentous.[19] Further, if we should not categorically affirm, on direct biblical grounds, the political right of present-day Israel to its claim on Jerusalem or the West Bank or any other territory, we can still leave open the question of whether, as a matter of relative justice, there may be some such entitlement.[20] Issues of entitlement to land are usually complex. If a claim to land is derived from a belief that it is

---

19. Ezekiel apparently entertains hope for the land more on the grounds of something like a new creation than because of the ancient promise to Abraham, though doubtless the two cannot be entirely disconnected (chs. 33–37).

20. It is worth referring to Reinhold Niebuhr's powerful insistence that relative, rather than absolute, justice is the proper goal of the political quest. For a general orientation to his work, see Rasmussen's "Introduction" to *Reinhold Niebuhr*.

God-given, that may complicate a question already complicated enough in relation to independent canons of political justice and international law. (It is not suggested here that "religion" invariably complicates "reason"!) Issues of nationhood, land, and right have moral and legal dimensions that pertain to Jews and Palestinians alike. All that is undercut, on my account of things, is a theological argument for the status of Israel as a land of promise drawn directly from the Old Testament. Of course, some argue that this undercuts everything.[21]

In the book of Joshua, Caleb reports that "Moses swore to me, 'The land on which your feet have walked will be your inheritance and that of your children for ever, because you have followed the Lord my God wholeheartedly'" (14:9). As this picks up what is earlier and more comprehensively vouchsafed about the "perpetual" nature of the bequest of land, it is not a text that holds interest simply for Caleb. God's promise and Caleb's obedience are connected. The precise relation of promise to requirement is not explored in the book of Joshua, even if we think that we can deduce from it the main elements of a thesis. We do not have a clear assumption in its pages that land is guaranteed in perpetuity irrespective of conduct within its borders, although it does have to be read in closest conjunction with Deuteronomy, which in turn has to be read in conjunction with Jeremiah and so forth (whatever view we take of the literary, historical, and theological relationship between the various books in the canon). For Joshua, it is important that the people does not presume that territorial right or retention is independent of the obedience of the people of God (14:9), even though that does not make void what is promised by God on the terms of the promise, correctly understood. The egregious enormity of national presumption emerges forcefully in the prophetic writings. The land belongs to the Lord (Lev 25:23); the absolute and sovereign right to it is his alone.

Christians speak of being "in Christ' rather than "in the land." This recalls an important feature of the book of Joshua. When it describes in detail the allocation of land amongst the tribes of Israel, it notes that Moses had given to the tribe of Levi "no inheritance, since the offerings made by fire to the Lord, the God of Israel, are their inheritance" (13:14). It is a point repeated at the end of the chapter, this time in the words that "the Lord, the God of Israel, is their inheritance . . ." (13:33). In Numbers (1:47), it is recorded that the

---

21. On any account of things, we have to ask what is the precise demarcation of "Israel" in various parts of the Old Testament and how this corresponds to modern Israel. There are other issues: e.g., the original gift of land was tied to what we might describe as a "theocratic" constitution, whereas modern Israel is not constitutionally a Jewish state in a cognate sense.

families in the tribe of Levi were not counted in the otherwise comprehensive tribal census. This is because they had been appointed to be in charge of the tabernacle. What is the connection between this and not being numbered? Is it not, amongst other things, that the tabernacle signifies something more important to take into account than this-worldly space, number and mathematics? When Deuteronomy describes the Levites' office, we read of high privilege: "The Levites have no share or inheritance among their brothers; the Lord is their inheritance" (Deut 10:9; cf. 18:2). Their priestly or ritual responsibilities are discharged in the land and they are dependent on the support of those who live off the land. They receive their allocation of towns (Joshua 21). But the form and substance of this inheritance differ from the treatment meted out to the other tribes. Yet the Levites suffer no deprivation. On the contrary, what they forgo in the way of physical appointment, they more than regain in the way of spiritual privilege.

While the priesthood was not designedly open to all Levites, the Levite responsibility of assisting the priests was a privilege derived from the privileges of priestly ministry. The designation of Israel at Sinai as a "kingdom of priests" (Exod 19:6 — a phrase unique in the Old Testament and patient of more than one interpretation) exalts both priesthood and people at the same time. Priests exercise an institutionally and religiously privileged ministry in a nation in which the institution of kingship and the religious role of prophet would emerge. The royal priesthood once ascribed to Israel is applied in the New Testament to a church that includes Gentiles against the background of a new inheritance which is not that of earthly land, but something imperishably preserved in heaven (1 Pet 1:4; 2:9).[22] It is an idea surely foreshadowed by the provision made for the Levites in the land. When Paul uses the spatial language of being "in Christ," he is describing in richest terms the priestly inheritance of the united Jewish and Gentile people of God in implicit contrast to the inheritance of the particular land of Canaan. While the book of Joshua is preoccupied with land and warfare, the priestly bearing of the ark and Levitical habitation of the towns point to something beyond war and even beyond land, displacing both of them in time. The Levites are a reminder that inheritance in land matters only if that which is greater than land is inherited by those who inherit it. Land is given in order to display righteousness, and it is better to be righteous without land (including in wilderness and exile) than unrighteous in the land.[23]

---

22. However, the fulness of New Testament witness speaks of a new *earth* as well: that particular phrase from Isa 65:17 and 66:22 is picked up in 2 Pet 3:13 and Rev 21:1.

23. The Levites are "an eschatological sign, an arrow into heaven, which pointed beyond

To go back to the land, however, we must also remember indications that do not come to the surface in the book of Joshua — at least, not clearly — but are there in the Pentateuch, that land given to Israel signifies wider divine concern for human possession of land.[24] Deuteronomy 2:1-19 advertises the fact that God has given land to the descendants of Esau and of Lot, and there is a parallel between this and the gift of Canaan to Israel.[25] We are still, of course, in the province of the family of Abraham, but a wider vista is opened out in Deut 32:8 (cf. Acts 17:26). God provides for the sustenance of the human race, and land is part of his provision. But behind the question of land looms the dark specter of violence. If anything problematizes Joshua for readers ancient and modern, it is the merciless extermination of Canaanites, to which we now turn.

The Question of Genocide

The Grim Tale

According to the book of Joshua, God did not only bestow a land upon the people of Israel, he also commanded acts of violent destruction and slaughter. Entry into the land was neither by negotiation nor by treaty, but by military force. "About forty thousand armed for battle crossed over before the Lord to the plains of Jericho for war" (4:13) in a formation bathed in covenant holiness, signified by the presence of the ark. Joshua's encounter with and obeisance to the commander of the Lord's army is "a symbol that all that is to follow is a liturgy of worship," the siege of Jericho constituting "the perfect liturgy."[26] War, victory, and devastation belong to the Lord. The fact that the inhabitants of the land melt in fear is an occasion not for sympathy but for joy and encouragement (2:9-11, 24; 5:1).

In many respects, matters turn out well for the people of Israel. Jericho, including everyone in it except Rahab and family, is destroyed and the city burned, "the silver and gold and the articles of bronze and iron" taken into

---

the land to what it signified"; O'Donovan, "The Loss of a Sense of Place," 51. Granted the reference to Hebrews here and the thought of Canaan as a "heavenly" possession, I should wish to gloss "heaven" as "new heaven and new earth."

24. For some implications, see O'Donovan, "The Loss of a Sense of Place," n. 154.

25. A "quite remarkable one" for C. J. H. Wright, *Deuteronomy*, on 2:9-12.

26. O'Donovan, *The Desire of the Nations*, 42 and 54. For the ark as the palladium of war, see Num 10:35. Childs highlights the distinctiveness of Numbers in connection with this; *Introduction to the Old Testament as Scripture*, 200.

the treasure of the tabernacle (6:24). Ai goes the same way as regards its inhabitants, while livestock and plunder are carried off. Then we have the fall of Makkedah (10:28), followed by a gruesome catalogue: Libnah, Lachish, Eglon, Hebron, Debir. Rounding up the tale of the defeat of the southern cities, the narrator tells us that Joshua "left no survivors. He totally destroyed all who breathed, just as the Lord, the God of Israel, had commanded" (10:40). As it was with the southern, so it transpired with the northern kings.

God was in the midst of it: "For it was the Lord himself who hardened their hearts to wage war against Israel, so that he might destroy them totally, exterminating them without mercy, as the Lord had commanded Moses" (11:20). God is directly involved: "As they [the armies of the Amorite kings] fled before Israel on the road down from Beth Horon to Azekah, the Lord hurled large hailstones down on them from the sky" with fatal consequences (10:11). Holiness and violence are fused. When God is with you, you win, and when he is not, you lose, and when he is not, on account of one man's disobedience, you destroy the entire family of those responsible for defeat (7:24-26). Achan and family go the way the Canaanites must go.

What are we to make of this? The question is an old one. Should we not treat the book of Joshua as Joshua treated the Canaanites, expunge it and seek out an alternative way of life, religious or otherwise, as far removed as possible from its evil influence?[27] Of course, the book of Joshua should not bear the punishment alone, more than Achan bore the punishment alone. Whatever is distinctive in it, Deuteronomy legislates for its actions and, whether or not we can satisfactorily square what is commanded in Deuteronomy with what is executed in Joshua, still Joshua is basically executing what the Lord commanded Moses. Which later canonical prophet would have clearly denounced what Joshua did and how he did it or have seen in the principle of his actions anything but the active hand of the Lord? There is certainly a *prima facie* justification for saying that "there is very little evidence" that either the Old or the New Testament authors "were embarrassed by the story in Joshua."[28] For our part, if we find contemporary notions and practices of holy war or ethnic cleansing abhorrent, much of the Old Testament will have to be dismissed along with Joshua, however we describe the range of Israel's subsequent military actions. So even if we allow that other Israelite wars do

---

27. Many will sympathise with those of whom John Chrysostom wrote long ago that "there are some even so low-minded, and empty, and unworthy of Heaven, as . . . to think that . . . whole books of the Bible are of no use, as Leviticus, Joshua"; *Homily on Romans* XXXI, p. 553.

28. Goldingay, "Justice and Salvation for Israel in Canaan," 1:184. Of course, lack of embarrassment does not of itself entail concurrence.

not take the same form as the military action that marked the occupation of Canaan, the problem will not go away.[29]

Matters are worse still if it turns out that Joshua's actions amount to more than an imitation or instantiation of extra-Israelite practices. In the course of the most poignant treatment of sin in the whole of the Old Testament, Jeremiah declares that Israel can educate the nations in the way of transgression (Jer 2:33). It is alleged that Israel actually introduced "ḥērem ideology and practice into world history" and educates the nations in the way of holy slaughter, *ḥērem* being a word used to describe some of the unsavory destructive practices under consideration — the devotion of people as well as of objects to the curse of destruction.[30] We concentrate here on "ideology"; there are a variety of views on what happened in practice.[31] The God of Joshua not only sanctions war, he orders it. He not only orders war, he leads it. He not only leads it, he commands total extermination. He not only commands total extermination, he abhors mercy. We may conclude that the fact that the battle belongs to the Lord breeds a perverted form of humility. But it does not exactly breed the peacemaker. The whole business, to put it mildly, is nauseatingly repulsive, and nausea is nothing compared to what the alleged victims of Yahweh must have suffered.

Is that how we should see things? Or is it time for "meditation"?[32]

Of course, there is no consensus today on the basis of moral judgment. We are long used to the truism that widespread moral relativism has replaced belief in moral absolutes in Western societies. So what is the presumed basis of our moral judgment when the book of Joshua is brought to its bar? Let everyone speak for her or himself. It is precisely as Christians, professing disciples of Jesus, that many readers are disposed to view the scene laid out before us in the book of Joshua with wordless dismay, the phrase "morally abhorrent" frozen on our lips only because it seems too weak. Is God actually capa-

---

29. A number of distinctions have to be made in relation to warfare which the narrow focus of this essay precludes from discussion, but see Goldingay, *Israel's Gospel*.

30. Cowles in *Show Them No Mercy*, 100. I am unable to judge this claim. What certainly appears to be unfounded is Bainton's general judgment about war in the form of a rhetorical comment on Joshua, that it "is more humane when God is left out of it"; *Christian Attitudes Toward War and Peace*, 49. While not agreeing entirely with his opinion on this book, I think that George Ernest Wright was right to indicate the superficiality of this judgment; Boling and Wright, *Joshua*, 35.

31. Remarks on general questions of historicity are deferred until "Reading Joshua Today," below. More pertinent to the treatment here is the literary question of hyperbole or stylization in the accounts in Joshua. However, our discussion in this essay is conducted independently of our judgments on those issues.

32. Wilson, *Our Father Abraham*, 154.

ble of commanding anything "morally abhorrent"? Could he actually have commanded anything like what he supposedly commanded in these accounts? Is such a representation anything but a religious monstrosity?

As we approach the task of interpreting the book of Joshua on this question, two things should be kept in mind. First, we may be wrongly picturing the situation depicted in Joshua. Whatever we do, we must not picture life in the land of Canaan as peaceful and happy before God's people came along. Before we have arrived at Moses' forthright statement that "it is not because of your righteousness or your integrity that you are going in to take possession of their land; but on account of the wickedness of these nations" (Deut 9:5), the book of Leviticus has graphically described the land of Canaan as "vomiting out" its inhabitants (Lev 18:25-28).[33] Sexual practices and the sacrifice of children to the god Molech are particularly responsible for this description. It is hard to be sure exactly what went on in the sacrificial or dedicatory ceremony that involved Molech, and whatever it was may not have remained constant over the centuries. But Deuteronomy alludes to the detestable practice of burning sons and daughters in fire as a religious sacrifice (Deut 12:31; 18:10), a practice to which there is increasing allusion as the story of the iniquity of the people of Israel reaches its climax in 2 Kings. Cult prostitution in Canaanite culture, both male and female, is implied by the prohibition of such practice in Israel (Deut 23:17-18; cf. Num 25:1-2). These practices were not adopted in Canaan by universal democratic suffrage and a self-determining popular vote. If we shudder at the thought of what happened to disempowered Canaanites at the hands of the people of Israel, let us pause to consider life in the land before they came along. If we assume that the people of Israel had no right to slay inhabitants of the land, let us not assume that the Canaanites had a right to stay in it.

This is not to explain away the problem before us, simply to get the picture as straight as we can. Canaanite life for a sizable number, as for so many in our world today, may have been so nasty and brutish that they might have preferred it to be short. The powerful people and fortified cities which the spies saw in the land testify to the fact that warfare was a standard feature of that scene (Num 13:28; Deut 1:28). Contrast the Laishites, a "peaceful and unsuspecting people" who should not have been attacked.[34] There is a dark and portentous verse as early as Genesis which declares that Abraham's descen-

---

33. Joshua scarcely needs to spell out the extremity of Canaanite decadence: Stone, "Ethical and Apologetic Tendencies in the Redaction of the Book of Joshua," 26.

34. This account is in Judges 18. On the Danites, who were involved in the attack, see Josh 19:40-48.

dants would not return to the land until the sin of the Amorites had "reached its full measure" (15:16).[35] Joshua's violence, however problematic, must be viewed, like the flood, as a form of counterviolence.[36] Nor must we make the subconscious assumption that, left to themselves, as it were, if they had never been fused together into a people, Israelite males, as we meet them in the Pentateuch, would have been nonviolent. This is a hypothetical way of putting the point, but the point itself is that the world in which the Israelites lived, moved, and were constituted as a people was filled with violence, and it is not as though God transformed peace-loving nomads into a fighting machine. The revenge exacted by Simeon and Levi for Shechem's treatment of their sister shows what stuff sons of Jacob could be made of (Gen 34:25-31).

The second point is that the book of Joshua is set in the canonical context of testimony to God's hatred of violence. Following the transgression of Adam and Eve, which disrupted the scene of creation, the first recorded action of humankind that reflects the disrupted order, after God has pronounced his judgment, is Cain's murder of his brother Abel. By the sixth chapter of the opening book of the Pentateuch and the Bible, God is so pained on account of human action that he even "grieved that he had made man on the earth" (Gen 6:6). It is violence that brings on the grief. Violence is not just symptomatic, it is largely constitutive of that corruption (6:5-13). Centuries after Joshua, prophets could look forward to swords being beaten into ploughshares and strife in the animal kingdom subdued "for the earth will be full of the knowledge of the Lord as the waters cover the sea" (Isa 2:4; 11:9). When Jesus arrives on the scene, announcing the kingdom of God and summoning people to discipleship, he acts in apparently stark contrast to his namesake, Joshua, but in line and not in contrast with the prophetic hope for peace.

Hence our revulsion at the scene of slaughter must be accompanied by perplexity because the God who commands slaughter hates violence. Only so long as we keep this in the forefront of our minds, and the picture of life in Canaan in the background of our minds, are we equipped to tackle the dark question that looms before us.

---

35. In light of this, Hamilton (translating the phrase as "run its course") regards "Joshua's invasion as an act of justice rather than of aggression," *The Book of Genesis: Chapters 1–17*, 428, 436. However, his remark strictly refers to the invasion of the land, not to the extermination of its peoples.

36. This is typical of divine violence. See, e.g., the chilling orchestration of killing by the man clothed in linen in Ezekiel 9, an action brought on by Ezek 8:17.

What and Why

What reason is offered in the book of Joshua for the command to practice what we might call "genocide"?[37] The book contains a large number of references to Moses, almost as many, in fact, as we find in the whole of the rest of the Old Testament outside the Pentateuch. Joshua is meant to execute what God has promised and commanded through and to Moses. In the first chapter of Joshua, we hit a note sustained throughout the book: Joshua commands not just *as* Moses commanded, but he also commands *what* Moses commanded. To follow such a command is to do all that God wants done (22:2). Among the commands of Moses that apparently bind Joshua is the command to wipe out all the inhabitants of the land (9:24). After Joshua has totally destroyed the kingdoms of Hazor, "not sparing anything that breathed" (11:11), we read that his total destruction of the northern kingdoms was in accordance with Moses' command. His troops spare livestock and take plunder "but all the people they put to the sword until they completely destroyed them, not sparing anyone that breathed" (11:14). If we perceive apparent discrepancies between the command in Deuteronomy and execution in Joshua, it does little or nothing to alleviate the difficulties that we are considering.

Deuteronomy gives us the reason for what is enacted in Joshua. It is all about idolatry, understood not just as a narrowly religious practice but as a spring of moral and social practice as well. The first commandment following the declaration of deliverance from Egypt reads: "You shall have no other gods before me," and this entails: "You shall not make for yourself an idol in the form of anything" (Deut 5:7-8; cf. Exod 20:3-4). Exodus anticipates the importance attached in Deuteronomy to the question of idolatry (Exod 23:24). Commands both to build and to destroy religious altars are framed by the extreme contrast between the worship of God at Sinai and the apostasy of the golden calf. Upon entry into Canaan, the people of Israel must above all not follow other gods (Deut 6:14). So entry must involve not just the defeat, but also the total destruction of the resident nations. Neither treaty nor intermarriage is permitted and no mercy is to be shown because "they will turn your sons away from following me to serve other gods" (Deut 7:4). The Israelites are to "break down their altars, smash their sacred stones, cut down their Asherah poles and burn their idols in the fire" (7:5). A distinction is drawn

---

37. We are not concerned here about whether the action recorded in the book of Joshua should be technically labelled "genocide." On the omission of any reference to "violence inspired by politics and ideology" in the definition of genocide adopted by the United Nations Convention on the Prevention and Punishment of the Crime of Genocide, see the comments by Amstutz, "Who Is My Neighbor?" 18.

between rules that obtain for warfare in general and those which obtain for the occupation of Canaan in particular. In the former case, battle is to be joined only when a city refuses to make peace and submit to the requirement that its inhabitants must play the role of slaves to the Israelites. In such a case, if hostilities break out, all the men are to be killed, but "as for the women, the children, the livestock and everything else in the city, you may take these as plunder for yourselves" (20:14). Thus with the cities that do not belong to the neighboring nations. By way of contrast, "in the cities of the nations the Lord your God is giving you as an inheritance, do not leave alive anything that breathes. Completely destroy them — the Hittites, Amorites, Canaanites, Perizzites, Hivites and Jebusites — as the Lord your God commanded you. Otherwise, they will teach you to follow all the detestable things they do in worshiping their gods" (20:16-18).

Why is idolatry handled by wholesale extermination rather than edifying assimilation into Israel of, for example, women and children? Does Joshua's policy amount to "a virtual admission that in free and open competition with Canaanite religion, Yahweh worship would lose out"?[38] The question really requires a wide-ranging discussion in socio-anthropology and socio-psychology about how inherited patterns of behavior function and are transmitted; on the effects of trauma on a spared, remnant population; on what male children, once grown, would do to exact vengeance for the slaughter of their fathers. It invites sober consideration of the practical options in light of all of this, but inquiry along these lines is beyond the scope of this essay. So at this point, let us just ask this: if Eve and Adam are portrayed as having transgressed under the most favorable conditions imaginable and the solemn covenant at Sinai was quickly followed by the worship of the golden calf, was it to be expected that the level of Israelite godliness would suffice to absorb and overcome the remnants of idolatry in a subdued and captive population?[39] And if idolatry wins out in Canaan, then where in the world is Yahweh to be known and worshipped? Further, the hypothetical sharing of the land by some sort of treaty arrangement would have kept the Canaanite gods in place.

How crucial an issue idolatry is emerges in the final chapter of Joshua, which reports his speech and the covenant renewal at Shechem. Joshua starts out by reaching back beyond the days when Abraham was called by God: "Long ago your forefathers, including Terah the father of Abraham and

---

38. Cowles, *Show Them No Mercy,* 98.

39. "Israel as it then was, and as its history showed, was not competent, by reason of its own sinfulness, to reform them. Instead of reforming the Canaanites, the Canaanites would have corrupted them, and thus righteousness would have perished from the earth"; Clarke, *The Eternal Saviour-Judge,* 33-34.

Nahor, lived beyond the River and worshiped other gods" (24:2). And Joshua ends: "Now fear the Lord and serve him with all faithfulness. Throw away the gods your forefathers worshiped beyond the River and in Egypt, and serve the Lord. But if serving the Lord seems undesirable to you, then choose for yourselves this day whom you will serve, whether the gods your forefathers served beyond the River, or the gods of the Amorites, in whose land you are living" (24:14-15). When the people responds affirmatively, Joshua presses his point (24:19-20). The people correspondingly presses its response. So Joshua concludes the matter: "Throw away the foreign gods that are among you and yield your hearts to the Lord, the God of Israel" (24:23). The battle for the land is a clash between Yahweh and the gods, just as the slaughter of the Egyptian firstborn, which broke Pharaoh's opposition, was a blow in the battle with the gods of Egypt (Exod 12:12; Num 33:4).

This is the context of the *ḥērem* which is a feature of this "holy war" or, better, "Yahweh war."[40] The word is not easy to translate with succinct precision. It contains the element of destruction, but, more specifically, it is to "place under the ban." We might formulate the idea in terms of "uncompromising consecration without possibility of recall or redemption."[41] If we regard the literal sense of the word as applying to objects, then we could say that, just as objects were literally devoted to the ban, so the Canaanites are metaphorically devoted to destruction as *ḥērem*. However, the metaphor can be used in a different way. In Deuteronomy, *ḥērem* has been termed a "metaphor for religious fidelity which has only two primary expressions, neither of which involves the taking of life."[42] In Joshua, of course, the taking of life is involved.[43] The practices followed in the course of occupation vary. Jericho,

---

40. "Yahweh war" may be preferable because, among other reasons, it can signify that Joshua's military action should not be regarded as just one instance of a generic transreligious, transcultural phenomenon which goes under the name of "holy war."

41. So Lilley, "Understanding the *Herem*," 177. See also Lilley, "The Judgment of God." On the complexity of the biblical materials, see Niditch, *War in the Hebrew Bible*. For an important essay on the semantic field of *ḥērem* and the appropriateness of talking about genocide, see Nelson, "*Hērem* and the Deuteronomic Social Conscience."

42. Moberly, "Toward an Interpretation of the Shema," 135. For some important conceptual issues, see also Moberly, "A Dialogue with Gordon McConville on Deuteronomy," including McConville's response. See too Moberly's allusion to McConville's discussion of metaphor on 525, n. 29.

43. It is also possible to contrast *ḥērem* as an ideal with a realistic application of it. The contrast between "real" and "ideal" should not be collapsed into the distinction between "literal" and "metaphorical." When *ḥērem* applies to the literal taking of life, the question arises of whether such application should be a total, wholesale, and comprehensive one or one that is circumscribed in some way. If it is the former, we might call it "ideal"; if the latter, "real."

the first fruits of the conquest, retains its booty intact whereas Ai is plundered.⁴⁴ In neither case is the people spared.

Disturbingly, to all appearances, the practice of destroying people is a particularly apt expression of love for God. "The nature of Israel's love for YHWH is particularly expressed in the *ḥērem* command."⁴⁵ Deuteronomy spells this out. We may want to take *ḥērem* as a metaphor for radical obedience and argue for a reading of Joshua as an edifying (!) type or allegory of spiritual warfare. But however we strive to mitigate difficulties by distinguishing different readings of Joshua and contexts for reading Joshua, we are textually faced with a divine command to slaughter an entire population on grounds of idolatry, a command textually obeyed in savagely literal form. What contribution do we make to the peace, safety, and well-being of our world if we worship and commend a God who, the book of Joshua tells us, issued such a command?

Did God Really Say . . . ?⁴⁶

Whether or not it is right to say that his "is the most direct and honest commentary on Joshua," there is no doubt that Calvin's approach to divine command has been massively influential.⁴⁷ And although voices will scream that the last thing we must consider doing is to take his approach to divine command, his bold way of grasping the nettle, along with his influence, entitles it to be given special consideration. The bottom line, as far as Calvin was concerned, is that what God commanded was just, simply because it was God that commanded it. On the slaughter in Jericho, Calvin commented: "As he, in whose hands are life and death, had justly doomed those nations to destruction, this puts an end to all discussion."⁴⁸ As to why a whole people was pun-

---

44. Campbell remarks that it "is as if Jericho bore the initial symbolism of total ban, total dedication to Israel's God, and the subsequent experiences in the narrative could be relaxed once the high point had been established"; "The Growth of Joshua 1–12 and the Theology of Extermination," 78.

45. MacDonald, *Deuteronomy and the Meaning of "Monotheism,"* 3. MacDonald's treatment of *ḥērem* as metaphor is also important. See too Moberly on the connection between Deuteronomy 7 and the love commandment, "Toward an Interpretation of the Shema," 134. We recall that Abraham's fidelity to God was supremely tested at the point where he was willing to raise the knife to kill his son Isaac.

46. Gen 3:1. Thus spoke the serpent.

47. Goetz, "Joshua, Calvin, and Genocide," 263.

48. *Commentaries on the Book of Joshua.* This comment is on Josh 6:20. From now on, I refer in the text to the chapter and verse in Joshua on which Calvin is commenting.

ished for the sin of Achan, our minds are to be kept "in suspense until the books are opened, when the divine judgments which are now obscured by our darkness will be most perfectly clear" (7:1). And as for the apparent cruelty to the children executed along with Achan, "what here remains for us, but to acknowledge our weakness and submit to his [God's] incomprehensible counsel?" (7:24). Joshua's destruction of the southern cities admittedly constituted a "detestable cruelty . . . surpassing anything of which we read as having been perpetrated by savage tribes scarcely raised above the level of the brutes." Yet, because it was commanded by God, the action was morally right, for "the judgment-seat of heaven is not subject to our laws" (10:40). This is not the first time that Calvin has made the point that what would have been horribly inhuman if perpetrated through human bloodthirsty motivation is not inhumane if commanded by God (6:20). Further, when commenting on the crossing over of Reuben, Gad, and Manasseh into Canaan, Calvin discusses the question of why only forty thousand crossed, just one third of the number in the recent census. His answer is: because Moses did not intend every man to leave his wife and children behind, for "it would have been harsh and cruel to leave an unwarlike multitude unprotected in the midst of many hostile nations" (4:12-13). So harshness and cruelty are normally morally reprehensible.[49]

At the same time as he appeals to God's inscrutable justice, Calvin seeks to provide some explanation for the ways of God. God had borne with Jericho for a long time — four hundred years — before destroying it on account of its defilement. The southern kingdoms were polluted; hence Joshua's action. And children? Infants, reprobate offspring of Adam's accursed race, deserve to die. If God willed to exempt any who died in the slaughter from the Adamic curse — that is, if some infants were among the elect — "it may be that death proved to them a medicine" (7:24). However, what matters is that the justice of divine command is axiomatic and the justification for Joshua's obedient action is consequently and indisputably established. The main line of Calvin's exposition is sustained in contemporary treatments. In a volume which aims to set out four views on God and Canaanite genocide, three contributors are close to each other and to Calvin on this point.[50] "The issue . . . cannot be whether or not genocide is intrinsically good or evil — its sanction by a holy God settles that question."[51] The holiness, justice, and wisdom of

---

49. Slaughter of Canaanite animals provides no problem for Calvin because animals "were created for the sake of men and thus deservedly to follow the fate of their owners" (7:24).

50. Cowles et al., *Show Them No Mercy*. These four views are not meant to be representative of contemporary theology or biblical studies, but are meant to comprise intra-"conservative" options.

51. These are the words of Eugene Merrill in Cowles et al., *Show Them No Mercy*, 93.

God make the slaughter unquestionably right. In fact, what is amazing in life is that anyone is ever spared: "It is divine mercy . . . that the human family is allowed to continue to exist."[52] The squeamish might remember that Jesus' eventual triumph over his enemies will make Joshua's slaughter seem like a picnic.[53]

With words like these ringing in our ears, and given our topic in any case, is it not heinous to approach our subject dispassionately? No, the boot is on the other foot. A dispassionate approach, in the appropriate and proper sense of that word, is all the more necessary when such a direly emotive matter is before us and when people's beliefs on God, humanity, life, and death are in practice so momentous. So let us pick out at least three suppositions that inform versions of the argument that we are considering. First, the people of the land were corrupt and deserved what they got. Second, infants who played no active part in such a corrupt scene deserve neither life nor mercy, for they are damnable and damned in Adam. Third, God's ways are unquestionably just, wise, and good as well as holy. Are we to believe this?

The third point is the only one to which we can attend. In relation to the first, some who reject the other two points will maintain that culpable perpetrators of corruption deserved death. Constraints of space forbid discussion of the question of how far we are in any position to apply appropriate notions of guilt, desert, and penalty to the situation under consideration and of the wider question of slaughter in war and the judicial sentence of death. We pass them by especially because the extermination of the powerless, rather than the relatively powerful, is what normally troubles people most.[54] In relation to the second point, the question of God's condemnation of infants born in solidarity with Adam and in original sin also raises too many independent questions to be addressed here. Similar theologies of original sin will not necessarily yield similar perspectives on the question of infant destruction. And the notion of original sin, never mind what use we make of it in connection with the destruction of the Canaanites, has been described by the most thorough and erudite of contemporary conservative theologians as a "riddle" not satisfactorily resolved for two millennia.[55] In allowing considerations of space

---

52. Daniel Gard in Cowles et al., *Show Them No Mercy*, 104.

53. Or, as Gard puts it: "The final judgment with its utter destruction of the heavens and the earth and all those at enmity with God makes the most bloody warfare narratives of the Old Testament seem like children's bedtime stories"; Cowles et al., *Show Them No Mercy*, 56.

54. When Horton says that holy wars are no more unjust than final judgment (*Covenant and Eschatology*, 163), he invites the question: "Is the final judgment relatively indiscriminate?"

55. Blocher, *Original Sin*, finds himself dissatisfied with previous attempts to resolve the problem and proposes his own resolution.

to veto discussion again, I do not for a moment doubt the importance of our views on children and original sin for the question at hand or pretend that they can be the subject of cool appraisal.

So we move on to the third proposition. Some who are disposed to reject one or both of the first two arguments may remain convinced that there exists a God who commanded the slaughter of the Canaanites; this we must believe even if we cannot explain it. The justice of God is unimpeachable, though inscrutable, and we can say little more than this. To put in syllogistic terms what may seem utterly callous to handle syllogistically:

(1) Anything God commands is just, by virtue of the fact that God commands it.
(2) God commanded the slaughter of the Canaanites.
(3) Therefore, the slaughter of the Canaanites was just.[56]

The reasoning is valid because the conclusion follows from the premises.[57] Are the premises correct?

The first premise, even if it is granted, needs explanation. For what do we mean by "just"? In the Torah, God taught Israel how to behave "justly," and he loves to see justice practiced towards widow and orphan, as the prophets particularly bring to light. Christians view Jesus Christ as the revelation, within appropriate limits, not just of the divine will but also of the divine nature. God's justice therefore has an open and public dimension which not only permits but actually compels us to ask what meaning we assign to the word "just" when it appears in this argument. Not all God's ways must lie open before us before we can say that he is just in all his ways. But if Christians subscribe to the first premise, it must be in awareness that "God" names "the God of Jesus Christ," "the God who revealed himself in Jesus Christ," "the God who was in Jesus Christ," and that his justice is partly a revealed justice.

However, should we not cut to the chase and insist that the difficulty lies in the second premise? Why not hold a view that has been around for a very long time, namely, that the book of Joshua records a culturally-relative per-

---

56. The argument is stated generally. It could be tightened up to allow for the fact that impure human motives might have operated in the slaughter (such as glee in hacking someone to death), thus qualifying the justice of the action. And the first premise calls out to be unpacked in order to explain more exactly the relation of commandment to justice. Calvin himself denied that the justice of a commandment was separable from the justice of God's nature; see Helm, *John Calvin's Ideas*, ch. 11.

57. Though, strictly speaking, the verb tenses in the premises should be aligned to secure validity.

ception that God commanded genocide, not a commandment actually issued by any "God"? This point of view advertises what has been in any case clear from the outset of our discussion, namely that our conflicting positions on slaughter in Joshua characteristically come down to differing views of Scripture. However, this means that, yet again, the importance of this question is matched only by the impossibility of addressing it in an essay dedicated to this particular issue. So I just note that, if we deny the second premise, much in the Old Testament unravels. God allegedly promised Abraham a land. But was it truly promised? If so, how was it meant to be possessed? Does the book of Deuteronomy, and so the Torah, radically misrepresent what any living deity might have told a people? Were the prophets rooted in traditions and assumptions about what God had willed for Israel which were mistaken at their heart and not just rough at the margins? Many will find the answers to these questions tolerably straightforward, one way or the other. All we can do here is to note the far-reaching nature of denial (and, of course, affirmation) of the second premise.

For some adherents of the Christian Scriptures, the dilemma faced here may be poignantly described in terms of being forced to choose between God and Scripture.[58] Either we protect the authority and integrity of Scripture, Joshua included, and so place God's reputation under a black cloud, or we insist that no such cloud be allowed to pass over his character and instead devote Joshua, along with much of the Old Testament treated in the New as the word of God, to something of a significant ban. But must anyone at all be impaled on the horns of this dilemma? In what follows, I hope that I can accommodate the concerns of at least some of those readers who completely reject the terms in which I have been stating the dilemma and their underlying presuppositions.

Radical Accommodation

At the root of the difficulty facing us as we read the book of Joshua is the existential reality of evil and suffering. The problem of evil is not thrust upon the Bible; it is paraded within its pages. The presence of the serpent in Eden, made by God who made all things good, constitutes a blatant theological problem on the very surface of the text and implies a warning against metaphysical explanations of the existence of evil. But whatever it is that incites the original couple into disobedience, it is not God — in fact, his antithesis.

---

58. To get a handle on some broader issues and discussion surrounding this in contemporary theology, see Vanhoozer, *First Theology*, 141-58.

The evil which proceeds in flood from the human heart, once sin has set in, is, correspondingly, the antithesis of what God wanted to see there. But if God does not cause evil, neither does he eliminate it.[59] Nor does he passively allow it to rage. If the river that bears the muck of human violence does not flow from the throne of God, it is nevertheless not left to its depradations unchannelled. "The Lord detests the way of the wicked" (Prov 15:9), and "the Lord detests the thoughts of the wicked" (15:26). Even so, while "to man belong the plans of the heart . . . from the Lord comes the reply of the tongue" (Prov 16:1), and while "in his heart a man plans his course . . . the Lord determines his steps" (16:9). The course of evil, tracked all the way from the disposition of the heart through desire, motive, intention, and plan to concrete action, and considered in all the varied phases of its unfolding and congealing, is not the product at every stage of a pure (or impure) autonomous impulse. If good divine action in creation has allowed space for evil human action in the fall, human action in a fallen world cannot expel concurrent divine action in that same world. We may not be able to synthesize the Old Testament materials so as to produce one neat scheme of divine action, but one thing that God does is to channel the actions of the human heart, evil and deceitful as it constitutionally is (Jer 17:9). If and where God ever commands what he abhors, we may be sure that he does so with a heavy heart and as the alternative to wiping out evil and suffering at a stroke, on the one hand, and turning his back on it so that it follows its own godless course, on the other.[60]

What is missing from Calvin's account, and that of many who agree with him, is any sense of this.[61] If God commands violence, it is part of a whole concessionary scheme of operation, an accommodation to the fact of rampant evil which he detests but has not abolished. If Canaanite genocide was divinely commanded, must we not think along these lines? In that case, the commandment expresses divine nature — particularly holiness and goodness — only in the most partial and qualified way and under universally

---

59. The conclusion that God does not cause evil indeed assumes a reading of Scripture that goes beyond the narrative in Genesis. Perhaps it is worth remarking that Isa 45:7 in particular should not be taken as a claim that God fashioned metaphysical evil, an impression which we might gain from some translations.

60. Goldingay makes a point similar to this when he speaks of God "getting his hands dirty"; "Justice and Salvation for Israel in Canaan," 184.

61. I include contributors to Cowles et al., *Show Them No Mercy.* However, Calvin's general position should not be judged solely by his commentary on Joshua. For some of the complexities in his position, see David Wright, "Calvin's Pentateuchal Criticism." This was one of many of Wright's contributions to this question. See now Balserak's helpful essay on *Divinity Compromised;* some discussion of Joshua is included in this work, e.g., pp. 72 and 85.

fractured conditions of violence.⁶² Moreover God has a specific historical purpose in mind. It is impossible to emphasise this too strongly.⁶³ To justify genocidal practice under any other conditions is to eliminate the context in which this particular act is narrated. It is to refuse Jesus Christ as the Lord of Scripture and it is to read Scripture as the product of another God than the one revealed in him.⁶⁴ The book of Joshua does not justify genocide. It narrates a particular history. If anyone says that it nevertheless invites imitation today, that can only be on condition that the revelation and imitation of Christ is rejected. And if these are rejected, we are no longer authorized to use the Old Testament as Christian Scripture.

Jesus insisted that Old Testament regulations governing divorce were evidence not of divine approval of the practice but of divine permission in a world of hard-heartedness (Matt 19:8). *Something* of God's nature is revealed in the relevant Mosaic legislation, for, within the bounds of accommodation to the status quo, care is shown for the unprotected woman and that is to the good. While we cannot use this as an exact analogy to what God *commands* in the case of Joshua, the words of Jesus aid our interpretation.⁶⁵ Joshua's action was designed to be the decisive step towards establishing in the land a people that would be holy and conduct itself in ways that would be a witness to the beauty of divine justice, compassion, and, ultimately, peace. In contrast, Canaanite practice was ethically opposite to the principles God had laid down for his people, principles laid down ultimately for the sake of his world. In that respect, *something* of divine holiness comes to light in the account of Joshua's actions. But God works within a situation radically alien, completely opposite, to his nature. What the Israelites presumably did not know, and did not need to know, was that God commanded with a heavy heart. We can say both that genocide is evil and that God commanded genocide if we distinguish the presence of evil in the world, which God can never command, from the manifestation of its forms, which he is at liberty to direct. This is not to

---

62. Barth's words thus need to be qualified: "Either we hear it [his command] as the command of His goodness (even though it is a command to shoot) or we do not hear it at all"; *Church Dogmatics*, II/2:712. See Craigie's judicious comments in *The Problem of War in the Old Testament*, 42.

63. Cf. Bonhoeffer's wider-ranging comment: "Israel's wars were the only 'holy' wars the world has ever known"; *Discipleship*, 138.

64. I make no assumptions here about what Jewish commentators on Joshua are bound to affirm or deny.

65. The different forms of the question and answer in the two accounts in Matt 19:3-8 and Mark 10:2-5 are interesting for anyone who wants to look into the distinction between divine commandment and divine permission. The "casuistic' formulation of divorce injunctions in Deut 24:1-4 constitutes a disanalogy with the command to slaughter Canaanites.

say that Joshua was an evil and not a good man. He is not a "dark Messiah."⁶⁶ It is to say that he was instrumental in God's hands according to the evils of our world in his place and time.

It would be possible to submit a more refined and rigorous formulation of the position adopted here, though without pretending to offer a full resolution of the problem that we face. And I am taking the narrative as it stands. For now, we simply indicate what appears to be a promising direction in dealing with matters so painful that refined and rigorous formulations sometimes seem better vomited out than spelled out.⁶⁷

Conclusion

As the book of Revelation draws to its close, a rider on a white horse, called "Faithful and True," rides out to conquer. "With justice he judges and makes war. . . . He is dressed in a robe dipped in blood, and his name is the Word of God. The armies of heaven were following him . . ." (Rev 19:11-14). Discussing the Canaanite genocide, one writer has described this as the scene of the "great and final *ḥerem*."⁶⁸ While this description is not committed to the view that eschatological divine action will be literally martial, the implication is that this apocalyptic imagery should deter us from being too squeamish about Canaanite genocide.

This is profoundly mistaken. The Christ of the apocalypse is portrayed as identical with the Jesus that was heard, seen, and touched, and this Jesus is surely his interpreter. Doubtless it is dangerous to presume to understand and to know all about Jesus by excessively confident inferences from the Gospel materials or uncritical appeal to our own experience. But let us judge the apocalyptic portrayal by the man of flesh and blood, for he who has seen the Son has seen the Father and the flesh of the Son is the medium through which the eyes of the spirit are illuminated (John 14:9). While the imagery of war conveys with unparalleled force the conflict described in the book of Revelation, it is precisely the contrast between the slain Lamb and the slaying pow-

---

66. Wolfe's characterisation of Hitler, *You Can't Go Home Again*, ch. 38.
67. Gordon McConville is a native of Northern Ireland and Stephen Williams has lived and taught there since 1994. We are familiar with the chilling sight of murals portraying texts from Deuteronomy that advocate the extermination of the enemy, designed for contemporary application in the days of "the Troubles" in Northern Ireland. For an account of the impact on political histories of notions of covenant rooted in the Old Testament (although he is a little shaky on the Old Testament itself), see Akenson, *God's Peoples*.
68. Daniel Gard in *Show Them No Mercy*, 102-106.

ers of evil that informs the book.⁶⁹ Far from diminishing it, this fact makes the thought of divine wrath extremely sobering. The reality and consequences of judgment in all their force and weight cannot be gainsaid. The literary form of apocalyptic writing should not conceal from us the truth that the day of accommodated action will be over. God's judgment will not only be perfect in purity, love, and justice; it will be seen to be so.

God's revelation of himself in Jesus Christ shows how profound is that grief of God over human violence which is described in the opening chapters of Genesis, and it shows us that the divine will of the Warrior God is not our guide to the divine nature of the Crucified God.⁷⁰ Jesus' life, ministry, and death do not simply witness to the way in which God temporarily operates in a new dispensation, only to be superseded by the eschatological return of the Warrior God with a vengeance, trading in the inexperienced colt of Luke 19:30 for the white horse of Rev 19:11.⁷¹ There *is* a new eschatological dispensation still to come, but our best guide to the nature and disposition of the figures in its drama is the nature and disposition of God as he has been revealed to us in Jesus. It does not detract from the apocalyptic revelation of Jesus Christ if we center our notions of God on the revealed character of Jesus Christ. On the contrary, we rightly appropriate apocalyptic insight only when we do so from a center in historical revelation.⁷²

In our day, it is the servant-king that gives guidance on how to relate to friend and antagonist alike. This is to contextualize and not to scorn the Old Testament. It is to allow God to give Joshua the instructions fitting for him when there was a land to be possessed and allow God to give us the instructions fitting for us when Christ is possessed.⁷³

---

69. For valuable guidance here, see Bauckham, *The Climax of Prophecy*, ch. 8; and, more generally, *The Theology of the Book of Revelation*. Note that Rev 22:3 can be translated in terms of the "curse of war," which connects it with *ḥērem*: see Aune, *Revelation 17–22*, 1178-79.

70. "Over and over again, Christians have forgotten that God the Warrior became the Crucified God"; Craigie, *The Problem of War*, 100.

71. See the rich commingling of motifs in this respect in Zech 9-14.

72. Nothing said here implies denial of judgment and perdition or of their seriousness. But surely it is the scriptural testimony to Jesus rather than the scriptural testimony to Joshua that must primarily mold our thinking on these matters.

73. Among the relevant hermeneutical issues debated in specifically conservative circles that we have been unable to address, see those that feature in the discussion between I. Howard Marshall and Kevin Vanhoozer in Marshall, *Beyond the Bible*, 66-67 and 85. A recent study which furnishes a useful broader context for our discussion is that of Swartley, *Covenant of Peace*, which includes a discussion of Revelation (ch. 12). Barth characterizes God as "eternal peace" in *Church Dogmatics* II/1: 505 and later observes that "Christian thinking revolves around God's Word of the covenant of peace"; *The Humanity of God*, 57.

Idolatry

At Stake

"The principal crime of the human race, the highest guilt charged upon the world, the whole procuring cause of judgment, is idolatry. For, although each single fault retains its own proper feature, although it is destined to judgment under its own proper name also, yet it is marked off under the *general* account of idolatry."[74] In a nutshell, "in idolatry all crimes are detected, and in all crimes idolatry." So Tertullian began his treatise on this subject. If the Old Testament is our guide, this is on the mark. As idolatry brought the judgment of God upon the Canaanite occupants of the land, the same thing happened with their Israelite successors. If extermination was the penalty for the one, exile was the penalty for the other.

What was idolatry and what made it evil? Although it is directly treated more often in the Old than in the New Testament, its significance is not on that account diminished in the New. The last book in the Christian canon, after striking an Old Testament note with reference to "idols of gold, silver, bronze, stone and wood — idols that cannot see or hear or walk" (Rev 9:20), refers to those excluded from the holy city as "the dogs, those who practice magic arts, the sexually immoral, the murderers, the idolaters, and everyone who loves and practices falsehood" (22:15; cf. 21:8).[75]

We have noted how Joshua highlights the issue of idolatry in his final speech. Israel has a "fundamental option."[76] It can worship Yahweh or it can associate itself religiously with the peoples remaining in the land. The latter will involve invoking, swearing by, bowing down to, and serving their gods (23:7). Religious obeisance is inseparable from doing the will of the gods. The first time that the worship of other gods is prohibited after the Decalogue in Exodus, this connection is explicitly stated: "You are not to worship their gods, you are not to serve them, and you are not to do their will."[77] If Israel nonetheless does this, it will be violating the covenant made with God. Indeed, idolatry is the essence of covenant violation (23:16). This is the case whether the gods in question are those worshipped in the past by Abraham, before his summons from Mesopotamia, or those worshipped in the present

---

74. Tertullian, *On Idolatry*, p. 61.
75. Rev 9:20-21, which refers to "demons" just before idols, also lists "murders . . . magic arts . . . sexual immorality" and "thefts."
76. Rahner's *option fondementale*, which phrase I am borrowing, is expounded in "The Theology of Freedom."
77. Exod 23:24 as Durham renders it in *Exodus*, 310.

by the Amorites resident in Canaan (24:15) and whether or not the same gods are involved in both cases. Israel as a whole eventually not only chose idolatry, but persisted with this option, a persistence with long temporal roots when we remember Joshua's allusion to gods worshipped "beyond the River and in Egypt" (24:14).[78]

In sliding terminologically from speaking of "idols" to speaking of "gods," we are true to an identification found within the compass of the Old Testament itself. Its language of "god," "gods," or even "God" is not too readily susceptible to the kind of conceptual analysis that has been such a constant feature in the Western intellectual tradition. The pages of the Old Testament do not offer a deliberate account of the relation between the act of fashioning an idol by human hands and the question of the independent existence of gods. Over the centuries, diverse concepts and categories have been deployed in both the wider study of religions and study of the Old Testament in particular: monotheism (worship of or belief in the existence of one god/God); henotheism (a tribe or people cleaves to one god with monotheistic devotion, but without being committed to strict monotheistic belief); kathenotheism (worship of one god at a time); polytheism (belief in and worship of many gods). Although such categorical distinctions doubtless risk imposing on the Old Testament data inappropriate classificatory schemes, they may be helpful in principle, if the risk is taken into account. Having said that, applying them confidently to all the religious phenomena encountered in the Old Testament is difficult, not least because we have to reckon with the development of Israelite belief, worship, and response to other religious practices over the course of many centuries. It is not denied that we could come up with a reasonably clear, if rather broad, account of the relation of "idol" to "god" and to "demon" and that this might yield a fruitful, if cautious, theological or philosophical account. But we shall not attempt this and shall instead concentrate attention on preoccupations on the surface in the biblical texts.[79]

Israelite idolatry is both one with and distinct from the idolatry of surrounding peoples. The idols may be the same ones, producing the same ill ef-

---

78. Cf. the treatment of Egypt in Ezekiel 20 and 23; also Lev 17:7, which presumably refers to the wilderness period.

79. For some relevant identifications and distinctions from the most influential of the Latin Fathers, see the sustained treatment in Part 1 of Augustine's *Concerning the City of God against the Pagans*. Reference to "idol" or "image" is less frequent in this part of his work than to "demons," "gods," and "unclean spirits." Augustine's use of the LXX is significant; for one example among many, see his appeal to Ps 96:4 in IX.23. Idols, demons, and assorted gods all appear together in Deut 32:16-17, although the word here rendered "demons" is rare in the Old Testament. Cf. 1 Cor 8:4-6; 10:19-21.

fects. However, in the case of Israel, idolatry is a breach of the covenant, unfaithfulness to Yahweh. If we regard idolatry strictly in terms of external practice, then unfaithfulness to Yahweh compounds rather than constitutes the wrong of idolatry; that is, there is an intrinsic wrong attached to it even when practised outside of the covenant. This does not diminish the enormity of Israel's peculiar transgression. Unfaithfulness is more than a supplementary misdeed to the practices of the nations. Nowhere is idolatry more poignantly described than by the prophet Jeremiah and he sums up, on God's behalf, the dual aspect of Israelite idolatry: "My people have committed two sins: They have forsaken me, the spring of living water, and have dug their own cisterns, broken cisterns that cannot hold water" (2:13). What practices are we looking at?[80]

Practices of the Nations

Names of various deities pepper the pages of the Old Testament. Before we reach the book of Joshua, the figure of Molech, for example, has turned up in Leviticus (20:2-5) and makes its detestable return as Israel heads towards rupture and then exile (1 Kgs 11:5-7; 2 Kgs 23:10-13). Before we are half way into the book of Judges, we learn that the Israelites have served "the gods of Aram, the gods of Sidon, the gods of Moab, the gods of the Ammonites and the gods of the Philistines" (Judg 10:6). Two specific references preface this list: Israel "served the Baals and the Ashtaroth" (RSV). This is not the first that we hear of them in the book of Judges. After Joshua's death and that of his generation, "there arose another generation after them, who did not know the Lord or the work which he had done for Israel . . . and they provoked the Lord to anger. They forsook the Lord, and served the Baals and the Ashtaroth" (Judg 2:10-13 RSV). No words or names more darken the Old Testament.

We start with Baal. The word "Baal" has a wide range. It can denote "protector," so that God can be Israel's "Baal"; it can apparently denote a *type* of deity and is used in the plural, or it can be used as a proper name, like "Molech." Between the exodus from Egypt and entry into Canaan, two major incidents of idolatry in Israel are recorded. One is the incident of the golden calf which took place when Moses was still with God on Sinai. In a grotesque

---

80. There is a raft of issues here that is worth probing, but must be left to one side, particularly in connection with the way in which God's covenant with Israel raises the question of the proper referent of the word "god"/"God." See N. T. Wright's "Preface" to *The New Testament and the People of God*. Intriguing and potentially significant questions of detail arise as well, e.g., what exactly is going on with Naaman in 2 Kgs 5:18?

parody of what was rightfully owed to Yahweh, the calf was crafted from gold earrings and credited with the deliverance of the people from Egypt. An altar was built for it, and it was the recipient of both burnt and fellowship offerings. The worship of the calf was accompanied and followed by something of an orgy (Exod 32:1-6). There is no explicit allusion here to Baal or the Ashtaroth, nor does Joshua explicitly allude to the incident. It is otherwise, however, in the second case, and there may be an important connection between the idolatry involved here and the idolatry of the golden calf.[81]

When describing God's blessings on the journey from Egypt to the promised land, Joshua picks out the way that God prevented Balaam from putting a curse on Israel, turning his words into reiterated blessing (24:10). But Joshua did not do what Moses had done, which was to draw attention to the dark side of that story in his opening speech to the people of Israel in Deuteronomy, shortly before addressing in detail the question of idolatry (Deut 4:3, 15-31). The dark side featured Baal of Peor. Israel's journey along the plains of Moab excited the worry of Balak, king of Moab, who instructed Balaam to curse Israel (Num 22:6). Balaam did not do so, but another kind of curse fell on the people because "while Israel was staying in Shittim, the men began to indulge in sexual immorality with Moabite women, who invited them to the sacrifices to their gods. The people ate and bowed down before these gods. So Israel joined in worshipping the Baal of Peor. And the Lord's anger burned against them" (Num 25:1-3). The outcome was memorable. A devastating plague reputedly killed twenty-four thousand (25:4-18). Worship of other gods involves indulgent promiscuity, bringing down the divine curse. Baal subsequently leaves his imprint on the pages of the Old Testament more prominently than any other deity.

Ashtoreth was a consort of Baal and associated with him in 1 Samuel as well as in the book of Judges (1 Sam. 7:4; 12:10). Like "Baal," the name comes in singular or plural form, as a proper noun, or what we might call a kind of "classifying" term. As the references to Baal accumulate in the two books of Kings, so Ashtoreth appears on the scene. Solomon's wives lead him astray in his old age and he follows "Ashtoreth the goddess of the Sidonians," along

---

81. This rather depends on how much we make of the sexual connotation of the "revelry" of which we read in Exod 32:6 (the Hebrew text is more forthcoming than the LXX at this point). The calf idolatry is highlighted in Neh 9:18 and memorably captured in Poussin's painting "The Adoration of the Golden Calf." It is a matter for debate what exactly Jeroboam was doing, or thought he was doing, or was taken by the Israelites to be doing when he made two golden calves and referred to them as deliverers from Egypt (1 Kgs 12:28). See also 2 Chr 13:8 and the references in Hosea which begin at 8:5. Indeed, what is the connection in the people's mind between Yahweh and the calf, according to the account in Exodus itself?

with "Molech the detestable god of the Ammonites" (1 Kgs 11:5). Later, we learn that Chemosh, god of the Moabites, was also implicated (1 Kgs 11:33). When Josiah waged war against idolatry in the second half of the seventh century in what turned out to be practically a last-ditch attempt to purge Judah of idolatry before the exile, these three are named again, Ashtoreth being described as "vile," in line with the way the others are described (2 Kgs 23:13).

There was a city called "Ashtaroth," presumably historically associated with the goddess Ashtoreth, and most of the few biblical references to that city occur in the book of Joshua. What is especially dark is its wider connection with the Sidonians (to which 1 Kings 11 alludes) and not the connection with ruler Og in particular (Josh 9:10). To see why, we go back to Genesis. When we are introduced to Canaan in Genesis, we are introduced to wrongdoing. Ham, son of Noah, is guilty of some kind of lewd behavior in relation to his drunk and naked father (Gen 9:22-24). Just before the incident is narrated, Ham is described as the "father of Canaan," and his action is subsequently pointedly ascribed to "Ham, the father of Canaan." While Noah blesses by name Ham's brothers Shem and Japheth, who had covered their father's nakedness, it is a case of: "Cursed be Canaan" (Gen 9:24-27). Canaan's firstborn son was called Sidon. The place called Sidon at one time defined one of Canaan's borders (Gen 10:19). The Sidonians who appear in Josh 13:6 (and see 13:4) stand under the curse brought on by the sexual indecency of Sidon's grandfather against the great-grandfather who had found such favor with God. The notorious Jezebel is daughter to the king of the Sidonians (1 Kgs 16:31).[82]

The Old Testament makes a profound and consistent connection between the worship of other gods and evil conduct.[83] It is the other side of the decalogical coin that joins the worship of God with holy conduct. Baal and other gods corrupt. No biblical book is bleaker than the book of Judges in its account of lawless violence, an account offered under the rubric of large-scale, sometimes wholesale, heedlessness of Joshua's warning and exhortation. The Baals moved in with a speed (Judg 2:11) — or, rather, did not move out with an intransigence — that reminds us of how quickly the affair of the golden calf followed the giving of the Ten Commandments, or how soon after the covenant Ham transgressed against Noah, and even brings to mind the story of the fall occurring so swiftly after creation. If any passage in the His-

---

82. Note Jesus' reference to Sidon in Matt 11:21-22 and Luke 10:13-14.
83. So I wonder whether Barth should be as surprised as he is when he says that "in the Old Testament the rejection of heathen religion is directed with a surprising onesidedness against its idolatry"; *Church Dogmatics* I/2:303.

torical Books sums up the story of Israel from exodus to the exile of the northern kingdom, it is 2 Kings 17, which gives a theological explanation for exile. Worship of other gods has involved both public evil practices and clandestine evil, both imitation of other nations' practices and supplementary practices of the Israelites' own. According to Jeremiah, the people of Israel could teach the nations a thing or two in this respect (Jer 2:33).[84] Calf idols, Asherah poles, bowing down to the starry hosts, and worshipping Baal are joined to the practice of divination, sorcery, and the sacrifice of sons and daughters in fire.[85] It is a sorry catalogue of which we are constantly reminded later in 2 Kings as well, as the rest of the book goes on to tell of what happened in Judah so that it, too, experienced exile. Manasseh, one of its kings, rebuilt the high places, brought Baal and Asherah poles back into play, worshipped the starry hosts even within the temple precincts, went in for sorcery, divination, consultation of mediums and spiritists, and sacrificed his own son in the fire (2 Kings 21; cf. Ps 106:34-39). On top of all this, he "shed so much innocent blood that he filled Jerusalem from end to end" (2 Kgs 21:16). In the saddest of indictments, the author comments that, under Manasseh's leadership, the people of Judah "did more evil than the nations the Lord had destroyed before the Israelites," and he himself had done "more evil than the Amorites who preceded him" (21:9-11).

On the surface, where misconduct is associated with idolatrous worship in the Old Testament, it centers on two areas: murderous violence and sexual licentiousness. Violence takes us back to the early chapters of Genesis, to Cain and Abel, universal violence and the flood. Human sexuality in those chapters is a more complex affair, but sexual morality is an important issue throughout Scripture.[86] Israelite idolatry will involve at least the breach of the sixth and seventh commandments, along with the first two. It involves the breach of the moral law enshrined in the covenant. More below the surface, perhaps (as regards the connection with idolatry), the prophets, in particular, take us beyond sex and violence. It is impossible to dissociate the social injustice per-

---

84. We connect 2 Kings 17 with Jeremiah 2 here, although we always have to ask whether we are reading about the northern kingdom, the southern kingdom or "Israel" as a whole.

85. The poles which somehow imaged the goddess Asherah are often mentioned in the Old Testament in connection with Baal; and although the famous clash between Elijah and his foes is often recalled in terms of Yahweh against Baal, Asherah has almost as many of her prophets on the scene (1 Kings 18:19). The two books that flank Joshua make significant reference to Asherah (Deut 7:5; 12:3; Judg 6:25-28; cf. Exod 34:13 and perhaps implicitly 23:24).

86. The complexity comes in connection with the interpretation of Gen 3:7. In 1 Corinthians, Paul gives particular attention to questions surrounding both idolatry and sexual immorality, using the same verb in his injunction to flee both of them (1 Cor 6:18; 10:14).

petrated in Israel from the pursuit of false gods practiced in Judah (Amos 2:4-8) and to detach the failure to defend the cause of the poor and needy from the evil of forsaking of God for other gods (Jer 22:9-17). If we also bring into play prophetic allusion to the desecration of the Sabbath, we must conclude that the prophets not only expand our horizons from the sixth and seventh to the eighth and tenth commandments, in connection with idolatry, but introduce us to the breach of the fourth as well. Killing through sacrifice in fire and sexual promiscuity might mark the more narrowly cultic aspects of idolatry, but the whole of social life unravels when idolatry is practiced. "In practice idolatry (hatred of the true God) comes down to oppression (hatred of the neighbor)."[87] And Israelite idolatry goes beyond that of the nations.

The Practice of Israel

Nothing in the Old Testament exceeds in emotional intensity the prophetic utterances generated by the idolatry of the nation of Israel, although they may be equalled in that respect by descriptions of divine grace. Only three prophets — Obadiah, Haggai, and Joel — fail to touch explicitly or directly on idolatry.[88] The three longest prophetic books — Isaiah, Jeremiah, and Ezekiel — are replete with allusion to it and, of the "minor prophets," Hosea is its prophet *par excellence*. The best that can be said of idolatry is that it is the high point of folly. If comparison be made between God and idol, it is extreme to the point of being ridiculous. Taking our cue from Isaiah: God is the Creator of heaven and earth. He foreknows and foretells the future. He can save. "To whom, then, will you compare God?" (Isa 40:18).[89] An idol is created and not Creator.[90] It can say nothing, foretell nothing, do nothing. Crafted by a goldsmith hired for the job, it has to be carried around and set mutely on its spot. Yet it gets worshipped (46:6-7). The situation is crazy. In a classic and devastating account, Isaiah concludes that "no one stops to think" about the significance of the fact that the idol made by the blacksmith started life as a tree; the wood was cut down; some of it is used for fuel — and the rest of it is a god! (Isa 44:12-20). Jeremiah joins in the indictment: "Every man is sense-

---

87. Brueggemann, *Theology of the Old Testament*, 697.
88. Though perhaps there is an allusive hint in Joel 3:3.
89. Although the great monotheistic chapters are found in 40-55, a great trial has taken place in the preceding chapters pitting Hezekiah's stark assertion, "The Lord will deliver us," against the rhetorical confidence of Sennacherib, king of Assyria, "Has the god of any nation ever delivered his land from the hand of the king of Assyria?" (Isa 36:18-20).
90. We find this approach and contrast in the Psalms as well (see Pss 97 and 135).

less and without knowledge; every goldsmith is shamed by his idols. His images are a fraud; they have no breath in them. They are worthless, the objects of mockery" (Jer 51:17-18).

This is the best that can be said, for Israel should have known — indeed, did know — better, and this renders the objectively absurd subjectively inexplicable.[91] It is one thing if Sennacherib and company were ignorant, speaking "about the God of Jerusalem as they did about the gods of the other peoples of the world — the work of men's hands" (2 Chr 32:19).[92] But what in heaven or on earth accounts for the fact that Israel went the way of idol worship? The situation is too astonishing for rhetoric. "'Has a nation ever changed its gods? (Yet they are not gods at all.) But my people have exchanged their Glory for worthless idols. Be appalled at this, O heavens, and shudder with great horror,' declares the Lord" (Jer 2:11-12). Is it that God has been like "a desert to Israel or a land of great darkness?" (Jer 2:31). If so, that might explain it. But not so, of course. The situation is profoundly puzzling and not just a profoundly foolish one to get into. Yet we are still nowhere near the depths of the problem. We do not even get there when we recall that Israel is guilty of an ingratitude more base than folly. No one paints the horror of idolatry in darker hues than does Ezekiel and when we get to him, we get to the depths. In the course of one of many searing chapters, he not only pins the label of "prostitution" on to Israelite conduct. He also points out that this is no standard form of prostitution. "In your prostitution you are the opposite of others" (Ezek 16:34). How so? Well, prostitutes get a fee and people go after them. Jerusalem, on the other hand, runs after lovers and gets no fee. It is adultery of a singularly gratuitous kind.[93]

It is in and with such language that we attain the high point of indictment of Israelite idolatry. By comparison with it, Jonah's succinct formulation — "Those who cling to worthless idols forfeit the grace that could be theirs" (Jonah 2:8) — or the historian's succinct summation — "They followed worthless idols and themselves became worthless" (2 Kgs 17:15) — sound rather tame. The language of adulterous prostitution is not confined to

---

91. It is because the Wisdom of Solomon does not go as deeply into matters as do the prophets that Godet regarded its explanation of idolatry as "tame and superficial," quoted in Stott, *The Message of Romans*, 71. At the same time, note that the account in Wis 13:10-19 is in the spirit of Isaiah 44.

92. See the narrative to which I allude in n. 89 above, which seems to indicate a more specific misunderstanding on the part of Sennacherib.

93. The rhetorical treatment of female sexuality here is an important study in itself. But when Brueggemann talks of the "pornographic propensity of Ezekiel," we must ask how many pornographers are horrified by what they write. See *Theology of the Old Testament*, 442.

Ezekiel. Hosea is saturated with it. "Go, take to yourself an adulterous wife" are God's first words to the prophet (Hos 1:23). "What more have I do to with idols?' are practically the last (14:8). If no prophet exceeds Ezekiel in conveying the divine wrath incurred by adulterous prostitution, none exceeds Jeremiah in conveying the divine sorrow at the "adulteries and lustful neighings," the "shameless prostitution" (Jer 13:27).[94] Yet the situation is acknowledged, if not so expressed, by other prophets aware of what it means to break a covenant.[95]

Idolatry is as bad as it gets. It is bad enough when it marks the life of extra-Israelite peoples. It is worse still when it marks the life of Israel. We need to say more about why.[96]

A Matter of Life and Death

Just before Joshua succeeded Moses, Moses put the issue squarely before the people. "I set before you today life and prosperity, death and destruction. . . . Now choose life" (Deut 30:15-19). The "life" referred to here includes social and economic well-being, but another note, persisting into the New Testament, sounds even louder, for spiritual life and death are at stake. Moses' exhortation is generated by the specter of idolatry. Likewise, the book of Joshua closes with Joshua setting before the people a choice and pessimistically urging the abandonment of idolatry: "You are not able to serve the Lord. He is a holy God; he is a jealous God. He will not forgive your rebellion and your sins" (Josh 24:19). Unless we view it against the background of the language of life and death in Deuteronomy, we shall misunderstand the nature of the appeal to divine jealousy and its connection with holiness. And if we misunderstand that, we shall misunderstand idolatry and suspect that behind its prohibition (at least in the case of Israel) lies a somewhat tyrannical divine possessiveness.

There are both a "jealousy" and a "possessiveness" that are proper to human relationships, even though the words normally have pejorative connotations. There is nothing untoward or tyrannical in one partner in a marriage expending all his or her energy in thwarting threatened amorous inter-

---

94. And none, we might add, was entrusted with the revelation of divine triumphant grace, to compare with the prophet we know as Isaiah.

95. E.g., Mal 2:11-14 deploys some but not all of the strong language used by Hosea, Jeremiah, and Ezekiel.

96. Israel fails, as Eve and Adam failed, and was expelled into exile as Adam and Eve were expelled out of paradise. In fact, Canaan, egregiously underadvertised in the description "flowing with milk and honey" (Deut 11:9; cf. 8:7-9), is a miniparadise. But Israel's is the failure of humanity; the people of Israel is not, qua people, worse than anyone else.

vention by a third party. On the contrary, it is moral energy well directed. Marriage institutionalizes a partnership in which each rightly belongs to the other; it is a relationship which ought to be jealously safeguarded incorporating a possessiveness which marks but not mars a healthy relationship.[97] If one partner spoils the relationship by acting destructively, then questions are appropriately asked as to what lengths another should go in preserving it. But such was not the case on the part of Yahweh in relation to Israel. That is, he had done Israel no disservice. In fact, as Savior of the nation and giver of the land, Yahweh had far exceeded the requirements or performance even of the ideal husband. Not so Israel in its bridal role.[98] The untold pain suffered by Yahweh is expressed in the language of the prophets. What is extraordinary is not the appropriate "jealousy" of God. It is the fact that God requires only repentance from his people, from its side, to restore the relationship (Hos 14:1-2; Jer 3:12-13) and, once it has set in, that God is so swift to put behind him his own pain and feel the pain of the people.[99] Behind divine jealousy, as behind human jealousy at its purest, lie two things: holiness and love. Marriage violation defaces the holiness of the marriage bond; not only so, but the love of the one who is wronged causes the pain of jealousy, for divine jealousy is associated with the possibility of pain, not with power-crazed domination. If the Old Testament narrative represents Yahweh as able to experience pain, the life and ministry of Jesus confirm that this is no mutable anthropomorphism, while the teaching of Jesus, for those who will receive it, removes any suspicion that divine pain is mingled with unsavory emotions. "The divine jealousy is one that is holy and not one that is envious."[100]

However, an Old Testament perspective which locates the story of Israel within the story of creation and a New Testament perspective which christologically confirms it combine to assure us that divine holiness and divine love range in their concern far beyond Israel and apply to the whole world. God's is a universal holiness and universal love towards all human creatures, so it is not just the holiness and love bound up with God's partnership with Israel that makes idolatry the evil that it is. In opposing idolatry, God is concerned not just about himself or his relationship with Israel, but

---

97. It goes without saying that there are a wrongheaded possessiveness and wrongminded jealousy.

98. Of course, Israelite idolatry can be conceptualized in terms of its filial rather than bridal role. See, e.g., Isaiah 1 (which forges a strong alliance between social wrongdoing and idolatry), while Hosea noticeably combines both metaphors.

99. Judg 10:16, translated more strongly in the NIV than Soggin's "his heart felt sorry for the sufferings of Israel"; *Judges*, 202.

100. I. A. Dorner, quoted by Horton, *Lord and Servant*, 63.

about others. At this point "jealousy" joins hands with the issue of life and death. Sin is in its nature profoundly destructive. Hosea reports: "But when they came to Baal Peor, they consecrated themselves to that shameful idol and became as vile as the thing they loved" (Hos 9:10). The connection between person and action is not external and contingent, as though the deed is in no sense the making of the person. What the heart worships and the life practices form the person at the core of his or her being. It is often said that Western and Eastern Christianities have accented the nature of sin differently. In the Western case, sin is understood in judicial categories: it is the violation of divine law and incurs judicial guilt and condemnation. In the Eastern case, it is understood in ontological categories: it is the forfeiture of life, the loss of existential communion with God. However we understand the relation of Western and Eastern Christianities, both notes are struck in Scripture. The Creator is Judge and maker of holy law, to whom all are accountable. But sin is also and equally an existentially distorting phenomenon: the self becomes corrupted and entangled in the opposite of the good, the beautiful, and the true. On both counts, these are matters of life and death.

God's summons to and deliverance of the people of Israel are his rescue plan for a cosmos in the grip of sin and death. The significance of the phrase "the living God" easily slips by us, but it is an eloquent descriptive, contrasting not only the actually existent with the actually nonexistent, but also the place where life is found with the place where death reigns.[101] Humanity indwells the sphere of sin and death; we are in Adam. Its rescue takes place in Christ, in whom there is life and in whom there was life from the beginning (Rom 5:12-17; John 1:4). As Israelite idolatry is bewildering, so too the transgression of Eve and Adam. True, the tree of the knowledge of good and evil was attractive to Eve, but why turn a blind eye to the other tree in the middle of the garden, no less pleasing to the eye or good for food? Why regard the scene through the lenses of the serpent's hermeneutic rather than in light of the divine commandment? Why was Adam complicit? Correspondingly, violence, greed, and promiscuity may have their allurement, but why did this attract Israel more than did God and his word? The same question is asked of all the sons and daughters of Adam and of Israel, Jew and Gentile. Reflecting on the fact that idolatry sprang from a darkening of mind and heart, Paul would conclude that the overweening power of sin rendered soteriologically

---

101. The first section of the first part of Jacob's *Theology of the Old Testament* draws attention to the significance of "The Living God, center of Revelation and of Faith." Note Paul's simple characterization of the Thessalonians' conversion as turning "to God from idols to serve the living and true God" and expecting the reappearance of Jesus as savior (1 Thess 1:9).

powerless the statements of the law (Rom 1:21–8:3). The gospel that met human need and powerlessness was thus described first and foremost as "power" and not as intellectual illumination of the human predicament (Rom 1:16). As a power to save, it is the archenemy of all that destroys humanity. "Idolatry" is both cause and sign of human destruction according to Testaments Old and New.[102]

It is as well to touch on two questions that arise on the basis of the biblical materials. The first is whether Scripture says or implies that all worship not explicitly directed to Yahweh or the God and Father of the Lord Jesus Christ should be regarded as idolatrous. Focusing on the question of idolatry does not enable us to answer that question, for it does not enable us to survey the whole range of religious belief that lay and lies outside Israel and the church from earliest times to the present. For example, how different phases of Zoroastrianism appear in the light of the Old and how Islam appears in the light of the New Testament are questions that cannot be answered on the basis of the materials that we have looked at, taking our trajectory out of the book of Joshua. Neither the specifics nor the principle of the biblical condemnation of idolatry entails that all extra-Israelite religious belief and practice throughout the course of religious history should *ipso facto* be regarded as idolatrous, and we might argue that this implies a similar stance towards extraecclesial religious belief and practice. In other words, narrow attention to "idolatry" does not allow us to decide definitively one way or another. But what is said in Scripture about idolatry may be profoundly instructive and applicable to a whole range of religious beliefs and practices now as then and applicable to Jewish and Christian along with other religious communities now as then.

The second is how biblical treatments of idolatry bear on the concept as we familiarly use it with reference to such things as power, celebrity, sex, or money. Such usage is quite generally warranted by biblical usage. Connecting idolatry with immorality, Paul makes a statement of principle that is widely applicable: "They exchanged the truth of God for a lie, and worshiped and served created things rather than the Creator" (Rom 1:25). In both Col 3:5 and Eph 5:5, covetousness is regarded as a form of idolatry. The background in Colossians is the contrast between setting mind and heart on things above, the domain of the risen Christ, and setting heart and mind on earthly things.

---

102. Hence Paul moves straight into the question of idolatry in Rom 1:20-25. The high profile that he gives to the question of homosexual activity in 1:26-27 is accounted for by his conviction that it illustrates in the sphere of basic interhuman relationships the principle of exchange which characterizes idolatry.

Theology in the Book of Joshua

According to Ephesians, the idolatry that consists in covetousness excludes people from inheritance in the kingdom of Christ and of God. The word "inheritance" also features in a similar context in 1 Corinthians, the Pauline letter which contains his most sustained treatment of idolatry in the narrower sense of that word; in fact, it is a word resonant with associations of the inheritance of the land of promise (1 Cor 6:9-10). "Covetousness" is closely connected with specific sins in the passages in Colossians and Ephesians. It is prohibited in the tenth commandment, as idolatry is at the beginning of the commandments. There is a kind of circle here, for to covet is to idolize, in that we seek to go beyond what God desires us to have and so the object of our spiritual affection displaces God as our proper end. The opposite attitude to idolatrous covetousness is not resigned acceptance of the provision of a grudging lawgiver; rather, it is thanksgiving (Eph 5:4, 20). Had Israel properly given thanks, there would have been no idolatry. If all things are ours in Jesus Christ, the same applies to us *a fortiori* (1 Cor 3:22). "What must not he possess who possesses the Possessor of all?"[103]

Touching on Beauty

Idolatry has lost sight both of the claims of God and of the grace of God, both of truth and of goodness. It has also lost sight of what we might term the "beauty" of God, to import a notion that has been linked in Western thought with goodness and truth. Constructing the golden calf was prohibited, but building a tabernacle (later, a temple) gave plenty of scope for the work of fashioning hands and the creation of what is materially pleasing to the eye.[104] Speaking generally and using the familiar language of aesthetics rather than biblical language, whether we should connect notions of beauty as applied to God and as applied to craft and sculpture is a moot point. But is there no connection between Ezekiel's sustained concluding interest in rational and aesthetic proportion and his opening vision of "the appearance of the likeness of

---

103. Savonarola, quoted in Perowne, *The Book of Psalms*, 1:197. My discussion of idolatry in the extended sense of the word has been extremely narrow. Among the hundreds of examples of the wider scene, see a by now older account of Stalin as a "super-Pharaoh" in Deutscher, *Stalin*. The phrase itself is found on p. 326, but the succeeding chapter is entitled "The Gods Are Athirst."

104. I am not assuming that the tabernacle is necessarily a "harbinger" of the temple: see Brueggemann, *Theology of the Old Testament*, 339, whose treatment builds somewhat on Terrien, *The Elusive Presence*. In light of the reference to Ezekiel below, see also Brueggemann, 427-28 and 665.

the glory of the Lord" (1:28), the aesthetics, we might say, of his religious experience?[105] We are admittedly on speculative terrain as we try to ferret out the antique perspective of a Near Eastern *homo religiosus* who had the moral sense of a prophet and the aesthetic sensibility of a priest. Yet, for all the different senses of our word "beauty" and for all the disanalogies between its different forms, in accordance with these different senses, Exodus and Ezekiel alike combine features in their literature that may leave (what I shall vaguely term) a reader with the impression of profound unities. The beauty of the material, the skill of the craftsmanship, and the form of their unity are presumably meant to be appropriate and not arbitrary signs of Yahweh on the assumption that the "being," "action," "law," and "command" of God are not conceived separately in the Hebrew mind (i.e., what God enjoins may tell us something about his being). The stern prohibitions against idolatry in both Exodus and Ezekiel indict an activity which lies on the other side of the chasm separating it from the glory of God, the morality that he commands, and the aesthetically pleasing. The logic of the argument against making idols in Deut 4:15-16 — at Sinai, God was heard but not seen — should not allow us to overlook the significance of Exod 33:8-11, let alone 33:22-23 and 34:35.[106] What is seen, whether God or his appearance, the tabernacle or the temple, constitutes, in an important sense, a single visual field. It suggests, albeit in a general and limited fashion, a connection of beauties.

However, we are in the business neither of inquiring into the relation of aesthetics to "beauty" nor of pronouncing on aesthetic theory in general or theological aesthetics in particular. But as the aesthetically beautiful may attract us just on account of its beauty, so the God of Scripture is attractive just on account of his. He is glorious in his being, and this glory can quite properly be conceptualized as a form of beauty. We are right to retain, honor, and emphasize today the language of the right, the good, and the true in a culture where their reality is eclipsed and their meaning obscured. Yet we can be too prone to speak only in the language of "law," neglecting to ask whether or

---

105. Reference to this and to subsequent visions recurs in the course of describing the temple (Ezek 43:1-5). The fact that chs. 40-48 present an idealized picture does not affect my observation but, if anything, tends to reinforce it. I do not imply that aesthetic beauty always requires some kind of "rational" proportion. Immanuel Kant spoke of beauty as the "symbol of the morally good"; *Critique of Judgment*, 198 (this older translation is unproblematic at this point). Ezekiel conceives of the ugly as the symbol of evil (Ezek 8:10). See De Gruchy's account of *Christianity, Art and Transformation*, a study motored, in part, by the perceived connection between apartheid and aesthetic ugliness in South Africa.

106. I am not suggesting that an idol cannot be beautifully crafted: see Williams, "The Response of a Theologian."

how we should speak of God in the language of "beauty" and "attractiveness." It is indeed the most sobering paradox that God is nowhere revealed more clearly than in the extremity of unattractiveness (Isa 53:2). But the very fact that we can describe this as a paradox is telling. Isaiah's depiction, certainly as christologically understood, is a cause for wonder because it is a transformation of the glory revealed in Exodus and Ezekiel into an opposite appearance. Yet, the Christ of the cross will undergo a further, eschatological transformation which warrants our remembering Old Testament appearances of the likeness of the glory of the Lord as long as we train our minds on God.[107]

Scarcely any critic of Christianity has been less compromising and surely none more influential on the twentieth century than Friedrich Nietzsche. In a central section of what he regarded as his greatest book, Nietzsche exhorts us to "shatter, shatter ... the old tablets" of the law.[108] In his immediately preceding volume, he had written words which aptly define our epoch: "What decides against Christianity now is our taste, not our reasons."[109] This applies to more than just our modern Western epoch, and Nietzsche may not have wanted to divide too neatly an era of rational objection from an era of spiritual revulsion towards Christianity. Throughout his work, he notices no divine glory underlying divine promulgation of truth and law. Correspondingly, he has no truck with religious lamentations about what idolatry amounts to in its opposition to God and transvaluation of the values which he gave to the people of Israel.[110]

There is nothing egotistical about the jealousy and holiness of God which Joshua brought to the people's attention in his warning against idolatry. Remembering the catastrophe in Eden and the saving covenant with Abraham and his descendants should have alerted us to this before we got to Joshua and long before we have arrived at those formulations in Ezekiel where God speaks of rescuing Israel for the sake of his own holiness (Ezek 36:22). Talk of God

---

107. This admittedly stretches Ezekiel's phrase beyond what is exegetically warranted to cover other Old Testament manifestations of divine glory. As regards the New Testament, the transfiguration of Jesus arguably points us in the direction of this eschatological transformation (e.g., Matt 16:27–17:5).

108. *Thus Spoke Zarathustra*, 175. Nietzsche tells us in *Ecce Homo*, 104, that the chapter containing these words is the "decisive" one in his book.

109. *The Gay Science*, 123.

110. Nietzsche wished to see in Europe a transvaluation or "re-evaluation" of Christian values. The outcome of idolatry leads to a radical transvaluation, according to Hos 9:7, when the prophet comes to be regarded as a fool, his inspiration judged manic. Schleiermacher *(On Religion)* made a celebrated pitch for cultivating the taste of "cultured despisers" so that they warmed to Christianity, but Nietzsche's analysis assumes a wider gulf between religious and nonreligious tastes than Schleiermacher could discern in his time.

saving Israel for the sake of his own holiness rings egotistical in our ears only because we measure the being and rights of God with our own crooked and self-interested measuring stick, missing the depths of God's love and humility towards humanity. We misunderstand because we do not ask ourselves where else glory is to be found but with and in God and, when we do, do not see it there. If, as a matter of fact, only divine holiness brings life and only divine glory brings joy to humankind, God's directing of human creatures to himself is no egoism. On the contrary, to conceal from human creatures knowledge of the true fount and glory of goodness would be to rob them of both the meaning and the joy of creaturely existence. Glory and goodness are intrinsically connected in God (Exod 33:18-19), and God's direction of his action to his own glory is a comprehensive and inclusive movement designed to unite God and humankind perfectly in participation in eternal life.

Habakkuk, who contrasted the worthlessness of idols with the Lord in his holy temple, perceived that a true vision of God is not for now. It is in the future that "the earth will be filled with the knowledge of the glory of the Lord, as the waters cover the sea" (Hab 2:14-20). What is for now is faith (Hab 2:4), a conviction picked up by Paul and the writer to the Hebrews alike (Rom 1:17; Heb 10:38). Faith is not intrinsically irrational, but it is against the grain of our native and distorted mental processes. In observing the tree from the standpoint of its superficial attractiveness, Eve broke with the most deeply rational mandate to heed instead the word of God. In indulging in idolatry because it had some sort of immediate appeal, the people of Israel broke with the most deeply rational mandate to adhere instead to the law of God. In opting for the gratification of the senses or the untutored instinct, we all break with the most deeply rational mandate embedded in the law of our being, which is to love God above all else and our neighbors as ourselves. Idolatry is a practical atheism and, as such, the most hopeless, as well as the most faithless — ultimately, the most loveless too — of all practices. If the biblical treatment of idolatry overwhelms us by its intensity, we might at least heed the words that close the book of Hosea, moderate in tone, but sobering in simplicity. "Who is wise? He will realize these things. Who is discerning? He will understand them. The ways of the Lord are right; the righteous walk in them, but the rebellious stumble in them" (Hos 14:9).

Covenant

Idolatry is a blight on humanity in general and on Israel in particular. In the latter case, it is a breach of the covenant. How should we understand "covenant"? The language of "blight" is the language of moral and existential devastation, but the language of "breach" is the language of law. And, indeed, covenant and law are intimately connected in the Old Testament, a connection which receives a measure of elucidation when we scrutinize parallels in the socio-legal arrangements of other ancient Near Eastern cultures. Staying within the confines of the biblical text, we have noted that what the prophets have to say about idolatry highlights the metaphorically marital dimensions of covenant, and marriage is both a legal institution and a properly personal, relational affair. Covenant is not just about law. In the first essay in this part of our commentary, we touched on the question of covenant in connection with land. Although we do not return here to the question of land, consideration of the covenant brings us back full circle in some respects.[111]

The book of Joshua more or less climaxes with the account of a covenant ceremony at Shechem (24:1-28). We can invoke the image of a full circle here too, up to a point. At the beginning of the book, God tells Joshua that he is about to fulfil the promise that he made to Moses and to give the people the land. On that basis, Joshua is exhorted to "be strong and very courageous" and also "to obey all the law my servant Moses gave you; do not turn from it to the right or to the left" (1:7). Now, in ch. 23, Joshua reminds the people how God has been true to his word and on that basis transmits the exhortation he first received. "Be very strong; be careful to obey all that is written in the Book of the Law of Moses, without turning to the right or to the left" (23:6). He proceeds to warn the people of the consequences of covenant violation (23:16). That done, he constitutes the people in assembly, placing the issue squarely before them: either Yahweh or foreign gods. Which? The people voice their allegiance to Yahweh, and Joshua makes a covenant, drawing up "decrees and laws" and recording it all in "the Book of the Law of God." A large stone is erected to mark the occasion as a witness to the promises of the people. Joshua then speaks a final word, sends "the people away, each to his own inheritance," and himself departs the land in death.

Among the uncertainties that surround our reading of this account is the difficulty of identifying the book in which Joshua wrote. Whatever the solution, this is not the first time that some form of covenant ceremony is recorded in the book of Joshua. After the devastation of Ai, which was a sign of God's renewed favor after the costly disobedience of Achan, Mount Ebal becomes the scene of a sober proclamation by Joshua of the words of the bless-

---

111. The next and last of the essays which make up the present part of this volume is on miracles and connected more loosely with the preceding four than these four are with each other.

ings and curses of the law as laid down by Moses. Declaration is accompanied by sacrifices on the altar with the people in solemn attendance and the ark of the covenant in their midst (8:30-35). The account is a key to interpreting the book of Joshua.[112] Yet again, the themes of the book of Deuteronomy are closely tracked in Joshua. "Covenant" is obviously central in Deuteronomy, its climactic treatment coming in chs. 27-30, where we have an account of the ceremony at Moab. We have touched on divine jealousy in connection with the question of idolatry. Now we turn to the question of divine favoritism in connection with covenant. The question will be somewhat misdirected as long as we read the account of the Sinaitic covenant against the background of the covenant with Abraham, but then fail to go further back than Abraham and also narrow our gaze from Abraham onwards so that it becomes focused only on the people of Israel.[113] However we view the relation of these two covenants, the question arises of what theological account we shall give of the privilege or privileges of covenant or covenants made with Abraham and his descendants. What are we to make theologically of divine favoritism? Christians believe that Gentiles are included in a new covenant made through Jesus Christ so that favor towards the Jews is not the terminus of God's covenantal ways. But does this not alleviate worries about *racial* or *national* exclusivism in connection with the covenant only to perpetuate them in relation to *religious* exclusivism, as Jewish and Gentile *Christians* inherit the mantle of previously Jewish privilege? Boundaries are redrawn here, but boundaries they remain. Even if we think, as some do, in terms of two existing covenants, one embracing Jews and Gentiles within the church, the other embracing non-Christian Jews, a significant exclusion zone applies in the case of the majority of humankind, which belongs to neither company. Does the book of Joshua offer uncompromising testimony to a form or phase of divine partiality enshrined in the very notion of covenant?

Behind the Covenant

Behind the covenant with Israel lies God's creation of humanity. How creation and covenant are connected has been a subject of lively discussion in Old Testament study, but, on any account, we cannot detach the summons to

---

112. See, e.g., Woudstra, *The Book of Joshua,* 144. See also the commentary on the passage above, which shows the significance of the symbolism of the act prescribed here for the covenantal life of Israel in the land.

113. I refer to the "Sinaitic" covenant as though the phrase were uncontroversial. In fact, it is not. For a brief attempt to balance the arguments here, see Goldingay, *Israel's Gospel,* 370.

Abraham in Genesis 12 from the story told from the beginning up to that point. One theological tradition interprets the narrative of the creation of Adam in terms of covenant.[114] Whether or not we follow it, the language used in the call of Abraham harks back to the account of creation. Abraham is a new beginning but not detached from the past. Before him stretch out his descendants and the beneficiaries of the covenant made with him; behind him lies the universal human drama played out in Eden. The world created by God is destined for eschatological restoration after the debacle of Genesis 3, something highlighted especially, within the pages of the Old Testament, in the prophecy of Isaiah.

Between Genesis 3 and Genesis 12 a crucial figure supervenes, his significance for the casual reader all too easily circumscribed by an ark and nearly swamped by a flood — Noah. Noah, once described in the New Testament as "a preacher of righteousness" (2 Pet 2:5), exhibits that righteous conduct which God finds wanting in his contemporaries (Gen 6:9). The covenant that God establishes with Noah, when he rescues him from the flood, is extensive in scope. It is a covenant made not just with Noah but also with his descendants and not just with humanity but also with nonhuman creatures and creation. The rainbow "is the sign of the covenant I have established between me and all life on the earth" (Gen 9:17). Abraham, descendant of Shem, is heir of the Noahic covenant. Noah, like Abraham after him, experiences a new beginning. But the narrative in Genesis shows a marked interest in the family fortunes of descendants that are not heirs of special promise, as are Isaac and Jacob. This is illustrated in the case of Ishmael's progeny (Gen 17:20; 25:12-16). Prophecy can also display an interest in the nations, nowhere more so than in the case of Isaiah. The New Testament draws out the significance of the fact that nations are to become beneficiaries of the covenant blessings bestowed upon Israel.[115]

Adam plunged posterity into unrighteousness. God purposes to unmake the devastation by establishing righteousness. Noah and Abraham are intimately connected according to this purpose. Both are summoned to righ-

---

114. This is the Reformed tradition. For a detailed contemporary exposition and defense of this, see a series of volumes authored by Horton and not yet completed: *Covenant and Eschatology, Lord and Servant,* and *Covenant and Salvation.* A firm distinction is drawn in this tradition between a covenant of grace, made with Abraham, and a covenant of works, made at Sinai. A covenant of works was also made with Adam, but a covenant of grace is made with believers in Jesus Christ.

115. As mention has been made of other covenants, we dare not forget the significance of the "Davidic" covenant, to which both Testaments bear witness at several points in one way or another.

teousness. "In the unfolding Genesis narrative this premise of Abraham's *tsedaqah* [righteousness] follows unmistakably on the characterization of Noah as *tsaddiq* [righteous], and the parallel is strengthened by Yahweh's making a covenant with Abraham in the immediate context (15.18)."[116] How divine covenant and human righteousness should be related is a question far too big for us to address. But the question of a behavior dignified by the weighty religious term "righteous" does not arise in the Old Testament simply in the case of those who are bound together by the specific Abrahamic and Sinaitic covenants. This seems to be the premise of the discussion between Yahweh and Abraham about the destruction of Sodom, a premise "accepted by both Abraham and YHWH and [which] indicates that it is possible for those outside the covenant between Abraham and YHWH to be considered 'righteous.'"[117] We are to hope for righteousness even in Sodom; its possibility is not the exclusive preserve of the covenant people in the narrower sense. If God's interest in righteousness embraces, at its heart, his interest in moral action, then Abimelech is capable of displaying a quality of righteousness that exceeds that of Abraham in a given case (Gen 20:1-6).[118] None of this is subversive of Pauline justification by faith, a theme which must remain at best on the margins of this essay.

If this theological outlook is applied to the New as well as to the rest of the Old Testament, it turns the edge of at least one form of the protest that "covenant" is a sign of problematic divine partiality, a divine interest only in a narrow band of people. Israel is immeasurably privileged to be a special covenant people. One sign of the privilege is that its breach is treated even more seriously than the sins of extra-Israelite nations, as Amos's logic makes devastatingly clear (Amos 3:2, culminating the previous discussion). In the Old Testament, election, which is what Amos is talking about, applies not to the ultimate eschatological destiny of individuals, but to the purposes of God in history. It is not focused on the felicity of the covenant people in the afterlife.[119] Correspondingly, those outside the covenant are not treated as sub-

---

116. McConville, *God and Earthly Power*, 43. This volume constitutes a sustained exposition, from the standpoint of "political theology" of the Old Testament, of the link between Israel, creation, and the nations.

117. Lyons, *Canon and Exegesis*, 183.

118. Although my interest here is in the substance of Abimelech's action and not the vocabulary in which it is described, it is interesting that, in the LXX, Abimelech protests that he took Sarah to himself *en dikaiosynē cheirōn*, in the "righteousness" of his hands, "with righteous hand," "righteously."

119. But that does not mean that it has no reference at all to it: see Matt 22:32; Mark 12:26-27; Luke 20:37-38.

jects of postmortem eschatological doom. We must leave as an open question whether this pattern is perpetuated in the New Testament.

In one of his sermons, Peter announces his discovery that "God does not show favoritism but accepts men from every nation who fear him and do what is right" (Acts 10:34-35).[120] The context is the participation of Gentiles in the blessings of the gospel. Cornelius, the high-minded centurion whose vision occasioned Peter's visit and his fresh insight into the nature of God's provision for the world, exercised faith in Christ and received the gift of the Spirit only after hearing the preached word. Far from implying that people outside Israel can do without the gospel, Peter's words are a triumphant celebration of the exact opposite. But the canonical writings in their totality witness to the unimpeachable nature of a divine justice which is not flawed by an unworthy favoritism, and Peter's words pick out God's regard for all "who fear him and do what is right." Cornelius himself was in the orbit of specifically Jewish life and worship (Acts 10:22), and his "righteous action" is in the context of "fearing God." Consistently, in Scripture, human life is standardly judged on the basis of the life lived, even if the implication of the atoning death of Christ is that no life is so lived that it qualifies us for entry into the eschatological kingdom of God and is exempted from the need to be justified by the grace of God in Jesus.[121] None of this reduces one whit the privilege of covenant.

Covenant and Privilege

When the covenant is renewed at Shechem, in that final dramatic chapter of the book of Joshua, the priests and the Levites are not particularly in evidence. We meet elders, leaders, judges, and other officials. It is different in the case of the earlier and rather more impressive ceremony at Mount Ebal. Here, the priests occupy a central place, along with the ark. Burnt and fellowship offerings are sacrificed in a ritual predictably tied to Mosaic injunctions. The people had consecrated themselves before the Lord in preparation for the great theophany and giving of the law on Mount Sinai, and, before the cross-

---

120. The word here translated "favoritism" is a biblical *hapax legomenon*.

121. Paul's most comprehensive statement of these principles comes in Rom 2:2–3:26, although their interpretation is controversial. As Paul appears to assume a universal knowledge of God that is available, if not always actual, the question does not arise about cases of "doing right" but not "fearing God." I speak of the way in which human life is "standardly," rather than invariably, judged so that we neither forget dying thieves nor neglect the importance of what they teach us.

ing of the Jordan, Joshua called again for a public consecration. But the priests are by now in greater evidence alongside the people, although they were also there at Exod 19:22. Between Sinai and the Jordan, the priests have assumed the privileged role of ministering in the tabernacle to deal with the sins of the people. The dilemma of Israel throughout the Old Testament turns out to be the dilemma of the world: sin. According to the New Testament, sin requires unprecedented and unparalleled divine action at a particular point in history in order for it to be dealt with. The history of Israel is the locus of this action, but it is action undertaken for the sake of the world as well as for the sake of Israel or for the sake of Israel for the sake of the world. It is undertaken in vital connection with the promise that the blessing of Abraham is for the sake of the world.

Unique action in unrepeatable history is action that conforms precisely to the reality of human existence. For in contrast to ideas characteristic, for example, of some oriental philosophies or religions, Israel does not believe that humans live and die more than once on this earth. Humans are uniquely and unrepeatably embodied in time and space. Even when the Messiah of Israel dies and rises again, his is not a resurrection to the self-same mortal life. The humanity of the Messiah secures his unique earthly existence in a particular body, place, and time. The Christian doctrine of the incarnation assumes this. "Incarnation" is precisely that — incarnation and not theophany or angelic manifestation. Whoever Joshua's mysterious interlocutor outside Jericho was, it was not God incarnate as a human being, someone who had been born, was living, would die, and would rise again. God's design was to achieve the salvation of the human race and institute the new covenant in flesh and blood, that is, within particular space and time. It was action motivated not simply by covenant holiness but by universal love. Covenant favoritism seems to imply limits to the love of God and its expression, but how is love for the whole of sinful humanity more deeply expressed than by the taking on of human flesh? Incarnation is as close as God can get to humanity. And how is human flesh assumed except by confinement, in accordance with the human condition, within specific place and time? A covenant rooted in unique action in particular space and time is the opposite of exclusivist action that reduces those outside the covenant to underprivileged status or maintains them in it. It is the very concrete locus of God's action that is the sign of universal love. Saving action is a bridge from God to the world, and the bridge must come down somewhere in particular.[122]

---

122. Even if we could make sense of the notion of multiple incarnations or divine reincarnations of the Son of God on this earth, it would scarcely diminish the problem of exclusive

If God intends to become incarnate in his own world and if incarnation entails true humanity and not theophany, the savior of the world must belong to a particular people, community, culture, place, and time. There must be a kind of privilege. Hence the calling of Israel. As often as covenant or election is spoken of, privilege is assumed. Israel is not chosen on account of inherent virtue or any other positive qualification. According to the election of grace, God is creative precisely at this point. An idolatrous descendant of Noah, named Abram, and his family are selected. The extended family, descendants, and nation look rather like any other family, extended family, or nation in that there are more and less virtuous people in their ranks. To this the history of Israel testifies. Maintenance of a covenant which climaxes in divine redeeming action in place and time does not depend on the quality of covenant people any more than the initiative of election ever depended on the religious worthiness of the elect patriarch. If incarnation is necessarily designed for space, time, and community, then space, time, and community have to be kept open for it and preserved. So "I took your father Abraham from the land beyond the River and led him throughout Canaan and gave him many descendants. . . . I gave you a land on which you did not toil and cities you did not build; and you live in them and eat from vineyards and olive groves that you did not plant" (24:3, 13). Joshua and his companions rightly took the formation of a satisfied community as a sign of divine favor. What remains hidden from their eyes is how divine favor to Israel in the form of a gift of fine land is for the sake of divine favor upon all flesh.

In Deuteronomy, Moses reminded the people: "I have taught you decrees and laws . . . so that you may follow them in the land you are entering. . . . Observe them carefully, for this will show your wisdom and understanding to the nations, who will hear about all these decrees and say, 'Surely this great nation is a wise and understanding people.' What other nation is so great as to have their gods near them the way the Lord our God is near us whenever we pray to him? And what other nation is so great as to have such righteous decrees and laws as this body of laws I am setting before you today?" (Deut 4:5-8). The objective is not to provoke the nations to incensed jealousy and accusations of divine injustice. It is, as the prophets saw most clearly, that the nations might be attracted to walk in the light of the Lord. An angry Jesus called the temple "a house of prayer for all nations" (Mark 11:17). He was quoting a prophet who had spoken both of walking in the light and of

---

privilege, as many see it. For, at any one time, only one earthly space would be occupied by the incarnate presence of God and the rest of the world would be deprived of it. See Williams, "On Religion and Revelation"; and Caputo, "On Being Clear About Faith."

the temple (Isa 2:2-5; 56:7).[123] Righteousness is communally displayed within the borders of a specific land. The temple becomes the religious heart of the land. Righteousness is meant to be on parade before the nations so that an exclusive privilege might flow into an inclusive destiny. That is the logic of the covenant. Israel is God's way into the world.[124] But he does not just use, he loves, Israel.

We should not unreflectingly leap from the logic of a covenant that includes messianic (or, more generally, future) promise to the assumption that a "New Testament" covenant built on the presence of the Messiah must enshrine exactly that same logic. Nevertheless, we are now in a position to place in its proper light the logic of at least one aspect of Christian particularity, with its possession of unique Scriptures and its missionary mandate. The Scriptures, written in known languages, are translatable into all languages, so that all languages might be privileged by receiving witness to the saving presence and action of God in the one world that he created. Mission is the proclamation of the universal lordship of Christ so that all places might be privileged by the possibility of confessing him. Neither land nor language, neither covenant nor law are symbols of exclusion. The privilege of one nation is the privilege of all.

Covenant and Law

If "covenant" on the face of it seems to denote exclusiveness and partiality with reference to Israel, what about "law"? In Jewish context, it is a covenant privilege. When Paul enumerated the blessings of his people, he was doing nothing novel in listing "the receiving of the law" in company with "the divine glory, the covenants . . . the temple worship and the promises" (Rom 9:4). One way or another, there is an accent on "law" throughout the book of Joshua. When Joshua built the altar on Mount Ebal, he did so according to the law of the Lord, copied "on stones the law of Moses," and "read all the words of the law — the blessings and the curses — just as it is written in the Book of the Law" (Josh 8:30-34). The performance was nothing if not meticulous and exhaustive (8:35). Joshua was heeding the divine word given to him

---

123. Note the reference to "covenant' in Isa 56:6.

124. After saying that "God had not chosen Israel and given them all that he did in order to shut out the world, but to bring in the world," Oswalt puts it well: "All of Israel's separation from the world was in order to keep Israel from being absorbed into the world and thus losing the ability to call the world out of itself into the blessings of God"; *The Book of Isaiah: Chapters 40–66*, 460-61.

from the inception of his leadership "to obey all the law my servant Moses gave you" and not to "let this Book of the Law depart from your mouth" (Josh 1:7-8). We have come across the "Book of the Law" as recently as the end of Deuteronomy when Moses determines to write the law which he has delivered and commands the Levite bearers of the ark of the covenant to place it beside their ark. Joshua figures prominently at this point in the narrative in Deuteronomy and, in time, comes to express that same foreboding conviction as Moses expressed here concerning the future conduct of the people of Israel (Deut 31:14-29; Josh 24:19-27). By the time that he does so, land has been allocated and cities of refuge provided, whose function is regulated according to the instruction given to Moses (Josh 20:2). The provision for the Levites likewise follows those instructions (21:2-8).

How should we understand the law in relation to the covenant? It has been a commonplace of Christian theology, peculiarly accented in Protestantism, that we enter into the new covenant in the blood of Christ by faith and not by observing any form of law. In proclaiming this, Paul took pains to establish that this was not a new-fangled Christian principle but a principle of divine action that informed the Old Testament, established decisively with reference to Abraham some centuries prior to the giving of the law. However, he hastens to quash the supposition that this undermines the law. "Do we, then, nullify the law by this faith? Not at all! Rather, we uphold the law" (Rom 3:31). The law is "holy" (Rom 7:12). Indeed, when God sent his son "in the likeness of sinful man to be a sin offering" because the law is powerless to save, it was "in order that the righteous requirements of the law might be fully met in us" (Rom 8:3-4). Paul twice quotes the command to love our neighbor as ourselves as something definitive of the Christian life and precisely as the fulfilment of the law; in fact, he does so in those very letters which most highlight justification by faith.[125] However we plot the various possible significations of "law" in relation to "gospel" or "faith," it remains that God's covenant with the Jews in the Old or with Jews and Gentiles in the New Testament has as its end the production of a people who will live lives of holy love, the fruit of an atonement and forgiveness of sin, which no human is in a position to make or to merit and which issues in eternal life.

Where law features in Joshua, it is taken for granted that an ethic of gratitude is foundational for the people of Israel. The first commandment of

---

125. Rom 13:8-10; Gal 5:13-16. It is interesting that the only other New Testament reference to this command outside the Synoptic Gospels is in Jas 2:8-11, the epistle sometimes believed to contain teaching on justification antithetical to that of Paul. James too thinks of it as fulfilment of the law.

the Decalogue was prefaced with the words: "I am the Lord your God, who brought you out of Egypt, out of the land of slavery" (Exod 20:2; Deut 5:6). Deliverance has been experienced. The law is given to a freed people who should be grateful for their liberation. When Joshua enjoins the people to keep the law and "to love the Lord your God, to walk in all his ways, to obey his commands, to hold fast to him and to serve him with all your heart and all your soul," he commends no cold or formal legalistic duty (22:5).

If we attend particularly to the provision for the Levites, we gain a helpful perspective on what the law entails. In an earlier discussion of the land, we noted the significance of the fact that Joshua gave no inheritance to the tribe of Levi "since the offerings made by fire to the Lord, the God of Israel, are their inheritance, as he promised them" (13:14). They are deprived of land in the form routinely allocated to the other tribes because they receive the privilege of ministering to God in a peculiar way. And, of course, Joshua is following Moses here again. "To the tribe of Levi, Moses has given no inheritance; the Lord, the God of Israel, is their inheritance, as he promised them" (13:33). Behind the law and greater than the law is God, whom Moses longed to behold (Exod 33:18). Even if the priest does not share in Moses' religious privilege (Num 12:8), his privilege remains immense. He serves in the holy place, and the high priest enters it once a year to make atonement.[126]

Priestly practice is governed by law. Surrounded by holiness represented in beauty, the high priest solemnly enters into transaction with Yahweh himself on the part of the people, when blood is shed and sin atoned for according to strictly prescribed rite. If the Decalogue at Sinai is embedded in the fact of once-for-all divine deliverance from Egypt, the priestly ritual is embedded in the grace of ongoing divine covering of Israelite transgression. The law which governs offerings by fire (8:31-33) is part of a system of privilege, and the misunderstanding over the affair of the altar recorded in ch. 22 (and mercifully cleared up) is no petty issue, but turns on how Israelites rightly and obediently honor the God of grace. When we further survey the provisions specified in Joshua, we find that what meets us as law always amounts to privilege. Land allocations are possible only because God has blessed. Not only was the land given, but the land given is good and great (5:6; 23:13; 24:13). All the promises were good in the first place (23:14). Legislation regarding the cities of refuge is protective and therefore conduces to human good (20:1-9).

When, then, we connect covenant and law, we are not in the first place connecting divine commitment with human duty or even divine grace with human duty; we are connecting divine grace with human gratitude. God, in-

---

126. My conflation of priests and Levites in this account does not affect the argument.

deed, has the right to command. But he commands under concrete circumstances of grace. Even if some homiletic accounts of David's heroic and good character can be idealistically one-sided, David stands out in the pages of the Old Testament from all who went before him in terms of the reality and warmth of his portrayed humanity. The overt and glowing confession of love for the law which is found in the Psalms (Davidic or otherwise) draws out the implications of the religious situation which the Pentateuch and the book of Joshua depict, as it impinges on the psalmist's experience.[127] Meditation on the law of God produces delight because humanity is constitutionally designed for its precepts and its precepts for humanity. In its way, the book of Proverbs bears testimony to the same thing where obedience constitutes wisdom, not because of craven fear of doing otherwise but because divine law is suited to human nature and not a heteronomous imposition on it.[128] "Theonomy," the law of God, stands in contrast to "autonomy," our being a law to ourselves, but it is not a form of "heteronomy," the law of another understood as an alien law inflicted by an alien being.[129] The law of God is the life of men and women. Yet again, we revert to Genesis. Humanity is not created to know good and evil. It is created to know the good alone and God our good.[130] Knowledge of good and evil is a sign of self-division and alienation from God, a forbidden fruit which has been tasted. Divine commandment, which is the law of life, is now experienced as an unwelcome imposition. The very word "law" in a moral context now connotes repression and restriction upon human freedom.

We should bear in mind that when we speak of "law" in English, we sometimes use the term descriptively rather than prescriptively. If I speak of the "law of gravity," I describe how things work, I do not refer to an obligation externally imposed upon an otherwise separate cosmic order. The law that the cheetah obeys in hitting 70 mph for up to 600 meters when it is firing on all its feline cylinders is not an external, still less an irksome, imposition on an otherwise independent cheetah. It is precisely the law of its being. It is not otherwise with humanity. The Genesis account of creation describes the creation of humankind as good; the environment in which Adam and Eve are set is good, with pleasant-looking trees that are good for food. A single prohibi-

---

127. Psalm 119 is outstanding in this connection.

128. However, there is more to Proverbs than this; it certainly urges us to fear the consequences of not following the way of wisdom.

129. "Theonomy" is sometimes used today to refer to a particular position taken on the nature of law and associated with "Christian Reconstructionism." I use it in a different sense, akin in salient respects to that of Tillich, *Systematic Theology*, 1:94.

130. Bonhoeffer, *Ethics*, 299-302.

tion is enjoined: that the fruit of the tree of the knowledge of good and evil should not be eaten. It is not an arbitrary, intrusive, heteronomous, or provocative law. It is information conveyed in imperative form, as when we command a child not to put its hand into the fire. Fire is destructive to humans according to the law of their mutual being — that of fire and of humanity. And so with the Torah: "Torah is not an imposition of an arbitrary God, Israel insists. It is, rather, a discernment of the reality of things."[131] Knowledge of good and evil is infinitely more destructive of human beings than is fire. A mysterious primal disobedience results in permanent inclination towards evil. Left to itself, humanity accordingly shrivels rather than flourishes when it is ensconced within a realm where good and evil are known.

If "morality" is a term that we apply to the scene of ordinary human life, a term which presupposes an active evil impulse within us, then we must say that humans were not designed for morality. Morality is the sign of the fall, of self-division. On that scene, moral law, often enshrined in social institutions, both signifies and, as Paul came to see, actually accentuates self-division (Rom 7:7-8). Yet moral law is also a recall to our created nature. It is the form in which we are beckoned to our own proper being under universal conditions of existential self-alienation, the product of alienation from God. God's covenant with Israel was doubly gracious. It was gracious by virtue of being made at all. And it was gracious in terms of its provision, for what it required in the way of obedience was conformity to the law proper to our being. If this is not explicit in Joshua, it is because only training in obedience enables the heart to apprehend the goodness of the law, and Joshua is concerned more with the training than with the depths of the law.

However, does not the New Testament frequently take a negative view of law and of any form of covenant that emphasizes law? Paul and the author of the Letter to the Hebrews are, in their different ways, the apparent proponents of this line of thought. We have already indicated some Pauline texts pertaining to law. In relation to law, the most arresting Pauline persuasion that comes across in his letters is that the law is powerless to deliver salvation. Indeed, it was never meant to. It is not just the law in its substance but also the whole epoch marked by its nominal sway which fails to deliver what sinful humanity needs for salvation. Paul is capable of strong language when he speaks of the ministry of Moses as a dispensation of death (2 Cor 3:7). Considered from the standpoint of the letter and spirit of the law, the law is our nemesis, for who has so lived by it as to fulfill the plenitude of its requirements (Gal 3:10)? But Paul does not object to the law as a way *of* life given by

---

131. Brueggemann, *Theology of the Old Testament*, 598.

God to the Jewish people; it is just not the way *to* life, which way is barred until the coming of Christ (Gal 3:24). If it seems extravagant to cast law in terms of a dispensation of death, the language reflects the underlying conviction that death has held sway since before the law made its formal appearance in the life of Israel and it is powerless to burst through the shroud of death which engulfs post-Adamic humanity.

In the case of Hebrews, the "challenge" to the law emerges in the writer's treatment of the sacrificial system and its inability to cleanse the conscience. Like Paul, he views law as a provision for a time. The covenant which enshrines that provision is now obsolete. But the author's theological point in elaborating this includes pastoral responsibility to secure the perseverance of Christian converts in a life of obedience to God through Christ. They are en route to the promised land of heavenly inheritance. Forgiveness through atonement becomes the permanent foundation of the Christian pilgrim's life, who daily comes to God through Christ. Christian life stands under the covering of an atonement and a need for a forgiveness provided by a permanent high priesthood in the heavenly place. Hebrews arrives at much the same point as does Paul when Paul declares that works of the law cannot save. The law did not save in its day and our works will not save us now that its day is done. Yet when atonement renews and redraws the community of the people of God, it is so that Jew and Gentile, saved by grace, may abandon sin and "do good works, which God prepared in advance for us to do" (Eph 2:10). Hebrews speaks consistently with this (e.g., Heb 10:24). "Requirements" are attached to the new as much as to the old covenant, if such a heartless and legalistic word may be used for the privilege of growth in holiness. Any emphasis on justification by faith which overlooks or denigrates this misunderstands the nature of covenant in its relation to law.

Conclusion

The essays which comprise this part of our volume began with the question of the land. God's covenant with Abraham and his seed included the design that they should receive the land and that the land should be a place for the demonstration of righteousness. The land is not an end in itself. The book of Joshua, which describes the occupation of the land, begins and ends with the insistence that righteousness be practiced within it. With Deuteronomy behind it and a stretch of history and prophecy before it, it refuses to comfort the people with any clear assurance that the gift of land will never be rescinded, even under conditions of persistent disobedience. An ominous verse is tucked away in Deuteronomy: "The Lord will send you back in ships to Egypt on a journey I said you should never make again" (Deut 28:68). Israelite breach of the covenant does not leave God unilaterally bound to preserve the land on behalf of any generation to which he promised it. If the book of Joshua is nonetheless implicitly undergirded by a covenant promise that cannot be broken, it is of little comfort to those who flout the law, for they will forfeit their status as beneficiaries of even an immutable promise. Only God knows and only history will disclose how promise and performance coalesce and to what precisely God has bound himself by irrevocable covenant.

Land and promise, covenant and law, are all contextualized by the prospect of a new heaven and new earth where righteousness will dwell, a promise twice mentioned in the Old and twice mentioned in the New Testaments.[132] It is a hope which does not come to light in the book of Joshua. Yet the perspectives on covenant and on law which do come to light therein not only belong to that epoch but also stand as a direct address and enduring testimony to all generations. As disobedience to the covenant could mean exclusion from the privileges of the land, so those Scriptures which set before our eyes the grand vision of the new heaven and earth do not withhold reference to those who remain outside that eschatological land (Rev. 22:11-15). The covenant has a wide reach, but it is not unconditional to the point that human righteousness is deprived of an ultimate significance. In its way, this is the sobering and permanently relevant message of Joshua too.

God of Miracle and Mystery

Something Rich and Strange

The God of whom we read in the book of Joshua gives land, commands slaughter, forbids idolatry, and enters into a covenant relationship with his people. It goes without saying that he is a God of remarkable power over the nonhuman and human worlds. Within the covers of this book, we encounter some of the most celebrated miracle stories in the Old Testament, including the fall of Jericho and the sun's arrest in the middle of the sky for the space of what we should normally reckon about a day. The narrator was no less impressed than we are by this last account, observing that "there has never been a day like it before or since, a day when the Lord listened to a man." What does it prove? "Surely the Lord was fighting for Israel!" (10:13-14). Earlier, and be-

---

132. Isa 65:17; 66:22; 2 Pet 3:13; Rev 21:1.

fore the collapse of Jericho, we have read of the people of Israel crossing the Jordan into the land of Canaan. As it was a time of flood, the river was particularly turbulent. "Yet as soon as the priests who carried the ark reached the Jordan and their feet touched the water's edge, the water from upstream stopped flowing. It piled up in a heap a great distance away" so the people crossed over on dry ground (3:15-17). The miraculous is compounded by the strange in this part of the book, for after this and before the unorthodox campaign against Jericho, Joshua meets a mysterious figure with a drawn sword in his hand, commander of the army of the Lord (5:13-15).

Many readers will quite simply read these accounts as the expression of a primitive worldview and that is that. Are they not obviously mythological, whether we use that term in a rather loose or rather more technical sense? In Old Testament studies, there was an interest in myth long before Rudolf Bultmann, in the twentieth century, influentially proposed his distinction between the existential meaning and the mythological form of biblical stories. The eighteenth century witnessed a major assault on the traditional belief in miracles.[133] Belief in both their possibility and their actuality was a significant component in Christian apologetics at the time because miracles were evidence for the existence of God. For some, denying the factual truth of biblical accounts of miracle was not an invitation to grasp the religious truth of the Bible in a positive, subtler, and more sophisticated way. Rather, it contributed to the case for rejecting belief in a transcendent deity.[134]

Since at least the eighteenth century, it has been widely held that scientific explanation rules out the miraculous, and scientific culture has been foundational in the modern West. But in the twentieth century the logic of scientific explanation came under fresh scrutiny. What we loosely term "postmodernity" is perhaps the most celebrated intellectual-cum-popular expression of the position that there is no universal "reason" and hence no pure scientific reason around with a right to function as an arbiter of what everyone should believe. On this view, there is no one standard of rationality which all right-thinking humans should deploy. Those who think otherwise may be judged guilty of exhibiting a colonial mentality, as though Westerners had a rational grip on reality superior to inhabitants of less scientific cultures. If this challenge to rationality is in order, the question arises: by what criterion do secularized Westerners presume to dismiss non-Western worldviews as

---

133. For an illuminating account, see Burns, *The Great Debate on Miracles*.

134. For the way in which German-speaking and English-speaking theologians could differ in their judgments about the religious significance of the "historical" reading of the Bible, see Frei, *The Eclipse of Biblical Narrative*, ch. 3.

primitive and subrational? The West is not uniform anyway: witness the proliferation of religious groups and cults whose worldviews are anything but scientific in a modern sense.

Given all this, is it misguided to ponder science in relation to Scripture as we step our third-millennial feet into the waters of discussion about the Jordan or contemplate walls that collapse and suns that stop? Surely not. The Enlightenment and post-Enlightenment critique of miracles still holds considerable sway. If it appears passé to approach Joshua with this in mind, we might ask to what extent those who professedly relegate "Enlightenment" questions to the margins of importance actually tacitly assume the basic validity of a scientific outlook that squeezes out miracle even as they concentrate their literary, socio-anthropological, or theological efforts on understanding the text of Joshua. The miraculous is prominent in the book of Joshua, and it is right to ask how we should think about it today. Certainly, we do an injustice to the biblical accounts of miracles if we scrutinize them simply with the narrow question in mind of whether something of the kind could or did happen. On even the most conservative reading, the stories are fraught with a significance way beyond considerations of mere fact. Yet the signifier (the miracle) is worth considering along with whatever it signifies. And if we are interested in universally popular and not just professionally academic readings and appropriations of Joshua, we should not too readily shunt off "Enlightenment"-type issues into an intellectual siding.

Approaching the Miraculous

The Bible neither outlines a concept nor sets forward a definition of miracle. However, if miracles are up for theological discussion, do we not need to start with a definition? How are we to conceive of miracles? Are they supposed to be violations of the laws of nature? Or are they violations just of our current ways of understanding those laws? Or should we drop talk of "laws of nature" altogether and talk about "observed regularities" which miracles allegedly defy? In a philosophical investigation, we might proceed by deciding on our definition and then ask whether, on that definition of miracle, miracles could possibly occur. If we conclude that they could, we should then ask whether any miracles actually have occurred. But biblical authors obviously do not proceed like that. Their language, when it comes to what we call "miracles," is the language of observation and testimony rather than of conceptualization. Further, although the word "miracle" can be found in English translations of the Bible, it can translate more than one word in the original languages and, correspondingly, a variety of terms and descriptions may be found in the Bible for what we, in standard English, tend to dub "miracle" or "the miraculous." Accordingly, the proper focus of our inquiry is the actual phenomena recorded in Joshua, not words and definitions, even if there are significant biblical words and concepts that we could profitably track down in a more comprehensive study of miracle.

Speaking generally, from a biblical point of view, God does many things in this world, some more and some less extraordinary. His acts are not neatly classifiable into the miraculous and nonmiraculous and may be regarded as marvellous, however one distributes them. God "performs wonders that cannot be fathomed, miracles that cannot be counted. He bestows rain on the earth; he sends water upon the countryside."[135] If it seems natural to most of us to isolate a group of occurrences and call them "miraculous," we shall probably include more than one type of event within our group. For example, there are cases of "freak" occurrences which nonetheless do not completely defy scientific explanation. The crossing of the Jordan in Joshua recalls the crossing of the Sea of Reeds recorded in the book of Exodus. In the Exodus account, we read of the agency of an outstandingly powerful east wind which divides the waters, enabling the people of Israel to cross (Exod 14:21). What is extraordinary in this occurrence is not just that a freak wind arises ("freak" is here used loosely and nontechnically) but that it should do so just as a large number of people stood at the water's edge, desperate to escape. This scenario has given rise to the description "coincidence miracle."[136] The presence of a "natural" component in "miracle" — in this case, the explicable, if extraordinary, wind — may be something frequently assumed by writers of biblical accounts, as far as we know, even when they do not say so. For example, what is supposed to be marvelous about Jesus' securing a huge haul of fish is presumably not that he or God suddenly created the fish *ex nihilo*, but that he knew by prophetic or more than prophetic insight that a congregation of fish — a phenomenon not in itself inexplica-

---

135. Job 5:9-10. "Miracles" is a possible, but certainly not necessary, translation of the Hebrew here; "wonders" is no less felicitous. Much of what Job deemed inexplicable is now deemed scientifically explicable. Eichrodt remarks that "even the course of Nature itself counts as a 'miracle' in the Old Testament," *Theology of the Old Testament*, 2:162. His brief account (162-67), proceeding from a succinct report on the relevant Hebrew vocabulary, brings out the evidential and redemptive significance of miracles, although it contains the questionable judgment that the blowing of the east wind at the Sea of Reeds was among "ordinary everyday events."

136. We are not concerned with this account in its totality, which introduces not just the unexpected wind, but implies a long duration for the physical conditions which followed if we count the number of people who allegedly crossed the sea at the time.

ble — was present in the vicinity where future disciples had been engaged in fruitless search (Luke 5:1-11; cf. John 21:1-14). It has been claimed that most Old Testament miracles are of this kind.[137]

But not all biblical accounts can be viewed in this light. Stories of turning water into wine or the feeding of the five thousand, taken as they stand, look like events of a different order; *par excellence,* this is the case with the resurrection of Jesus of Nazareth from the dead. So we might stipulate four things as we approach Joshua. First, what we commonly refer to as "miracles" might turn out to cover different types of events. Second, Scripture does not, in any case, directly conceptualize what we term "miracles." Third, we cannot approach the miraculous in Joshua either by looking up the English word "miracle" in a biblical concordance or by selecting particular Hebrew and Greek words to see if they occur in the narrative. Fourth, we should not approach Joshua armed with an independently acquired definition of "miracle." So where do we go from here?

What Exactly Are We Told?

Leaving aside, for a moment, the story of Joshua's encounter with the stranger outside Jericho, three "miracle" incidents stand out in the book of Joshua: the crossing of the Jordan, the collapse of Jericho, and the sun standing still over Gibeon. In the first case, the crossing of the Jordan, we are not told that a wind was responsible for the heaping up and cutting off of the waters, but the account is strongly reminiscent of what happened at the Sea of Reeds (4:23); the earliest transmitters, writers, and readers might have assumed, or at least allowed for, the presence of a wind, if we can rather anachronistically describe their intellectual processes in that way. In the second case, the fall of Jericho, the cause of collapse appears to be the yelling of the people. An "Enlightenment" reader who wanted both to defend the historicity of the account and to offer some scientific explanation for it could do so by postulating a tremor, a kind of earthquake, divinely synchronized with the yells of the people. Whether or not there is any point in pursuing such an explanation, it does not formally collide with the biblical account.[138] The point is that the "rationalist" who takes a "conservative" view of the historicity of these two accounts — the crossing of the Jordan and the collapse of Jericho — can, in

---

137. Jacob, *Theology of the Old Testament,* 225.
138. However, I am not persuaded that Brueggemann is correct to regard this type of approach as injurious to biblical salvation history; see *Theology of the Old Testament,* 35.

principle, invoke scientific explanation, at least within limits, whether or not he or she is well advised to do so.

Do matters stand on the same footing in the case of the sun? Initially, we may think not. It is not just that no natural forces are *mentioned*, as they are in the case of the crossing of the Sea of Reeds, or are perhaps *assumed*, as in the case of the crossing of the Jordan. It is that no natural forces seem to be *possible*, in the way that we might posit in the case of Jericho. The cosmic consequences of the state of affairs described in the account of the sun's arrest in midsky are of a different order from those that would obtain if the river Jordan had dammed or the walls of Jericho did collapse. They are rather earthshaking.

> In order for the sun to stand still to permit Joshua to kill more Amorites the earth would have to stop rotating. We must think about the consequences of that. The circumference of the earth at the equator is only slightly less than 25,000 miles. The earth rotates once every 24 hours. This means that any object at the equator has a linear velocity of more than 1,000 miles an hour. If the earth were suddenly to stop rotating the law of inertia tells us that anything not securely tied down would continue to move in a straight line tangent to the surface of the earth at its original velocity of 1,000 miles an hour. If this happened there would still be bunny rabbits and toad frogs in orbit, not to mention cataclysmic geological disruptions of the earth's surface. The enormous inertial forces generated by such a sudden halt would have destroyed everything on the planet if not the earth itself.
>
> Since there are no such curious objects flying around in space and no evidence of any such geological disturbances, we can only conclude that the earth did not stop rotating.[139]

Now it may be thought that anyone who seriously believes today that Joshua's sun stood still deserves this sort of riposte and should be sent packing on unpaid leave to prosecute a search for flying bunnies. And may they fall into black holes in the company of white rabbits. But if we pause to inquire into what we are actually told, Joshua does not tell us that, as a matter of scientific fact, the sun stood still. In the sixteenth and seventeenth centuries, controversy was famously generated over the scientific claim that the sun did not go round the earth but that the earth orbited the sun. There was a worry abroad that this claim contradicted Scripture. Ecclesiastes says baldly, inasmuch as it says anything baldly: "The sun rises . . ." (Eccl 1:5). Yet, no informed reader today assumes any collision between science and Scripture on this

---

139. Tilghman, *An Introduction to the Philosophy of Religion*, 108.

point; indeed, plenty of readers did not do so at the time.[140] Whatever biblical authors and readers thought was really going on in the heavens, statements like these are observation statements and not scientific statements, indicating what was perceived and not propounding a scientific statement. We, in our own time, do not hesitate to speak of the sun's rising. In the account in question, the sun over Gibeon and the moon over Aijalon certainly emanated a light that made them extraordinarily visible to the naked eye, and the account just as certainly picks out the unique nature of what went on, including God's heeding the voice of a man. Indeed, this last is a key theological point in the narrative. Here we merely note that talk of the sun and moon stopping is observation language just as in the case of the sun rising and going down. The person of tender scientific conscience with an interest in reading about Jordan and Jericho in a scientific light need not worry that the light over Gibeon is bound to blot out the light of science.

But does this whole approach to the narrative belong in a time warp, to the eighteenth and nineteenth Enlightenment centuries, if not the sixteenth and seventeenth Copernican centuries? Are we missing a rich vein of theology or myth in a misguided quest for history? At points in this commentary, the question of the historicity of the accounts in Joshua has briefly raised its head. We take up this question at greater length not in this essay but in "Reading Joshua Today," below. A long tale can be told about the history of biblical interpretation in its bearing on the question of history and historicity.[141] The question of historicity is itself perched on the back of other questions, including the question of literary genre. What kind of accounts are we looking at? Were they crafted as historical or mythical or some combination or something else? Did author or tradent mean to say that such and such an event happened as described or was he happy to incorporate myths, legends, sagas, or whatever we should name them, for this or that purpose? How does a "canonical" reading affect these questions?[142] And are we to expect anything but provisional and tentative answers?[143]

---

140. For a quick way into the history, see McGrath, *Science and Religion*, ch. 1. See too his *The Foundations of Dialogue in Science and Religion*, 122-29. However, I shall be using the language of "observation statements" rather than his "accommodation."

141. For an angle specifically on Old Testament theology, see Perdue, *The Collapse of History*.

142. See the work of Childs, esp. *Introduction to the Old Testament as Scripture*; and *Biblical Theology of the Old and New Testaments*.

143. "From where we stand we probably have no way of recovering what might have figured as a fact in the ancient Hebrew mind, whether the narrative data of centuries-old oral traditions were assumed to be facts, or to what extent the writers consciously exercise a license of

However we answer these questions, it may be widely presupposed that scientific considerations rule out a fruitful pursuit of history and miracle in Joshua even if literary considerations should legitimize the inquiry by suggesting that the accounts were designed to be read basically as report. But suppose that we do conclude on literary grounds that things are much as they superficially appear, i.e., that the canonical book of Joshua proposes to us that we believe in the literal historical occurrence of what is narrated.[144] If so, is not science sufficiently culturally important to warrant some rumination on the question of miracle? In any case, behind the two sets of questions — the significance of science, on the one hand, and the appropriation of Scripture, on the other — lie theological issues which make it worth sticking to the trail on which we have embarked. For those theological questions lead us to the heart of matters to which the book of Joshua bears witness.

The Scientific Question

Scientific and religious domains are often contrasted in terms of knowledge and opinion, or proof and subjectivity, or public truth and private belief. Developments in twentieth-century philosophy of science, independently of the philosophy of religion, challenged this contrast. Questions were asked about what makes a statement scientific; whether a statement could only rightly be called scientific if it was falsifiable; whether we have a right to speak of scientific certainties; how scientific theories change.[145] What should scientific and philosophical laypersons make of all this? In all likelihood, most of us will intuitively fight shy of total scepticism and will assume that human beings can know or judge probable at least *some* things of scientific significance. On the other hand, we shall be unclear about what kinds of things we might sensibly claim to know and wonder whether a sound philosophy of science leads us to

---

invention," observes Alter, *The World of Biblical Literature*, 54. With reference to responses to his early and important work, *The Art of the Biblical Narrative*, see Alter's clarification, in the volume from which I have quoted, on the subject of "fiction" (39). See too Alter and Kermode, *The Literary Guide to the Bible*.

144. To talk of the "canonical book" as "proposing" is shorthand and not strictly accurate: see Barr's legitimate complaints in "Childs' Introduction to the Old Testament as Scripture." The phrase "literal historical occurrence" does not imply that historical occurrences can only be literally, and not pictorially, described.

145. The names of Kuhn, Popper, Lakatos, and Feyerabend became particularly associated with challenges to received opinion. There is a brilliant, if deliberately limited, account and critique of some of these tendencies in Stove, *Popper and After*.

suspend confidence about at least *some* beliefs standardly and confidently held. So the question of scientific "knowledge" is quite independently complex without wheeling religious issues into the fray.

On the religious front, Judaism, Christianity, and Islam have traditionally shared the conviction that God is the Creator and sustainer of the world. He has purposes for it which he is able to achieve. Nature does not possess independent power of the kind that constrains God. It may bear the marks of a rational order. Genuine causal powers are operative within it. But if we are right to speak of laws operating within it, they do so because they are created forces subject to their Creator. Winds and waves behave in ways that scientists can describe, but that is consonant with the fundamental conviction that they are subject to the living, active, omnipresent Creator. This theological dimension informs and is fundamental to the whole of Scripture, Joshua included. Anyone who believes in the existence of such a Creator — for whatever reason, whether good or bad — is bound to approach the question of miracles in that light. Scripture testifies to a God who has created a world in which he can act in various ways whose outward forms may be perceptible but whose inner nature may or may not be more or less fathomable.

Does this mean that, for all we know, God might have made the sun stop in the sky and not just look as though it did? Is this not obviously possible for the God of Joshua? We have to tread carefully here, and we shall approach this question by what may look like a roundabout route. Scripture does not actually go so far as to commit us to the theoretical conviction that just anything could have happened and can happen in the world. It is true that God is powerful over all. The word "omnipotent" has been used traditionally to pick out this characteristic of God, but the meaning we should attach to it has proved so difficult to specify precisely that even hardened philosophers have wondered whether we should give up any attempt to define "omnipotence."[146] Defenders of omnipotence have sometimes qualified this attribute by saying that there are some things that God cannot do, such as love evil or destroy himself. It may also seem clear that God cannot do something logically impossible, such as make a square circle. Both questions of truth and questions of meaning arise here, and it is not always clear wherein their boundaries lie. If you tell me that you were in London yesterday, I normally know what you mean, but I may have no idea whether your statement is truthful. However, if you tell me that you drew a square circle yesterday, I might say that this cannot be true, but I might and

---

146. See Kenny, *The God of the Philosophers*, ch. 7. It is another matter whether "omnipotence" is the optimal description of God's power as portrayed in the Bible.

Theology in the Book of Joshua

should more strictly say that I just do not know what you mean.[147] Let us pursue this for a moment.

The difficulty of establishing in principle or at least of drawing in practice exact boundaries between questions of truth and questions of meaning emerges if we consider this question: Can the God of the Bible turn a human being into an animal?[148] Some might answer: "Yes," on the grounds that God is omnipotent. Others, however, might say that the question cannot be directly answered, for it is not clear what it means. Do we mean that the human ceases to be human? If so, is there any difference between saying that the human was *changed into* an animal and saying that an animal miraculously appeared on the spot where the human was physically located a moment ago? Or are we saying that the human has morphed into a kind of hybrid, a kind of human soul in an animal body? Some might insist that it is impossible to decide on the matter of *truth* of such claims until we have answered these questions about *meaning*. But there is still another approach from the perspective of the "God of the Bible." It might be granted that the question has meaning, but that it does not follow that even the all-powerful God could have changed and can change a human into an animal. Why not? Because this God, for all we know, may have created a world in which certain things are just not possible. And this may be one of them. This does not demean God. It was his decision to create this kind of world. We might not know what is or what is not possible in this world. Nor might we know the difference between a possibility within our world that God *could* actualize if he wanted to, but never would, and a possibility whose occurrence God has *categorically* eliminated in constituting the world as he did. So, we could say in principle, without detracting from divine power, that, for all we know, God has set up a world where certain things, such as turning humans into animals by some sort of metamorphosis, cannot happen.

We are not bound, then, to approach the text in Joshua assuming that it testifies to a God who has created a world where just anything can happen. If the text does not actually tell us that the world stopped rotating, more than Ecclesiastes tells us that the sun actually rises, is it a total waste of time — as

---

147. More strictly still, talk of square circles is not obviously meaningless: see Morris, *The Logic of God Incarnate*, 21, n. 4.

148. This is not an idle question; I was myself confronted with it when I first visited West Africa, because it had allegedly been witnessed. Cf. Augustine, *Concerning the City of God against the Pagans*, 782-84. Commenting on Dan 4:13, 29 (16, 32) and Ps 73:22, Jacob remarked that "the worst punishment a man can suffer is to be reduced to the state of an animal"; *Theology of the Old Testament*, 152. Of course, those passages do not say that a human turned or can turn into an animal.

some will judge that it is for other reasons — to ask whether the God of Joshua *could have* stopped the world rotating? Perhaps not. Hermeneutical issues arise that affect the way that we read Joshua. The empirical findings of science have helped the church to read Scripture aright. Copernicus and Galileo convinced a number of people that Scripture could not be saying that the sun went round the earth because science had shown that this was not the case. Of course, a scientific demonstration cannot determine exegesis. It may be that science and Scripture cannot be harmonized and that one is right and the other wrong. But Galileo and company promoted a way of reading Scripture which chimes in with the results of appropriate hermeneutical sensitivity to the literature in its own right, quite apart from anything that we learn from science. Nobody now thinks that we read biblical language about the sun rising as an observation statement only in a desperate hermeneutical maneuver to find a way of harmonizing science with Scripture.

So what is the hermeneutical significance of the flying bunny for our reading of Joshua? In principle, exactly the same as that of the Copernican discovery. We might conclude that the earth cannot have stopped rotating; that, if we have some reason to defend the historicity and truth of Joshua's account, it cannot be saying that the sun actually stood still; and that, on literary grounds, we should in any case never have read it as making that scientific statement more than we should have read talk of the rising sun as a scientific statement. But suspicion might linger that we have herein abandoned the God of Joshua — that the price we pay for reading this story in a way that does not violate scientific truth, and so reading it broadly in line with the way that we are reading of the Jordan and Jericho, is a denial of divine omnipotence. Hence our earlier discussion. As far as we know, there are certain things that just cannot happen in our world. Maybe God cannot stop suns in the sky without sending frogs into orbit. There is much about what God can or cannot do about which we are in the dark. Joshua's religious sensibility may have instructed him that his God could do *anything that he wanted*. But the book that bears his name does not formulate the belief that God can do *anything whatsoever* in the world that he has created, of which the stopping sun is an example. Nor does it deny any such belief.

We may believe that the background, history, genre, or ideology in and of the text before us has not required of us this whole discussion. However, the question of miracle cannot be a matter of indifference to anyone who believes that God raised Jesus from the dead and maintains that this lies at the heart of Christian faith. Hence our conceptual sortie into the realm of miracle, prominent as it is in connection with the book of Joshua. Quizzed by a philosophical Gibeonite, Joshua would scarcely have paused in the middle of battle to fire back: "Is anything too hard for the Lord?" (Gen 18:14). And no philosophical Israelite should have been ashamed of his answer. Reference to the resurrection helps us to clarify a further point. Our discussion has not implied that we suspend decisions on the meaning and truth of all Scriptural accounts in the light of science. The Gospels direct us both to read (the question of meaning) and to believe (the question of truth) that Jesus rose bodily from the dead. If folk are persuaded that scientific knowledge makes it impossible to subscribe to such a belief, that does not entitle them to suspect that they have misread Scripture. It means that they have to choose between science and Scripture.[149] Copernicus put us on the trail to a better hermeneutic and allowed those with an interest in defending the historicity of the incident at Gibeon to do so without scientific worry. But it does not follow that science makes Scripture pliable or that all the "miracles" of which we read in Scripture are explicable in the same way. The power of Joshua's God remains hermeneutically significant.[150]

The Half-Seen World

"Now when Joshua was near Jericho, he looked up and saw a man standing in front of him with a drawn sword in his hand. Joshua went up to him and asked, 'Are you for us or for our enemies?' 'Neither,' he replied, 'but as commander of the army of the Lord I have now come.' Then Joshua fell facedown on the ground in reverence, and asked him, 'What message does my Lord have for his servant?'" (5:13-14). This incident is sandwiched between the unorthodox crossing of the Jordan and the unorthodox razing of Jericho. In the Old Testament, we occasionally encounter figures that refuse to fall neatly into our categories, figures that leave us wondering not only whether we are reading about God, a manifestation of God, an angel, or a human being but also whether we even understand much about our own distinctions. In the scene before us now, we meet someone who apparently turns out to be a sort of angel. Joshua initially takes him for a mere mortal, so he presumably looks like one, but he manifests in person and word the presence of Yahweh himself in a way that transcends mere humanity. What are we to make of him? Does he not clearly inhabit a primitive worldview which no longer holds? Is there

---

149. It is not suggested here that we must make the choice; my own position, along with that of many theistic scientists, is that it is impossible for scientific reason to disprove the possibility of resurrection.

150. For some useful remarks not usually cited in connection with the discussion of miracle, see John McLeod Campbell, *The Nature of the Atonement*, xxxvi-xliv.

any objection to Thomas Thompson's acid remark that romantic folktales like this "taste so much of free-floating fantasy that they are washed of their grue"?[151] Or, if a little space has been cleared for those who believe in miracles, will we now believe anything?

The questions as stated assume a particular cultural background, a secular formation. Life is experienced differently in those large tracts of Africa, for example, which are immune from the Western influences that increasingly pervade their towns and cities. Why on earth do we so often talk as though both theological questions and theological norms ought to derive from the West?[152] Is it really an absurdity if the world of "spirits," including God, gods, demons, and angels, is experienced as fully as real as the world of "matter"? More tamely, a dualistic separation of "spirit" and "matter" is foreign to cultures such as we find in Africa and, as far as this goes, Africa is quite near to the biblical world or worlds.[153] For one reason or another, dualism may be widely rejected in the West as well; however, what appears odd to many non-Westerners is not Joshua's story but the fact that Westerners are so blinkered and provincial that they have serious difficulty with believing the story at face value. An opposing point of view is that, while it is perhaps possible that there exists some sort of God and that strange and inexplicable things happen in the world, it is sheer superstitious primitivism to read today accounts such as we find in Joshua and actually believe that commanders of the Lord's army merrily jaunt across earth and sky and sea. Others again will conclude that both outlooks incorporate strengths and weaknesses and that neither has an entirely satisfactory purchase on reality.

Discussion of miracles shows to what extent our reading of biblical narratives is dependent on our convictions about the existence and nature of God. Although our convictions do not actually determine our reading, from our belief or disbelief at this point much flows. The hermeneutical force of a positive

---

151. "Holy War at the Center of Biblical Theology," 224. He goes on to remark that, "viewed historically, one must surely find it an odd religion which has a God who chooses an ever-worthless folk for his own, while viewing all the world's peoples with murderous enmity," 224. I leave the reader to assess this observation.

152. Although his thesis is not strictly à propos of our inquiry (and I am not persuaded by it anyway), Oden's recent contribution on *How Africa Shaped the Christian Mind*, acts as something of a spur to cultural humility.

153. See, e.g., Taylor, *The Primal Vision: Christian Presence amid African Religions*. Jenkins observes that "if there is a single key area of faith and practice that divides Northern and Southern Christians, it is this matter of spiritual forces and their effects on the everyday world"; *The Next Christendom*, 123. As I tend to use "West" loosely where other descriptions might be more accurate, so "Northern" is used somewhat loosely in this quotation, in light of what has just been written about South Korea.

Theology in the Book of Joshua

belief in the existence of God is significantly diminished unless belief is accompanied by a lively sense of divine reality. In traditional Christian thought, God is a personal reality who is both transcendent (existing apart from the world and not identified with it) and immanent (present throughout the world in power).[154] The being of God is unlike that of anyone or anything else and knows no parallels. God thus transcends our comprehension. Neither divine transcendence nor divine immanence can be described according to their innate ontological reality. But if God exists in a form of being radically different from, while sustaining, the forms that we standardly experience in the world, this opens up a space for the possibility of an angelic world, an ontological dimension different from that of the created human and visible nonhuman worlds. Theism, if such a cold and abstract word be allowed, broadly makes angels possible, whatever we make of Joshua 5 in particular.

Our beliefs about angels are by no means culturally marginal, even in the West.[155] Some years ago, Frank Peretti's work, *This Present Darkness*, reported on a whole world of supernatural powers, figures, and territories.[156] Although the author apparently intended his work to be read as fiction, it lit a fire of convinced imagination in a large number of readers, and the topography of spiritual warfare has been mapped out in military detail in schemes of religious thought that take seriously belief in the territorial spirits that roam the earth. It is not surprising that Scripture is sourced as this way of thinking. In Job, Satan is said to roam the earth (Job 1:7). In Zechariah, where Satan puts in another appearance, horsemen patrol the earth and report to God on what they find (Zech 1:10-11; 3:1-2). A character named Michael is in the thick of conflict in the book of Daniel (Dan 10:13–12:1) and reappears in Revelation (Rev 12:7; cf. Jude 9). Jesus contends with a number of demons, some of which move between arid places and human bodies (Luke 11:24). Joshua's commander of the army of the Lord may cut a dramatic figure, but he does not stand canonically alone in supernatural combat.[157]

The Joshua scenario, not to mention the broader biblical one, understandably perplexes a body of readers who wish neither to discount various

---

154. But see the "quiet revolution" that has taken place in the twentieth and twenty-first centuries in a panentheistic direction; Clayton and Peacocke, *In Whom We Live and Move and Have Our Being*. And, of course, there have been a number of other alternatives around for a long time.

155. The angel logos that pop up all over Western towns and cities breed a familiarity with angels; many contemporary youth and adults apparently do not regard them as just a subject of playful superstition.

156. Peretti, *This Present Darkness*.

157. See Lane, *The Unseen World*.

angelic possibilities nor to adopt them uncritically. They are persuaded that God exists and was incarnate in Jesus Christ, through whom we have the forgiveness of sin; also, that Jesus rose from the dead. Astonishing as the thought is that Jesus shall reappear and establish a future kingdom, such a notion at least interlocks with testimony to the resurrection and belief in God as Creator. They believe in the Holy Spirit, too. They do not lack intellectual space for belief in angelic powers, both good and evil. For some, it is a short step from this, and none too difficult, to believing in conversations with the commander of the Lord's army held several centuries before Christ. For others, however, there is a significant difference between admitting the principle of the existence of an angelic realm and believing in such a conversation. The difference may not be easy to account for in terms of any solid logic. Still, it may be uneasily experienced — felt more than explained.

Of course, the question of literary genre has priority here, as with the miracle accounts in Joshua, but in this case, as in the case of miracles, theological questions obtrude. Whatever we make of genre in respect of Joshua 5, both testaments indicate a cosmic order in which heavenly commanders can indeed hold converse with earthly mortals. It does look as though, if we consistently maintain that Jesus rose from the dead by the agency of a Creator God, we really should not have too much trouble in principle with believing the account of Joshua's encounter with the stranger outside Jericho. Draped in the numinous as the story is, the numinous should be credible. That being said, two checks must be placed on those habits of thought that uncritically receive the account as it stands.

First, there is and always has been a huge amount of superstition abroad, a frame of (perhaps untutored) mind which believes without any foundation, tests nothing and scrutinizes nothing, assuming that the question of biblical meaning and truth is problem-free once one or two easy presuppositions are in place. But if there is such a thing as blind unbelief as well as blind faith, there is also such a thing as a healthy skepticism. In 1777 David Hume's influential chapter on miracles saw the light of day.[158] Among other things, Hume pointed out that folk are prone to lap up accounts of the extraordinary, which transmit an agreeable feeling of excited pleasure. Even if we dissent from Hume's overall conclusion, which effectively rules out the propriety of believing in miracles, his point here is importantly correct. It may appear arrogant to affirm that "Western rationality" puts us in a superior position to "non-Western" cultures. But if some non-Western cultures have much to teach us in the way of a lively sense of spiritual realities, the tradition

---

158. Hume, *An Enquiry into Human Understanding*, section 10.

of critical thought in Europe rightly instructs us to beware of unfounded, untested fantastical notions, to say the very least. Such notions easily infect the addlepated brain, injecting it with ideas of an exciting world whose traffic weaves in and out of our own, like Harry Potter's Night Bus.[159] It is salutary to remember how Paul instructed Christian converts. He was persuaded of the reality of principalities and powers and, indeed, perhaps the main and fatal weakness of our churches today is that they consider their struggle to be merely with flesh and blood (Eph 6:12). But those Pauline and non-Pauline pastoral exhortations that have been preserved in the Scriptures of the Christian church discourage us from indulgence in foolish supernatural excitement and curiosity.

The second check kicks in when we bear in mind that Joshua does not provide a blueprint for later experience. Ludwig Feuerbach somewhere made a scathing remark to the effect that nothing ever happened normally in Old Testament Israel. It was a neat and mischievous comment, but very wide of target. "Normal" life is the assumed background against which the Israelites experienced all that they experienced. "Miracle" is no more portrayed in the Old Testament as a representation of daily life than highly selected Premiership football or NFL Super Bowl highlights are meant to represent what happens in the world of football. "In the contemporary world," a contemporary Old Testament scholar remarks, "asses do not talk, prophets do not ascend to heaven in whirlwinds."[160] We should take his verb tenses entirely seriously and add: "They do no such thing in Israel either." Further, we should remember that the course of Israel's history and the character of its witness are not meant to be typical of universal human experience. We are dealing with a single nation with a single history and a particular destiny.

This is not to say that a range of religious phenomena found in Israel is unparalleled outside it, either in literature or in experience. Neither is it to deny the possibilities of dramatic "supernatural" encounters in the third millennium anywhere in the world; on the contrary, only dogmatic atheism or Western provincialism will deny or play down this possibility. It is simply to issue a warning. We may give credence to what we read about Joshua at the Jordan, outside Jericho, at Jericho, and at Gibeon. But credence is not credulity and what happens in one time and place is no blueprint for all times and spaces in a world which progresses through various stages to its divinely-

---

159. Delightfully featured in the film of *Harry Potter and the Prisoner of Azkaban* (2004).

160. Perdue, *The Collapse of History*, 259. We should complete his sentence: ". . . and holy war is a nightmare of terrorist insanity." In light of the earlier reference to Eichrodt (n. 135), we note that Eichrodt emphasises that miracle stories are unevenly distributed in the Old Testament and hence are not typical of all phases of national life.

appointed end. Scripture is best read and studied in the company of people of a different background and culture from the one familiar to us in our personal experience. The more we do that, the humbler we shall become in interpretation. And the less we do so, the more we should refrain from dogmatic judgments in interpretation. As a result, we might learn of spiritual encounters that transcend anything that we presently imagine. But we might also develop a tough-minded, hard-nosed rigor in ferreting out the facts surrounding putative claims about the supernatural, across times, spaces, religions, and cultures. In either case, the heart of the matter is that the God who summoned Israel to be his people and who revealed himself in Jesus Christ is the reality of all realities, miraculous or otherwise. There is no substitute for a rigorous interpretation of biblical literature, but no credible interpretation will deny that this reality is the substance of its testimony.

Joshua and Biblical Theology

Introduction

The purpose of the present section is (a) to draw out the theological themes of the book of Joshua and (b) to discuss them in their biblical context. These two aspects of interpretation cannot be absolutely separated, as the theology of Joshua is bound up with its function within the narrative of Genesis to Kings. We begin, therefore, by locating Joshua in that narrative.

In undertaking this it is necessary to enter a note of caution. The reader of a narrative is confronted by many possibilities of interpretation. No full account of the meaning of a narrative can be given, and any reading of it will be colored by the reader's own interests and questions. This is evident not least in the myriad of narrative studies that now exist on individual sections of Genesis-Kings, quite apart from the corpus as a whole. One example is those readings of Genesis which have highlighted the roles of women in many of the stories and shown that they have frequently been overlooked in traditional readings. Or again, parts of Exodus have been appropriated in the interests of a politics of liberation. Many such readings can justify themselves by looking at the texts from certain angles or focusing on particular features, though in principle they remain open to critical scrutiny, and the notion of misreading, on the grounds that there are limits to what the text will bear, should be maintained.

The reader of the present commentary may suspect that our understanding of the narrative is too much influenced by the overarching narrative of Christian theology, with its themes of universality, and the ultimate prevailing of the divine will to save over the impulse to come in judgment. In the nature of the present task it is not possible entirely to assuage that suspicion, since our interest is precisely to bring biblical study into dialogue with theological. We are indeed looking for themes that feed into the broad concepts and structure of Christian theology. A politically-interested reading would no doubt look different, though there would certainly be significant correspondences between theological and political readings. If we find much that echoes the Christian narrative, it does not follow that we have become detached from the details of the text, and indeed the relationship between text and theology is woven together in a long history. Yet the story of Joshua, like that of Genesis-Kings as a whole, does not render the Christian narrative in any simple way. With that in mind, we must be sure that the reading of Joshua presented here is subject to the discipline of reading the text itself. We shall reflect a little more on the nature of this text's relationship with the Christian narrative in a conclusion to this section.

The aim of the present offering is furthermore somewhat limited, namely to highlight resonances between Joshua and its wider narrative context.

Key Themes of the Book of Joshua

The book of Joshua forms a crucial part of the story of God's purpose for the world he created, as unfolded in Genesis to Kings. Its special significance lies in its position as the first book, following the foundations laid in the Pentateuch, to tell of Israel's life in the land promised to Abraham. This structural position is an important clue to its theological significance, since it is both a culmination (as promise fulfilled) and a beginning. To understand its character as a culmination, we need to observe the ways in which it makes connections with all five books of the Pentateuch.

Joshua and Genesis

Beginning in Genesis, the Old Testament tells of the one God, who creates the heavens and the earth, and who seeks fellowship with human beings. He pursues this universal purpose through the particularity of a people descended from Abraham. This people, Israel, is always rooted in and unavoidably connected with the other nations. Joshua's final address to Israel, in the covenantal assembly at Shechem, expressly recalls the origin of Abraham in Mesopotamia, as a worshipper of other gods (24:2). The life of Israel is thus conceived, paradoxically, in both separation and continuity. This necessary two-sidedness in Israel's existence derives from its mission, disclosed to Abraham, that "all the families of the earth" should be blessed (or "bless themselves") in them: it exists in its separateness for the sake of the others. Yet this mission becomes a danger to its very existence, because by virtue of its exposure to the ways of the nations it may lose its vocation to demonstrate allegiance to the one God.

By the same token, the prospect of divine judgment on the nations is raised, for while Abraham might conduct polite business with the people of the land (Genesis 23), it is already intimated that his descendants' possession of it will come at a cost to others, that the possession will involve a dispossession, and this will be a judgment on human sin (Gen 15:16-21). If the book of Joshua tells of a fulfilment for Israel, it does the same in obverse for Canaan. If Israel is to bring blessing to the nations this mission is not such as to preclude the possibility of judgment.

It is undoubtedly a complication of the story that the divine plan for Israel's salvation entails a judgment on Canaan. Yet this equation does not have permanent or absolute status in the biblical portrayal of judgment and salvation in human affairs. It is rather only one form in which these possibilities are played out; it is contingent in the way that the election of Israel is itself contingent. The unfolding story makes it clear enough that Israel, the vehicle of salvation, may fall under judgment, while Canaanite Rahab may be saved. The role of Israel in the story is not to signal a preference for Israel for all time; rather, its story provides an entrée into the topics of judgment and salvation universally. Israel as opposed to Canaan has always to be tempered with Israel as representative of all humanity.

In this way, the book of Joshua participates in the tense drama that puts in question the possibility of humans relating to God. This fundamental issue is raised in the early pages of Genesis, in which humanity, as God's "image," is called to "subdue" the earth (Gen 1:28), that is, to realize and preside over God's purpose for order and justice in the creation. But this is swiftly followed by that human bid for a different kind of power in the world, a form of godlikeness that arises from the fantasy of temptation rather than obedience (Gen 3:5), known to Christian theology as the "fall." In one sense Joshua is indeed a fulfilment of promise, in that Abraham's descendants enter the promised land to possess it. It is even said that "the land lay subdued before them" (Josh 18:1 NRSV), in an unmistakable echo of the mandate of Gen 1:28 (since "land" and "earth" are the same word; see Comment on the passage). Yet the book of Joshua does not let us think that that might be the end of the story, for resonances of the lustful bid for power and control still intrude, as in the sin of Achan, who takes what is God's for himself (Joshua 7); or in Joshua's astonishing rebuke to Israel at Shechem: "You are not able to serve the Lord"

(24:19), with its implication that they will be drawn to idolatry. In these vignettes we are reminded that, even in the moment of fulfilment, humanity's (and Israel's) character and destiny remain unsettled.

Nevertheless, the fulfilment of promise is a real and vital vindication of God in his ancient commitment to Abraham and to the creation. If Israel's occupation of Canaan is not in itself the triumphant end of God's history with humanity, it is an earnest of it, though it shows too that the way lies through judgment.

Joshua and Exodus

The book of Exodus once again intertwines the story of Israel with that of the world. At its heart is the deliverance of Israel from the enslaving power of the exodus Pharaoh into the sphere of Yahweh's rule, which is freedom. The great divide placed between Israel and Pharaoh's Egypt is symbolized by the Passover and the miraculous crossing of the Reed Sea. Joshua provides a powerful echo of this when Israel miraculously crosses the Jordan, then celebrates the first Passover in the land. The conflict with Canaan under Yahweh as divine warrior corresponds to the former conflict with Pharaoh. In this way, Joshua continues a story about deliverance into freedom in the service of Yahweh.

Exodus also establishes the marks of this freedom, namely covenant, law, and the worship of the holy God. The exodus and Passover lead to Sinai and tabernacle. At Sinai, the uniqueness of the creator God is expressed in commandment and law, with the first commandment ("You shall have no other gods before me"; Exod 20:3) towering over all the rest. The preface to the Commandments, with its assertion that Yahweh is the God of the exodus (Exod 20:2), shows that the gift of law is a function of the deliverance into freedom. It is situated within a covenant, because it is essentially about Israel's acceptance of its role in loyal relationship to Yahweh and thus its commitment to his purpose for the world. This relationship is expressed in worship, with the provision for the tabernacle occupying a large swath of the book. It is also expressed negatively, in the story of the golden calf, which stages an Israelite apostasy at the very moment when the covenant is concluded (Exodus 32–34).

The book of Joshua also brings this combination of covenant, law, and worship to a certain culmination, since these patterns of Israelite life are now planted in occupied land. There are major covenantal ceremonies and speeches in 8:30-35; chs. 23 and 24. The Mosaic law provides the substance of these: in the ceremony at Mount Ebal, forming a bridge with Mount Sinai, Joshua writes "a copy of the law of Moses" on the altar of stones he builds there (8:32). And in the final two chapters, Joshua recalls Israel to covenantal renewal and to obedience to the law, in particular to the first commandment, which informs the strong emphasis on the danger of idolatry in those speeches (23:6, 15-16; 24:14-15, 23-27). The conflict between Israel and Canaan in Joshua can be understood as a conflict in the world of nations about the unique claims of Yahweh to be creator of the heavens and the earth, as focused in the first commandment.

The close connection between law and worship follows from this prominence of the first commandment. For example, the call to exclusive worship of Yahweh underlay the conflict with the Transjordanian tribes in Joshua 22. Indeed, the very entrance to the land was an act of worship, as seen especially in the role of the ark of the covenant. This central item of the furniture of the tabernacle in Exodus symbolized the presence of God to Israel in worship (esp. Exod 25:10-22). In Joshua, it symbolizes God's presence in the sense of his leading Israel in war, yet in such a way that the connotations of worship are also present. The possession of land and the act of judgment on Canaan are portrayed together as an act of worship.

The Exodus theme of divine presence is further present in Joshua in the role of the tabernacle, in the key text of 18:1. Here the Genesis perspective on the whole creation converges with the Exodus perspective on God's presence with Israel. The biblical narrative's opening scene, with a unified humanity in the earth, gives way to a chosen people contracting a relationship with God outside land, then bringing its covenanted life into a place of its own in the world. The human mandate to bring all creation into obedience to God is now expressed in Israel's occupation of a space on earth in which, through law and worship, God's reign is fully acknowledged.

Joshua and Leviticus

Closely connected with the divine presence, Joshua presupposes a theology of holiness, met first in Exodus but elaborated in Leviticus. Holiness may be defined as belonging particularly to God. This has to be understood in terms of the concept of a "holiness sphere," an area of life visibly and symbolically set aside to express the divine presence and God's ultimate claim on all of life. In the religious geography of the Old Testament, the sphere comprises the holy space of the tabernacle (or temple), the holy personnel of priests and Levites, the holy times of feasts and set sacrifices, and the holy actions that happened in the tabernacle precincts.[1] Within this structure, which has much in common with ancient Near Eastern worship arrangements, devotion to God is typically expressed by gifts taken from ordinary life made over into the holy sphere (such as tithes, firstfruits, and sacrifices).

This holiness theology, systematically elaborated in Leviticus, informs Joshua profoundly, even though the language of holiness is infrequent. The ark of the covenant, the tabernacle, and the priests and Levites are essential elements in the holiness geography, and thus the holiness idea underlies the procession into the land in Joshua 3–4. It also underlies the "devotion" of Jericho to God as Israel's first act in the land. In holiness terms this becomes a kind of recognition that the whole land is God's in a particular way. The language of holiness surfaces in this connection. It is on the verge of the attack on Jericho that the mysterious "commander of the army of the Lord" confronts Joshua with the command, like the Lord's to Moses (Exod 3:5), to remove his shoes for he was standing on holy ground (meaning the vicinity of Jericho; Josh 5:13-15). Jericho is then to be "devoted to destruction" (see Comment on 6:15-21). The only exception is silver and gold (6:19), which is "holy" (קדש/qōdeš, not חרם/ḥērem), and must be kept for Yahweh's sanctuary.

An individual note in the Joshua narrative of this holy action is the prominence of the "ram's horn" (יובל/yôbēl; 6:4, 5, 6, 8, 13) as the type of trumpet used by the priests as they proclaim that this is an action of God and lead in it. As we noted in the Comment section (6:1-7), this is curiously evocative of another Leviticus theme, namely the Jubilee (also yôbēl). By this linguistic means, a powerful combination of holiness concepts with those of freedom and justice is achieved.

Finally, the holiness of God is invoked in the covenantal context of the ceremony at Shechem, in the strong and strange rebuke to Israel that they cannot serve him (24:19). God's holiness is thus brought into connection with Israel's obligation to be faithful, meaning in effect to keep the law, especially the first commandment. This connection of thought recalls particularly the latter parts of Leviticus (sometimes called the Holiness Code, chs. 17-26), with its call to Israel to "be holy because I, the Lord your God, am holy" (Lev 19:2). To be holy in this context means in practice obedience, both in the sphere of worship and in that of social ethics. The creation of a just society is therefore bound up with the worship of God. Joshua's rebuke to Israel sounds a pessimistic note about their capacity to match this standard of holiness. But the connection is made nevertheless. And ultimately in biblical theology, the

---

1. This typology of the holiness sphere is indebted to Jenson, *Graded Holiness*, who has elaborated it most helpfully.

Joshua and Numbers

Connections between Joshua and Numbers appear first in strong narrative links. It is in Numbers that the people move away from Sinai, in orderly fashion (beginning at Num 10:12), and proceed to the borders of the promised land, whence in Joshua they will enter. In several ways, the narrative and themes of the former book prepare for the latter. Numbers dwells on the composition of the people, both by tribe (Numbers 1–2) and by respective roles in relation to holiness: priests distinct from Levites, and both from the rest of Israel (chs. 3–4, 8). This emerges as a powerful theme in chs. 16–17, where the terrible fate of the Korahites, who tried to transgress the boundaries laid down for them, marks the rigor with which the divinely commanded ordering of Israel would be maintained. Further on the theme of due order, the people are presented as carefully organized around the tabernacle as they march, in a formation that is both military and liturgical (Numbers 2; 9:15–10:10). They celebrate a Passover at Sinai prior to their departure (9:1-14). As they approach the land the anticipation of it becomes intense. The end of the forty-year delay imposed on Israel because of their first refusal to enter the land by faith (Num 14:33-34) begins to appear on the horizon. A census of the new generation is taken (Numbers 26). Joshua is appointed as Moses' military successor (Num 27:12-23), just as Aaron's death had initiated the priesthood to his son Eleazar (Num 20:22-29), so setting up the dual leadership that is in place in the book of Joshua. In the closing stages of the book, the notion of land as inheritance is introduced via the particular situation of the daughters of Zelophehad (Num 27:1-11; 36). The first steps in the conquest and settlement are taken in Transjordan, with the defeat of the Kings Sihon and Og (Num 21:21-35) and the occupation of their territory by the tribes of Reuben, Gad and half-Manasseh (Numbers 32), though some doubt is raised as to whether this is properly the promised land (32:29-30). Directions are given for the war against Canaan (33:50-56), and the boundaries of the land are outlined (34:1-15). Finally, issues arising from the distribution of territory are dealt with: cities for the Levites, cities of refuge, and associated regulations for governing blood revenge (Numbers 35).

Much of this is continued or echoed in Joshua, in ways which distinguish the two books from Deuteronomy. (Such features lay behind the literary-critical interest in sources that may have underlain the Pentateuch, or

Hexateuch, especially the distinction between the Priestly source, P, and the Deuteronomic, D, and the question whether P continued into Joshua.) The entrance to the land is the culmination of the forty-year delay, with only Joshua and Caleb of the original spies surviving to take part in it (Josh 14:6-15). The settlement of Transjordan is a *fait accompli* (1:12-15), and its status is again addressed, with the resolution that Israel is defined by the worship of Yahweh rather than the boundary as such (ch. 22). The organization of the people is largely taken over from Numbers, with its tribal divisions and the dual leadership of Joshua and Eleazar (Josh 14:1). The military-liturgical march into Canaan continues at the crossing of the Jordan and defeat of Jericho, and a Passover is kept (chs. 3–6; recall Num 9:1-14). The notion of inheritance now bulks large, with the leadership of Joshua and Eleazar defined specifically as a commission to enable the tribes to enter into their share in the land as inheritance (14:1, and see Comment there). The war with Canaan, adumbrated in Num 33:50-56, becomes an immediate preoccupation. Further, as Numbers laid emphasis on the composition of the people (Numbers 1–4; 26), Joshua correspondingly stresses the composition of the land, in its close description of tribal boundaries (Joshua 13–19). Cities of refuge and cities for the Levites arise again as issues consequent upon occupation (chs. 20–21).

The comparison with Numbers serves to highlight the will of God to bless Israel by bringing them into the land he has given them. The theme of the gift of land, often associated with Deuteronomy, is already strong in Numbers. The withholding of a territorial inheritance from the tribe of Levi is a powerful symbol of land as gift (Num 18:20; Josh 14:3-4), bespeaking the dependence that comes from landlessness. By the same token, it manifests the relative detachment of all Israelites from their grasp on possession, since they must tangibly renounce parts of their territories for the maintenance of the priestly tribe. Moreover, God's gift of land is not only a blessing to Israel but a demonstration before the nations of God's power and love, as shown above all by the failed attempt of King Balak of Moab to prevent Israel's advance by means of Balaam's magic (Numbers 22–24).

The emphasis on order in both books symbolizes the divine ordering of all of life, and submission to it corresponds to obedient acceptance of his command. In tandem with God's purpose, gracious as well as commanding, is the ever-present possibility of human rebellion. This is manifest not only among the nations, as in Moab, Balaam, and the Baal of Peor (Numbers 22–25), but is also vividly portrayed in Israel's first refusal to enter the land (Numbers 13–14), in the sin of Achan (Joshua 7), the ambiguous relationship with Gibeon (ch. 9), and Joshua's declaration, "You are not able to serve the Lord"; 24:19). Yet over against these human tendencies, with their attendant implicit threat of death, are set examples of humble acceptance, none more so than Joshua himself, who not only asserts and practices his obedience to God and his Torah, but finally withdraws to a place of obscurity (19:49-50). The concept of inheritance betokens fundamentally the acceptance of one's due place within the people as a whole. Whatever that place, the right attitude to it is humility. It is such a vision, with the moral courage to follow it through, that can make Israel what it ought to be.

Finally, the status of the land itself is raised. What really constitutes this promised land? Is it boundaries as such? This appeared to be questioned not only by the doubtful status of Transjordan in both Numbers and Joshua, but also by the impreciseness of some of the boundary descriptions (see Comment on Josh 16:1-10; 19:49-51). Israel's land exists where Israel is true to its vocation.

Joshua and Deuteronomy

It is almost possible to read directly from Numbers to Joshua as if Deuteronomy were not there, but not quite. Deuteronomy develops themes of covenant, law, and worship already established in Exodus-Numbers, but establishes these in a new way in Israel's life and thus provides its own characteristic foundation for the action in Joshua. It does this in three ways: (a) a stance on leadership, succession, and Israel as a body politic, (b) a theology of land and worship, and (c) a view of Israel's destiny.

Succession

The spring of the action of Joshua is the death of Moses. Henceforth Israel must live without the leader who gave them the covenant and the law, and at the outset, Joshua is called to be completely faithful to these (1:6-8). The themes and action of Joshua are predicated entirely on the need for succession to Moses. As the pentateuchal narrative closes in on the promised land, an important subtheme is the death of Moses. The leader who brought Israel out of Egypt cannot accompany them into the land. Responsibility for covenant-keeping devolves at last upon Israel. Succession to Moses, therefore, is not entirely concentrated in the person of Joshua, whose responsibilities are limited to military victory, facilitating the tribes' settlement in their territories, and leading in Torah-keeping and covenant renewal.[2] In any case,

---

2. The theme of Joshua as successor to Moses has been most fully developed by Schäfer-Lichtenberger, *Josua und Salomo*. See also Olson, *Deuteronomy and the Death of Moses*.

Joshua himself must one day cease to lead, just as Moses had done, and the narrative places some emphasis on his withdrawal from public life after his work is done (19:50-51). Moreover, no one succeeds Joshua in the way that he had succeeded Moses. The combined leadership of Moses and Joshua is revealed finally as a transitional phase, an act of midwifery to bring Israel to the beginning of its life in the land, where it must learn to grow and walk. The book of Joshua prepares the reader for this next stage by depicting a somewhat collaborative style of leadership, with Joshua, Eleazar, and tribal leaders playing their different parts (e.g., 14:1). This arrangement is most helpfully read in conjunction with the laws that deal with the administration of Israel in Deut 16:18–18:22, which anticipate a polity for Israel that looks beyond the time of both Moses and Joshua. Deuteronomy and Joshua together lead into a "citizenly" model for Israel's covenant-keeping.[3]

The devolved responsibility for Torah-keeping is reflected also in Joshua's portrayal of the land in relation to the people. Whereas in Deuteronomy, there is very little evidence of the tribes of Israel, since these largely disappear behind the powerful notion of a united people,[4] in Joshua the tribes reappear strongly in the distribution of land (Joshua 13–19), in relation to Levitical cities (ch. 21), and again in the matter of Transjordan (ch. 22). While Deuteronomy plays down internal divisions, whether among people or territorially, Joshua is deeply concerned about these. The two books thus provide contrasting but complementary perspectives on the notion of the covenant people in its land, namely unity and particularity. In Joshua, the integrity of the covenant people is played out in a thousand mundane localities.

Theology of Land and Worship

Deuteronomy's forward look is predicated throughout on its anticipation of Israel's possession of land, as expressed in the recurring formula: "When you enter the land the Lord your God is giving you" (e.g., Deut 17:14). Joshua as fulfilment of the pentateuchal narrative is therefore most directly hinged to Deuteronomic expectation.

The theology of land and worship in Deuteronomy-Joshua is realized particularly in relation to the place of worship. The prominence of this topic in Deuteronomy is expressed in the recurring formula found in Deut 12:5 and

---

3. The most comprehensive modern statement of this is Carrière, *La théorie du politique dans le Deutéronome*. I have dealt with the topic in McConville, *God and Earthly Power*, esp. 74-98.

4. The tribes appear in relation to the occupation of Transjordan (Deut 3:12-22) and in the Blessing of Moses (Deuteronomy 33); otherwise hardly at all.

frequently in chs. 12-18, with its reference to a place of worship that the Lord would choose, not only for Israel's acts of worship, but also as a symbol of his ownership of the land.[5] Later in the narrative the mantle of "chosen place" would fall on Jerusalem (2 Kgs 21:4), and indeed the Deuteronomic formula is often considered to be a veiled reference to Jerusalem. However, other places predominate in Deuteronomy-Joshua. These two books are stapled together by the command to hold a covenant renewal ceremony in the vicinity of Shechem (Deut 11:26-32; 27) and its performance there (Josh 8:30-35; 24). The events at Shechem declare that possession of land is tied to covenant loyalty and the keeping of Torah. But why Shechem? From the perspective of the end of the narrative of Genesis-Kings, Shechem is an odd choice, since it lay in the north, and therefore in that part of Israel, the northern kingdom, that eventually suffered exile first, and irrevocably (2 Kings 17). At the end of Kings, future hope for the covenant lies rather with Judah and Jerusalem. In view of the prominence of Jerusalem in Israel's history in the land, it seems strange that it plays at best a minor role in Deuteronomy and Joshua. But in the era of Moses and Joshua, the outlook is different. Shechem is in the northern heartland. The tabernacle is set up in Shiloh (Josh 18:1), and it is Shiloh that stands as the place of worship for all Israel in the contention with the Transjordanian tribes about the people's unity (in ch. 22). Finally, "the place the Lord would choose" is referred to but unidentified in 9:27.

In one sense the story of worship in Israel leads to the establishment of Solomon's temple (with the foundation of the Davidic dynasty in Samuel and the temple construction in Kings). Yet there are pointers here in the charter documents for Israel's life in the land to the provisionality of all established places, with the systems and interests that accompany them. In the context of the larger narrative, it seems important that the worship of Yahweh is not tied once for all to a specific place. This fits well with a picture that is building up in Joshua, in which the promises to Israel are always greater than the historic people or any particular form that it might take. The point is similar to the one made about boundaries (above, on Numbers). As it is when Israel is true to its vocation that Israel's land may be said to exist properly, so it is then that the people is truly at worship. It follows that the vision of worshipping Israel is not congruent with the supremacy of any particular sanctuary. Joshua renews covenant at Shechem and inscribes the words of Torah on Mount Ebal, but the life of Israel will in the end not depend on this place, nor the keeping of Torah on the inscription of its words on stone there. Similarly, Solomon's

---

5. This understanding of the "place formula" has been well elucidated by Richter, *The Deuteronomistic History and the Name Theology*.

temple in Jerusalem will not enshrine worship once for all in a building (1 Kgs 8:27-30). It is one of the paradoxes of the biblical narrative that the particular and historical is essential to the vision, yet always points on to the universal and eschatological.

Israel's Destiny

The destiny of Israel is obviously attached, in Deuteronomy and Joshua, to its possession of the land that Yahweh is giving them, together with the *dis*possessing of nations already there, and indeed the subjection of these to the *ḥērem*, in an act of Yahweh's judgment. In these political and geographical images, the destiny of Israel is portrayed, namely in the covenantal obligation of exclusive loyalty to Yahweh, and the attendant responsibility to create a society that derived its whole manner of life from that relationship. The *ḥērem* is thus expressive of a cultural revolution, a radical rejection of the religious-political tyrannies over mind, spirit, and body symbolized by the kingdoms of Canaan, as earlier by Pharaoh's Egypt. The content of that radical new vision of society is given form in the Torah, with the implications of the Decalogue spelled out in numerous laws, the heart of it all being in the command to "love Yahweh" (Deut 6:5). That love of Yahweh, with "heart, soul, and strength," implied that Israelite society in its breadth, height, and depth should bear witness to Yahweh's character and will. This mission affected not only ordinary social ethics (e.g., in regard to debts and slavery, Deuteronomy 15), but also the very political organization of society, the theme of Deut 16:18–18:22, which defines Israel as distinct in warp and woof from surrounding political systems and which explains the highlighting of the Canaanite *kings* in the war of Joshua (Joshua 12). Once again, the shared leadership in Joshua, and Joshua's final retreat, correspond to this shared and disseminated responsibility on all Israel to do right. It is in relation to all of this that the *ḥērem* is to be understood in both books. (The problematical issues raised by the *ḥērem* are addressed below.)

This picture of Israel's destiny, however, is ominous as well as promising, in ways that have been adumbrated above (on Genesis). The "reality" of Israel will not finally be contained or expressed in terms of a fixed tenure within permanent borders. In tension with the gift of land is always the demands of covenant and Torah. And in this respect the outlook is decidedly mixed. In fact, a final echo of Deuteronomy in Joshua is in the somewhat pessimistic view in both books concerning Israel's likely future success in keeping the covenant. A remarkable feature of Deuteronomy is that, alongside its consistent exhortation of Israel to keep the covenant, it expresses serious doubt about their moral capacity to do it. This occurs in its record of the archapostasy at Sinai in the making of the golden calf (esp. Deut 9:4-6, as prelude to 9:7-24), and in Moses' anticipations of Israel's life after his death, when he gives instructions for the book of the law to be kept beside the ark of the covenant (31:27-29), and in the Song of Moses (ch. 32). The effect of this is both rhetorical and theological. Deuteronomy is deeply concerned about the possibility of apostasy as a consequence of the good life in the land (cf. 8:11-20). Its rhetorical strategy therefore keeps a fine balance between a strong doctrine of sin and grace on one hand and the real moral responsibility of the people on the other. Joshua's declaration, "You are not able to serve the Lord" (Josh 24:19), has presumably a similar function.

Joshua and Judges–Kings

In a sequential reading of the Old Testament, Joshua builds, as we have seen, on the whole cumulative narrative since Genesis. Critical scholarship recognized this continuity in its concept of a Hexateuch (the idea that Genesis-Joshua once formed a redactional unity). The idea is now less popular, partly because, since Martin Noth, the book of Deuteronomy has been taken to be the beginning of a separate body of literature stretching to Kings and partly because of the more recent interest in the redactional unity of Genesis-Kings as a whole. The last of these approaches is most compelling, in my view, because it does best justice to the forward and backward links in both Deuteronomy and Joshua (of which more below). Thus far, I have tried to place it in the flow of the "Hexateuch." The main advantage of this is to strike a balance between the universal scope of the creation theology of Genesis and the concentration on Israel: the story of Israel is at the same time that of God and humanity, even when Israel enters land formerly occupied by other nations and subjects them to the "devotion to destruction." I have tried to bring out the cosmic and universal implications of this in the Commentary.

However, the book of Joshua has also to be seen as part of the continuing story. We shall review the books following Joshua more summarily, because we shall return to them also in the next section.

Joshua and Judges form a contrast, since while Joshua tells of the first possession of the land, Judges depicts the life of Israel in it in its early generations. The contrast is not exact, however, since Judges begins with a continuing account of the first possession after Joshua's death (Judges 1), which resonates with those parts of Joshua that concede that the conquest was not swift and complete (such as Josh 13:1-7; 15:63; 16:10). Judges, however, brings out the tremendous moral struggle in Israel, with accompanying loss of land and ultimate destruction and exile. We have seen that Joshua's narrative is by no means triumphalist, but knows already that it will be no easy matter for Israel to keep the covenant. Judges, with its repeating episodes of Israel's idolatry and consequent failure to hold its land effectively, demonstrates the profound difficulty of the task facing the people. While Joshua leaves us with a memory of God's leadership and victory, and indeed of Joshua's faithfulness, effective leadership in the Judges phase is sporadic and Israel lacks cohesion. Furthermore, the key ingredients of life before Yahweh set out in Deuteronomy and Joshua retreat into the background, namely covenant and Torah and a faithful priesthood. The leaders of Israel in Judges, in each case called by Yahweh to answer particular crises, hardly correspond to the types of leadership envisaged in Deuteronomy-Joshua (whether we look for these in Deut 16:18–18:22 or in Joshua's alignment of priests and tribal leaders alongside himself, as in Josh 21:1). While they are raised up to deliver Israel in their time, they nevertheless seem to typify weaknesses of Israel, and in their fragility its fragility.[6] There is no covenant renewal here, and in the end only a refrain that looks for a king to keep order, an office that, though permitted in Deuteronomy (Deut 17:14-20), lay outside the stipulated authority pattern and about which Joshua held out no expectation (the only kings in Joshua are enemies).

Samuel and Kings tell of the institution of kingship in Israel and the history of monarchy, first in the united kingdom and then in the separated Israel and Judah. In this long stretch of narrative, Joshua is curiously absent. His name is conspicuously missing from the list of Israel's early heroes (1 Sam 12:8, 11), from the brief account of the nations Israel could not expel at its first possession of the land (1 Kgs 9:20-22), and from the reference to the non-observance of Passover throughout the times of the judges and kings (2 Kgs 23:22, neglecting mention of Joshua's Passover, Josh 5:10-12). Only an allusion to the rebuilding of Jericho by Hiel of Bethel (1 Kgs 16:34), in defiance of a curse laid on anyone who did this (Josh 6:26), suggests direct knowledge of the book of Joshua by the authors of Samuel and Kings.

The reasons for Joshua's elision from Samuel-Kings are not our immediate concern. But we are bound to ask in what way the book of Joshua anticipates the things that are narrated thereafter. The figure of Joshua has widely been seen as an adumbration of King Josiah, the reforming king of Judah, who surpassed all others in faithfulness to Yahweh and the covenant (2 Kgs 23:24-25), though his righteousness proved insufficient to avert the Babylonian exile which came within a couple of decades of his death. Yahweh's

---

6. A number of studies have brought this out. See Webb, *The Book of the Judges*.

words to Joshua in Josh 1:7-8 are reminiscent of both the instructions in the law of the king (Deut 17:18-20; see also Josh 8:32) and of King Josiah, who most closely conforms to the Deuteronomic ideal.[7] The analogy is not perfect, not least because Joshua himself does not aspire to kingship and has no successor. His disappearance from the narrative after the book that bears his name chimes intriguingly with his withdrawal into anonymity at the end of his life.

In fact, between Joshua and Josiah lies a massive transition in the way in which human power is carried. The story of the inception of kingship in Israel raises some of the narrative's most profound theological issues. Can Israel in covenant with Yahweh embrace within it a dynastic style of kingship that resembles in important ways the autocratic monarchies of the ancient Near East? This eventuality is precisely precluded by the limitations laid on kings in Deut 17:16-17, and there are notes in both Judges and 1 Samuel that bring the project of dynastic kingship into conflict with the premise of Yahweh's kingship (Judg 8:22-23; 1 Sam 8:4-22). The narrative thus testifies to the underlying issue of how political power may be borne, in relation to the authority of God and the supreme guidance of his Torah. It is often held that the block of material from Deuteronomy to Kings has been edited so as to promote the type of rule exemplified by King Josiah. It seems to me, rather, that the narrative of Israel between Joshua and the exile exemplifies both the imperative of political power and the extraordinary challenge entailed in exercising it in faithfulness to God. The issue cannot be expressed entirely in terms of one type of government as opposed to another type, although I think Deuteronomy's concern to disperse political authority makes an instructive contrast with the ancient Near Eastern autocratic model. Rather, the story contains the general warning that political power is to be exercised in obedience to God's command. Power can be abused in any kind of political system. It is held properly only when its bearers acknowledge that it is derived from God, whose own authority is supreme.[8]

---

7. The idea of Joshua as a type of Josiah has been forcefully expounded by Nelson, "Josiah in the Book of Joshua"; and also *Joshua*, e.g., 22, 29, 79, 119.

8. The most significant statement in recent times of the entailments of political power in relation to the story of Israel is O'Donovan, *The Desire of the Nations*. See also Bartholomew et al., *A Royal Priesthood?* I have suggested a way of reading Genesis to Kings politically in *God and Earthly Power*.

Conclusion

I have tried to review major themes in the book of Joshua by placing it in the context of Genesis-Kings. We have seen that the book functions as part of the great narrative that leads from creation, through the disclosure of God's special purpose for Israel and the account of its possession of a land, to its loss of that land. The great theme that underlies the narrative is that of God's purpose to bring peace and justice among his creatures on the earth. This choice of a people that should exemplify his purpose becomes the means to this end, but also has within it that which illustrates the problems that impede its realization. Those problems beset both Israel and the other nations.

The story is always a story of Israel, its special elect status, its laws and its worship, its rights to a land, and in all these things its differentiation from other peoples. Yet at the same time it is a story of the nations. It is such both in the sense that Israel's significance derives from its being part and parcel of the humanity God created and in the sense that it has its being among other nations whose destiny is bound up with its own. The account that takes Israel into a land "flowing with milk and honey" is never told for its own sake alone, and therefore could not culminate simply in a narrative of possession. Israel's blessing is inseparable from the blessing that God desires to bring to all nations. And running through the story is the ever-present problem of human resistance to the divine will.

The place of Israel is never unequivocally assured in this narrative, primarily because it is subject to the demand of covenant loyalty. And the story shows its reluctance to treat the people's status as absolute. We saw that neither people nor land is given absolute status, but that both exist properly only when Israel is faithful. This means that the narrative of land possession carries within it a notion of its provisionality, expressed in the kind of polarity that I have tried to bring out in the exegesis of Joshua, between total conquest and the idea that much possession still remains ahead. This is not a merely historical fact, but a typology of blessing and fulfilment. We might say that when God promises to show Abram a land (Gen 12:1), the promise involves an entire understanding, yet to unfold in the narrative, of what a chosen people in a God-given land ought to look like. The land that God gives always remains to be possessed. Moreover, if Israel will not possess land according to God's purpose, it will lose the foothold it has and others may come in in its stead. The tension between Amos 3:2 and 9:7 (i.e., between Israel as privileged elect and Israel as no more elect than any other nation) is never far away in the theology of Genesis-Kings.

Israel stands before the real possibility of lasting possession and blessing; it would be hard to read Deuteronomy, the necessary prelude to Joshua, in any other way. Yet equally, both books know of the immense challenge ahead. Joshua, in its larger context, affirms both the real human obligation to possess land in due obedience to the purpose of God and the strong possibility of judgment and failure. The story is played out between these poles.

The book of Joshua is part of a story that leads on to an end. The "end" may be located in different places, including the loss of the kingdoms of Israel and Judah; the restoration of exiles to the ancient land as promised by prophets, often by clear analogy with Joshua's possession of it; the coming of Jesus, whose very name ("savior") is a Hellenized form of "Joshua"; or the culmination of human existence in the Resurrection life, often symbolized by a crossing of the spiritual "Jordan," as in the wonderful hymn of William Williams, "Guide Me, O Thou Great Jehovah." In reading Joshua in this way, we are calling upon some of the layers of biblical interpretation used by early Christian theologians, in which, for example, the "anagogical" sense encouraged an interpretation in relation to God's ultimate purposes for humanity and even the renewed creation itself.[9]

There is also a "moral" sense, however, and perhaps at this level we can think of Joshua as an example of piety, integrity, and good leadership. At the heart of this narrative stands one of the towering figures of the Old Testament. He accepted the mantle passed to him by none other than Moses without demur, having been trained from early days as the great lawgiver's servant. And he led Israel without any sign of self-aggrandizement. In that respect he exemplifies as well as any other the ideal of a covenant-keeping Israelite.[10]

Joshua in Biblical Theology

My question in approaching the book of Joshua is in what way it makes a contribution to the theology of the Bible, and especially how it helps elucidate the meaning of the Gospel. At first approach, the material is unpromising. Here is a book in which a people is commanded and empowered by God to go to a land occupied by others and drive them out, indeed destroy them, so that they might settle in their place. It would be hard to imagine a more

---

9. For the "fourfold sense" of Scripture, developed in early Christian interpretation, see Rogerson, Rowland, and Lindars, *The Study and Use of the Bible*, 77-78, 275.

10. For more on reading the Old Testament ethically, see Barton, *Understanding Old Testament Ethics*, 10; cf. Wenham, *Story as Torah*.

unpalatable message for today's world. Indeed, the strain of the Old Testament of which Joshua is the prime example has been arraigned by many critics as illustrating all that is worst in religion. The God of Joshua is seen as partisan and violent. The sentence of death on the Canaanites in the cause of clearing a land for the occupation of a distinctive people with its own God resembles too much the modern horror of "ethnic cleansing" and the savagery of militant jihad. Critics have rejected its violence and exclusivism, and some of them, looking nevertheless to the Bible for the word of God, have contrasted it with what they see as a quite different strain whose accents are compassion and inclusiveness. This latter tendency finds a voice in a prophecy like that of Isaiah, with its concept of a salvation that reaches the uttermost limits of the earth, and leads to Christ, who commanded the love of enemies, was himself the victim of excluding hatred, and stood as God's "light to the nations."

It is not only hardened critics of religion who find Joshua intolerable, but many ordinary readers and worshippers who simply ask: can God really have commanded Israel to destroy the Canaanites, women, children, and all? What has this bloody book to do with the idea of a God of love or the Gospel of Jesus Christ? Can it be that the book of Joshua (and with it a good portion of the "primary history" of Genesis-Kings, not to mention a number of Psalms) has a merely oppositional role in theology, the cruel schoolmaster who leads by negative example to Christ? Or should we, with a number of modern commentators, seek refuge in a separation of form and content, so that the violence against the Canaanites becomes a metaphor for the rejection of all that leads away from God?

The Problem of Evil and Violence

In attempting to face these formidable questions one feels a little like the Irishman who, when asked the way to Cork, replied: "Ah, if I were you I wouldn't start from here!" When the question is framed as: How could God do such violence? there is an unconscious elision of the deep-lying problem of violence that has been a powerful leading idea of the narrative about humanity since Genesis. The biblical story of humanity becomes very quickly a story of sinful rebellion against God, and the heart of this sinfulness is, not sex as often imagined, but violence. Violence asserts itself primevally in Cain's brutal murder of his innocent brother Abel, a paradigm for all the cruel ruthlessness in the world that sets the life of the other at nought, as so well brought out by such writers as the South African theologians Itumeleng

Mosala and Allan Boesak.[11] Cain's murderous act escalates to Lamech's murderous habit. It is the violence of humanity that precipitates the flood; violence is the sin of Sodom; the reign of Pharaoh is violence enshrined in the apparatus of state. Violence cannot be removed from the record, because it belongs intrinsically to it. The story of the Bible confronts and aims to deal with precisely this problem. That is why any attempt to understand Joshua has to face up to its violence. It is part of the story of God's purpose to establish justice and righteousness in the world and to do so by means of human action and responsibility.

The story of creation can be told as one of God's overcoming of Chaos. In a sense, the Old Testament stands in critical opposition to the mythological ideologies of the ancient world, in which universal order is established when the dominant god slays the primeval monster that represents the Chaos of disorder. Genesis 1 has been said to "demythologize" such accounts of creation, by insisting on the unchallenged power of the one God over everything in heaven and on earth. There, the sun, the moon, and the stars, elsewhere the objects of worship, are mere inanimate objects. And Chaos lacks all overt monstrous features and is merely תהום/tĕhôm, "the deep" (Gen 1:2). Even so, the Genesis account retains something mythic itself, in the sense that it asks the kinds of questions that ancient peoples asked and shares somewhat in their terms. Here something remains of creation as a subjugation of disorder. The mysterious serpent of Genesis 3, though introduced as one of the "beasts," hints at dark power. The Old Testament's memories of the creation often recall the defeat of "chaos monsters" in ways that are less dismissive than Genesis 1 (e.g., Psalm 74; Job 41), and here the line between the image and the concept is not easy to draw. The biblical account of the world does indeed emphasize God's unrivalled power. Yet there is a kind of Chaos that threatens in drought, barrenness, disease, and flood. And Israelites, like their neighbors, could fear that such powers might overwhelm.

But if Chaos constantly threatens in the Old Testament's narrative, the distinctive thing is that it often takes on a human aspect. This is evidently the case with Pharaoh's Egypt, an instance of Chaos erupting in the sphere of human politics, as Terence Fretheim has convincingly argued.[12] The service of Pharaoh is a powerful challenge to the claims of Yahweh upon Israel, a dedication to the enslavement of human beings in violent opposition to the service of Yahweh that is freedom, so strong that it will go to the lengths of sacri-

---

11. Boesak, *Black and Reformed*; Mosala, *Biblical Hermeneutics and Black Theology in South Africa*.
12. Fretheim, *Exodus*, 12-14, 19-20.

ficing its firstborn in the desperate attempt to maintain its iron grip on the human spirit. When Israel is delivered through the "sea" (Exodus 14-15), there is a memory of the Chaos-deep, and the defeat of Pharaoh's forces becomes a case of God's victory over the primeval forces hostile to creation itself. Israel's unnatural fear of the inhabitants of Canaan at first approach to the land rests in part on the belief that the Anakim (inhabitants of Hebron) were descended from the Nephilim, a primeval race of giants associated with monstrous liaisons between gods and humans (Num 13:28, 33; Gen 6:4; cf. Deut 1:28). The crossing of "sea" is repeated at the entry to the promised land in Joshua, prior to the collapse of Jericho's walls, in a sequence that places that contest too in the line of the confrontation between God and the hostile forces that do cosmic battle with him. In all these cases, human confrontations take on an extra dimension that has to do with powers in the world opposed to God.

It is in this seam of the biblical story that the overcoming of the Canaanites must be placed. They are in a direct line from Pharaoh, that embodiment of antithetical, enslaving power that constitutionally refuses freedom. Liberty from Pharaoh's Egypt entails liberty from the satellites of slavery in Canaan; exodus and settlement are part and parcel of the same story, and in each case freedom comes through conflict. If Joshua has history in it, this is no ordinary history. It is in the strict sense mythic, because in the act of divine judgment that it stages there is an overcoming of Chaos at the cosmic level and human violence as its counterpart in the world.

Joshua–Kings: Chaos, History, and Violence

If the confrontation between Israel and Canaan in Joshua reflects a certain universal contest between the power of God and the forces of Chaos, in what sense does historical Israel carry forward the divine purpose, and how is this purpose served by the Israelite conquest of Canaan? The Old Testament story unquestionably is or becomes a story of a particular people in its relationships with other historical peoples. And the Old Testament witness is that in this people God has made known his purposes for the world. The question just posed is a form of the question about the relationship between the universal and the particular. In Genesis that relationship is stated thus: Abraham is called by God to go to a land that God would show him, where his descendants would become a populous nation — and in them the nations would be blessed (Gen 12:3). This theme of God's purpose to bless the nations emerges strongly in a number of places in the Old Testament: where Ruth the Moabite is drawn into the family of God and becomes the ancestress of King David

(Ruth 4); where the prophet Jonah is sent to bring the Assyrians of Nineveh to repentance; where the Syrian commander Naaman becomes a worshipper of the God of Israel (2 Kings 5); in certain Psalms which call the whole world to praise (Psalms 65; 67) and extend the divine birthright to other peoples (Psalm 87); and in many prophetic texts, supremely in the book of Isaiah, which anticipate a turning of the nations to God (Isa 2:2-4; 49:5-6) and reapply the language of intimacy between God and Israel to others (19:24-25). Even in those parts of the Old Testament which, like Deuteronomy, put Israel in confrontation with other nations, there is a sense that Israel is manifesting to the world its knowledge of God (Deut 4:6-8) and that God's providential hand has been at work in their histories too (Deuteronomy 2-3).

Israel's role in this purpose of God is as witness and representative or mediator. The witness dimension has been noticed in Deut 4:6-8. The mediatorial role is announced in Exod 19:5-6 and pursued through the portrayal of tabernacle worship, in which God's presence in the innermost sanctuary is a partial restoration to humanity of that which was lost in Eden. In Israel's approach to God in worship, and especially in the high priest's annual entry to the holy of holies, is symbolized humanity's presence to God, still very imperfect, but containing the hope and promise of fuller restoration in due course.

If Israel is God's chosen instrument to bring his salvation to the world, does this mean that it fulfils this purpose faithfully and well? The end of the "primary history" (Genesis-Kings), with the northern kingdom ruined forever and the people of Judah subjugated and exiled, shows clearly that it did not. But might it be that in Joshua, at least, Israel is manifesting God's ideal in a more pure way? Such is sometimes implied, when the narrative of Genesis-Kings is divided into two phases, a period of "salvation-history" up to and including Joshua, followed by a period of "judgment-history," comprising the story of decline and fall that begins in Judges.[13] Yet this simple typology of success followed by failure does no justice to the nature of biblical narrative, in which heroes are typically flawed from the start. (King Solomon is one of the best examples of this. Though he asks for wisdom rather than wealth, and gains God's commendation as well as wealth in consequence, it is impossible to discern a point in his story at which he alters from righteous to wicked. On the contrary, he appears to be compromised from the beginning; 1 Kings 1-11.[14])

The problem with Israel itself is expressed in Deuteronomy, in its con-

---

13. The typology is that of Schmid, *Erzväter und Exodus*.
14. See treatments of Walsh, *1 Kings*, e.g., 34, 77, 113; Eslinger, *Into the Hands of the Living God*, 156-58.

cern to guard against the idea that the people was chosen by God because of some special intrinsic merit: on the contrary, it is insisted, Israel was chosen neither because of its great size (Deut 7:7-8) nor because of its righteousness (9:4-6), since Israel is portrayed as temperamentally resistant to God's word, as the episode of the golden calf (now repeated) makes evident (Deut 9:6-29). The notion of Israel acting as God's righteous instrument in the acts of judgment on Canaan in Joshua is complicated by Joshua's own accusation of them in the covenant renewal at Shechem that they "are not able to serve the Lord" (Josh 24:19).

Israel too is a flawed hero, unable to take the land without compromise with its inhabitants, as I have tried to show in connection with Rahab and the Gibeonites. This point can be misunderstood to suggest that if only Israel had more rigorously prosecuted the ban of destruction it would have been acting more righteously and would have been more successful in the project of keeping God's covenant in God's land. How different the whole history might then have been! I do not mean it in this way. In my view, the chosen people's proneness to rebellion against God's purpose is too deeply embedded in the biblical portrayal for this to be a real possibility. I mean rather that, though Israel goes against Canaan at God's command, its response is still imbued with that spirit which, at the report of the spies, had first manifested fear then false confidence (Deuteronomy 1). In the enactment of land possession, Israel is somehow implicated in the problem of violence. The story of Joshua is bound up with that of Israel's successes chronically intertwined with the lust for power (Samuel, David), its own succumbing to God's judgment, and the moral blank at the end of Kings. It plays its part in the larger story of jeopardized possession, not least in its pervasive counterpoint between announcements of total success and intimations of failure.

For these reasons, Joshua cannot be a mere exemplary tale (the "good" Israelites overcome the "bad" Canaanites). "Joshua won the battle of Jericho" cannot translate into a simple recipe, certainly not a permanent warrant for Israel to make war. Nor can it be passed off as a metaphor for some spiritual reality that does not involve actual violence. The conflicts over Jericho, Ai, and the rest are a contact point between the divine purpose and human violence, but they do not in themselves accomplish that purpose. Joshua shows that the life of Israel lies between present reality and the future realization of the kingdom of God. It is part of the story of the long postponement of that kingdom. When we read that "the land lay subdued before (Israel)" (Josh 18:1 NRSV), we hear, as we recall, an echo of the creation mandate to "subdue the earth" (Gen 1:28). Yet this is far from the end of the story of humanity's response to that mandate. In its context, this subduing of land/earth can only point forward, somewhat poignantly, to the hope of a fuller accomplishment, a hope that might be called eschatological.

We can, I think, go further than this. When God commands Joshua to destroy the Canaanites, yet the Joshua mission is bound into failure from the beginning, how then can we view the divine command? Are we to think God thought that this strategy would work? Surely not. But in that case the story has meaning only as part of the larger story in which the achievement of the divine purpose of planting a righteous, witnessing people among the nations comes by means other than the overcoming of nations by force. It follows that the vision of conquest in Joshua does indeed function theologically as a counterpoint and contrast to the means of such witness constituted by the notion of Suffering Servant. And this affects how we read: "God commanded Joshua." The narrative that includes "God commanded Joshua to destroy the people of Jericho" (and here "narrative" is understood to embrace the whole gamut of Old Testament discourse about God) knows that this ultimately is not God's way.

In the meantime, human politics must proceed in the grey area between Chaos and new creation and is subject to both Torah and divine judgment. While there is no mandate here for bringing the kingdom of God by violent means, nor for the permanent right of any people to hold any territory at all costs, Joshua nevertheless affirms the ideal of godly leadership. He resolves to follow Moses by leading Israel in the light of God's Torah. He declares that he "and his house" will adhere loyally to Yahweh. And his final act of humility, in which he retires from public view to take his place as an ordinary Israelite in an ordinary place, is unparalleled in the history of the leadership of Israel in the land. There is a cooperation in leadership that comes close to the Deuteronomic ideal of mitigated central power (elaborated in Deut 16:18–18:22). And in paradoxical ways, the inclusion of Rahab and the Gibeonites, though from one perspective a compromise, chimes from another angle with a notion of openness that is recommended especially in the laws of Leviticus (in respect of the "alien," who in many ways is to be treated just as the "native").

Joshua, Chaos, and History in the Rest of the Old Testament

I have been arguing that the Old Testament's portrayal of God's conflict with Chaos does not finish with Joshua, nor indeed with the primary history of Genesis-Kings. The sin of Judah in its failure to keep the covenant has cosmic effects, as in Jeremiah's vivid picture of uncreation (Jer 4:23-26), strongly evoking Genesis 1-2 with its "heavens and earth," its "formless and empty"

(תהו ובהו/*tōhû wābōhû*, cf. Gen 1:2), its abandonment by creaturely life (Jer 4:25b), and especially "there was no human" (האדם/*hā'ādām;* cf. Gen 2:5). Famine is side by side with sword in the ills that fall on the people (Jer 11:22; 15:2), and the land's languishing under famine is portrayed at length in Jer 14:1-10 (cf. 5:24-25). These natural disasters are inextricable from the war against Judah brought by the Babylonians, which is described in "holy war" terms, mirroring the language of holy war formerly conducted by God in Israel's favor (Jer 21:5-6; cf. Deut 4:34). In this way Jeremiah turns on its head the primary history's close connection between God's creative and historical actions on Israel's behalf, while reasserting the affinity between creation and history themselves. Such affinities are reflected elsewhere in prophetic texts, notably in Joel, where the locust imagery neatly combines the threat of both military and natural ravages.

If the prophets thus confirm the impression of a war of God against all the forces of evil, in humanity and in the natural order, this may be taken a step further when chaotic evil appears in mythological dress. The historical memory of a way of deliverance through the "sea" is mingled with the mythological imagery of a primeval monster defeated, whether Rahab (Isa 51:9-10)[15] or Leviathan (Ps 74:13-14).[16] Even the word "sea" itself in such contexts recalls the name of the sea-god Yam, who in Canaanite mythology monstrously personified the cosmic threat to life and order, and was overcome in a crushing battle by the god Baal, who thus made possible the ordinary rhythms of life.[17] The vivid anthropomorphisms of the language applied to Yahweh in these biblical texts strongly evoke violent battle.[18] And similar imagery and ideas underlie other texts even if it is not so immediately obvious there (e.g., Ps 93).[19]

As in the "primary history," mythological language is closely bound up with historical people and events. The texts in both Psalm 74 and Isaiah 51 point towards God's reaffirmation of his sovereignty through the overcoming of Babylon and the restoration of his people and his worship in Jerusalem.[20]

---

15. This Rahab is spelled differently in Hebrew from the Rahab of Joshua 2, and there is no connection between the two names.

16. See also Job 3:8; 9:13; 26:12; Ps 89:10; Isa 27:1. It is not known if the biblical writers are alluding in these texts to known Canaanite myths or to similar Hebrew myths now lost.

17. For this myth, see Hallo and Younger, *The Context of Scripture*, 250-51.

18. The "thou"-address in Isa 51:9-10 is strictly not to Yahweh but to his "arm," and so is feminine (since the word זרוע/*zĕrôa'*, "arm," is grammatically feminine).

19. Ps 93:3-4 uses the terms נהר/*nāhār* and ים/*yām*, "river" and "sea," which are also used in parallel in the Canaanite Yam myth. Their personification in the Psalm increases the effect of the mythical allusion.

20. The exodus connection is particularly clear in Isa 51:9-11 (see also Isa 52:11-12). The Psalm is directly concerned with the restoration of worship.

There are therefore clear parallels between Egypt and Babylon, first and second exodus into promised land. These texts from prophets and Psalms reinforce the view that Israel's war on Canaan in Joshua is part of a comprehensive, cosmic war between God and the powers of evil, within which human evil has an integral place.

In one other place the human-historical and the beastly-mythological appear together, namely in the book of Daniel. Here the succession of empires that dominated Israel and its world throughout most of the first millennium is imagined in the form of fierce and unnatural beasts rising from the sea. The connection with the myths of Chaos monsters opposing the creative, ordering power of God is clear.[21] But especially striking is the interplay between the beastly and the human. The first beast, which was like a lion with eagle's wings, has its wings stripped off and is made to stand upright "like a human being" (Dan 7:4; Aramaic אנש/'ĕnāš). The implication is that this monstrous rule is a perversion of a rule that is properly human. The human connection continues in the chapter, as the successive beasts become ever more weird and cruel. The second beast is told to "eat your fill of flesh (בשר/bĕsar)," meaning human flesh. The third is given "dominion" (Aramaic שלטן/šolṭān), recalling the "dominion" given to human beings at creation (Gen 1:26). And the fourth, the strongest and most vicious, is a gross perversion of humanity, having human appearance, but only a superficial resemblance to the truly human, and falsely arrogating greatness to itself (having "eyes like the eyes of a human being, and a mouth," Dan 7:8). The specific allusion in this case, as predominantly in the visions of Daniel, is Antiochus Epiphanes IV, the Seleucid king who lives in infamy because of his desecration of the Jerusalem temple in 167 B.C. But the whole sequence speaks forcefully of the terrible abuse by human beings of the God-given privilege of "dominion" that was theirs from the beginning.

To this parade of brutal inhumanity is opposed a vision of truly human dominion, the "one like a human being" [or "son of man"] (Dan 7:13), whose everlasting kingdom finally overcomes and displaces all the violent pretenders (vv. 11-14) and is placed in the hands of "the saints, the people of the Most High" (v. 27). Moreover, there is a correspondence between truly human rule on earth and the ultimate source of all rule in heaven. In Daniel, therefore, is envisaged a final realization of God's creative purpose, a humanity that is able at last to shoulder the responsibility of proper dominion.

How does the bestial imagery function in this picture? Is it merely a colorful metaphor, intending to show how vicious the empires of biblical times

---

21. For the imagery of the sea and the beasts, see Lucas, *Daniel*, 168-72, esp. 170.

were? I think that the imagery goes deeper. Its evocation of ancient myths takes us into the realm of cosmic opposition to the rule of God. This is confirmed by the book's continuing analogy between powers in heaven and on earth, and even war in heaven corresponding to war on earth (e.g., Dan 10:10-14).[22] The unnatural symbolism for human rule gone wrong presses into a sphere beyond ordinary human reach. Power is not only corrupted, but takes on a kind of destructive intensity, as if something truly demonic has been unleashed.[23] The vision of Daniel knows that the overcoming of oppressive empires can be achieved only by a massive disturbance in both heaven and earth.

Joshua and Daniel are two parts of the same story. In each, human history is placed into a drama or narrative that sees an unbreakable connection between powers in heaven and on earth. The heavenly dimension is more muted in Joshua, yet it is present in the crossing of the "sea" (Joshua 3–4, recalling in turn Exodus 15 with its Chaos connotations), in the mysterious appearance of the "commander of the Lord's army" (5:15), and in the ritualized account of the overcoming of Jericho, which required no human action (ch. 6).

Conclusion

The book of Joshua is no mere account of a phase in the history of Israel. Rather, it belongs to the biblical drama of salvation, in which the people of Israel played a special part, but where issues are at stake that go deeper than surface historical events. Joshua tells of a conflict of God with "the powers." The war between Israel and Canaan is a reflex in history of a conflict that encompasses heaven and earth.

It may be objected to the view taken here that the Old Testament story is essentially one of failure, and therefore that Joshua is less about the salvation of the world than I have suggested. Does not Joshua belong to a narrative in which Israel's mission to the nations, as signalled by the call of Abraham (Gen 12:1-3), ends in failure, only finally to usher in the Gospel? Does a reading of the Old Testament not cohere more satisfactorily with the picture in Romans 9–11, especially 11:11, in which the divine judgment on Israel becomes the occasion of the salvation of the Gentiles in Christ?

---

22. Lucas, *Daniel*, 275-76. Lucas thinks the figure of Michael may be a development of the commander of Yahweh's armies in Josh 5:14 (p. 276).

23. I have in mind here something close to the sense of "the powers" as developed in a number of books by Walter Wink, where institutions can take on a moral or spiritual character that goes beyond that of the sum of their members; e.g., *The Powers That Be*.

In response, it seems to me that the Old Testament always assumes the possibility in principle of a true turning to God, and so of salvation, and that this view of it is borne out by a reading of the text in its own terms. I think there are biblical clues that counsel against taking a text like Rom 11:11 as a pointer to a univocal reading of Old Testament prophetic texts about Israel and the nations. The point may be illustrated by the different New Testament readings of the controversial text in Isa 6:9-13, where the prophet receives a commission from God to

> Make the mind of this people dull,
> and stop their ears,
> and shut their eyes, so that they might not look with their eyes,
> and listen with their ears,
> and comprehend with their minds,
> and turn and be healed (v. 10 NRSV).

Isaiah's ensuing question, "How long, O Lord," receives one New Testament answer in Acts 28:23-28, where Paul, having met resistance to his message in a Jewish congregation in Rome (though "some were convinced"), takes the word of Isaiah as a confirmation of the mission to the Gentiles. Does this determine our reading of Isaiah? If we compare Matt 13:10-17 and Mark 4:10-12, we find a different application of the prophecy, to a division between the disciples, to whom it was given to understand the "secrets of the kingdom of heaven," and others to whom it was not. The New Testament, therefore, does not have a single exclusive interpretation of Isaiah's prophecy. Furthermore, the book of Isaiah has its own answer to the prophet's question "how long?" In Isa 6:11-13 the initial response to Isaiah is that the hardening of Israel will continue until a severe judgment has fallen on the people. But when will that be? The answer to this question appears in texts in the book which portray Israel as the "blind" and "deaf," yet no longer under judgment, but on the point of knowing salvation. The key text runs from Isa 42:14 to about 43:21.[24] The passage is an extended allusion to the blindness and deafness of "my servant" Israel, in a clear reminiscence of Isa 6:9-10, but its thrust is to declare the "new thing" that God is about to do, namely to release Jewish exiles from captivity in Babylon and bring them home in triumph to Jerusalem (43:14, 18-19). The book of Isaiah's answer to the question in 6:11, therefore, is that the hardening of Israel will continue until the judgment of God on his people that was con-

---

24. Other texts include Isa 35:5; 42:6-7 (where indeed the new thing includes a giving of "light to the Gentiles"). On the context of 6:9-13 in the book of Isaiah, see Williamson, *The Book Called Isaiah*, 46-51; Beuken, *Jesaja 1–12*, 164-67.

stituted by the Babylonian exile has had its full effect, so that he may "comfort" them (Isa 40:1) and lead them home to Zion.

This example means that specific prophecies may be shown, by a range of biblical texts, to be fulfilled in various ways. It follows that individual interpretations can be taken to point to something more fundamental. The book of Acts, for example (in 28:23-28), surely does not mean that all Jews forever were excluded from salvation. Rather, what is at stake is a structure of history, in which judgment and salvation are permanent possibilities. This is represented in the Old Testament narratives and prophecies by judgment-salvation as a sequence. The Old Testament has its own prophetic and rhetorical aspect, rendering the possibilities of judgment and salvation. The New Testament rides on the Old Testament pattern, and certainly in the biblical macronarrative, the Christ event is decisively new. Yet the theological and rhetorical force of the Old Testament's literature remains.

It is true that the biblical drama, with its pattern of salvation rather than judgment, embraces a move from the particular (Israel) to the universal, as exemplified especially in Isaiah 40–55. However, this progression is not from particular to universal *as such*, since the universal scope of the divine activity is signalled in the Old Testament from the beginning and is always more or less latent in the story. It is not, therefore, that Gentiles will succeed where Jews failed. It is rather that Israel plays a unique role in the story of humanity and has representative aspects as well as missionary ones. The issues go far deeper than who is "in" and who is "out," but are about the place of humanity before God in a contested world. These issues lend a "mythic" aspect to Joshua, as I have suggested.

The story of Joshua, which is nevertheless placed within history, occupies a particular place in the drama and does not know of or disclose its ultimate end. To illustrate the point in one way, while the book of Joshua knows of "servants of the Lord" in both Moses (1:1) and Joshua (24:29), it lacks a "Servant" in the sense of the Suffering Servant of Isaiah 53. In Isaiah's Servant is the other indispensable strand of that prophecy, alongside the powerful overcoming of Chaotic rule in history. In the Servant, violence is portrayed in a new way, and only in him is human violence finally borne redemptively. The Old Testament story is taken up in numerous ways by the New in its witness to Jesus Christ, including the figures of the Son of Man and the Servant. Here are new realizations of the drama of human power in God's world, definitive for Christian belief.

In the book of Joshua the conflict is staged in a particular way. Because in its account of war it is part of a cosmic drama, it cannot be employed as a model for action in that respect. Rather, it provides a language for victory-salvation over the forces most hostile to human life in its fullness and freedom, though it cannot yet narrate that victory completely. There are both "now" and "not yet" in this narrative. The "not yet" is clear from the foregoing. In the "now," however, there are an affirmation that all possession and place are God-given; a positive portrayal of leadership and organization of a nation by prayer, Torah, and fidelity to God; an ideal of a united people, and space in which a Joshua may "serve the Lord" ("me and my house"), keep Torah, retire to his Timnath-serah in the hill country of Ephraim, and bequeath an "inheritance" to a new generation.

A Response to Gordon McConville

Stephen Williams

I have profited immensely from reading Gordon McConville's work over the years, and it has been a pleasure to collaborate with him on this volume. In particular, I have recently learned much from, and been persuaded by, his *God and Earthly Power*. It is not surprising, then, if I react in a similar way to the bulk of this essay. Although I have questions here and there, they are set within the framework of overwhelming agreement. If we differ in a way profitable to discuss, it is in the way that we conceptualize the interrelationship of Bible, theology, and church. So I shall studiously concentrate on differences and, in particular, on the "Introduction" to his essay.

Attention is drawn in this introduction to the possibility of readers' worries "that our understanding of the narrative is too much influenced by the overarching narrative of Christian theology." In response, Gordon says that "our interest is precisely to bring biblical study into dialogue with theological." It looks as though the contrast between the narrative in Joshua and the Christian theological narrative is equated with the contrast between biblical and theological approaches to the material.

But are these contrasts rightly described? The complexities of the issues in question are effectively brought out by James Barr in his study of *The Concept of Biblical Theology*, including, but only as the best example, in his detailed criticisms of Brevard Childs. Many reject both Barr and Childs, of course. We are not investigating an area where there are likely to be easy answers. But is it right to distinguish Scripture and theology quite as Gordon does? Three phenomena must be kept in mind: Christian theology, the New Testament, and the Old Testament or Hebrew Bible. The binding together of the Old and New Testaments in a single canon (I shall not worry here about the canonical differences between Catholicism, Protestantism, and Orthodoxy) is a declaration of unity and continuity between the two Testaments.

An allegorical reading of the Old Testament in the earliest Christian centuries was largely displaced by more "historical" readings in post-Reformation and modern biblical study. But the logic which is critical of allegory — whether or not we agree with the criticism — does not entail that we should not read the Old Testament in a christological light. The assumption behind the single Bible of the Christian church is that the New Testament definitively interprets the Old.

Now the whole notion of a definitive interpretation will darken many a brow and induce postmodern apoplexy. Even before it begins to have those physiological effects, we have to ask what is meant by "definitive interpretation" anyway. What is meant is, roughly, this. The New Testament proclaims the coming of Jesus Christ onto the human scene for human salvation. In the same breath it proclaims that salvation is the question which the human creature must attend to above all, because the human predicament lies in human need of salvation, acknowledged or not.[1] Jesus Christ is qualified for his role because he, however we understand this, was the one through whom all was created. If there is salvation in no other name, it is because there was creation in no other name. Faith and discipleship mean a corresponding orientation of the whole of intellectual life to Jesus Christ; it is to find the meaning of all existence, as far as meaning can be found, in and through Christ. It is to believe that the Old Testament has meaning as the word of God ultimately only in relation to Christ, for all good things have their meaning only in that relation. That does not involve applying every text, or as many texts as possible, directly to Christ. It does not involve straining the text to make it mean something that it never could. It does not involve the exclusion of various types of meaning, various ways in which texts can be meaningful or various contexts in which they can be studied and yield meaning. It does mean that, as a coherent canonical — Hebrew or Septuagintal — whole ("coherent" here simply signifies that there is such a thing as a canon), its theologically proper and plenary religious intelligibility lies in its relation to Christ. That, as I see it, is the logic of the Christian Scriptures, whether or not we like it, whether we accept or reject its premises or conclusion.

The narrative in Joshua, then, is not something on which Christian theology imposes, something which Christianity threatens to swallow up in an overarching narrative in the mode of alien imperialism. The terms "Jewish" and "Christian" have become used in an unfortunate way, though the occasional use of language in the New Testament and the historical relationship be-

---

1. I hope that no one will conclude that I am assuming here just one particular view of salvation or emphasizing the human predicament at the expense of the fate of the cosmos.

tween Judaism and Christianity make this usage understandable. The fact is that the New Testament constitutes a Jewish interpretation of the Old Testament.[2] To read Joshua in a Christian light is to read it in a Jewish light, though, obviously, not the only Jewish light. Certainly, canonization of the New Testament books took place in a church where leadership had become Gentile. Certainly, the early churches largely used the Greek Old Testament as their Scripture. And, certainly, we may distinguish Christian theology from the New Testament if, by the former, we mean "post–New Testament theology." But, as long as the New Testament is our guide, after the narrative in Joshua is integrated into the story from Genesis to Kings and further integrated into later prophetic and other writings, it finds its deepest theological integration when integrated into the witness to Jesus Christ in the New Testament.

Speaking as a Christian theologian, I think that one of the great weaknesses, indeed, we should probably say "tragedies," in the history of theology has been the loss of contact with the Hebrew Bible or Old Testament. Patterns of thought became deeply ingrained in theology that ignored the Jewishness of the New Testament and were even further estranged from the First Testament. When John Goldingay, for example, says that we need to read the New in light of the Old Testament more than the Old in light of the New, simply because we have done so much of the latter, I sympathize up to a point.[3] But he then goes over the top, insisting that the New Testament approach to the Old "need not influence an attempt to work out the inherent theological significance of the Old Testament — indeed we must resist its doing so."[4] This is surely an impossible position from a Christian point of view, at least as formulated. As though those Jews who first confessed Jesus as Messiah and Lord could ever have consistently believed that the promises to Abraham or the sin-bearing servant of Isaiah had an *inherent* theological significance detachable from Jesus Christ! Are Christians to be so different today from early Jewish believers? I hasten to say that I mention this in a response not because I think that Gordon takes Goldingay's line nor to insinuate guilt by any kind of association, but to bring out the general hermeneutical point.

In relation to Gordon's essay in particular, I question also whether the distinction between the narrative in Joshua and the "overarching narrative of Christian theology" is to be identified with a distinction between biblical study and a theological perspective. That band of pilgrims which is set on the integration of biblical with theological study is the most worthy of compa-

---

2. In the salient respect, this includes Luke's signal contribution.
3. See the "Introduction" to Goldingay, *Israel's Gospel*.
4. Goldingay, *Israel's Gospel*, 25.

nies. But mutual suspicion remains. Biblical scholars regard theologians as prone to more or less systematic constructions which are a world away from the text of Scripture — which might be okay, except that theologians are as blissfully ignorant or careless of that fact as they might be of the biblical languages. Theologians regard biblical scholars as consistently deploying presuppositions in their reasoning that are logically untested and as operating *de facto* on undeclared or unconscious theological assumptions. In this case, the most peaceful thing to say is also the truest: both are right.

But a Christian perspective on Joshua is not "theological" in any way that contrasts with the "biblical." At any rate, not necessarily. Indeed, the more that theologians set about the elaboration of Christian ideas and the more inferential, not to mention speculative, their reasoning becomes, the more frustrating it is when they clamp the biblical text in their seared hands and mold it into something theologically, but certainly not textually, suitable. However, it does not have to be like that. A perspective on Joshua that is derived from the New Testament — not that I assume a single New Testament perspective or a single New Testament theology — is a biblical perspective on Joshua. If "New Testament theology" can be used in a sense that is equivalent to "Christian theology," then a "biblical/theological" distinction has to be modified, to say the least. It is true that many, after years of immersion in both Testaments, feel that they are in different worlds when they turn from one to the other. But it is also true that Luke (though sometimes identified as the one Gentile author in the New Testament) crafts the material in his earliest chapters to make sure that the worlds are not kept apart (though he evokes the atmosphere of the LXX, not of the Hebrew Bible). And he is no New Testament maverick. The Christian church has regarded the Old and New Testaments as belonging significantly to a single world, while admitting that there are significant differences within that world. That world is the one world where a "New Testament" joins the "Old Testament" as a single biblical witness, embracing diversity, to the creation of the world by God, the election and history of Israel, the coming of Jesus Christ to fulfill God's purposes for creation and for Israel, and the consummation of these purposes in church and world. Many, after years of immersion in the Christian Bible, feel that they are in one world, that in Christ there is no Greek and Hebrew, and not even a little Aramaic.

Arguments over the hermeneutical use of the New Testament in the interpretation of the Old (or even Christian theology in the interpretation of the whole Bible) may logically be fundamentally an argument over the justification for Christian belief. Reading the Old Testament narratives through Christian eyes can be an exercise in culpable naivete, even assuming that there are many pairs of Christian eyes; but it can also be a matter of the simple logic of Christian conviction. Similarly, the claim that the New Testament is the hermeneutical key to the Old can seem to be an exercise in colossal arrogance; but it can also be a matter of the simple logic of believing in the resurrection of Jesus from the dead.[5] What is the religious position of Gentile Christians, bearing in mind that the majority of Christians are Gentile? Gentile Christians believe that salvation is of the Jews. They sit under the Jewish (Pauline) admonition that they do not support the root, but that the root supports them (Rom 11:18). If they read in the Hebrew Bible that Jews can be as bad as non-Jewish idolaters, they read in the New that they, Gentile Christians, can be cut off from the root as surely as any Jew (Rom 11:22). If they assent to the belief, rightly or wrongly, that the history of Israel is the history of failure, they will ask why this should not be equally true of the history of churches (no human being has enough information to view "the church" as a single entity). The point of this digression is to indicate that theological hermeneutics cannot be legitimately grounded in arrogance.

My considerable agreement with Gordon's essay indicates how different ways in which we might describe the hermeneutical situation need not entail general disagreement when it comes to interpreting Joshua. Yet there are particular points where hermeneutical differences might affect our reading. In the discussion of "Joshua and Genesis" in this essay, Gordon remarks: "It is undoubtedly a complication of the story that the divine plan for Israel's salvation entails a judgment on Canaan. Yet this equation does not have permanent or absolute status in the biblical portrayal of judgment and salvation in human affairs." Perhaps I am not quite convinced that the judgment on Canaan emerges clearly as a "complication" so long as we are reading the story within the context of Genesis-Kings given the way that 2 Kings ends, as Gordon says, in a "moral blank." Perhaps things look different if we go a step further in the Hebrew Bible and go on to read Isaiah, or in the Christian Old Testament and read to the end of 2 Chronicles, for example. Still, Gordon may have this wider scene in mind. Where the New Testament witness, if we align ourselves with it, is surely bound to impinge on our reading of Joshua, is in relation to the "permanent or absolute status" of Joshua's action against the Canaanites. The New Testament has traditionally been read in the Church in terms of an eschatological separation, not an eschatological unity, of human-

---

5. David Yeago criticised Hans Frei, as Vanhoozer describes it, "for leaving the impression that what modern hermeneutics lost was the technique of figuration rather than the knowledge that Christ had indeed been raised from the dead"; *The Drama of Doctrine*, 222, n. 38. From a theological point of view, Frei struggled hard with the resurrection; see *The Identity of Jesus Christ*, ch. 13.

kind. A universalist alternative has become increasingly widespread in recent decades, and there is a variety of ways of understanding human eschatological destiny. It seems to me that whether or not one reads Joshua's action as at least a *sign* of "permanent or absolute" *destiny* can *in principle* be affected by our reading of New Testament eschatology. So the different ways in which we might understand the hermeneutical foundations of our reading of Joshua may have a rather specific bearing on that reading in this instance.

But this response is situated within giant parentheses. I write, first, as one who has learned and, second, as one who agrees.

Reading Joshua Today

Stephen Williams

How should we read Joshua today? If we ask this question against the background of contemporary biblical studies, we must prepare for a sortie that goes far beyond the borders of the text of Joshua, and we shall encounter currents as dangerous and countervailing as any swirling in the Jordan during a harvest-time flood. How are we to read and interpret any Old Testament text or any New Testament text or any text at all? As I sit before the text, scholarly voices remind me that I or the community of which I am part must pay heed to context, interests, motivations, presuppositions, and a raft of considerations all the way through to the particularities of gender as I presume to engage with the text. I must be aware of my identity as a reader. Nor does the text itself get off more lightly. I am bidden to go beyond attending to its literary form and structure, its historical, religious, or theological dimensions and sociological background; I am bidden also to detect its ideological bias and deconstruct it and/or read it in its canonical context, not forgetting that there is more than one canon.[1]

A mass of what we can broadly describe as "hermeneutical" issues clamors for attention as we confront biblical (and many extrabiblical) texts. The significance of the issues and the clamor must be acknowledged; the considerations above are not listed in the service of a snide complaint. However, they are impossible to treat in an essay on reading Joshua today. It is something of an encouragement, if something of a surprise, when the author of a work that helpfully surveys various ways of reading the Old Testament and argues that there is no one correct method of doing so, announces that the "meaning of very many passages, even of very many books, is not very seri-

---

1. A range of positions and approaches is described by Perdue, although his particular concern is with *Reconstructing Old Testament Theology*.

ously disputed."² What is indisputable is that the book of Joshua offers an account of entry, slaughter, occupation, and land allocation by and for a covenant community identified as the people of Israel, all taking place in narrative and religious succession to the ministry of Moses, whose death concludes the previous book, Deuteronomy. This is what we are reading when we are reading Joshua, whoever we are, whatever we are about, whatever more we are reading into it, and whatever more there is to be read out of it.

The Question of History

This brief and bland summary of what Joshua is about makes an obvious assumption: we appear to be reading history. Why state an assumption so obvious or why qualify it with the word "appear"? It is because "history" is a broad category, and "history" as we encounter it in Joshua raises contentious issues. Debate on the relation of the Bible to history and debate on the importance of the debate have gone on for a long time. Should questions of historicity matter when we read Joshua today? Do they matter in some contexts but not in others?

"Historicity" is a rather broad term, though not as broad as "history." By "historicity" I am not picking out the genre of a work or a passage, but, assuming that a given text purports to describe something that actually happened — to give us a history — I take the word to refer to the actual veracity of its report. Various distinctions can be drawn between "core" historicity and detailed historicity, or between fundamental and less significant, or between general and more specific elements in the accounts that we have in the text. All this is but the beginning of distinctions. Indeed, it is not really the beginning. For these distinctions make an assumption about genre; they are appropriate when we have concluded that a specific kind of material is presented to the reader, but genre assignment obviously has a logical priority. "Genre" itself turns out to be a broad term as well. Broadly, it denotes the kind of material under consideration when we categorize something as "chronicle," "poetry," "prose," or "fiction," or some mixture of them, or something different.³ Perhaps we are destined always to be in the dark as regards much in the narrative and poetic conventions embodied in the Hebrew Bible, as we are in the case of

---

2. Barton, *Reading the Old Testament*, 245.

3. For some warning shots pertaining to "genre," see Porter, "Hermeneutics, Biblical Interpretation, and Theology." On "supergenre," see Knierim, "Criticism of Literary Features, Form, Tradition, and Redaction."

authorship, authorial intention, and the stages and types of authorship in the transmission of the material embodied in a canon. Yet, the lay reader will encounter in the book of Joshua an apparently clear design, which is to describe how, at a specific point in space and time, a people entered a precisely identifiable territory, putting many inhabitants to the sword and razing some property in the process. Even sophisticated scholarship will scarcely gainsay that, at a general level, this is what it looks like. The complexities of historical transmission and subtleties of literary rendering do not induce much doubt that this is the design, even if there is much more to the design than that and even if we might qualify the description in some way. If Joshua is meant to be read as history at least in the basic respect just described, however that history comes or is presented to us, should it matter to anyone whether the fundamental story line of Joshua describes what happened once upon a time? Does it matter whether the attempt to convey history got it anything like right?

There is wide-ranging disagreement on this. One view is that, for theological or practical purposes, it does not matter. What matters and what has shaped readers' attitudes from an early time right to the present is not what may have happened independently of what the text says, but the content of the text itself. That is what has come down to us as Scripture. As Goethe observed: "Once written the thing has rights of its own, and will assert them."[4] But "rights" is a word that might point us in an opposite direction when we consider the political situation in the Middle East and impel us to insist that, on the contrary, historical truthfulness *does* matter. Many believe that Joshua's interpretation of history is dangerous to world health. What if we find that the underlying history is basically "constructed" without objective foundation in historical event? We would seem to be confronted with a portrayal that is not only grotesque in itself but is also painted on water, as it were, a religious monstrosity mounted on a historical fake.[5] Will this not affect our talk of contemporary political rights? On the other hand, what if we believe the history and believe that it *legitimately* grounds a contemporary political claim? Brevard Childs is right to say that "because of the material in Joshua, it is not surprising that the problem of using the biblical text in reference to historical phenomena should be an acute one."[6] Leaving aside sociopolitical repercussions, the trend in Old Testament studies away from interest in questions of history and historicity has not swept the question of history

---

4. Quoted by Constantine, "Kafka's Writing and Our Reading," 23.
5. The language of painting on water is borrowed from Anselm, *Cur Deus Homo*, 1.4.
6. Childs, *Introduction to the Old Testament as Scripture*, 252. Cf. Goldingay, *Israel's Gospel*, 486.

off the field. "Minimalists" find a minimum, "conservatives" a maximum of reliable history in the biblical accounts, and both agree that there are important issues at stake. The book of Joshua is at the heart of all this.

Is there a Christian perspective on this question — the question of basic historicity and whether it matters? The New Testament presents Jesus of Nazareth as the Messiah of Israel, risen from the dead, and declares that the one God to whom the Old Testament bears witness as creator of the world and savior of Israel has, by his action, forged a new covenant that includes Jews and Gentiles. When John declared that his testimony was to what "we have heard, which we have seen with our eyes, which we have looked at and our hands have touched," he captured the empirical foundation of the whole New Testament witness (1 John 1:1). The narrative conventions deployed in the New Testament, however they are related to those found in the Old, are at the service of empirical testimony.[7] The *prima facie* effect of the New Testament witness is to confirm any conviction formed independently from the Old Testament itself, that the historical facticity of the grant of land to an exodus people is a foundational piece of history and grounds the claim of both Testaments to be speaking truly of the God who acts. From a schematic point of view, the land in which Jesus purged his people from their sins was the land that Israel was meant to purge from idolatry. The Israelites themselves eventually became the focus of divine cleansing action. This happened not by a physical expulsion from a land in the time of Jesus, but by the bearing of sins on a cross in the land, set up outside Jerusalem. The bearing of sins and the cleansing of conscience (Heb 9:14) are supposed to impact Gentile as well as Jew. Jew and Gentile, Israelite and Canaanite, meet at the cross in the land. In his zeal for cleansing, Jesus is Joshua with a difference. What happened in the land, what was heard and seen and touched, is the object of testimony.

Of course, the possibility of reading Joshua, land, and Jesus on this scheme does not establish the importance of reading Joshua as history; still less does it even remotely suggest the truth of that history, even if we conclude that the narrative is designed to convey to us its historical truthfulness. It is

---

7. In his impressive study of *The Poetics of Biblical Narrative*, Sternberg bitterly complained about the way in which the New Testament evangelists breached the narrative conventions of the Hebrew Bible (e.g., 86, 127). However, his distaste for the New Testament witness prevented him from reading it properly on its own terms while effectively chastising those who will not read the Hebrew Bible on its own terms. For example, he supposes that Luke has a "yearning for eyewitness-like authority" and presents him as an author under the sway of an unfortunate theologico-literary compulsion, but he does not allow that Luke might have thought that eyewitnesses had something to say which mattered to him and should matter to his readers (Luke 1:1-4). See Bauckham, *Jesus and the Eyewitnesses*.

possible to believe in the importance of the Messiah's birth, teaching, atonement, resurrection, and exaltation in the land of Israel and allow for its suggestive contrasts and similarities with the story of Joshua as handed down to us in the canonical Scriptures without thereby being committed to some fundamental historicity in the book of Joshua. The latter is an independent question, whether we are thinking of establishing the genre or of the success of its historical reference, if it aspires to be history.[8] To establish something about history in relation to Joshua on the basis of empirical testimony in relation to Jesus seems at best highly precarious, and that is to put it generously. But is it really as bad as that?

One of the perennial dangers in scholarship, and nowhere more than in biblical scholarship, is that the purported realities which are the subject of discussion are treated quite unrealistically as mere ideas. It is not just a problem in scholarship. The doctor who loses sight of the patient because of preoccupation with her liver and the psychoanalyst who counsels the abused and thinks only of his technique have lost touch with reality by blocking out context. Biblical and theological scholarship can be totally unhinged from the purported realities that they investigate.[9] If someone seriously believes the New Testament witness that God raised Jesus from the dead, it forms or transforms an outlook on everything. Where it does not have that effect, it is not seriously believed.[10] There are thinkers who find an examination of the reports of overwrought female reactions at the tomb of a crucified Jew extremely boring. Others do not, but will undertake the examination dispassionately. In either case, contact has been lost with reality. To find these accounts boring is rather like finding my doctor's diagnosis of cancer (mistaken or otherwise), stated in professional prose, boring. Dispassionate examination, unless we simply mean examining with appropriate objectivity, makes as much sense as a dispassionate examination of whether a leopard is crouching outside my front door. At least this is the case unless we have reason to

---

8. To talk about "it" aspiring to be history is admittedly a lazy way of speaking; accounts do not strictly have aspirations. But while precision is sometimes important, I trust that the shorthand here does not get in the way of the discussion. James Barr, rightly a stickler for precision in such matters, will himself very occasionally and harmlessly refer to the way the biblical text "sees" or "understands" itself, but his parenthetical criticism of Brueggemann is justified; *The Concept of Biblical Theology,* 550.

9. Those liberation theologies that had their literary beginnings in around the 1960s (e.g., Latin American and feminist) often injected into academic biblical and theological studies a welcome dose of realism in this respect.

10. Reference to "New Testament witness" is meant to take us beyond the position adopted by someone like Pinchas Lapide, to take an admittedly unusual example; see N. T. Wright, *The Resurrection of the Son of God,* 24, n. 37.

rule out the testimony *a priori* as fundamentally unbelievable or improbable. If it is possible that Jesus rose from the dead, it is not possible sanely to treat the proposition just as a piece of information for analysis.[11]

Those persuaded of this witness have a world of possibilities opened out to them, which is not to say that belief in this witness is a necessary condition for entertaining these possibilities. If Jesus was raised from the dead, then Elisha may have had more than a legendary encounter with the son of the Shunammite (2 Kings 4). If Jesus ascended from the earth, then perhaps Elijah did not die an entirely natural death (2 Kings 2). If Jesus performed miracles, then perhaps something strange did happen when Joshua and company crossed the Jordan and after they crossed it. We can not merrily leap from the resurrection over issues of literary genre, archaeology, and ideology to establish the basic historicity of the account in Joshua. But this latter begins to look at least plausible. The resurrection of Jesus tends towards the vindication of what is presupposed in the New Testament witness, namely, that Israel had rightly staked its claim to know God and that concrete history, in its more and less extraordinary aspects, was a locus of revelation. And it rather matters that Israel knew what it was talking about.

Conservative defenders of the historicity of the accounts in Joshua (and in the rest of the Old Testament) sometimes struggle with the question of the significance of "noncore" as opposed to "core" elements.[12] Speaking both generally and particularly in relation to Joshua, it is impossible to divide components of narrative categorically into "essential" and "minor" components. Consider all the possibilities when we conceptualize the relation of "narrative" to "event," even when we fight shy of technical language like "satellite" or "kernel" elements in relation to narrative. A narrative can chronicle events; it can offer literary adornment; it can embellish on the edges; it can be meticulous in its report of when and where something happened, but inventive as regards the speech of its characters; it can be meticulous as regards the speech of its characters, but inventive as regards the when and where, and so on and so forth to more tenuous connections between event and narrative and to the entire dissociation of narrative from any event independent of it. Nevertheless, there is justification for the familiar cultural practice of assuming that different elements in historical accounts carry different weights. Mistaking the color of a house on a street is not like mistaking the presence of a house on the street.

---

11. Watson rightly draws attention to the sober hermeneutical implications of Christian belief in the resurrection in *Text, Church and World*, e.g, 291-92.

12. It is interesting that when Long tries to nail down and not duck the question of commitment to the historicity of noncore elements, he reverts to talking about "core" or "central" matters even when he is trying go beyond them; *The Art of Biblical History*, ch. 3.

It is hard to see how the claim that a significant group of people who worshipped Yahweh entered and partly occupied the land of Canaan by military force is not a core claim, even if we might wish to formulate it a bit differently or add to the core. Is it at least important to maintain this much?

I think that it is. If this is fiction, ideology, or whatever without real basis in fact, the grounds for Israel's claim to know God, as testimony is borne to it in the Old Testament, are surely removed to a very significant degree. And if these are removed, the attitude assumed in the New Testament to the history is questionable; and if this is questionable, the New Testament witness as a whole is questionable. To be sure, I am having to take rather great strides at this point, and, even if space permitted, I have couched the question that I am treating in such a way that a lot of conceptual and detailed ground has to be covered, if it is to be treated aright.[13] Further, in practice and perhaps in principle, it is difficult to handle separately questions about (a) "core" as opposed to "noncore" elements, assuming that we are reading a purported account of history, and (b) genre, issues of whether what we are reading even purports to be history.

Christian defenders of the fundamental historicity of the accounts in Joshua by no means simply appeal to a principle of faith. Take the claim that the description of Canaan in the book of Joshua simply does not fit our archaeological information about the Late Bronze Age. A variety of responses is possible for those who dissent from this judgement, including some combination of them: (a) difficulties in harmonization arise because people read into Joshua a description of conditions in Canaan that it simply does not give; (b) difficulties arise because allowance is not made for deliberately hyperbolic and stylized features in its literary presentation; (c) perhaps the whole scene described in it should not be set in the Late Bronze Age; (d) the "findings" of archaeology are notoriously subject to change with the scholarly generations.[14] But, aside from this, to proceed on the basis of "faith" to an affirmative judgment on the fundamental historicity of the accounts in Joshua is by no

---

13. Witness the general way in which Long has to state his conviction with regard to the destruction of Jericho in particular, despite being able to give the question of history far more attention than I am giving it here. If archaeology showed that it could not have been destroyed, "our confidence in the general trustworthiness of Scripture would not necessarily be destroyed, but neither would it be entirely unaffected"; *The Art of Biblical History,* 117. I do not criticize him for this generality.

14. Strategies of this kind can be deployed by thinkers who take the challenge of sceptics or minimalists entirely seriously — in fact, precisely because the challenge is regarded as forceful. See, e.g., essays in Baker and Arnold, *The Face of Old Testament Studies,* such as those by Chavalas and Adamthwaite on "Archaeological Light on the Old Testament" and Younger, "Early Israel in Recent Biblical Scholarship."

means intellectually indefensible if we understand "faith" aright and describe our procedure aright. Suppose we believe that evidence external to the Scriptures which would enable us to draw confident positive or negative conclusions on credibility on purely historical grounds is rather scant, susceptible to more than one interpretation, and these interpretations liable to shift. There is nothing in principle irrational in giving credence to the Old Testament historical testimony on its own terms, certainly for those who believe in the resurrection of Jesus from the dead.[15] Lack of supporting or corroborating evidence need not increase the possibility that biblical accounts are inaccurate. It may simply signify that there is no means of digging up external attestation several centuries on. This is merely an epistemological remark about the principle of historical credibility. Many, of course, believe that the external evidence positively undermines the historical reliability of Joshua.[16]

My discussion hitherto will appear to some to be culpably trapped in a modern or Enlightenment frame of reference, "culpably" because we should long have known that the narrow question of historicity is a distraction from engagement with the text as text.[17] It certainly can be a distraction.[18] Yet, in the midst of late-twentieth-century and early-third-millennium scholarship, the question of historicity, in its narrower and quite traditional sense, remains alive and well in some quarters, despite and along with literary, postmodern, feminist, and other interests, and it is by no means the preserve

---

15. The case for this both in principle and in detail has been well stated by Provan, Long, and Longman in *A Biblical History of Israel*. However, I think that the authors too quickly apply to the Old Testament materials the general principle of credulity in relation to testimony (see 48). It is a principle that is hard to state satisfactorily when it is stated generally. "Credulity" is used here in its technical philosophical, not normal pejorative, sense; see Swinburne, *The Existence of God*, ch. 13. It is as well to note here the importance of the declaration by Provan, Long, and Longman, that *"biblical accounts must be appreciated first as narratives before they can be used as historical sources"* (93). I am not for one moment suggesting that only believers in the New Testament can take this approach.

16. My concentration on the "core" elements is without prejudice to what may be held about "noncore" elements in the narrative. I hope that it is clear that I do not mean to do literary injustice to Joshua, proposing that the above is the only way in which we should conceptualize issues of literature, narrative, and history.

17. Note Perdue's prediction "that the Enlightenment's epistemology will continue long after the demise of its most ardent critics"; *Reconstructing Old Testament Theology*, 13.

18. So Vanhoozer, *Is There a Meaning in this Text?*, 426. Origen may lend unexpected help in some quarters, when he struggles with the problems of triviality and irrelevance in the interpretation of Joshua and asks, e.g., exactly what the method of hanging of the king of Ai has to do with him; *Homilies on Joshua*, 91, and see, e.g., the whole of Homily 8. Spiritually read, of course, Origen believes that the fate of the king has a lot to do with him and with everyone in the church.

of theologically more conservative scholars. Without a doubt, the whole range of methods of engaging with and interpreting the Old Testament text over the last quarter of a century or so — certainly in principle and often in practice — both enriches our reading of the text and constitutes a welcome corrective to any narrow preoccupations with historicity, and the proportion of space that I have accorded to the issue here is not meant to be an indication to the contrary. Yet the Old Testament landscape stubbornly resists being cleared of its bedrock historical references.[19]

Let us now move on from history.[20] For the main problem as we read Joshua today, as it has been through the centuries, is not the mere fact but the celebration of the violent occupation of land and the accompanying portrayal of God. What should we make of the God of Joshua?

The God of Joshua

Although Joshua tells its own story about the actions of Yahweh, there is nothing obviously very distinctive about its portrayal of God, compared with the rest of the Old Testament. Three features come to the fore in its depiction.

---

19. "In general," says Goldingay in the course of a frank "Appendix," "the First Testament talks about history because the events that happened matter"; *Israel's Gospel*, 868. Despite the considerable gains of and illumination provided by literary approaches, I sympathize with the critical refusal to let these approaches marginalize historical issues as voiced by, e.g., Thompson, one of the leading "minimalists," in his *Early History of the Israelite People*. Of course, just as minimalists can disagree among themselves, so major proponents of the "literary" approach, who are the target of his criticism, differ somewhat among themselves. See, e.g., Alter, *The Art of Biblical Narrative*, on Perry and Sternberg (19), but also Sternberg, *The Poetics of Biblical Narrative*, on Alter (24); and see too Sternberg's well-aimed shafts at the history of biblical scholarship (23). Thompson's own approach is vitiated by an ambiguous use of the term "ahistorical." He often means "nonhistorical," for he is referring not to genre but to performance — to the lack of success of the biblical narratives as history (109). It seems to be a habit that he picked up from one of the other minimalists, Nils Lemche (131), in whose work the problem of terminological unclarity sets in early; see Lemche, *Early Israel*, 56.

20. Even those who approach the Old Testament differently from von Rad may sympathize with the fact that he found himself faced with a constellation of issues here "that vexed him but he could not overcome it," as Barr puts it; *History and Ideology in the Old Testament*, 94. Vos makes a number of sober comments on the questions that have occupied us in his "Christian Faith and the Truthfulness of Bible History," although many will, of course, reject his presuppositions and many who basically accept them may find the treatment dated. One does not have to buy into his whole thesis to assent to George Ernest Wright's crisp and straightforward way of ordering history to narrative: "Israel's theology involved such a concentration on history, that the art of narration was highly developed"; *The Old Testament Against Its Environment*, 73.

First, God is characterized by immense power. He is able to promise credibly because he can deliver on what he promises. He is in control of nature. He can drive out the foes of Israel. Why did God treat the waters of the Jordan as he had treated the Sea of Reeds? "He did this so that all the peoples of the earth might know that the hand of the Lord is powerful and so that you might always fear the Lord your God" (4:24). The account of the controversy over the erection of the altar at Geliloth enshrines the most exuberant of praises to God in the book of Joshua, and it is God's power that is the subject of exultation: "The Mighty One, God, the Lord! The Mighty One, God, the Lord. He knows!" (22:22). Omniscience is a form of power.

Second, God exhibits what we might very loosely and perhaps rather inadvisedly call "moral" characteristics, although this is a terribly weak analogical word to apply to the unique and holy being of God. God is not sheer untrammelled power. He is not even mainly power. Joshua describes him as "holy and jealous" (24:19), words which pick out broadly moral characteristics (whether or not readers are attracted to them) so that God is not just a mysteriously numinous existence. The "moral" aspect of God's being accounts both for his opposition to idolatry and for his mercy towards Israel. God is behind the extermination of the Canaanite peoples, but he is also behind the background Mosaic legislation designed to protect those who are guilty of manslaughter without malice aforethought (20:1-9). Legislation after Sinai describes the ways of justice and of equitable discrimination. Of course, it may be said that these standards are patriarchal and that patriarchy should be viewed in a negative light, but we are not evaluating anything at this point. Perhaps, as we read the Pentateuch, we shall reckon that divine power is in certain respects more immediately discernible than "moral" qualities — that the former is practically contained in a definition of God while the latter are to be learned progressively (e.g., Exod 34:6). Be that as it may, as far as Israel is concerned, God possesses the quality of mercy. The God of Israel is apprehended and portrayed as holy and jealous in the first place only because his initiative in revelation was and is generous and saving, starting with the promises to father Abraham of the gift of land. In his farewell speech, Joshua reports that God delivered Abraham from idolatry; provided him with a family and a pledge; delivered the Israelites from Egypt; delivered the Israelites in the wilderness; delivered the Israelites in the land of Canaan. The catalogue of mercies culminates in the reminder: "I gave you a land on which you did not toil and cities you did not build; and you live in them and eat from vineyards and olive groves that you did not plant" (24:13).[21]

21. Schwartz appears to miss this entirely when she alludes to the "*vague* sense that Israel

Third, although the Lord is often described as the God of Israel, he is also Lord of all the earth. Rahab, an extra-Israelite prostitute, is the first to make the confession: "The Lord your God is God in heaven above and on the earth below" (2:11). The point is soon repeated. Joshua tells the people before they cross the Jordan that "the ark of the covenant of the Lord of all the earth will go into the Jordan ahead of you" (3:11). Two verses later, the Lord is emphatically described as "the Lord of all the earth." A God of power on this scale can not be a merely local or merely Israelite deity. He has already displayed his might further afield, for example in Egypt. We are not told that Joshua pondered the question of whether or not there were seas and rivers somewhere else that were not subject to the power of God, but his confession and that of Rahab formulaically indicate confidence that all the earth is subject to the Lord. Certainly the reader who has read Joshua after reading Deuteronomy has no doubts in the matter. It may be significant that these references to the universal presence and power of God (presence and power are inseparable) come so early in the book of Joshua. The Former Prophets immediately introduce us to no lesser deity than the one we have hitherto encountered in the Pentateuch.

Although these three features are not peculiar to the book of Joshua, our encounter with the action of land seizure and merciless, indiscriminate, divinely-mandated slaughter immediately and soberly forces us to reflect on them according to the expression that they find in this book. Even if the characteristics of God that I have picked out are fairly ubiquitous in the Old Testament, we can not simply assume that they are integrated and ordered in the book of Joshua in the same way as elsewhere. But I shall not embark on a comparative investigation. What matters here is that reading Joshua today brings to more or less its sharpest point a cardinal problem in Old Testament religion, whatever its internal varieties — the portrayal of a personal being allegedly possessing dubious, unprepossessing, or universally perilous attributes. If there indeed exists such a God as the book of Joshua conveys to us, and if such a God is capable of commanding what the book of Joshua says that he commands, we are all in trouble. It would be a bit better if such a God turned out to be a projection of human religious consciousness based on some ideological or quasi-ideological suppositions. For, in such a case, there is a glimmer of hope that we might be able to do something to disabuse and enlighten religious people and alter their con-

---

is *somehow* undeserving of this land" that "hovers over this passage" (italics mine); *The Curse of Cain*, 56. It is somewhat, though not exactly, akin to the mistake that she makes in referring to an Israelite "boast" over tearing down Jericho's walls (61).

sciousness. The God of Joshua is trouble either way, but the less the chance that this God is projected, the greater seems the plight of our world. So it looks to the anxious eye.

What does a Christian reading of the Old Testament look like here? Particularly difficult, some will say.[22] Getting our hermeneutics right might be a matter of life and death for all too many people. Of course, I do not imply that all non-Christian readings of the text doom our world to the possibilities of multiple violent repetitions of Joshua-type actions. Other religious traditions must account for their readings; I simply describe what I take to be entailed in a Christian reading without doubting the independent resources found in the Old Testament itself in aid of a pacific hermeneutic. If a Christian reading of Joshua is justified — a reading which understands the religious and theological import of the text in the light of Jesus Christ — the vital practical contemporary significance of such a reading is clear. The revelation of the nature of God in Jesus is the vantage-point from which Christians must construct their understanding of that God to whom the Old Testament bears witness.[23] But before attempting to shed christological light on the three characteristics noted above, it is important that we attend to the underlying supposition of the book of Joshua, shared with every other Old Testament book. It is the supposition that God is personal.

God as Personal

In the New Testament, the Lord God of Israel is identified as the Father of Jesus Christ. The book of Joshua may well rank on top of the list of Old Testament books that appear to place an intolerable strain on this identification. If we were able to extract from this book some sign that God the Creator and universal Lord intended to have fatherly eschatological mercy on Israelite and non-Israelite alike, it would not remove the difficulties, but it might at least encourage us to seek out a positive connection between the God of Joshua

---

22. See Barr's example of Joshua, *The Concept of Biblical Theology,* 57.

23. As Childs puts it: "The task of a Biblical Theology is to test the reality of God witnessed to in the Old Testament by the reality of Jesus Christ testified to in the New"; *Biblical Theology of the Old and New Testaments,* 706. I agree with much in the detailed criticisms of Childs offered by some who disagree among themselves, such as Barr throughout *The Concept of Biblical Theology* and Watson, e.g., *Text, Church and World,* 43-45, and *Text and Truth,* 209-16. Moberly also seems to be in weighty agreement with Watson against Childs, "The Theology of the Old Testament," 467 n. 51. I do not wish to defend Childs comprehensively on "biblical theology," but I think that this particular statement is apt.

and the God and Father of Jesus Christ. But it seems difficult to extract it.[24] So what positive connections can we legitimately make?

The testimony of the New Testament, as it was apprehended in the early centuries, led the Christian church to formulate a belief in God as Trinity. A justified warning that we should not read patristic theology back into Scripture can obscure the logical implications of this conviction. Those who confess God as triune are bound to regard the monopersonal portrayal of God which pervades the Old Testament as a form of divine accommodation, shaping religious understanding in a way appropriate to the time. The God of Joshua is an accommodated God. And this should make us pause at the portals of what we deem our righteous indignation. Reading Joshua today, as in the past, easily elicits appalled anger at and/or incredulous disbelief in this monopersonal deity, and deconstructive surgery is the least that is needed. Actually, anger, especially angry disbelief, is quite a complex phenomenon. If we disbelieve in the existence of a deity remotely like the one portrayed in Joshua, then we cannot consistently get angry towards Yahweh, for there is no Yahweh to be angry at. We can get angry at the textual figure, as we can get angry at a villain in fictional literature, and we can get angry at believers in Yahweh past and present who have sickeningly taken that figure for real. But the order of existence contains no Yahweh to get angry at. Yahweh transcends our anger in sublime indifference not because he is despotically unconcerned about Canaanite infants, but because his lifeless nonexistence renders him as blind, deaf, and dumb as the most paltry of idols. This is not to reduce anger to absurdity; the prophets treated with contempt and asperity idols made of wood and stone crafted by human hand. It is just that one gets the marked impression at times that some of those who profess disbelief in Yahweh nonetheless get angry with him, as though suspecting that he is not altogether nonexistent.

Be this as it may, why import the notion of God as Trinity? Because, where Joshua's God is in view, the object of anger is a monopersonal deity. A monopersonal deity is to some extent an object of our thought as well as of emotional response, even if our thought is limited in scope. What we are reflecting on is at least clear enough to our imaginative or conceptualizing capacities for us to direct a personal anger towards it. But the triune God can strictly not be thought in that way. The powers of human thought are unable to come up with categories that enable us to get a conceptual grip on the Trinity. I do not wish to exaggerate this point of difference; but does not divine commandment to Joshua begin to look different in a trinitarian light?

---

24. However, see the argument in McConville, *God and Earthly Power,* ch. 6, in the context of the overall argument in the book.

Reading Joshua Today

For a monopersonal God is a being who first experiences relationship with another only when he creates another. For the first time, love is experienced, including disappointed love and holy jealousy. Divine grieving over humanity, as portrayed to us at the beginning of Genesis, is a lonely grief. However, on the Christian understanding of God as Trinity, divine command issues forth from the heart of an eternal triune love which knows no inner ground for anger, jealousy, or disappointment. It is not the command of a powerful, glory-seeking lonely monad. Mindful of this, we shall be less disposed to rail against the God of Joshua than to puzzle at the alleged command to slay.[25]

To import trinitarian considerations into a reading of Joshua may appear like the sort of bizarre move that only a certain type of theologian is capable of. However, in point of fact, it is the only consistent thing to do if Jesus Christ is confessed as Lord in an affirmation of deity.[26] The man Joshua was warned to approach God cautiously. Sandwiched between the story of the crossing of the Jordan, a drama witnessed by all the Israelites, and the story of the collapse of Jericho, a drama witnessed by both Israelites and non-Israelites, there is an account of a personal meeting with a commander of the Lord's army, an equally dramatic but private experience. Reading Joshua today, it is a fragment all too easily marginalized, but it may have a greater hermeneutical significance than appears at first blush. Joshua had been there or somewhere not unlike it before, for he was with Moses on Sinai (Exod 24:13; 32:17). And Moses had been there, or somewhere not unlike it, before that, for he was with God at the scene of the burning bush, the account of which has resonances with this account in Joshua (Exod 3:2). Peter, James, and John were not complete strangers to the scene. In an account redolent of Sinai, three of the four evangelists record the transfiguration of Jesus Christ. In fact, one commentator on the book of Joshua alludes to transfiguration in connection with Joshua's experience.[27] This incident in the book of Joshua contains more than a warning about how Joshua is to approach the commander of the Lord's army. It constitutes a warning about how we are to ap-

---

25. I am well aware that adherents of nontrinitarian views of God can appeal to the mystery of divine being which transcends its monopersonal representation.

26. Pneumatology is not up for consideration here. The hermeneutical significance of the doctrine of the Trinity is well brought out by Watson in *Text and Truth* and, in a previous work, Watson remarked that "this trinitarian hermeneutic presents itself as a framework within which the exegesis of texts will at the same time be an exegesis of reality"; *Text, Church and World*, 255. Cf. Vanhoozer, *Is There a Meaning in this Text?* ch. 8.

27. Hess, *Joshua*, 127. The accounts of the transfiguration are found in Matt 17:1-8; Mark 9:2-8; and Luke 9:28-36. The transfiguration of Jesus Christ is a narrative and theological hinge on which the Synoptic accounts turn.

proach the text of Joshua, a reminder that its portrayal of God may reflect only the surface of God's being and ways.[28] Mystery surrounds the personal reality of God long before we get an inkling of the Trinity. Mystery does not dissolve the problem of the commands of the God of Joshua. But we might find his ways as difficult to fathom as we do the words of the commander of the Lord's army. The better part of wisdom is to let silent unknowing displace angry bewilderment along the lines of the movement from Hab 1:2 to 2:20. As long as we puzzle over the God of Joshua, the incident outside Jericho should be lodged at the forefront of our minds. We now return to the features picked out earlier and inquire about the power, character, and lordship of God.[29]

God of Power

> God lets himself be pushed out of the world on to the cross. He is weak and powerless in the world, and that is precisely the way, the only way, in which he is with us and helps us. Matt. 8.17 makes it quite clear that Christ helps us, not by virtue of his omnipotence, but by virtue of his weakness and suffering. Here is the decisive difference between Christianity and all religions.... The Bible directs man to God's powerlessness and suffering; only the suffering God can help.[30]

These words, penned by Dietrich Bonhoeffer in his prison confinement, are some of the most quoted words in twentieth-century theology. They appear to distance the book of Joshua from Christianity. In light of the fact that the healings recorded in Matt 8:17 are connected with the display of signs and wonders that mark the pages of the Gospels and the book of Acts, Bonhoeffer's words contain an element of rhetorical exaggeration. Yet they also contain a significant element of truth, and this challenges us as we set about the task of reading Joshua today in the light of the New Testament.

---

28. It may be worth recalling that nowhere in the Old Testament is divine wrath portrayed more starkly than in the prophecy of Ezekiel, but no book of the Bible opens with a more dramatic scene, one which implicitly warns us about the limits of our intellectual apprehension of God. Caird felicitously characterized the language of Ezek 1:28 as a "triple guard against literality"; *The Language and Imagery of the Bible*, 175.

29. Eichrodt wrote that it was "patent that those whose task it was to proclaim the divine will regarded it as far less damaging that men should have to grope in the dark on the subject of Yahweh's spiritual nature, than that they should remain unconscious of the personal quality of his behaviour and operations"; *Theology of the Old Testament*, 1:212. That is true as far as it goes, but pertains to the monopersonal disclosure in the Old Testament.

30. Bonhoeffer, *Letters and Papers from Prison*, 360-61.

Jesus suffered and summoned his disciples to do the same. This is a prospect surely invisible on Joshua's map. Divine power and might were supposed to translate into victory in battle for the people of Israel, just so long as the people harnessed obedient conduct and trust to its belief in the promise of God. In contrast, the New Testament authors discovered that divine power was exercised at a (literally) crucial juncture through the efficacy of a cross and a sacrifice for sin. Seven verses after Israel has disposed of twelve thousand inhabitants of Ai, and two verses after hanging its king on a tree, Joshua leads the people in the ritual of burnt and fellowship offerings. But Jesus, also designated a king and also suspended from a tree, belongs more to the world of the offerings than to the world of the preceding military action. And when Jesus is called a priest, he is unlike those priestly accomplices of military action that bore the ark into war.

How should we read Joshua today in the light of all this? If we merely see in Jesus a revelation of divine power that contrasts with or surpasses what we find in Joshua, we are thinking along lines of what has traditionally been called "progressive revelation." But we are witnessing not just novelty in divine *revelation*, but also novelty in divine *action*. (This is not to deny that revelation is a form of action.) We are faced not just with contrasting modes of divine *appearance*, but contrasting *dispensations* as far as divine action is concerned. That is, we are proposing that God has reserved to himself the right to exercise his power in different forms in different epochs, not just that we *view* him in a changed light. The contrast should not be exaggerated. The incidence of miracles in Joshua and the Gospels provides some kind of continuity that places a question mark against Bonhoeffer's generalization about power. There is not only a cross, but a resurrection, in the New Testament, not only divine power but divine suffering in the Old.[31] But God's suffering in the New Testament is embedded in a new economy, the kind that spells the death of a commandment such as Joshua received.

In the discussion of genocide above, it was argued that we should answer in the affirmative the question of whether or not God commanded the slaughter of the Canaanites, only if we do so with a proviso. There, I read the command as a concessionary or compromise divine action in a world already filled with violence. The suggestion was that divine command is related to divine nature by supposing that the command issued from a heavy heart. Ac-

---

31. The "passibility" of God, roughly his capacity for suffering, has admittedly been denied through long centuries in Christian theology. In relation to the Old Testament, Heschel's treatment remains valuable in *The Prophets*, chs. 12-14. In relation to the cross, see Frei's discussion of the "increasing dominance of God's initiative over that of Jesus in the last stages of the Gospel story"; *The Identity of Jesus Christ*, 71.

cording to the way that the New Testament interprets history, our present epoch is defined by the advent of the Spirit of Christ following the exaltation of Christ to a lordship which is universal and not simply exercised in relation to the church (Matt 28:18). The problem of evil remains with us in the New Testament no less than in the Old for, while the lordship of Christ is universal, yet "the whole world is under the control of the evil one" (1 John 5:19). The conundrum of evil and suffering, which underlies our struggle with the book of Joshua, is no more theoretically soluble when we view Christ than when we read Joshua. The revelation of evil is greater in the New Testament; Joshua would surely have been surprised to learn that the whole world could ever be under the control of the evil one.

What baffles many readers of the book of Joshua is God's *perpetration* of slaughter and suffering, although we have been prepared for it in the book of Deuteronomy. When we are not baffled by that, we are baffled by a cosmic state of affairs which involves God's *endurance* of evil and suffering. From the earliest chapters of Genesis, we have been warned not to identify divine command automatically with God's preferred way of acting towards and upon humanity. The prohibition on slaying animals is rescinded after the Flood, but this is a concessionary measure and presumably of a piece with divine grieving over human violence on earth, for the animals are objects of his covenant care (Gen 9:9-17). In the unfolding economy of the New Testament, as it is described by Matthew, Christ's declaration of authority is immediately followed by the summons to reach the nations with the message of the gospel and to make disciples (Matt 28:16-20), but we have learned earlier that discipleship entails self-denial and suffering (16:24). The Messiah will not command his own to possess and retain a land entered and taken in battle; the donkey replaces the warhorse, if we may take metaphorical liberties in our description of Joshua's military forces. In Joshua's day, God exercised his power in a form consonant with the epoch before the advent of Christ. In our day, God exercises his power in a form consonant with the epoch after the advent of Christ. In fact, distinctive divine action serves to define the distinction of epochs. If all this is too sweeping and too little nuanced, it captures an important feature of the distinct economies.

It is easy to assume that the God of power portrayed in Joshua is the projection or construct of an ideal of masculine military power. On that assumption, those who transmitted to us the story about Joshua and his kind have modelled God on their own understanding of prowess and might, transposing a cultural perception of human power onto the divine plane. On my reading, it is better to think of a twofold accommodation on the part of God. First, there is a divine accommodation to human perception, so that God is portrayed as mysterious but monopersonal. Second, divine action is accommodated to the times: *given* evil, expressed in violence, God uses it instrumentally. The New Testament does not discourage the notion that Joshua heard and obeyed the word of God. Rather, it speaks to us a different word. The new word exposes the absence of divine weakness, in the sense exemplified in the life and death of Jesus, in the narrative of Joshua. Of course, the Old Testament is consistently rich in subtleties. In the book of Judges, which follows immediately after the book of Joshua, the Laishites are described as a "peaceful and unsuspecting people" (Judg 18:7-10). Does this description contain or imply an evaluation, a repudiation of violence that even makes us pause to consider how we should read Joshua? It would not be uncharacteristic of Hebrew narrative, broadly speaking, to seal its lips in this matter and let the reader try out the possibilities. As it is, the text is difficult to translate and to understand with confidence. All we can certainly say is that the God of power who features in the book of Joshua authorizes a specifically-directed violence whose day has gone. Of course, the God of war long survives Joshua in the rest of the Former Prophets. In light of the account of Israel's faithless move towards monarchy, we wonder to what extent this survival is a sign of Israel's failure to trust Yahweh. But it does seem certain that divine power knows different dispensational forms. Perhaps the classical prophets, with deepened insight into God, including the revelation of the divine lover as early as Hosea, open out the prospect of a new dispensation. At any rate, it awaits the coming of Jesus Christ for its establishment. So the Bible does not authorize anyone to do today what Joshua did then. On the contrary, such action will come under a judgment as severe as the judgment experienced by the Canaanites in Joshua's day — severer, it may be.

The Character of God

In thinking about the nature of God as he is represented in the book of Joshua, we are liable to forget the kind of ground on which we ought to set the feet of the mind. An exercise in reflection easily becomes an exercise in mastery. "We are masters of what we can apprehend."[32] The object of our thought presents itself to us as exactly that — an object of thought and there-

---

32. Barth, *Church Dogmatics* II/1:188. This sentence is embedded in Barth's discussion of "The Hiddenness of God." Barth's discussion of divine hiddenness in *Church Dogmatics* I/2, which contains a brief reference to the time of Joshua, should be read alongside it; 84-94; 104-113. Whether or not we can go along with all its formulations, it is also worth consulting Barth's brief discussion of power in *Dogmatics in Outline*, ch. 7.

fore a kind of object. In conscious thought, we tacitly assume that mind possesses a significant measure of control. God, whether the God of the book of Joshua or of any other book, becomes an idea. This applies even to those who most strongly insist that "God," like Adam's animals, names a reality apart from our naming and who equally insist that this reality, unlike Adam's animals, names himself to us. As long as "God" is thought, talked, or written about, an *idea* tends to parade itself before our minds, an idea whose content may be that of a dynamic being, but whose form is static or manipulable as long as it is an object of thought.[33] Speaking generally, thought is a constructive process and not just a passive reception, so even conservative readers of Scripture who demur from the language of "construction" in the cause of safeguarding "revelation" in the Bible are entirely prone to be manipulators and movers of religious ideas even as they robustly defend the realism of biblical language about God. Within limits, this is in order, just as long as we do not forget that all theology is carried out *coram deo*, before God.

The words of the stranger outside Jericho (5:13-14) are as significant for our meditation on the character of God as was his sheer appearance for our meditation on the being of God. No doubt is entertained anywhere in the book of Joshua that its hero was bidden to take the city in the name and strength of the Lord. Yet the figure whom Joshua met declares that he is neither for nor against Joshua and his fellow Israelites. We surely domesticate and reduce the religious force of his words if we hear them merely as a statement to the effect that commanders of the Lord's army are never part of any regular terrestrial force, as though we could paraphrase thus: "I am obviously for you, not for your enemies, for you and I and our armies are on the Lord's side. It is just that my support does not take the form that you think. So, to draw attention to that fact, I shall answer: 'Neither' when you ask me whose side I am on."[34] The stranger's words are a warning against the easy invocation of God as being on any side, except on the side of the holy and true against the unholy and untrue, and the warning is not only for the ears of Joshua in his time or for a selection of preexilic and postexilic readers.[35] In

---

33. I use the word "idea" in the broad sense frequently used by John Locke, e.g., as that which the mind is occupied with when it is thinking: *An Essay Concerning Human Understanding*. It is admittedly, to use Gilbert Ryle's phrase, a "Pandora's box of a word" in Locke; Ryle, "John Locke and the Human Understanding," 17.

34. For a persuasive reading of this account, see Hawk, *Joshua, ad loc.*, in addition to the exegesis in the first part of the present volume.

35. Abraham Lincoln's insight into divine purpose was, in many and relevant respects, remarkable. See Noll, *America's God*, 426-38. "In the present civil war," said Lincoln in "Meditation on the Divine Will," "it is quite possible that God's purpose is something different from the pur-

the Old Testament, it turns out that God is not always on the side of Israel against her foes, even as the mysterious force of election and promise course their way through the bleak career of Israel's history and failure.[36]

In considering the "character" of the God of Joshua, holiness is surely the place to begin. In holiness, God is revealed as most unlike and least liable to be confused with created humanity. Some read the text as though an irascible, rather capricious disposition to violence is partly constitutive of divine jealousy. If so, we shall judge that this, along with mercy, is a phenomenon encountered on the human scene, even if we are cautious about joining language about God and about ourselves within a single analogical bracket. Holiness is different. "Holiness" in the Old Testament does not always, and sometimes not primarily, meet us as a "moral" quality at all, i.e., a quality immediately apprehended in moral categories. If it were, readers might place it alongside "jealousy" and "mercy" and "disposition to violence" as something with at least a parallel on the human scene. But holiness is not necessarily like that. The "holiness" of impersonal vessels designed for priestly use in the Pentateuch did not pick out a moral quality in the vessels, but set them apart. So it can be with the holiness of God, though we shall come on to its "moral" nature in a moment.[37]

Divine holy apartness is not the apartness of sheer otherness, something that leaves us unable usefully to attribute to God any positive qualities or characteristics. It is through accounts set forth in speech that Israel testifies to its religious consciousness of God's holiness and gives it some positive content. Yet, because God is Creator of all, himself uncreated, his holiness com-

---

pose of either party"; Lincoln, *His Speeches and Writings*, 655. Cf. the words of the Second Inaugural Address: "The Almighty has His own purposes"; *Collected Works of Abraham Lincoln*, 8:333.

36. Many take exception to this characterization offered by Rudolf Bultmann (a "history of failure") at the end of his essay on "Prophecy and Fulfillment," 75. Bultmann's reasoning was that Israel was seduced into identifying God's eschatological activity with what happens in secular history, and so it is interesting that Goldingay, who does not agree with Bultmann here, remarks that "we live as if God had already taken us to the place of our destiny"; *Israel's Gospel*, 371; cf. 696 (see too 640 on *Unheilsgeschichte* and Martin Buber on "the history of God's disappointments," 614). It is possible to accept Bultmann's conclusion in a qualified form, at least for the Genesis-Kings narrative, without subscribing to his reasons for coming to that conclusion. For a different emphasis, see Bultmann's essay on "The Significance of the Old Testament for the Christian Faith." Barr is understandably intrigued by the thesis on the Christian interpretation of failure advanced by Sweeney, "Tanak versus Old Testament"; see Barr, *The Concept of Biblical Theology*, 307-9. But note Barth's reference to "the fact that a history of Christianity can be written only as a story of the distress which it makes for itself," *Church Dogmatics* I/2:337.

37. Otto, *The Idea of the Holy*, remains in some respects an illuminating treatment.

pounds our sense that it is inappropriate to imagine, as we read the Old Testament, an order of Being that can be subdivided into a number of different kinds of beings, of which God is numerically one, albeit the only one of his kind.[38] We are compelled to speak and think of God as personal and, in Christ, we have every reason to affirm the propriety of doing so. But our thought of God never penetrates to the inner constitution of his being. Our language should not allow us to forget a living holiness, mercy, and power that is far more overwhelming in reality than the richest analogical imagination can conceive.[39]

Readers may be wondering whether, if all this is implied in the book of Joshua, their copies are missing a chapter or two. But we are asking about reading Joshua today, which means reading it against a background of centuries of intellectual history during which the question of language about God has become an explicit theme of conscious reflection in parts of the world. Against the background of these intellectual habits, our consideration of holiness, divine being, and divine mystery in Joshua will lead us to qualify carefully, though not analyze definitively, our thinking and speaking about God as "good," "merciful," or "jealous." The intellectual and emotional confidence with which we seize on the meaning of such predications signals a failure to keep in mind the holy otherness of the one to whom they apply.

It was observed that the descriptives "irascible" and "disposition to violence" commend themselves to some readers as appropriate to Joshua's God. But Joshua's God is not rightly described in those terms. Take the case of a gentle and peace-loving human individual who is confronted with a violent threat to home or territory over a sustained period of time. This individual conscientiously but reluctantly decides against pacifism. We might opt to describe such an individual as "disposed to violence" in terms of short-term disposition to action, but we might equally regard the description as misleading or false. Certainly we are not, in such a case, describing a disposition of the heart. Dietrich Bonhoeffer was introduced earlier. It would be misleading to

---

38. The way that the Bible speaks of "Yahweh" does not make it consistently impossible to subdivide things that way, but theological reflection on the biblical witness to God, particularly if we think that the New Testament witness is trinitarian, enhances our sense of the radical ontological incomparability of God.

39. I agree with Vanhoozer that we should not shun the language of ontological reference: "When God speaks, he is present as the one who transcends (is ontologically distinct from) the world order"; *The Drama of Doctrine*, 100. Brueggemann is rightly criticized on this point: see Barr, *The Concept of Biblical Theology*, 545 and 559, and Moberly's discussion of Brueggemann in "Theology of the Old Testament." Mackintosh well captures the attitude that is appropriate when we consider the holiness of God in *The Christian Apprehension of God*, ch. 6.

describe Bonhoeffer as "disposed to violence," because the phrase is typically used to indicate "nature" or "character." Yet he was practically disposed towards the violent assassination of Hitler. The God of Joshua is "disposed to violence" only along these lines, and we fail to rise above the surface of anthropomorphism and to stand back before the wider biblical picture if we regard God as "irascible." As for Joshua, speaking generally, he may have rightly understood the divine command, although it was presumably not given to him to know the relation of divine command to divine disposition.

Holiness certainly has a deep moral dimension. Joshua's concern with idolatry, which underlies the slaughter of the Canaanites, makes this clear. The divine qualities of jealousy and mercy, as exhibited in Joshua, probably best come into view in connection with this dimension of holiness. God's antipathy towards evil indicates the purity of his jealousy and the passion of his mercy.[40] A christological reading at this point exhibits continuities with Joshua. "Jealousy" has its home and rationale in the context of faithful covenant relationships. It is an implication of holiness and of faithful covenant love. The jealousy that Yahweh shows in relation to Israel looks like a kind of exclusiveness and partiality only when we abstract it from the wider economy of God's dealings with the world. As Paul put it to the Romans, God "has bound all men over to disobedience so that he may have mercy on them all" (Rom 11:32).[41] Paul here concludes an argument that explains divine election not as the foundation of exclusive and possessive jealousy, but in terms of a universal mercy. The election of a people, in tandem with the gift of land to that people, has more than the people in mind. We do not know how far beyond the blessing of his own people Abraham personally looked, but the promise given to him looked forward to the wider blessing of the world, and so connected the creation of humankind with eschatological rescue in Christ.

In Deuteronomy, we read of Israel set apart. Why? One answer is: "So that the nations might be drawn in" (Deut 4:5-8). This positive attitude towards the nations, sitting alongside the exclusive attitude to Israel, is meant to inform our reading of Joshua, even if it does not clearly break the surface of the book when we consider it in isolation.[42] Read apart from Deuteronomy, Joshua lacks an inchoate Deuteronomic theology of the nations. It is not surprising, for Joshua is largely narrative. In any case, it should not be read apart.

---

40. The profound alliance of holiness with compassion is yet to emerge in Joshua, but see, e.g., the poignant representation of God in Hos 11:8 against the background of the prophecy as a whole.

41. This is certainly a verse that is variously interpreted, but my general point can be made without being dogmatic on its interpretation.

42. This is a thesis well developed by McConville in *God and Earthly Power*.

With Deuteronomy and the prophets, and still more when we go back to Abraham, we catch sight of the wider purposes of God. These wider purposes are perhaps set on the margins of the book of Joshua, but they constitute its vital canonical context.

We may suitably return to holiness at this point. As we pause on holy ground outside Jericho, we should become aware of the limitations placed on any view of God's character that is derived solely from the material found in the book of Joshua itself.[43] The phenomenon of holiness warns us to be careful about how we apprehend God's character even within the confines of that book. It suggests to us the possibility that the end of God's ways and the disposition of his heart contain mysteries neither revealed to the Joshua of whom we read nor in the book in which we read of him. Holiness indirectly indicates a trail whose end might just turn out to be mercy. Neither the trail nor its end is clearly visible in the book, but obedience to divine command is the way to follow it now as then, however difficult it is to comprehend the commandment or the God who commands it.

Divine Lordship

To read Joshua in christological perspective is to read it in eschatological perspective. Of course, to read it in eschatological perspective is not necessarily to read it in christological perspective, for eschatology is not a peculiarly Christian preserve. Neither, indeed, is Christology, if we think of Christology primarily under the rubric of "messianism." An eschatological reading of the Hebrew Bible may include a messianic reading without being a christological reading in the Christian sense. The eschatological context of a peculiarly Christian reading of Scripture is highlighted by the location of the book of Revelation at the end of the New Testament canon. From a Christian point of view, to offer a dispensational interpretation of the forms of divine power, as I have done above, is to think in dispensational terms of triune lordship.[44] Pneumatology takes us too far afield. But the apocalyptic and christological formulation is germane: "The kingdom of the world has become the kingdom of our Lord and of his Christ, and he will reign for ever and ever" (Rev 11:15).

43. I am taking "holy ground" as referring to far more than the physical location of Joshua's encounter in its proximity to Jericho.

44. Among modern theologians, Wolfhart Pannenberg has made a particularly notable attempt to follow this through in a *Systematic Theology* which culminates in the eschatology of vol. 3.

The Old Testament already knows of deferred lordship: "The Lord will be king over the whole earth. On that day there will be one Lord, and his name the only name" (Zech 14:9). This language of "deferred lordship" is designed to evoke memory of the phrase "deferred meaning" for those acquainted with discussions of Jacques Derrida and postmodernity.[45] In a way, what we mean in theology will not be clear until the eschaton; as Paul tells us that our present *knowing* is only in part (1 Cor 13:12), so the reference of our language outstrips the *meaning* that we can now give to our words. We can not expect either scholarship or reflection to grasp fully the contrasting forms of divine lordship respectively revealed in the creation of the world, the book of Joshua, the gospel of the cross, and the eschatological end of it all. We may be surprised that the Lord of all the earth, who does nothing but right, became entangled in the affairs of the humans of the earth, who mostly do wrong. How divine action, which is mysterious, is related to human action, which is also mysterious, is a mystery.

How and to what extent the actuality of God's being comes to light in the book of Joshua are questions which await eschatological resolution. The campaign against idolatry and for holiness which the Israelites waged against the Canaanites (and which God subsequently waged against the Israelites) is a campaign which, the prophets foresee, will end in the triumph of the Lord. That scene in Joshua 5 beyond the Jordan and before the taking of Jericho, which has inspired so much of the reflection in this essay, bespeaks a dimension and scope to the campaign of God that reaches infinitely far beyond even the most successful seizure of Canaanite land.[46] The furthest reaches of its meaning, and of the meaning of lordship, exceed anything that we can envision, let alone describe. All this impinges on the kind of confidence that faith possesses. But it does not detract from the confidence of faith. "For the revelation awaits an appointed time; it speaks of the end and will not prove false. Though it linger, wait for it; it will certainly come and will not delay" (Hab 2:3).[47]

---

45. For those unacquainted, Norris, *Derrida,* is a way in. Caputo, *The Prayers and Tears of Jacques Derrida,* pursues Derrida from a religious point of view.

46. George Adam Smith, though he was picking out a feature of them that I have not, viewed these verses in Joshua 5 as an Old Testament pinnacle. He is quoted on this in *IB,* 2:576.

47. Although there is a measure of fulfilment in the gospel of Jesus Christ (Rom 1:17, picking up the next verse in Habakkuk) the future-eschatological dimension is alive and well in the New Testament. Hab 2:14 is unfulfilled prophecy.

A Response to Stephen Williams

Gordon McConville

History and Theology in Joshua: A Concluding Reflection

In responding to Stephen Williams's preceding section, "Reading Joshua Today," I begin by expressing my deep appreciation for his contribution to the present volume generally. I have particularly valued the pains he has taken to ensure a genuine conversation between the somewhat different approaches of Theology and Biblical Studies, not least by engaging most effectively with Old Testament scholarship. But he has also drawn extensively on his knowledge of theological and philosophical issues and literature in ways that have enormously enriched the volume.

In rereading all the material for the volume while preparing this short response, I have been gratified to observe again the very large degree of unanimity that I think our separate contributions exhibit. I especially endorse Stephen's commitment to the exposition of theological themes of Joshua on the canvas of the whole Bible and Christian theology. Some of these themes are notoriously controversial, not least that of the land, and of course the violence of the book of Joshua. I welcome too his perception of the importance of the incident recorded in Josh 5:13-15, as a moment in the book that invites particular reflection on the reality behind the events that unfold on the surface. I think we are sufficiently close on the topics he has treated to make further comment from me on them unnecessary, except perhaps incidentally in what follows.

I want only to turn one more time to the question of Joshua and history, which Stephen has addressed in the preceding section. Stephen has articulated clearly how important is the location of the biblical message in historical times and places: it is in the land once given by God to Israel that the events at the heart of Christian belief were played out. The dimension of history, of event in specific time and place, cannot be bracketed out of Christian confession, nor therefore out of biblical story. The points that he makes about the indissoluble relationship between ideas and realities I take with the utmost seriousness. Theologically, it matters that God is able to act in history. Hermeneutically, it is true that a belief in the New Testament witness that God raised Jesus from the dead changes the way in which we read other biblical testimony to the nature and activity of God.

Therefore, in my final remarks in this volume, I want to turn again to the theme. They are in a sense a response to Stephen's preceding chapter, not in the manner of a disclaimer, but rather as a prompt to think a little further on the position I have generally adopted in the book, and on the relation between historical narrative and theological truth. My question is why, and in what way, we believe the Bible's story gives a true account of God and of the human condition. What is the connection between narrative and event, or reality?

It is not necessary to repeat here the points I have made in other parts of the volume about this connection, as in the commentary on Joshua 6, for example. I have argued that it is difficult, on a reading of the text itself, to suppose that events are described here in factual or realistic ways. There may be bad reasons for taking such a view, such as a reluctance to face up to the theological implications of doing so, or an undue skepticism about the credentials of the biblical writers as historians. But I think that the form of the narrative gives us clues which as readers we should attend to, and once again I have tried to say what these are.

One irrevocable gain of modern biblical study is the realization that the biblical writers wrote for their particular audiences and that the various horizons of those audiences affect the way in which the writers wrote. The point holds for history-writing as much as for any other form. I have referred earlier to the case of the books of Chronicles in comparison to Samuel-Kings — or better Genesis-Kings, since Chronicles too begins with Adam and a swift review of God's action in the world as told from Genesis on. The first and obvious point that follows from this is that a biblical writer could take it upon himself to tell that story in an entirely new way. He knew the older story, and assumed his hearers would know it, and his own would scarcely make sense without it. 1 Chronicles 1 makes the point, being both predicated on Genesis and offering a theological reading of it.

Why would a writer do this? The answer to this question tells us something important, I believe, about the way in which the Bible tells history. The two blocs, Genesis-Kings and Chronicles, were written for generations facing quite different situations. The precise settings for each cannot be known with certainty, but broadly speaking the former audience was probably still coming to terms with the conditions of the exile, while the latter faced new issues in a later postrestoration stage. The important point is that each is brought face to face afresh with its history, and the portrayal of the history owes much to the situation of the audience. This accounts, I believe, for the considerable variations between the two blocs not just on points of detail but in terms of the whole structure and tendency of each portrayal. This is not the place to rehearse these differences, which are well known in the scholarly literature. By way of illustration I merely mention the focus in Chronicles on the southern kingdom to the almost total neglect of the north and the heavy emphasis on the reigns of David and Solomon at the expense of Moses and Sinai.

Now it may be objected that the Old Testament does, after all, carry a single narrative. Stephen has spoken of the "twin peaks" of the Old Testament story, namely the occupation of land narrated in Joshua and the establishment of the Davidic dynasty in both Samuel-Kings and Chronicles (in his essay above on "Land"). And it is true that we possess in the finished Old Testament (inasmuch as we can speak of this)[1] an underlying narrative that can be constructed out of these canonical parts. The term "narrative," admittedly, is now being used somewhat differently, not in the sense of a unified composition, but rather as a person might think of his or her life story as a kind of narrative. Canonically we read Chronicles in the light of the "primary history" of Genesis-Kings and also in close association with Ezra-Nehemiah, with their account of a restoration and rebuilt temple. Land, dynasty, and (closely associated) temple are the indispensable constituents of the story and symbols of the life of Israel. Nevertheless, the underlying narrative is only constructed out of these disparate versions, its meaning emerging in cognizance of their different perspectives. And there are, I think, in these distinct histories, profoundly different conceptions of the relationship between the "present" Israel and its religious and historical heritage. In these circumstances the concept of an essential core of history is difficult. The notion is problematical, because such a core may elude definition. And I think that not only the books of Chronicles, but Joshua too, and Old Testament history generally, force us into this dilemma. If there is an essential "core" of Old Testament history, why are we not given it as such? Does it not make more sense to think of the writing of Old Testament history as a bringing to bear of a stream of tradition on a present exigency, with the prophetic purposes of reproach, warning, encouragement, and renewal of vision?

In one important attempt to portray history as an engagement between

---

1. I have in mind that there is not a single form of the extant Old Testament. Nevertheless, the point holds.

past and present, John Rogerson, following Jan Assmann, has used the concept of "cultural memory." Cultural memory is essentially "remembered history" (as distinct from "factual history"). It is cultivated in groups and is longer and more structured than the memory of any individual. Crucially, it functions not as straightforward record of the past, but for purposes of self-understanding and encouragement in the present.[2] In this context, history-telling selects what is of value to the present and discards what is not.

Rogerson is aware that an account of this sort is open to the objection that it is purely anthropological, and that God has apparently been left out of the reckoning. He answers with the notion of an "absent presence," and explains: "If a Communicative Theology concentrates upon the treatment of human dilemmas integral to modern existence, this will not exclude God."[3] Rogerson's account is one answer to the problem of determining a factual "core" in the Old Testament's record of Israel's history. It leaves open the question, however, how we are to understand the person of God and in what way he impinges upon the historical life of his creatures. Israel's faith in God in its various "presents" depends on its belief that he acted in their history in the past. And his capacity to do so underlies both their confidence in the future and their perplexity about aspects of their experience (as expressed, for example, in Lamentations). An account of Old Testament history must recognize both its orientation towards present exigencies and its predication on the real action of God in the world. The Old Testament's picture of Israel's life before God may be seen as a perpetually renewing dialogue between event and the reception of it. And the content of the action of God in history may be inseparable finally from the totality of the Old Testament's story, and indeed that of the New Testament.

The attempt made here to think about the relationship between the biblical text and divine action is necessarily theological. Theological inquiry into the Bible cannot bracket out historical, archaeological, sociological, anthropological, or literary questions. Such questions are properly and unavoidably raised by the texts, by virtue of their nature as the portrayal of the life of a people. They have informed my understanding of the book of Joshua, even though specific issues in these areas have not been treated at length. And they are inseparable from the theology of the Bible, in the sense that we are bound to reckon with a God who spoke in such ways that human authors were en-

---

2. Rogerson, "Towards a Communicative Theology of the Old Testament," 293-94. Rogerson refers in turn to Assmann, *Das kulturelle Gedächtnis*, 343-48.

3. He invokes an analogy with Friedrich Schiller's play *Wallensteins Lager* (Wallenstein's Camp), in which the figure of Wallenstein never appears, yet his personality affects the entire play; "Towards a Communicative Theology," 295.

trusted with writing this history and human readers with making sense of it by all the means given to them.

The Old Testament confronts us with a wide range of texts, which vary enormously in terms of their genre and even in their literary sophistication. They have in common, however, the assumption that heaven and earth are not radically separate, but are intersecting realities. This is the case when we read of the prophet Elisha miraculously making an iron axhead float (2 Kgs 6:4-7); when the same Elisha has a vision of a heavenly army protectively surrounding the camp of the Israelites (2 Kgs 6:15-18); when the Lord comes to Abraham by the oaks of Mamre in the form of three travellers in need of hospitality (Gen 18:1-2); when a sober narrative or an unpretentious genealogy shows God's hand at work in historical events in unexpected ways (as in the story of Ruth and the indication of King David's Moabite ancestry at its end; Ruth 4:13-22). The book of Joshua too moves easily between miraculous event and mundane boundary descriptions, all bespeaking God's presence in the human world. The geography of heaven and earth is such that God may be experienced at any time as either absent or present. Biblical writers are frequently exercised by the nature and conditions of that absence-presence. But they never doubt that God's hand is at work in the events of their lives. It is the fool who says in his heart: "There is no God" (Ps 53:1). In this understanding of the perspective of the biblical texts I believe I am in essential agreement with Stephen's lucid essay on Miracle in this volume.

I think a question remains, however, about how precisely the biblical writers' axiom about God's presence and active power in the world bears on the question of the nature of biblical texts as historical report. The author and readers of Jonah may or may not have thought that the story of Jonah was a fiction, but this would have been quite irrelevant to their belief in the reality of God's judgment on nations such as Assyria. Similarly, I think, the several accounts of God's actions in Joshua may be factual in different manners and degrees, without diminishing the book's point that God gave the land of Canaan to Israel. I am seeking here room for the judgment, on whatever grounds, that parts of the Old Testament's "historical books" may not be factual in the way that modern history is normally required to be. To think again of Abraham's encounter with three men who turn out to be the Lord, how does one conceive of this as historical event? It is at the least a type of event that challenges the imagination. Jacob's struggle with the mysterious figure at the Jabbok is a further case in point (Gen 32:22-32). Faced with accounts of incidents like these, I wonder if our categories of history can contain the kinds of truth that the biblical writers want to convey. Perhaps, and here I tread carefully for we are indeed close to holy ground, Joshua's meeting with the commander in the approaches to Jericho is another of the same. But I am suggesting at the same time that the book of Joshua's truthful reference to reality may not depend upon or be congruent with its accurate historicity as conceived in our terms.

I close with a comment about the purpose of biblical history-writing. The presence of God to human beings is not just the assumption of biblical texts, but also explains their nature and purpose. The reception of biblical texts is not a matter of hermeneutics in some academic sense. Rather, God speaks here and demands a response. The literature is predicated upon the need for decision. Elijah's prophetic exhortation to his generation who wavered "between two opinions" (1 Kgs 18:21) is a picture of the occasion and purpose of the biblical literature. The "absent present" God is not mute or coy, awaiting discovery as in a game.

Biblical history, like other literature, aims to say: will you believe in this God? Will you abandon other gods? Do you see what God has given? — will you *remember* that it was he who gave it (Deuteronomy 8)? Memory, for Israel, is enactment and commitment. Joshua is entirely at one with this biblical history. Its appeal to us is that of its last two chapters: to recall the faithfulness of God in times past; to acknowledge our natural resistance to the way of faith and obedience; and to enter again into covenant with him.

Bibliography

Akenson, Donald H. *God's Peoples: Covenant and Land in South Africa, Israel, and Ulster.* Ithaca: Cornell University Press, 1992.

Albertz, Rainer. *A History of Israelite Religion in the Old Testament Period.* 2 vols. OTL. Louisville: Westminster John Knox, 1994.

Albright, William F. "Archaeology and the Date of the Hebrew Conquest of Palestine." *BASOR* 58 (1935) 10-18.

Alter, Robert. *The Art of Biblical Narrative.* New York: Basic Books, 1981.

———. *The World of Biblical Literature.* New York: Basic Books, 1992.

———, and Frank Kermode. *The Literary Guide to the Bible.* Cambridge, MA: Belknap, 1987.

Amstutz, Mark R. "Who Is My Neighbor? The Moral Responsibility to Halt Genocide." *Books & Culture* 9/3 (2003) 18-20.

Anselm. *Cur Deus Homo.* In *Anselm of Canterbury,* ed. Jasper Hopkins, vol. 3. Toronto: Mellen, 1976.

Assmann, Jan. *Das kulturelle Gedächtnis: Schrift, Erinnerung und politische Identität in frühen Hochkulturen.* Munich: Beck, 1992.

Augustine. *Concerning the City of God against the Pagans.* Harmondsworth: Penguin, 1972.

Aune, David E. *Revelation 17–22.* Nashville: Nelson, 1998.

Bainton, Roland. *Christian Attitudes Toward War and Peace: A Historical Survey and Critical Re-Evaluation.* Nashville: Abingdon, 1960.

Baker, David W., and Bill T. Arnold, eds. *The Face of Old Testament Studies: A Survey of Contemporary Approaches.* Grand Rapids: Baker, 1999.

Balserak, Jon. *Divinity Compromised: A Study of Divine Accommodation in the Thought of John Calvin.* Dordrecht: Springer, 2006.

Barr, James. "Childs' Introduction to the Old Testament as Scripture." *JSOT* 16 (1980) 12-23.

———. *The Concept of Biblical Theology: An Old Testament Perspective.* Minneapolis: Fortress, 1999.

———. *History and Ideology in the Old Testament: Biblical Studies at the End of a Millennium.* Oxford: Oxford University Press, 2000.

Barth, Karl. *Church Dogmatics*, I/1-2: *The Doctrine of the Word of God*. Edinburgh: T. & T. Clark, 1955.
———. *Church Dogmatics*, II/1-2: *The Doctrine of God*. Edinburgh: T. & T. Clark, 1957.
———. *Dogmatics in Outline*. London: SCM, 1949.
———. *The Humanity of God*. Richmond: John Knox, 1960.
Bartholomew, Craig, et al., eds. *A Royal Priesthood? The Use of the Bible Ethically and Politically: A Dialogue with Oliver O'Donovan*. SHS 3. Carlisle: Paternoster, 2002.
Barton, John. *Reading the Old Testament*. Rev. ed. Louisville: Westminster John Knox, 1996.
———. *Understanding Old Testament Ethics: Approaches and Explorations*. Louisville: Westminster John Knox, 2003.
Bauckham, Richard. *The Climax of Prophecy*. Edinburgh: T. & T. Clark, 1993.
———. *Jesus and the Eyewitnesses: The Gospels as Eyewitness Testimony*. Grand Rapids: Wm. B. Eerdmans, 2006.
———. *The Theology of the Book of Revelation*. Cambridge: Cambridge University Press, 1993.
Beuken, W. A. M. *Jesaja 1–12*. HTKAT. Freiburg/Br: Herder, 2003.
Bienkowski, Piotr. *Jericho in the Late Bronze Age*. Warminster: Aris and Phillips, 1986.
Bimson, John J. "The Origins of Israel in Canaan: An Examination of Recent Theories." *Them* 15/1 (1989) 4-15.
Blocher, Henri. *Original Sin: Illuminating the Riddle*. Grand Rapids: Wm. B. Eerdmans, 1999.
Block, Daniel I. *The Book of Ezekiel: Chapters 25–48*. NICOT. Grand Rapids: Wm. B. Eerdmans, 1998.
Boesak, Allan. *Black and Reformed: Apartheid, Liberation, and the Calvinist Tradition*, Maryknoll: Orbis, 1984.
Boling, Robert G., and George Ernest Wright. *Joshua*. AB 6. Garden City: Doubleday, 1982.
Bonhoeffer, Dietrich. *Discipleship*. Ed. Geffrey B. Kelly and John D. Godsey. Minneapolis: Fortress, 2001.
———. *Ethics*. Ed. Clifford J. Green. Minneapolis: Fortress, 2005.
———. *Letters and Papers from Prison*. London: SCM, 1971.
Bright, John. *A History of Israel*. 2nd ed. Philadelphia: Westminster, 1972.
Brueggemann, Walter. *The Land: Place as Gift, Promise and Challenge in Biblical Faith*. OBT. 2nd ed. Minneapolis: Fortress, 2002.
———. *Theology of the Old Testament: Testimony, Dispute, Advocacy*. Fortress: Philadelphia, 1997.
Bultmann, Rudolf. "Prophecy and Fulfillment." In *Essays on Old Testament Hermeneutics*, ed. Claus Westermann, 50-75. Richmond: John Knox, 1963. Publ. as *Essays on Old Testament Interpretation*. London: SCM, 1963.
———. "The Significance of the Old Testament for the Christian Faith." In *The Old Testament and Christian Faith*, ed. Bernard W. Anderson, 8-35. New York: Harper & Row, 1963.
Burns, R. M. *The Great Debate on Miracles: From Joseph Glanvill to David Hume*. Lewisburg: Bucknell University Press, 1981.
Butler, Trent C. *Joshua*. WBC 7. Nashville: Thomas Nelson, 1983.
Caird, George B. *The Language and Imagery of the Bible*. Philadelphia: Westminster, 1980.

Calvin, John. *Commentaries on the Book of Joshua.* 1854. Repr. Grand Rapids: Wm. B. Eerdmans, 1949.
Campbell, Antony. "The Growth of Joshua 1–12 and the Theology of Extermination." In *Reading the Hebrew Bible for a New Millennium: Form, Concept, and Theological Perspective,* ed. Wonil Kim et al., 2:72-88. Harrisburg: Trinity, 2000.
Campbell, John McLeod. *The Nature of the Atonement and Its Relation to Remission of Sins and Eternal Life.* 3rd ed. London: Macmillan, 1869.
Caputo, John D. "On Being Clear About Faith: A Response to Stephen Williams." *Books & Culture* 12/6 (2006) 40-42.
———. *The Prayers and Tears of Jacques Derrida.* Bloomington: Indiana University Press, 1997.
Carrière, Jean-Marie. *La théorie du politique dans le Deutéronome.* ÖBS 18. Frankfurt: Lang, 1997.
Chavalas, Mark, and Murray Adamthwaite. "Archaeological Light on the Old Testament." In *The Face of Old Testament Studies,* ed. David W. Baker and Bill T. Arnold, 59-96. Grand Rapids: Baker, 1999.
Childs, Brevard S. *Biblical Theology of the Old and New Testaments.* Minneapolis: Fortress, 1994.
———. *Introduction to the Old Testament as Scripture.* Philadelphia: Fortress, 1979.
Clarke, James Langton. *The Eternal Saviour-Judge.* New York: Dutton, 1904.
Clayton, Philip, and Arthur Peacocke, eds. *In Whom We Live and Move and Have Our Being: Panentheistic Reflections on God's Presence in a Scientific World.* Grand Rapids: Wm. B. Eerdmans, 2004.
Clines, David J. A. "New Year." *IDBSup,* 625-29.
Constantine, David. "Kafka's Writing and Our Reading." In *The Cambridge Companion to Kafka,* ed. Julian Preece, 9-24. Cambridge: Cambridge University Press, 2002.
Coogan, Michael D. "Archaeology and Biblical Studies: The Book of Joshua." In *The Hebrew Bible and Its Interpreters,* ed. William H. Propp, Baruch Halpern, and David Noel Freedman, 19-32. BibJS 1. Winona Lake: Eisenbrauns, 1990.
Coote, Robert. "The Book of Joshua." *NIB* 2 (1998) 553-719.
Cowles C. S., et al. *Show Them No Mercy: 4 Views on God and Canaanite Genocide.* Grand Rapids: Zondervan, 2003.
Craigie, Peter C. *The Problem of War in the Old Testament.* Grand Rapids: Wm. B. Eerdmans, 1978.
Cranfield, C. E. B. *A Critical and Exegetical Commentary on the Epistle to the Romans.* Vol. 1. ICC. Edinburgh: T&T Clark, 1975.
Cross, Frank Moore. *Canaanite Myth and Hebrew Epic.* Cambridge, MA: Harvard University Press, 1973.
Davies, W. D. *The Gospel and the Land.* Berkeley: University of California Press, 1974.
———. "Jerusalem and the Land in the Christian Tradition." In *The Jerusalem Colloquium on Religion, Peoplehood, Nation, and Land,* ed. Marc H. Tannenbaum & R. J. Werblowsky, 115-54. Jerusalem: Truman Research Institute of the Hebrew University, American Jewish Committee, and Israel Interfaith Committee, 1972.
De Gruchy, John. *Christianity, Art and Transformation: Theological Aesthetics in the Struggle for Justice.* Cambridge: Cambridge University Press, 2001.

Deutscher, Isaac. *Stalin: A Political Biography*. Harmondsworth: Pelican, 1966.
Durham, John I. *Exodus*. WBC 3. Waco: Word, 1987.
Eichrodt, Walter. *Theology of the Old Testament*. 2 vols. Philadelphia: Westminster, 1961-67.
Eslinger, Lyle M. *Into the Hands of the Living God*. JSOTSup 84. Sheffield; Almond, 1989.
Finkelstein, Israel, and Neil Asher Silberman. *The Bible Unearthed: Archaeology's New Vision of Ancient Israel and the Origin of Its Sacred Texts*. 2nd ed. New York: Simon and Schuster, 2002.
Ford, David F. *Christian Wisdom: Desiring God and Learning in Love*. CSCD 16. Cambridge: Cambridge University Press, 2007.
Freedman, David Noel. "Canon of the OT." *IDBSup*, 130-36.
―――. "The Law and the Prophets." VTSup 9 (1963) 250-65.
Frei, Hans W. *The Eclipse of Biblical Narrative: A Study in Eighteenth and Nineteenth Century Hermeneutics*. New Haven: Yale University Press, 1974.
―――. *The Identity of Jesus Christ: The Hermeneutical Bases of Dogmatic Theology*. Philadelphia: Fortress, 1975.
Fretheim, Terence E. *Exodus*. Interpretation. Louisville: John Knox, 1991.
Goetz, Ronald. "Joshua, Calvin, and Genocide." *ThTo* 32 (1975) 263-74.
Goldingay, John. *Israel's Gospel*, 474-505. Old Testament Theology 1. Downers Grove: IVP, 2003.
―――. "Justice and Salvation for Israel in Canaan." In *Reading the Hebrew Bible for a New Millennium: Form, Concept, and Theological Perspective*, ed. Wonil Kim et al., 1:169-87. Harrisburg: Trinity, 2000.
―――. "Old Testament Theology and the Canon." *TynBul* 59 (2008) 1-26.
Gunn, David M. *Judges*. BBC. Oxford: Blackwell, 2005.
Hallo, William W., and K. Lawson Younger. *The Context of Scripture*. 3 vols. Leiden: Brill, 1997-2003.
Hamilton, Victor P. *The Book of Genesis: Chapters 1–17*. NICOT. Grand Rapids: Wm. B. Eerdmans, 1990.
Hawk, L. Daniel. *Joshua*. Berit Olam. Collegeville: Liturgical, 2000.
Helm, Paul. *John Calvin's Ideas*. Oxford: Oxford University Press, 2004.
Heschel, Abraham J. *The Prophets*. 2 vols. New York: Harper & Row, 1962.
Hess, Richard. *Joshua*. TOTC 6. Downers Grove: IVP, 1996.
Holland, Thomas A., and E. Netzer. "Jericho." *ABD* 3:723-40.
Horton, Michael. *Covenant and Eschatology*. Louisville: Westminster John Knox, 2002.
―――. *Covenant and Salvation: Union with Christ*. Louisville: Westminster John Knox, 2007.
―――. *God of Promise: Introducing Covenant Theology*. Grand Rapids: Baker, 2006.
―――. *Lord and Servant: A Covenant Christology*. Louisville: Westminster John Knox, 2005.
Howard, David M., Jr., *Joshua*. NAC 5. Nashville: Broadman & Holman, 1998.
Hume, David. *Enquiries Concerning Human Understanding*. 3rd ed. Oxford: Clarendon, 1975.
Jacob, Edmond. *Theology of the Old Testament*. New York: Harper & Row, 1958.
Jenkins, Philip. *The Next Christendom: The Coming of Global Christianity*. Oxford: Oxford University Press, 2007.

Jenson, Philip Peter. *Graded Holiness: A Key to the Priestly Conception of the World.* JSOTSup 106. Sheffield: JSOT, 1992.
John Chrysostom. *Homilies on the Acts of the Apostles and the Epistle to the Romans.* NPNF[1]. Repr. Grand Rapids: Wm. B. Eerdmans, 1989.
Johnston, Philip, and Peter Walker, eds. *The Land of Promise: Biblical, Theological, and Contemporary Perspectives,* Downers Grove: InterVarsity, 2000.
Kant, Immanuel. *Critique of Judgment.* Trans. J. H. Bernard. London: Macmillan, 1931.
Kenny, Anthony. *The God of the Philosophers.* Oxford: Clarendon, 1979.
Kenyon, Kathleen, *Digging Up Jericho.* New York: Praeger, 1957.
Kitchen, Kenneth A. *Ancient Orient and Old Testament.* London: Tyndale, 1966.
Knierim, Rolf. "Criticism of Literary Features, Form, Tradition, and Redaction." In *Reading the Hebrew Bible for a New Millennium: Form, Concept, and Theological Perspective,* ed. Wonil Kim et al., 2:1-41. Harrisburg: Trinity, 2000.
Kraus, Hans-Joachim. "Gilgal: ein Beitrag zur Kultusgeschichte Israels." *VT* 1 (1951) 181-99. Eng. trans. "Gilgal: A Contribution to the History of Worship in Israel." In *Reconsidering Israel and Judah,* ed. Gary N. Knoppers and J. Gordon McConville, 163-78. SBTS 8 (Winona Lake: Eisenbrauns, 2000).
Lacocque, André, and Paul Ricoeur, *Thinking Biblically: Exegetical and Hermeneutical Studies.* Chicago: University of Chicago Press, 1998.
Lane, A. N. S., ed. *The Unseen World: Christian Reflections on Angels, Demons and the Heavenly Realm.* Carlisle: Paternoster and Grand Rapids: Baker, 1996.
Lapide, Pinchas. *The Sermon on the Mount: Utopia or Program for Action?* Maryknoll: Orbis, 1986.
Lemche, Nils. *Early Israel: Anthropological and Historical Studies in Early Israelite Society.* VTSup 37. Leiden: Brill, 1985.
Lilley, J. P. U. "The Judgment of God: The Problem of the Canaanites." *Them* 22/2 (1997) 6-7.
———. "Understanding the *Herem.*" *TynBul* 44 (1993) 169-77.
Lincoln, Abraham. *Abraham Lincoln: His Speeches and Writings.* Ed. Roy P. Basler. Cleveland: World, 1946.
———. *Collected Works of Abraham Lincoln,* 8. Ed. Roy P. Basler. New Brunswick: Rutgers University Press, 1953.
Livingston, David F. "Location of Biblical Bethel and Ai Reconsidered." *WTJ* 33 (1971) 20-44.
Locke, John. *An Essay Concerning Human Understanding.* Ed. Peter Nidditch. Oxford: Oxford University Press, 1975.
Long, V. Philips. *The Art of Biblical History.* Grand Rapids: Zondervan, 1994.
Lucas, Ernest. *Daniel.* AOTC. Leicester: Apollos, 2002.
Lyons, William John. *Canon and Exegesis: Canonical Praxis and the Sodom Narrative.* JSOTSup 352. Sheffield: Sheffield Academic, 2002.
McConville, J. Gordon. *God and Earthly Power: An Old Testament Political Theology, Genesis-Kings.* London: T&T Clark, 2006.
McDermott, Gerald. "The Land: Evangelicals and Israel." *Books & Culture* 9/2 (2003).
MacDonald, Nathan. *Deuteronomy and the Meaning of "Monotheism."* FAT 2/1. Tübingen: Mohr Siebeck, 2003.

McGrath, Alister E. *The Foundations of Dialogue in Science and Religion*. Oxford: Blackwell, 1998.
———. *Science and Religion*. Oxford: Blackwell, 1999.
McKeown, James. "The Theme of Land in Genesis 1–11 and Its Significance for the Abraham Narrative." *IBS* 19 (1997) 51-64, 133-44.
Mackintosh, H. R. *The Christian Apprehension of God*. London: SCM, 1929.
Marshall, I. Howard. *Beyond the Bible: Moving from Scripture to Theology*. Grand Rapids: Baker, 2004.
Mazar, Amihai. "The Iron Age I." In *The Archaeology of Ancient Israel*, ed. Amnon Ben-Tor, 258-301. New Haven: Yale University Press and Tel Aviv: Open University of Israel, 1992.
Milgrom, Jacob. *Leviticus 1–16*. AB 3. New York: Doubleday, 1991.
Miller, J. Maxwell. "The Israelite Occupation of Canaan." In *Israelite and Judean History*, ed. John H. Hayes and Miller, 213-84. OTL. Philadelphia: Westminster, 1977.
Moberly, R. W. L. *The Bible, Theology, and Faith: A Study of Abraham and Jesus*. CSCD. Cambridge: Cambridge University Press, 2000.
———. "A Dialogue with Gordon McConville on Deuteronomy." *SJT* 56 (2003) 516-31.
———. "The Theology of the Old Testament." In *The Face of Old Testament Studies*, ed. David W. Baker and Bill T. Arnold, 452-78. Grand Rapids: Baker, 1999.
———. "Toward an Interpretation of the Shema." In *Theological Exegesis: Essays in Honor of Brevard S. Childs*, ed. Christopher Seitz and Kathryn Greene-McCreight, 124-44. Grand Rapids: Wm. B. Eerdmans, 1999.
Morris, Thomas V. *The Logic of God Incarnate*. Ithaca: Cornell University Press, 1986.
Mosala, Itumeleng J. *Biblical Hermeneutics and Black Theology in South Africa*. Grand Rapids: Wm. B. Eerdmans, 1989.
Nelson, Richard D. "*Hērem* and the Deuteronomic Social Conscience." In *Deuteronomy and Deuteronomic Literature*, ed. M. Vervenne and J. Lust, 39-54. BETL 133. Leuven: Leuven University Press, 1997.
———. *Joshua*. OTL. Louisville: Westminster John Knox, 1997.
———. "Josiah in the Book of Joshua." *JBL* 100 (1981) 531-40.
Niditch, Susan. *War in the Hebrew Bible: A Study in the Ethics of Violence*. Oxford: Oxford University Press, 1993.
Nietzsche, Friedrich. *Ecce Homo*. Trans. R. J. Hollingdale. London: Penguin, 1979.
———. *The Gay Science*. Trans. Josefine Nauckhoff. Cambridge: Cambridge University Press, 2001.
———. *Thus Spoke Zarathustra*. Trans. Graham Parkes. Oxford: Oxford University Press, 2005.
Noll, Mark A. *America's God: From Jonathan Edwards to Abraham Lincoln*. Oxford: Oxford University Press, 2002.
Norris, Christopher. *Derrida*. Cambridge, MA: Harvard University Press, 1987.
Oden, Thomas C. *How Africa Shaped the Christian Mind: Rediscovering the African Seedbed of Western Christianity*. Downers Grove: IVP, 2007.
O'Donovan, Oliver. *The Desire of the Nations: Rediscovering the Roots of Political Theology*. Cambridge: Cambridge University Press, 1996.
———. "The Loss of a Sense of Place." *ITQ* 55 (1989) 39-58.

Olson, Dennis T. *Deuteronomy and the Death of Moses*. OBT. Minneapolis: Fortress, 1994.
Origen. *Homilies on Joshua*. Trans. Barbara J. Bruce. Fathers of the Church 105. Washington: Catholic University of America Press, 2002.
Oswalt, John N. *The Book of Isaiah: Chapters 40–66*. NICOT. Grand Rapids: Wm. B. Eerdmans, 1998.
Otto, Eckart. *Das Mazzotfest in Gilgal*. BWANT 107. Stuttgart: Kohlhammer, 1975.
Otto, Rudolf. *The Idea of the Holy*. Oxford: Oxford University Press, 1923.
Pannenberg, Wolfhart. *Systematic Theology*. 3 vols. Grand Rapids: Wm. B. Eerdmans, 1991-98.
Pennant, David F. "The Significance of Rootplay, Leading Words and Thematic Links in the Book of Judges." Ph.D. diss., Council for National Academic Awards, 1988.
Perdue, Leo G. *The Collapse of History: Reconstructing Old Testament Theology*. OBT. Philadelphia: Fortress, 1994.
———. *Reconstructing Old Testament Theology: After the Collapse of History*. OBT. Minneapolis: Fortress, 2005.
Peretti, Frank. *This Present Darkness*. Eastbourne: Monarch, 1986.
Perowne, J. J. Stewart. *The Book of Psalms*. London: Bell, 1883.
Polzin, Robert M. *Moses and the Deuteronomist*. New York: Seabury, 1980.
Porter, Stanley. "Hermeneutics, Biblical Interpretation, and Theology: Hunch, Holy Spirit, or Hard Work?" In *Beyond the Bible: Moving from Scripture to Theology*, ed. I. Howard Marshall, 97-127. Grand Rapids: Baker, 2004.
Provan, Iain. "Ideologies, Literary and Critical: Reflections on Recent Writing on the History of Israel." *JBL* 114 (1995) 585-606.
———. "In the Stable with the Dwarves: Testimony, Interpretation, Faith, and the History of Israel." VTSup 80 (2000) 281-319. Repr. in *Windows into Old Testament History*, ed. V. Philips Long, David W. Baker, and Gordon J. Wenham, 161-97. Grand Rapids: Wm. B. Eerdmans, 2002.
———, V. Philips Long, and Tremper Longman III. *A Biblical History of Israel*. Louisville: Westminster John Knox, 2003.
Rad, Gerhard von. *Old Testament Theology*. 2 vols. New York: Harper & Row, 1962-65.
Rahner, Karl. *Theological Investigations*, vol. 6. London: Darton, Longman & Todd, 1974.
Rasmussen, Larry, ed. *Reinhold Niebuhr: Theologian of Public Life*. San Francisco: Harper & Row, 1989.
Richter, Sandra L. *The Deuteronomistic History and the Name Theology: lᵉšakkēn šᵉmô šām in the Bible and the Ancient Near East*. BZAW 318. Berlin: de Gruyter, 2002.
Rogerson, John. "Towards a Communicative Theology of the Old Testament." In *Reading the Law: Studies in Honour of Gordon J. Wenham*, ed. J. G. McConville and Karl Möller, 283-96. LHB/OTS 461. London: T&T Clark, 2007.
———, Christopher Rowland, and Barnabas Lindars, *The Study and Use of the Bible*. The History of Christian Theology 2. Grand Rapids: Wm. B. Eerdmans, 1988.
Ryle, Gilbert. "John Locke and the Human Understanding." In *John Locke: Tercentenary Addresses Delivered in the Hall of Christ Church, October 1932*, 15-38. London: Oxford University Press, 1933. Repr. in *Locke and Berkeley: A Collection of Critical Essays*, ed. C. B. Martin and D. M. Armstrong, 14-39. New York: Doubleday 1968.

Schäfer-Lichtenberger, Christa. *Josua und Salomo: Eine Studie zu Autorität und Legitimität des Nachfolgers im Alten Testament.* VTSup 58. Leiden: Brill, 1995.

Schleiermacher, Friedrich. *On Religion: Speeches to Its Cultured Despisers.* Trans. Richard Crouter. Oxford: Oxford University Press, 1996.

Schmid, Konrad. *Erzväter und Exodus: Untersuchungen zur doppelten Begründung der Ursprünge Israels innerhalb der Geschichtsbücher des Alten Testaments.* WMANT 81. Neukirchen: Neukirchener, 1999.

Schwartz, Regina. *The Curse of Cain: The Violent Legacy of Monotheism.* Chicago: University of Chicago, 1997.

Seitz, Christopher R. "Canon, Narrative and the Old Testament's Literal Sense." *TynBul* 59 (2008) 27-34.

———. *Word Without End: The Old Testament as Abiding Theological Witness.* Grand Rapids: Wm. B. Eerdmans, 1998.

Smelik, K. A. D. "The Inscription of King Mesha." In *The Context of Scripture*, vol. 2: *Monumental Inscriptions from the Biblical World*, ed. W. W. Hallo and K. Lawson Younger, 137-38. Leiden: Brill, 2000.

Smend, Rudolf. "The Law and the Nations: A Contribution to Deuteronomistic Tradition History." In *Reconsidering Israel and Judah: Recent Studies on the Deuteronomistic History*, ed. Gary N. Knoppers and J. Gordon McConville, 95-110. SBTS 8. Winona Lake: Eisenbrauns, 2000 (German original 1971).

Smith, Mark S. *The Origins of Biblical Monotheism: Israel's Polytheistic Background and the Ugaritic Texts.* New York: Oxford University Press, 2001.

Soggin, J. Alberto. *Joshua.* OTL. Philadelphia: Westminster, 1972.

———. *Judges.* OTL. Philadelphia: Westminster, 1981.

Soulen, R. Kendall. *The God of Israel and Christian Theology.* Minneapolis: Fortress, 1996.

Sternberg, Meir. *The Poetics of Biblical Narrative: Ideological Literature and the Drama of Reading.* Bloomington: Indiana University Press, 1985.

Stone, Lawson G. "Ethical and Apologetic Tendencies in the Redaction of the Book of Joshua." *CBQ* 53 (1991) 25-36.

Stott, John R. W. *The Message of Romans.* Leicester: IVP, 1994. U.S. ed. *Romans: God's Good News for the World.* Downers Grove: IVP, 1994.

Stove, D. C. *Popper and After: Four Modern Irrationalists.* Oxford: Pergamon, 1982.

Swartley, Willard M. *Covenant of Peace: The Missing Peace in New Testament Theology and Ethics.* Grand Rapids: Wm. B. Eerdmans, 2006.

Sweeney, Marvin A. "Tanak versus Old Testament: Concerning the Foundation for a Jewish Theology of the Bible." In *Problems in Biblical Theology*, ed. Henry T. C. Sun and Keith L. Eades, 353-72. Grand Rapids: Wm. B. Eerdmans, 1997.

Swinburne, Richard. *The Existence of God.* Oxford: Clarendon, 1991.

Taylor, John V. *The Primal Vision: Christian Presence amid African Religions.* London: SCM, 1963.

Terrien, Samuel. *The Elusive Presence: Toward a New Biblical Theology.* San Francisco: Harper & Row, 1978.

Tertullian. *On Idolatry.* ANF 3:61-77. Repr. Grand Rapids: Wm. B. Eerdmans 1993.

Thiselton, Anthony C. *The Two Horizons.* Grand Rapids: Wm. B. Eerdmans, 1980.

Thompson, Thomas L. *Early History of the Israelite People: From the Written and Archaeological Sources.* Leiden: Brill, 1992.

———. "Holy War at the Center of Biblical Theology: *Shalom* and the Cleansing of Jerusalem." In *Jerusalem in Ancient History and Tradition,* 223-57. JSOTSup 381. London: T&T Clark, 2003.

———. "A Neo-Albrightian School in History and Biblical Scholarship?" *JBL* 114 (1995) 683-98.

Tilghman, B. R. *An Introduction to the Philosophy of Religion.* Oxford: Blackwell, 1994.

Tillich, Paul. *Systematic Theology.* Vol. 1. Chicago: University of Chicago Press, 1951.

Vanhoozer, Kevin J. *The Drama of Doctrine: A Canonical-Linguistic Approach to Christian Theology.* Louisville: Westminster John Knox, 2005.

———. *First Theology: God, Scripture & Hermeneutics.* Downers Grove: InterVarsity, 2002.

———. *Is There a Meaning in This Text? The Bible, the Reader, and the Morality of Literary Knowledge.* Grand Rapids: Zondervan, 1998.

Vos, Geerhardus. "Christian Faith and the Truthfulness of Bible History." *Princeton Theological Review* 3 (1906) 289-305.

Vos, Jacobus Cornelis de. *Das Los Judas: Über Entstehung und Ziele der Landbeschreibung in Josua 15.* VTSup 95. Leiden: Brill, 2003.

Walsh, Jerome T. *1 Kings.* Berit Olam. Collegeville: Liturgical, 1996.

Watson, Francis. *Text and Truth: Redefining Biblical Theology.* Grand Rapids: Wm. B. Eerdmans, 1997.

———. *Text, Church and World: Biblical Interpretation in Theological Perspective.* Grand Rapids: Wm. B. Eerdmans, 1994.

Webb, Barry G. *The Book of the Judges.* JSOTSup 46. Sheffield: JSOT, 1987.

Weinfeld, Moshe. *Deuteronomy 1–11.* AB 5. New York: Doubleday, 1991.

Wenham, Gordon J. *Story as Torah: Reading the Old Testament Ethically.* OTS. Edinburgh: T&T Clark, 2000.

———. "The Structure and Date of Deuteronomy." Ph.D. diss., London, 1971.

Williams, Stephen N. "On Religion and Revelation." *Books & Culture* 12/6 (2006) 39-40.

———. "The Response of a Theologian." *ACPA [Association of Christians in Planning and Architecture] News Letter* 24 (1993) 52-59.

Williamson, H. G. M. *The Book Called Isaiah: Deutero-Isaiah's Role in Composition and Redaction.* Oxford: Clarendon, 1994.

Wilson, Marvin R. *Our Father Abraham: Jewish Roots of the Christian Faith.* Grand Rapids: Wm. B. Eerdmans, 1989.

Wink, Walter. *The Powers That Be: Theology for a New Millennium.* New York: Doubleday, 1998.

Wolfe, Thomas. *You Can't Go Home Again.* New York: Harper, 1998.

Woudstra, M. H. *The Book of Joshua.* NICOT. Grand Rapids: Wm. B. Eerdmans, 1981.

Wright, C. J. H. *Deuteronomy.* NIBC. Peabody: Hendrickson, 1996.

Wright, David F. "Calvin's Pentateuchal Criticism: Equity, Hardness of Heart, and Divine Accommodation in the Mosaic Harmony Commentary." *CTJ* 21 (1986) 33-50.

Wright, George Ernest. *The Old Testament Against Its Environment.* SBT 2. Naperville: Allenson, 1950.

Wright, N. T. *Jesus and the Victory of God.* Minneapolis: Fortress, 1996.

———. *The New Testament and the People of God*. Minneapolis: Fortress, 1992.
———. *Resurrection and the Son of God*. Minneapolis: Fortress, 2003.
Younger, K. Lawson. *Ancient Conquest Accounts: A Study in Ancient Near Eastern and Biblical History Writing*. JSOTSup 98. Sheffield: JSOT, 1990.
———. "Early Israel in Recent Biblical Scholarship." In *The Face of Old Testament Studies*, ed. David W. Baker and Bill T. Arnold, 176-206. Grand Rapids: Baker, 1999.

Author Index

Adamthwaite, M., 212
Akenson, D. H., 123
Albertz, R., 4
Albright, W. F., 4
Alter, R., 161, 214
Amstutz, M. R., 113
Anselm, 208
Arnold, B. T., 212
Assmann, J., 233
Augustine, 126, 163
Aune, D. F., 124

Bainton, R., 110
Baker, D. W., 212
Balserak, J., 121
Barr, J., 104, 161, 200, 210, 214, 217, 225-26
Barth, K., 122, 124, 129, 223, 225
Bartholomew, C., 185
Barton, J., 187, 207
Bauckham, R., 124, 209
Beuken, W. A., 197
Bienkowski, P., 6, 31-32
Bimson, J. J., 4
Blocher, H., 118
Block, D. I., 104
Boesak, A., 189
Boling, R. G., 110
Bonhoeffer, D., 122, 151, 220-21
Bright, J., 4

Brueggemann, W., 100, 102, 131-32, 137, 152, 158, 210, 226
Bultmann, R., 6, 225
Burns, R. M., 155
Buber, M., 225
Butler, T. C., 25, 51, 54, 62, 68

Caird, G. B., 220
Calvin, J., 116-17, 119, 121
Campbell, A., 116
Campbell, J. M., 165
Caputo, J. D., 147, 229
Carrière, J.-M., 180
Chavalas, M., 212
Childs, B. S., 10, 108, 160, 200, 208, 217
Chrysostom, John, 109
Clarke, J. L., 114
Clayton, P., 167
Clines, D. J. A., 25
Constantine, D., 208
Coogan, M. D., 31
Coote, R., 26
Copernicus, N., 164-65
Cowles, C. S., 110, 114, 117-18, 121
Craigie, P. C., 122, 124
Cranfield, C. E. B., 101
Cross, F. M., 21, 25

Davies, W. D., 100-102, 104
Derrida, J., 229

Deutscher, I., 137
De Gruchy, J., 138
Dorner, I. A., 134
Durham, J. T., 125

Eichrodt, W., 10, 157, 169, 220
Eslinger, L. M., 191

Feuerbach, L., 169
Feyerabend, P., 161
Finkelstein, I., 4
Ford, D. F., 9
Freedman, D. N., 2
Frei, H. W., 155, 204, 221
Fretheim, T., 189

Galileo, G., 165
Gard, D., 118, 123
Godet, F., 132
Goethe, J. W. von, 208
Goetz, R., 116
Goldingay, J., 10, 109-10, 121, 142, 202, 208, 214, 225
Gunn, D. M., 8

Hallo, W. W., 194
Hamilton, V. P., 112
Hawk, L., 9, 26, 28, 33-34, 38, 40-41, 48-50, 53, 55, 60, 62-64, 66, 77, 83, 85, 91, 224
Helm, P., 119
Heschel, A., 221
Hess, R., 6, 22, 24, 57, 67, 69, 71-72, 219
Holland, T. A., 31
Horton, M., 98, 118, 134, 143
Howard, D. M., 28-29
Hume, D., 168

Jacob, E., 135, 158, 163
Jenkins, P., 166
Jenson, P. P., 176
Johnston, P., 100

Kafka, F., 208
Kant, I., 138
Kenny, A., 162

Kenyon, K., 31-32
Kermode, F., 161
Kitchen, K. A., 4
Knierim, R., 207
Kovacs, J., 8
Kraus, H.-J., 25
Kuhn, T., 161

Lacocque, A., 10
Lakatos, I., 161
Lane, A. N. S., 167
Lapide, P., 210
Lemche, N., 214
Lilley, J. P. U., 115
Lincoln, A., 224-25
Lindars, B., 187
Livingston, D. F., 42
Locke, J., 224
Long, V. P., 211-13
Longman, T., 213
Lucas, E., 195-96
Lyons, W. J., 144

McConville, J. G., 98, 115, 123, 144, 180, 185, 218, 227
McDermott, G., 100
MacDonald, N., 116
McGrath, A. E., 160
McKeown, J., 103
Mackintosh, H. R., 226
Marshall, I. H., 124
Mazar, A., 6, 31-32
Merrill, E., 117
Miller, J. M., 4
Moberly, R. W. L., 10, 35, 115-16, 217, 226
Morris, T. V., 163
Mosala, I., 189

Nelson, R. D., 3, 14, 17, 19, 23-24, 27-28, 30, 33, 46, 48, 53, 84-85, 91, 115, 185
Netzer, E., 31
Niditch, S., 115
Niebuhr, R., 105
Nietzsche, F., 139
Noll, M. A., 224

Author Index

Norris, C., 229

Oden, T. C., 166
O'Donovan, O., 108, 185
Olson, D. T., 179
Origen, 213
Oswalt, J. N., 148
Otto, E., 25
Otto, R., 225

Pannenberg, W., 228
Peacocke, A., 167
Pennant, D. F., 65
Perdue, L. G., 160, 169, 206, 213
Peretti, F., 167
Perowne, J. J., 137
Perry, M., 214
Polzin, R. M., 9, 64
Popper, K., 161
Porter, S., 207
Poussin, N., 128
Provan, I., 6, 213

von Rad, G., 10, 214
Rahner, K., 125
Rasmussen, L., 105
Richter, S. I., 44, 75, 181
Ricoeur, P., 10
Rogerson, J., 187, 233
Rowland, C., 8, 187
Ryle, G., 224

Savonarola, G., 137
Sawyer, J., 8
Schäfer-Lichtenberger, C., 179
Schiller, F., 233
Schleiermacher, F., 139
Schmid, K., 191
Schwartz, R., 215
Seitz, C. R., 10
Silberman, N. A., 4
Smelik, K. A. D., 34
Smend, R., 14
Smith, G. A., 229

Smith, M. S., 5
Soggin, J. A., 68, 134
Soulen, R. K., 101
Sternberg, M., 9, 209, 214
Stone, L. G., 111
Stott, J. R. W., 132
Stove, D. C., 161
Swartley, W. M., 124
Sweeney, M. A., 225
Swinburne, R., 213

Taylor, J. V., 166
Terrien, S., 137
Tertullian, 125
Thiselton, A. C., 6
Thompson, T. L., 6, 166, 214
Tilghman, B. R., 159
Tillich, P., 151

Vanhoozer, K. J., 120, 124, 204, 213, 219, 226
Vos, G., 214
Vos, J. C. de, 69

Walker, P., 100
Walsh, J. T., 191
Watson, F., 211, 217, 219
Webb, B. G., 184
Weinfeld, M., 21
Wenham, G., 44, 187
Williams, S. N., 123, 138, 147
Williams, W., 10, 187
Williamson, H. G. M., 197
Wilson, M. R., 110
Wink, W., 196
Wolfe, T, 123
Woudstra, M. H., 142
Wright, C. J. H., 108
Wright, D. F., 121
Wright, G. E., 110, 214
Wright, N. T., 99, 127, 210

Yeago, D., 204
Younger, K. L., 8, 54-55, 194, 212

Scripture Index

OLD TESTAMENT

Genesis
Ref	Pages
1–2	193
1	34, 189
1:1–2:3	14, 33, 34
1:1	103
1:2	189, 194
1:26	195
1:28	75, 173, 192
2:5	194
3	143, 189
3:1	116
3:5	173
3:7	130
4:11-12	49
6:4	190
6:6	112
6:9	143
9:9-17	222
9:17	143
9:18-27	103
9:22-24	129
9:24-27	129
9:25-27	49
10:19	129
11:31–12:3	89
12	143
12:1	186
12:1-3	1, 89, 196
12:1-7	95
12:1	96, 103
12:2	24
12:3	102, 190
12:7	13
13:15	95
13:18	66
14	52
14:18-20	52
14:19	21
15:1-6	89
15:7	95
15:16-21	173
15:18-21	13
15:18	144
15:19	66
15:20	63
17:1	21
17:6	102
17:8	95
17:9-14	27
17:9	96
17:20	143
18:1-2	234
18:14	165
20:1-6	144
22:18	96, 102
23	173
25–33	89
25:12-16	143
26:4-5	96
27	70
28:10-17	38
28:13-15	14
28:19	71
29:31-35	69
32:22-32	234
34	69, 91
34:2	21
34:7	40
34:14	27
34:15-31	76
34:25-31	112
35:22	69
37–50	72, 89
48:5-6, 8-14	70
48:8-22	62
48:17-20	70
49:4	69
49:5-7	69, 91
49:7	76
49:22-26	73
50:22	91
50:25	91

Exodus
Ref	Pages
1–15	89
3:2	219
3:5	30
3:8	21, 95
3:12	13, 15
3:17	21
6:3	21

Scripture Index

Reference	Page	Reference	Page	Reference	Page
12:2-3	25	25:16	25	1–2	177
12:2	115	25:22	25	2	177
12:3	28	26:33-34	25	1:47	106
12:6-11	25	28–29	82	3–4	82, 177
12:6	28	29:42-43	74	3:5-10	20
12:13	23	29:45	74	4	20
12:14-20	28	32	37, 91	8	177
12:26-27	23	32:1-6	128	9:1-14	177, 178
12:26	25	32:6	128	9:15–10:10	177
12:44-48	28	32:10	96	10:12	177
12:48-49	81	32:11-14	38	10:35	108
13:5	21	32:12	39	11:28	13
14–15	9, 190	33:11	13	12:8	150
14:16, 21, 26-27	43	32–34	174	13–14	16, 21, 178
14:21-25	84	32:17	219	13:16	13
14:21	157	33:18-19	140	13:25-33	65
14:24-25	52	33:8-11	138	13:28	190
15	196	33:18	150	13:29	26
15:8	22	33:22-23	138	14	65
15:15-16	17	34:6	215	14:2-3	38
16:2, 7	49	34:11	21	14:5	38
16:10	74	34:13	130	14:6-10	38
17:1	74	34:14	21	14:6, 30	13
17:3	38	34:28	96	14:26-35	27
19:4-6	89	34:35	138	14:33-34	177
19:5-10	20	40:2-3	73	15:8-10	63
19:5-6	191			16–17	177
19:5	96	**Leviticus**		16:2	74
19:6	107	1–7	63	18:8-24	82
19:10-15, 22	20	2:1-2	63	18:20	178
19:13	33	2:3	63	20:12	39
19:21-24	20	17–26	176	20:22-29	177
19:22	146	17:7	126	21:21-35	15, 177
20:2	150, 174	18:25-28	111	21:21-32	32
20:3-4	113	19:2	176	21:21-35	89
20:3	174	20:2-5	127	21:34	32
20:17	40	23:5	25, 28	22–25	19, 178
20:25	45	23:6	28	22–24	32, 63, 89, 178
23:15	28	23:10	25, 28	22	26
23:23	21, 57	25	33	22:3	17, 50
23:24	113, 125, 130	25:9	33	22:6	128
23:27	52	25:23	106	25	63
24:3-8	45	26:11-12	74	25:1-9	85
24:7	96	27	33	25:1-3	128
24:9	13			25:1-2	111
24:13	13, 97, 219	**Numbers**		26	177, 178
25:10-22	20	1–4	178	26:29-34	71

Scripture Index

Reference	Pages	Reference	Pages	Reference	Pages
27	72, 177	1:28-29	18	7:2-5	41
27:4	72	1:28	26, 32, 59, 111, 190	7:2-3	35, 37
27:8-11	72	1:34-40	27	7:2	47, 57
27:12-23	177	1:36	65	7:4	59, 113
32	15, 60, 177	1:37-38	16	7:5	113, 128
32:1-5	84	2–3	191	7:7-8	192
32:2-5	82	2:1-25	22	8	235
32:5	60	2:1-19	108	8:7-9	133
32:6-15	84	2:9-12	108	8:11-20	183
32:7	60	2:11	63	8:20	97
32:12	66	2:20	63	9:1	15
32:15c	84	2:23	62	9:4-6	90, 183
32:21-22	84	2:24–3:11	60	9:7-24	183
32:25-32	24	2:26–3:22	15	9:5	34, 111
32:29-30	177	2:26–3:11	55	9:6-29	192
33:4	115	2:33-34	55	9:10	46, 74
33:48-49	16	3:3-6	55	9:14	96
33:50-56	177, 178	3:6	55	10:1-5	20, 25
34	104	3:11	63	10:5-6	26
34:1-15	177	3:12-22	180	10:8-9	81
34:2-5	66	3:13	63	10:9	107
34:16-29	64, 84	3:18-20	84	10:20	84, 87
35	177	3:18	24	11:1-2	12
35:6	80	3:23-29	16	11:2-4	17
35:9-28	79	4:3	128	11:9	133
35:12	80	4:5-8	147, 227	11:22	84
35:25	81	4:6-8	103, 191	11:24	13
35:26-27	81	4:15-31	128	11:26-32	44, 181
36	72, 177	4:15-16	138	11:29	44, 88
36:2-9	72	4:21	14	11:30	44
36:4	33	4:26-31	97	11:31	15
		4:31	13	12–26	44
Deuteronomy		4:34	19, 23, 194	12–18	181
1–3	89	4:41-43	79, 81	12	86
1	21, 65, 192	5:6	150	12:3	128
1:6-8	13	5:7-8	113	12:5	44, 74, 75, 86, 180
1:7	21, 26	5:22	46, 74	12:9-10	15, 34
1:8	83	5:32	87	12:31	111
1:15	15	6:1-9	86	13:5	39
1:19–3:17	43	6:4-5	84	13:6-18	39
1:19-46	87	6:5	182	15	182
1:21	15, 42, 54, 57	6:8	23	15:12-18	72
1:22-33	16	6:10-13	89	16:18–18:22	92, 180, 182, 184, 193
1:23	23	6:14	113	16:18	15, 20
1:25	38	7	116	17:2-7	39
1:26-40	54	7:1-5	87	17:4, 6-7	80
1:26-33	15	7:1	21, 89		

251

Scripture Index

17:7b	39	31	46	2–12	14		
17:14-20	184	31:3	13	2	37		
17:14	13, 180	31:6	13	2:1	18		
17:16-17	185	31:7-8	13	2:2-3	51		
17:18-20	14, 185	31:7	14, 15	2:8-14	35		
17:18	25, 45, 91	31:9-12	46	2:9-11	16, 108		
18:1-2	81	31:9	14, 20	2:9	16, 38		
18:1	20, 63	31:12	46	2:10	51, 60		
18:2	107	31:14-29	149	2:11	26, 35, 216		
18:3-5	82	31:14-15	14	2:12-14	47		
18:10	111	31:14	97	2:14	36		
19:1-10	79	31:21	97	2:22	20		
19:7	81	31:23	13, 14	2:24	16, 108		
19:8	81	31:24-29	90	3–6	5, 25, 178		
19:11-13	80	31:24-26	14	3–4	23, 73, 176, 196		
19:15-21	80	31:25	20	3:1	18-19, 34		
20:8	26	31:26	45, 91	3:2-4	19		
20:10-15	47	31:27-29	183	3:5	19, 39		
20:10-11	48	31:30	74	3:6	22, 25		
20:10	48	32	86, 183	3:7	24		
20:14	114	32:8	22, 108	3:8	19, 25		
20:16-18	35, 36, 42, 47, 114	32:16-17	126	3:11	216		
20:17	21	32:30	87	3:12	19, 23		
21:1-9	81	33	87, 180	3:13	19		
21:22-23	54	34:1-4	13	3:14-17	84		
22:21	40	34:7	65	3:15-17	155		
23:1-3	74			3:15-16	24		
23:17-18	111	**Joshua (excluding texts ad loc.)**		3:15	19, 25		
24:1-4	122			3:17	19, 23-24		
25:5-10	72	1–12	1	4:1-8	91		
26:1-2	28	1	16	4:1	22, 24		
27–30	142	1:1-8	24	4:2	19		
27	2, 44-46, 181	1:1-5	20	4:6-7	25		
27:2-3	45	1:1	198	4:6	23		
27:2	45	1:2-6	83	4:8-9	19		
27:4	45, 88	1:5-9	52	4:12-13	117		
27:11-14	88	1:5	36	4:13	108		
27:12-13	45	1:6-9	58	4:16-18	24		
27:14-26	45	1:6-8	179	4:19	22, 28		
28:15-68	97	1:6	64	4:20-24	3		
28:58, 61	14, 45	1:7-8	149, 185	4:20	19, 23		
28:68	154	1:7	141	4:23	19		
29:10-11	46	1:8	3	4:24	215		
29:18	39	1:9	38	5	167, 229		
29:20-21	45	1:11	20	5:1	38, 108		
30:1-10	97	1:12-18	84	5:6	22, 150		
30:15-19	133	1:12-15	24, 178	5:8	22		

Scripture Index

Reference	Pages	Reference	Pages	Reference	Pages
5:10-12	184	9:7	3, 21	13:6	129
5:10	22, 35, 67	9:8	49	13:8-33	15, 62
5:13-15	155, 176, 230	9:10	60, 129	13:11	62
5:13-14	165, 224	9:17	2	13:14	81, 106, 150
5:14	196	9:23	2	13:15-31	62
5:15	196	9:24	113	13:33	106, 150
6	5, 37, 89, 196, 231	9:27	2, 181	14	78
6:1-7	9, 176	10–12	61, 78	14:1	78, 178, 180
6:2	51	10–11	61	14:3-4	178
6:4-6	176	10	50	14:4	81
6:4	34	10:1-6	26	14:6-15	67, 178
6:7	24	10:5-6	26	14:9	106
6:8	176	10:6	67	14:13-15	82
6:9	24	10:11	109	14:13-14	83
6:12	34	10:13-14	154	15	64
6:13	24, 176	10:15	54	15:1	65, 69-70
6:15-21	176	10:16-27	26	15:5-12	76
6:15	19	10:27	2	15:13-19	65, 82
6:19	176	10:28–11:23	55	15:13	66
6:20	18, 40, 116-17	10:28	109	15:16	112
6:22-25	17-18, 47	10:36-39	67	15:20-63	76
6:24	58, 109	10:40	109, 117	15:26-29	76
6:26	184	11	54	15:35	55
7	35, 173, 178	11:1-2	26	15:63	21, 55, 67, 79, 82, 183
7:1	117	11:11	113		
7:3-5	42	11:14	113	16:3	56
7:5	26	11:16	56	16:7	31
7:7	41	11:17	62	16:10	56, 79, 183
7:16	19, 34	11:20	109	17:1	70
7:21	35	11:21-23	37, 87	17:16	77
7:24-26	109	11:22	62	18–19	75, 78
7:24	117	11:23	15, 70, 83	18:1	42, 46, 80, 181
8	5	12	26, 61, 87, 182	18:12-13	71
8:2	27	12:1-6	15	18:14-20	78
8:10	19, 34	12:1	17	18:15-19	67
8:14	19, 34, 51	12:5	62	18:21	31
8:19	40	12:7-8	55	18:28	70, 82
8:26	42	12:9-24	17	18:29	78
8:28-29	2	12:16	42	18:30-31	78
8:28	58	12:23	22	19	68
8:29	51	13–24	2	19:2-8	68
8:30-35	2, 42, 88, 142, 181	13–22	14	19:40-48	111
8:30-34	148	13–19	178, 180	19:41-43	76
8:32	175, 185	13	56, 64	19:46	71
8:33	20, 81	13:1-7	37, 183	19:47	71
9	2, 35, 71, 178	13:1	78, 87	19:49-51	179
9:1	26, 47, 51	13:4	129	19:50-51	179

253

Scripture Index

19:50	90	24:20	97	**1 Samuel**	
19:51	75	24:23-27	175	1:24	2
20–21	178	24:23	115	2:27-36	98
20	2, 79	24:26	3	2:34	23
20:1-9	150, 215	24:29	198	4–6	20
20:2	149	24:31	90	4:5	33
20:7	42			6	62
21	2, 63, 79-80, 107, 180	**Judges**		7:4	128
		1	183	8:4-22	185
21:1	184	1:1-2	69	12:8	184
21:2-8	149	1:5-7	51	12:10	128
21:43-45	84, 96	1:8	55, 70	12:11	184
21:44	15	1:9-15	56	13:3	33
22	60, 79, 150, 178, 180-81	1:21	70	15:3	42
		1:23	71	15:9	42
22:2	113	2:6-10	27	15:14	42
22:5	150	2:7	90	17:17	28
22:12	46	2:10-13	127	20:8	17
22:22	215	2:11	129	21:5	20
22:26-28	91	3:3	62	25:18	28
23	61, 86, 88, 141	3:9-11	68	30:25	91
23:1-3	61	3:13	30, 31		
23:2	20	5:14, 17	71	**2 Samuel**	
23:3-4	22	6:11-24	30	1:18	53
23:6	141, 175	6:25-28	130	2–4	67
23:7	22, 125	8:22-23	185	4:2-3	2
23:9	22	9:46	88	5:1-5	66
23:12-13	22	10:6	127	5:5-16	55
23:13	150	10:16	134	5:6-10	70
23:14	150	13:21-22	30	5:6	21
23:15-16	175	14:5	67	5:25	56
23:16	125, 141	16	62	6:15	33
24	2, 44, 61, 86, 181	18	77, 111	7:1	70
24:1-28	141	18:1	77	7:13	2
24:1	20, 42	18:2	77	8:15	52
24:2	115	18:7-10	223	10:5	31
24:3	147	18:10	77	11:11	20
24:10	128	18:27	77	18:21	235
24:11	21	19:23-24	40	21:1-6	2
24:13	147, 150, 215	20:36-48	43		
24:14-15	115, 175			**1 Kings**	
24:14	126	**Ruth**	72	1–11	191
24:15	126	2:20	80	2:2-4	87
24:19-27	149	4	191	2:4	98
24:19-20	115	4:13-22	234	6:1	4
24:19	50, 174, 176, 183, 215			6:4-7	234
				6:15-18	234

Scripture Index

8:27-30	182	10:13-14	37	132:13-14	51
9:15-16	56	10:13	85	135	131
9:16	71	17:17-27	98	135:8-12	17
9:20-22	184	22:13	98		
9:20-21	3	22:18	75	**Proverbs**	
11	129	29:25	24	15:9	121
11:5-7	127			15:26	121
11:5	129	**2 Chronicles**		16:1	121
11:33	129	1:1	24	16:9	121
12	71	6:16	98		
12:25-33	38	13:8	128	**Ecclesiastes**	
12:28	128	32:19	132	1:5	159
16:31	129				
16:34	36, 184	**Nehemiah**		**Lamentations**	233
18:17-18	41	5:5	75		
18:21	90	9:18	128	**Isaiah**	
				1	134
2 Kings		**Esther**		2:2-5	148
2	31, 211	7:8	75	2:2-4	191
2:7-8	19			2:4	112
4	211	**Job**		2:9-21	54
5	191	1:7	167	6:9-13	197
5:10-12	10	3:8	194	6:9-10	197
5:18	127	5:9-10	157	6:11-13	197
6:16-17	29	9:13	194	8:18	23
11	25	26:12	194	9:1-2	102
11:12	25	41	189	11:9	103
17	130, 181			19:1	26
17:7-23	98	**Psalms (EVV)**		19:24-25	191
17:15	132	27:6	33	27:1	194
19:29	23	47:2	52	35:5	197
20:8	23	47:5	33	36:18-20	131
21	130	50:1	85	38:8	53
21:4	74, 181	53:1	234	40–55	131, 198
21:9-11	130	66:6	19	40:1	198
21:16	130	73:22	163	40:18	131
23:1-3	3	74:12-17	19	42:6-7	197
23:10-13	127	74:13-15	19	42:6	103
23:13	129	74:13-14	194	42:14–43:21	197
23:22	184	76:2	51	43:14	197
23:24-25	184	89:10	194	43:18-19	197
24:20	98	89:15	33	44	132
25	2	93	194	44:12-20	131
25:27-30	2	93:3-4	194	45:7	121
		96:4	126	46:6-7	131
1 Chronicles		97	131	49:5-6	191
1	231	106:34-39	130	49:6	103

Scripture Index

51	194	34:25	100	Jonah	
51:9-11	194	36:22	139	2:8	132
51:9-10	194	37:26	100		
52:11-12	194	40–48	138	Micah	
53	198	43:1-5	138	6:5-6	19
53:2	139	47:13–48:29	100		
56:6	148			Habakkuk	
56:7	148	Daniel		1:2–2:20	220
65:17	107, 154	4:13	163	2:3	229
66:22	107, 154	4:29	163	2:4	120
		7:4	195	2:14-20	120
Jeremiah		7:8	195	2:14	103, 229
1:17-19	15	7:11-14	195	3:11	53
2	130	7:13	195		
2:11-12	132	7:27	195	Zechariah	
2:13	127	8:11	29	1:10-11	167
2:31	132	10:10-14	196	3:1-2	167
2:33	110, 130	10:12-14	29	9:14	124
3:12-13	134	10:13–12:1	167	14:9	229
3:12	85	10:13	30		
3:14	85			Malachi	
4:23-26	193	Hosea		2:11-14	133
4:25b	194	1:3	133	4:5-6	99
5:24-25	194	2:15	67		
7:12	74	4:15	38	APOCRYPHA	
7:31-34	67	5:8	38		
8:8-12	100	5:10	67	2 Esdras	
10:16-17	100	8:5	128	2:29	67
11:22	194	9:7	139		
13:27	133	9:10	135	Wisdom of Solomon	
14:1-10	194	10:5	38	13:10-19	132
15:2	194	11:8-9	177		
17:9	121	11:8	215	NEW TESTAMENT	
21:5-6	194	14:1-2	134		
22:9-17	131	14:8	133	Matthew	
34:16	75	14:9	140	4:16	102
51:17-18	132			5:22	67
		Joel	194	5:29-30	67
Ezekiel		3:3	131	8:17	220
1:28	137-38, 220			11:21-22	129
8:10	138	Amos		13:10-17	197
8:17	112	2:4-8	131	16:24	222
9	112	3:2	144, 186	16:27–17:5	139
16:34	132	4:4-5	38	17:1-8	219
20	126	4:4	67, 71	19:3-8	122
23	126	4:8	67	19:8	122
33–37	105	9:7	22, 186		

256

Scripture Index

22:32	144
26:28	100
28:16-20	222
28:18	222

Mark
4:10-12	197
9:2-8	219
10:2-5	122
11:17	147
12:26-27	144
14:24	100

Luke
1:1-4	209
5:1-11	158
9:28-36	219
10:13-14	129
11:24	167
19:30	124
20:37-38	144
22:20	100

John
1:4	135
14:9	123
21:1-14	158

Acts
7:45	100
10:22	145
10:34-35	145
17:26	108
28:23-28	197-98

Romans
1:16	136
1:17	140, 229
1:20-25	136
1:25	136
1:21–8:3	136
1:26-27	136
2:2–3:26	145
3:31	149
4:13	101
4:16	101
5:12-17	135
7:7-8	152
7:12	149
8:3-4	149
8:35	148
9–11	105, 196
9:4	101, 148
11:11	196-97
11:13-24	102
11:18	204
11:22	204
11:26	105
11:32	227
13:8-10	149

1 Corinthians
3:21-23	101
3:22	137
6:9-10	137
6:18	130
8:4-6	126
10:14	130
10:19-21	126
13:12	229
15:13-14	6

2 Corinthians
3:7	152
11:22	101

Galatians
3:10	152
3:16	101
3:24	153
5:13-16	149

Ephesians
2:10	153
3:5	136
5:4	137
5:5	136
6:12	169
5:20	137

Philippians
3:5	101

1 Thessalonians
1:9	135

Hebrews
4:8	100
9:14	209
10:24	153
10:38	140
11	18, 100
11:31	18
12:28	100
13:5	13
13:14	100

James
2:8-11	149

1 Peter
1:4	107
2:9	107

2 Peter
2:5	143
3:13	107, 154

1 John
1:1	209
5:19	222

Jude
9	167

Revelation
9:20-21	125
9:20	125
11:15	228
12:7	167
19:11-14	123
19:11	124
21:1	107, 154
21:8	125
22:3	124
22:11-15	154
22:15	125

www.ingramcontent.com/pod-product-compliance
Lightning Source LLC
Chambersburg PA
CBHW020644230426
43665CB00008B/312